MW01194376

NATO'S **Gamble**

DAG HENRIKSEN

NATO'S Gamble

COMBINING
DIPLOMACY AND
AIRPOWER
IN THE
KOSOVO CRISIS
1998–1999

NAVAL INSTITUTE PRESS
Annapolis, Maryland

Naval Institute Press
291 Wood Road
Annapolis, MD 21402

© 2007 by Dag Henriksen
All rights reserved. No part of this book may be reproduced or utilized in any form or by any means, electronic or mechanical, including photocopying and recording, or by any information storage and retrieval system, without permission in writing from the publisher.

Library of Congress Cataloging-in-Publication Data
Henriksen, Dag.
  NATO's gamble : combining diplomacy and airpower in the Kosovo crisis, 1998-1999 / Dag Henriksen.
    p. cm.
  Includes bibliographical references and index.
  ISBN 978-1-59114-355-0 (alk. paper) — ISBN 978-1-59114-358-1 (pbk. : alk. paper) 1. Operation Allied Force, 1999. 2. Kosovo (Serbia)—History—Civil War, 1998-1999—Aerial operations. 3. Kosovo (Serbia)—History—Civil War, 1998-1999—Participation, American. 4. United States—Armed Forces—Serbia—Kosovo. 5. North Atlantic Treaty Organization—Armed Forces—Serbia—Kosovo. 6. United States—History, Military—20th century. 7. Intervention (International law) I. Title.
  DR2087.5H46 2007
  949.7103—dc22

                                                                        2007018427

Printed in the United States of America on acid-free paper

14 13 12 11 10 09 08 07   9 8 7 6 5 4 3 2
First printing

All of the maps in this book were created by Christopher Robinson.

CONTENTS

ACKNOWLEDGMENTS

Although writing this book has often been a somewhat lonesome mental voyage, I am very conscious of and immensely grateful to those who made this journey possible. Invaluable contributions were provided by a number of influential individuals who were willing to share their experiences and perspectives from the Kosovo crisis; to them I am forever grateful. My sincere gratitude goes to friends and colleagues at the Royal Norwegian Air Force Academy, who have provided resources, backing, and advice to my work. Thanks also to the Naval Institute Press for believing in my project. I am indebted to my family and friends, who have been extremely patient with my often physical and sometimes mental lack of presence the past few years—and particularly to my fiancée, Anne Katrine, whose support has proved crucial both practically and emotionally. Thus, this book is dedicated to her.

Map 1. Operation Allied Force area of operation

INTRODUCTION

On 24 March 1999, the North Atlantic Treaty Organization (NATO) began an air campaign against the Federal Republic of Yugoslavia (FRY) that lasted for seventy-eight days until it formally ended on 10 June 1999. The air campaign—publicly known as Operation Allied Force (OAF)—was the first war NATO had fought against any sovereign nation after its creation fifty years earlier, and for some of the Alliance's smaller nations—like Norway—it was the first use of fighter aircraft in war since World War II.[1] It was the first major combat operation conducted for humanitarian objectives against a state committing atrocities within its own borders—thus a war challenging "long-established international relations and diplomatic principles, in particular the idea of non-intervention and non-interference in the domestic affairs of sovereign states."[2] It was the first time a theater war of the size of OAF had been fought predominantly by airpower, with ground forces having been publicly ruled out of the operation from the outset. As such, it was arguably a war conceptually different from any other war throughout history.

When the most powerful military alliance in history entered its first war, no one in the military leadership of NATO had received any political guidance or developed any strategy for what the situation in Kosovo should be like after the war. In effect, NATO had not planned for the war it was about to start. It had inadequately planned for a loosely focused bombing campaign perceived to last a few days and was politically and militarily unprepared for the possibility that the president of the Federal Republic of Yugoslavia, Slobodan Milošević, would continue to oppose NATO after that. As the French chief of defense, General Jean-Pierre Kelche, commented with regard to NATO's preparedness: "It was no political direction in the beginning—absent." Gradually the military effort improved, "but in the beginning—it was a mess."[3] Thus, the starting point for this book is to explain why NATO ended up being so unprepared.

When OAF commenced, the deteriorating situation in Kosovo had been the focus of the international community for about a year. With the killing of four Serb policemen in Kosovo on 28 February 1998 and the subsequent Serb crackdown in the Drenica Valley, the conflict in Kosovo—a conflict that had been brewing for years—passed a threshold of violence that made it rise quickly on the international political agenda. Within a few weeks, U.S. Secretary of State, Madeleine Albright, the president's representative in the Balkans, Robert Gelbard, and the Supreme Allied Commander Europe (SACEUR), Gen. Wesley K. Clark, were convinced that FRY president Slobodan Milošević was the source of the problem. In addition they considered that the threat of force to back diplomacy was essential—coercive diplomacy[4]—and that airpower could provide diplomacy with the necessary credibility to achieve a negotiated solution to the mounting crisis. Thus, airpower almost immediately became the key ingredient in the international effort to solve the crisis.

After the 1991 Gulf War, which General Clark describes as airpower's "persistent reference point," airpower promised a low-cost, low-risk statement of political intent and left open other more difficult and costly options. Combined with the perceived success of airpower in Bosnia in 1995, airpower seemed to many U.S. politicians and diplomats the preferable military tool to coerce an opponent. As Professor Michael Clark asserts, "Airpower is frequently regarded as embodying the ultimate instrument of military coercion."[5] Precision air strikes left the politicians in control; airpower could strike without affecting much else; it could send political "messages" to opposing leaders; and an air campaign could be called off and the force dispersed at any time.[6]

However, the Kosovo War was *not* like the Gulf War of 1991—it was a humanitarian intervention by a military alliance resting on the political will of nineteen sovereign member nations—nations with differing perspectives, commitment, and interests. Without a UN authorization of force, and with NATO struggling to find consensus for a viable strategy to address the crisis in Kosovo, airpower appeared to provide political and military flexibility—the room to maneuver that was so desperately sought.

As it turned out, airpower did not provide the immediate political leverage hoped for. Key individuals believed that two to four days of NATO bombing would suffice to alter the behavior of Slobodan Milošević—as they believed NATO airpower had done in Bosnia in 1995, when Operation Deliberate Force had triggered the peace negotiations that resulted in the Dayton Peace Accords. In fact, it was a gamble, and as Lord David Owen rightly observed with regard to the chosen NATO strategy of relying on a few days of "show of force" in late March 1999, "Their bluff was called by Milošević. That's what happened."[7] Instead of a three-day operation, NATO ended up bombing the FRY, mainly Serbia, for seventy-eight days.

This book focuses primarily on how the international community combined diplomacy and airpower in the handling of the Kosovo crisis. It examines the key political, diplomatic, and military processes that shaped NATO's crisis management and how airpower was utilized as the key instrument in NATO's strategy to coerce the Federal Republic of Yugoslavia to concede to its demands. It has been an ambition of mine to reveal the origins and content of NATO's strategic and conceptual thinking as to *how* to apply airpower in order to alter the FRY's behavior—at the time when NATO went to war.

A few things should be made clear to the reader. NATO was unprepared for the type of conflict Kosovo represented—a fact that a number of authors have pointed out in articles and books in recent years. To that extent, *NATO's Gamble* is battering an open door. However, the nature and level of NATO's unpreparedness have been inadequately described—particularly the *use of force* part of coercive diplomacy. Little emphasis has been put on the key ingredient in the international effort to solve the Kosovo crisis—airpower. The general perspective on this issue can perhaps be summed up by the somewhat simplified description provided by James Dobbins—the special adviser for Kosovo and Bosnia and Herzegovina of former U.S. president Bill Clinton and Secretary of State Madeleine Albright—who confided his belief in the chosen NATO strategy: "We'll bomb them a little bit, if that doesn't work, we'll bomb them a little bit more, and if that doesn't work, we'll bomb them a little more, and if that doesn't work—ultimately—we have to consider invading. I don't see anything that lacks clarity in that strategy."[8]

Instead, the immense complexity of how best to apply airpower to produce political results had been debated for the better part of the twentieth century; the perspective on this issue significantly shaped the way this military tool was integrated in the diplomacy to end the humanitarian disaster unfolding in Kosovo. When the Kosovo War started, the controversy regarding how to use airpower was a source of constant friction between the political and military leadership of NATO, on one side, and on the other, the professional airmen set to plan and execute the operation. This book argues that the latter too were unprepared for a humanitarian intervention in the midst of Europe—even though during the war they were quick to deflect the blame for failure to grasp the nature and potential of airpower to politicians and the military leadership at the Allied headquarters in Mons, Belgium.

This book focuses particularly on U.S. political and military structures leading up to and including the handling of the Kosovo issue and how these structures became pivotal in shaping the international response. U.S. airpower, which had performed extraordinarily well in the 1991 Gulf War, made up the bulk of the airpower in the 1995 air campaign in Bosnia, Operation Deliberate Force, and it provided significantly more aircraft in OAF than the other eighteen nations combined. The United States developed the air campaign plans of OAF almost unilaterally, was by far the dominant force contributing and shaping target generation—and it had all the top positions in the executing military wing of NATO.[9] The United States was the sole remaining superpower after the Cold War, played the key role in ending the war in Bosnia, and would be the driving political and military force all through the handling of the Kosovo crisis. Thus, to a large extent the key to NATO's resolve and strategy in 1998–99 was generated and shaped in Washington rather than in Brussels.

NATO's Gamble argues the international handling of the Kosovo crisis was marked by the different transatlantic perspectives on power, the role of diplomacy, and the use of force. The American author and journalist Robert Kagan argues that on the all-important question of power—the efficacy of power, the morality of power, the desirability of power—American and European perspectives are diverging. He adds, "That is why on major strategic and international questions today, Americans are from Mars and Europeans are from Venus: they agree on little and understand one another less and less."[10] Thus, as the crisis unfolded in Kosovo, the general European reluctance to use force and limited military capabilities would collide with the more pragmatic and forceful American approach. This book suggests there are lessons to be learned on both sides of the Atlantic on this issue.

This book is based on the author's PhD dissertation from the Scottish Centre for War Studies at the University of Glasgow (2006), with the title "Operation Allied Force: A Product of Military Theory or Political Pragmatism? An Examination of the Role of Air Power in Handling the Kosovo Crisis, 1998–99."

ABBREVIATIONS

ACSC	Air Command and Staff College (USAF, Maxwell AFB, Alabama)
ACTS	Air Corps Tactical School (from 1931 and onward; Maxwell, Alabama)
AFB	Air Force Base
AFSOUTH	Allied Forces Southern Europe
CAOC	Combined Air Operations Center
CJCS	Chairman of the Joint Chiefs of Staff
EU	European Union
FRY	Federal Republic of Yugoslavia (Serbia and Montenegro)
IADS	Integrated Air Defence System
IFOR	Implementation Force—The NATO-led force responsible for upholding the Dayton Peace Accords from December 1995 through December 1996
JDAM	Joint Direct Attack Munition
JNA	Yugoslav People's Army (JNA—Jugoslovenska Narodna Armija)
JTF	Joint Task Force
KFOR	Kosovo Force—International force organized and commanded by NATO to enforce an agreement in Kosovo
KLA	Kosovo Liberation Army (UCK—Ushtria Clirimtare e Kosovës)
KVM	Kosovo Verification Mission
MUP	Serbian Interior Ministry Police (MUP—Ministarstvo Unutrasnjih Poslova)
NAC	North Atlantic Council—the NATO policy-making body
NATO	North Atlantic Treaty Organization
NSC	National Security Council—senior U.S. policy-making body
OAF	Operation Allied Force

OSCE	Organization for Security and Cooperation in Europe
SACEUR	Supreme Allied Commander Europe
SFOR	Stabilization Force—second phase of the Implementation Force (IFOR)
SHAPE	Supreme Headquarters Allied Powers Europe—commanded by SACEUR
UN	United Nations
UNPROFOR	United Nations Protection Force
VJ	Yugoslav Army (VJ—Vojske Jugoslavije [FRY])

Part I
Operation Allied Force: How NATO Stumbled into War

The first duty and the right of the art of war is to keep policy from demanding things that go against the nature of war, to prevent the possibility that out of ignorance of the way the instrument works, policy might misuse it.

—Carl von Clausewitz

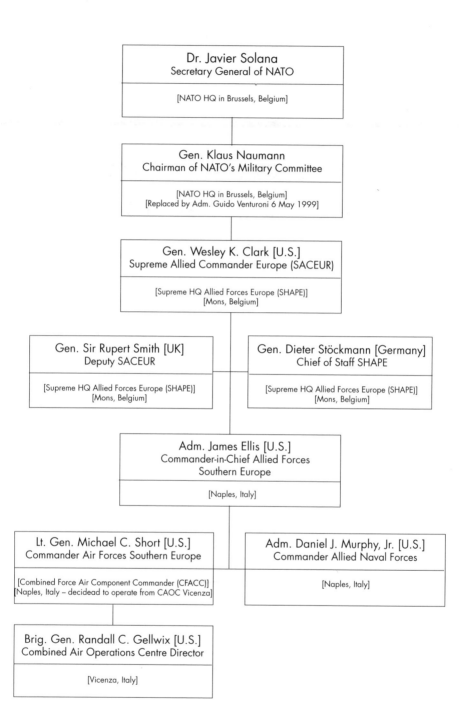

Figure 1. NATO chain of command during Operation Allied Force

Chapter 1
THE FIRST WEEK OF OAF

One of the most obvious features of the conflict [Operation Allied Force] was the West's lack of preparedness when conflict actually began.

– Gen. Wesley K. Clark[1]

When NATO went to war against the Federal Republic of Yugoslavia (or FRY, comprising Serbia and Montenegro) on 24 March 1999, it was adequately prepared neither politically nor militarily for what was to ensue. Evidence suggests it was not even close. This is the story of just how unprepared NATO really was when it entered its first war—and why the Alliance ended up in this situation. It is a story from which lessons may be learned.

In his memoirs, the Supreme Allied Commander Europe—Gen. Wesley K. Clark—says that the surprise of being at war and lack of preparedness at the outset were distinctive characteristics (features) of the initial phase of the air campaign. In fact, NATO went to war on the basic assumption that if exposed to its military force, President Slobodan Milošević would quickly accede to NATO's demands. It was thought by key individuals in Washington and many of the political leaders in NATO that this would be achieved in as little as two to four days.[2] Evidence suggests that SACEUR advised high-ranking politicians, at least in Washington and the United Kingdom, that once pressed hard enough to find a solution to the crisis in Kosovo, Milošević would crumble.[3] Two weeks into the war, the deputy chief of the British Defence Staff—Air Marshal Sir John Day—candidly admitted, "We hoped that he [Milošević] would quickly get the message and not continue his plans."[4] The perception that a few days of *show of force* would have Milošević agreeing to NATO's demands was to shape the level of NATO's preparedness, strategy, and targeting—the whole foundation of the air campaign. Gen. Klaus Naumann rightly observed, "[We] had three guiding principles: we had first of all to avoid if possible any of our own casualties and fatalities, secondly we were told to avoid collateral damage to the extent possible, and thirdly bring it to a quick end. If you take these three ingredients, it's very difficult to find a proper solution to make this equation fly."[5]

In a speech at the Royal Norwegian Air Force Academy after the war, the man in charge of the air campaign, Lt. Gen. Michael C. Short, asserted, "The phrase I heard used many times was 'NATO was going to demonstrate resolve.' Your Prime Minister probably, and my President certainly, my Secretary of State absolutely, they all thought that if we bomb Milošević for about three days, and demonstrate to him that we are serious, he will roll and accept our terms."[6]

Commenting on NATO's preparedness, Ivo H. Daalder and Michael E. O'Hanlon assert, "NATO neither expected nor prepared for an extended military confrontation."[7] NATO failed to develop a strategy to achieve their objective. In fact, they argued, NATO "had a hope, but not a plan. NATO stumbled into war, unready either for countering Serbia's massive campaign to forcefully expel much of the ethnic Albanian population from Kosovo or to do militarily what it would take to achieve its stated objectives. . . . NATO went to war in the hope it could win without much of a fight. It was proven wrong."[8]

After analyzing the conflict, Anthony Cordesman pointed out that NATO's "political leadership then operated under the military illusion that a limited number of focused air strikes could force a diplomacy based on political illusion to be successful."[9] On numerous occasions General Naumann says he told the North Atlantic Council (or NAC, the Alliance's principal decision-making institution) that it would take at least a week—under favorable conditions—to neutralize the Serb integrated air defense system (IADS). When asked why a lot of politicians seemed to think the intervention would be over in a few days, Naumann answered somewhat diplomatically, "Perhaps some of them made the mistake of believing that Kosovo was Bosnia, and in Bosnia it was a relatively short air campaign."[10] Cordesman says NATO did not fail to prepare for military action but rather failed to prepare realistically for the level of conflict it might actually have to face: "As a result, NATO was unready to deal with the military realities that followed. . . . The end result was that NATO was not ready in terms of an agreed strategy for going to war, the number of aircraft deployed, full scale targeting plans, and support capabilities."[11] In a similar assertion, Benjamin Lambeth says, "NATO leaders on both sides of the Atlantic had little to congratulate themselves about when it came to the manner in which the air war was planned and carried out. On the contrary, there was a dominant sense among both participants and observers that the desultory onset of Allied Force and its later slowness to register effects reflected some fundamental failures of allied leadership and strategy choice."[12]

The leader of the Defense Committee in the Norwegian parliament at the time, Hans Røsjorde, admitted that "the desired end-state and the exit strategy when NATO went to war was—to put it mildly—very unclear."[13] The Norwegian Chief of Defense, Gen. Arne Solli, similarly pointed out, "If you have not defined political objectives or an end-state, it is very optimistic to believe that the operation was going to be over within a few days."[14] In an interview after the war, Ivo Daalder said that NATO had not committed itself to winning the war—it had not even been committed to going to war: "It was a strategy designed to somehow convince somebody that we were committed to something we were not committed to."[15]

So, NATO went to war on the assumption that Milošević would quickly agree to NATO demands. It did not adequately plan for the eventuality that Milošević would not act according to its assumption. In fact, NATO hardly planned at all. The Pentagon was very reluctant to engage in a ground campaign, and from the outset President William J. Clinton ruled out ground forces in what became known as Operation Allied Force (OAF).[16] In many countries in Europe there was significant opposition to the use of force against the FRY; many politicians felt that preparing for war sent the wrong political signals, something they were reluctant to do. General Clark explains:

> In the case of Kosovo, there simply was no detailed planning. There was no strategic consensus in Washington. Even if there had been, U.S.-only planning would have been unrealistic, since we never had any intention of fighting alone. Nor could we have done effective U.S. planning without visiting the theater, which was impossible under the restrictive provisions of the Roberts Amendment, which forbade spending money for intervention in the Balkans unless certain prerequisites and reporting requirements had been complied with. Detailed NATO planning would have required political authorization that just wasn't possible. . . . In Europe and the United States, repeated political concerns inhibited the kind of detailed NATO planning in the summer and fall of 1998 that might have promoted a more credible and more effective threat.[17]

In his memoirs, Wesley Clark, the man in charge of the overall military effort to coerce Milošević to accede to NATO's demands, candidly admits, "The Desert Storm team had been assembled and was scrambling on the offensive plan and techniques for months before it attacked Iraq in 1991. We hadn't had that luxury. Our force came together at the last minute. . . . We were fighting, planning, and adapting simultaneously."[18]

The NATO force and effort did indeed come together at the last minute. Even the name of the operation was not clear by 23 March—the day before OAF started; it was the result of a call from Washington wondering what the name would be. Shortly before the air campaign started, Supreme Headquarters Allied Powers Europe (SHAPE) had neither a military press spokesman nor a media strategy. Eventually Air Commodore David Wilby was selected—he was on a planned ski vacation in the Alps and had to be "read into the operation" on his way to his sudden new assignment—something that hardly provided him the time to prepare adequately for the job.[19] By the end of the twentieth century, the overall significance of the media in handling most crises and wars could hardly have been overestimated. In his memoirs, General Clark makes the general point that the instantaneous news flow that could make distant crises into huge domestic governmental problems—the "CNN factor," as he describes it—"could put unrelenting heavy pressure on policymakers at all levels from the very beginning of any operation."[20] The British prime minister, Tony Blair, was aware of the importance of media, later commenting on the influence of television on this conflict: "When you fight an action like this in modern politics in our modern media world, you are fighting it on television! It is an extraordinary thing."[21]

In effect, when OAF actually commenced, Wesley Clark's media strategy appeared to be along the lines of: "We hoped to buy a few days by minimizing the initial public releases while we refined the system."[22] So when NATO went to war for the first time in its history, the media strategy appears to have been: say as little as possible, until we know what to say—not a particularly sophisticated approach. Later commenting on the lack of preparedness, the French chief of defense, Gen. Jean-Pierre Kelche, said, "There was no solid information cell at all. It is incredible to think that at the end of the 20th century, you can commit an alliance like NATO to start an air campaign without a trained information cell—it is simply unbelievable."[23]

As the NATO alliance went to war, the political objectives of the air campaign were not very concrete, concerted, or clear. In a press statement on 23 March, the secretary-general of NATO, Dr. Javier Solana, said:

> We are taking action following the Federal Republic of Yugoslavia Government's refusal of the International Community's demands: (1) Acceptance of the interim political settlement which has been negotiated at Rambouillet; (2) Full observance of limits on the Serb Army

and Special Police Forces agreed on 25 October; (3) Ending of excessive and disproportionate use of force in Kosovo. . . . Our objective is to prevent more human suffering and more repression and violence against the civilian population of Kosovo. We must also act to prevent instability spreading in the region.[24]

A press release on 23 March said, "NATO's overall political objectives remain to help achieve a peaceful solution to the crisis in Kosovo by contributing to the response of the international community. More particularly, the Alliance made it clear in its statement of 30th January 1999 that its strategy was to halt the violence and support the completion of negotiations on an interim political solution."[25]

This press release referred to a NATO statement of 30 January 1999 regarding its strategy: "The crisis in Kosovo remains a threat to peace and security in the region. NATO's strategy is to halt the violence and support the completion of negotiations on an interim political settlement for Kosovo, thus averting a humanitarian catastrophe."[26] According to the OAF After Action Report to Congress,[27] the United States and its NATO allies had three primary interests from the onset of the operation: ensuring the stability of Eastern Europe; thwarting ethnic cleansing; and ensuring NATO's credibility. In an address on NATO attacks on Yugoslav military forces, President Clinton stated:

> We act to protect thousands of innocent people in Kosovo from mounting military offensive. We act to prevent a wider war, to defuse a powder keg at the heart of Europe that has exploded twice before in this century with catastrophic results. We act to stand united with our allies for peace. . . . Our mission is clear: to demonstrate the seriousness of NATO's purpose so that the Serbian leaders understand the imperative of reversing course, to deter an even bloodier offensive against innocent civilians in Kosovo and, if necessary, to seriously damage the Serbian military's capacity to harm the people of Kosovo.[28]

The British secretary of defense at the time, George Robertson, stated on 24 March, "Our overall political objectives remain to help achieve a peaceful solution to the crisis by contributing to the response of the whole international community. More particularly, NATO made it clear in a statement of 30 January that its strategy is to curb the violence and support the completion of negotiations on an interim political settlement."[29]

So when Western leaders went to war over Kosovo on 24 March 1999, the official political objectives seem to have comprised a moral aspect, aiming to prevent a worse humanitarian disaster than was already unfolding in Kosovo; a strategic aspect, particularly ensuring the credibility of NATO but also aiming to prevent the conflict from spreading and destabilizing other parts of the region; and a pragmatic aspect, getting the parties to return to the Rambouillet peace talks in order to find a political solution to the issue of Kosovo. In public, a particular emphasis seems to have been put on the moral objective. Besides the fact that Western leaders probably genuinely felt they had to deal with it, the humanitarian issue was perceived to provide the legal basis for the operation; the combination of the two, in turn, influenced public support for an air campaign. It would be fair to assume that this particular aspect—the gaining of public support—was of paramount importance to the political leaders. Publicly, the way to achieve the moral objective of avoiding a humanitarian disaster was to coerce Milošević to negotiate. Looked at from this perspective, the third objective initially seems to have been the dominating one. According to General Clark, "The air campaign began with one objective—drive the Serbs back to the negotiations at Rambouillet—and quickly moved toward other aims, such as halting the ethnic cleansing, and then, after the NATO summit, the five conditions endorsed by the G-8 foreign ministers—a cease-fire, the withdrawal of all Serb forces, the return of all refugees and displaced persons, the presence of a NATO-led international force, and subsequent participation in a political settlement."[30]

In other words, at the outset there was no clearly defined political strategy explicitly defining the political objective to be achieved by the military planners. Evidently, there was no long-term strategy for the Balkans or a desired end-state for the issue of Kosovo. In fact, it could be claimed that the attempt to persuade Milošević to return to Rambouillet reflected not only a short-term focus, lack of unified strategy, and a rather naïve lack of understanding of both Belgrade's perspective and resolve, but also an inadequate appreciation of how to achieve a desired result through the use of force. The loosely stated ambition of getting Milošević back to Rambouillet was driven by the lack of consensus as to how to proceed and by an unsound reliance on the hope of success by using force—as if military force were an abstract political tool with standardized features that, when its use was threatened, could be counted on to generate political leverage. Evidence suggests that there was no conscious comprehensive strategy based on thorough, well-informed analysis of the perspectives and power structures of Belgrade. In their analysis, Daalder and O'Hanlon claim, "Operation Allied Force was in its early weeks a textbook case of how not to wage a war. The blindness of NATO's major members to the possibility that the war might not end quickly was astounding. As a result of that blindness, the alliance was caught entirely unprepared for what followed."[31]

The deputy chief of operations at SHAPE, Brig. Gen. Gunnar Lundberg, admitted that there was no long-term strategy for approaching Kosovo, which created problems for military planners, who had very limited and short-term guidance to work with.[32] This view seems to be backed up by the British Defence Committee's Fourteenth Report on lessons learned from OAF, which points out that at the outset there was little clarity concerning the purpose of the campaign: "The compromises forced upon the North Atlantic Council by the need to find consensus meant that the politicians and diplomats directing the NATO military planners did not demonstrate, by 24 March 1999, a clear grasp of the nature of the strategy they had committed themselves to pursuing."[33]

This lack of strategy pointed out in the above document coincides with SACEUR's perception. General Clark's insight is particularly important, because it was at this point in the exercise of coercive diplomacy based on credible force that the "use of credible force" part was set in motion. If it was to be credible both a strategy and clearly defined political objectives were required, and General Clark—the officer whose responsibility it was to organize and conduct the use of force—felt he had neither. General Clark writes about a conversation between himself, Javier Solana, and General Naumann after the campaign had started: "When the conversation moved into the diplomatic area, I raised the issue of the political objectives of the campaign. What really was our aim? I asked. Surely not just a return to Rambouillet?"[34] General Clark continues, in seeming candor, "However, operating without a clear, agreed strategy or a strong, unified Washington, made leadership feel like physical conditioning using some kind of 'resistance training.'"[35] A few days into the campaign, President Clinton commented that the chosen strategy was the best "among a bunch of bad options . . . to maximize the possibility of achieving our mission."[36] Since there was evidently no clear strategy at the outset, the press started asking what the objectives of NATO's air campaign were, and, General Clark admits, "a number of us had begun to ask in private about the political goals of the campaign."[37] During the first week, General Clark continued to press the point: "I raised the 'end-state' issue. What was our objective, to deter ethnic cleansing? Surely, no one could think that Milošević would now return to Rambouillet."[38]

By the end of the first week, the perceived lack of strategy, objectives, and "end-state" of the air campaign was becoming increasingly apparent;, General Clark admits that "the strategy had never actually been laid out and agreed to by Washington."[39] In a video teleconference (VTC) with his commanders, General Clark had a private discussion about the air campaign: "Were we meeting our military objectives? How were these linked to the political objectives? What were the political objectives? What is the end-state?"[40]

The lack of a clear and adequate strategy was so conspicuous and the public critique of the air campaign so intense by the end of the first week that the U.S. secretary of state, Madeleine Albright, received a call from German minister for foreign affairs, Joschka Fisher:

> Saying that it was vital for NATO to regain the political initiative, Fisher proposed that we issue a statement of war aims, the draft text of which he had already prepared. I liked the idea and also his statement. . . . The statement, soon endorsed by all NATO, would hold up with little alteration throughout the war. Before allied bombing would stop, Serb security forces must withdraw from Kosovo, a NATO-led force must be allowed to deploy, and refugees must be allowed to return home safely. "Serbs out, NATO in, refugees back," became our mantra.[41]

Shortly afterward (4 April), General Clark says, "the political end-state was being defined, and the NATO nations were toughening their expectations,"[42] and—according to the official *NATO Handbook*—these objectives were formally implemented on 12 April 1999. Thereafter, "throughout the conflict the achievement of these objectives, accompanied by measures to ensure their full implementation, was regarded by the Alliance as the prerequisite for bringing to an end the violence and human suffering in Kosovo."[43] At a NATO summit in Washington, 23–25 April, Wesley Clark says, the Alliance "at last" agreed formally on its objectives for the campaign: "(1) Stopping the violence in Kosovo; (2) withdrawing Serb military, police, and paramilitary from the province; (3) stationing an international military presence there; (4) allowing all Kosovar Albanians safe return home; and (5) working toward a political settlement based on the talks outside Paris (Rambouillet)."[44]

It had taken NATO about a week to address the distinct lack of an adequate political strategy for the air campaign, and, according to Wesley Clark, close to a month to agree formally on the objectives for OAF. As the chief of staff at SHAPE, Gen. Dieter Stöckmann, later commented, "We started strategic planning in June 1998 with assumptions, long term strategic visions and military advice regarding an intended end state. And even informal principal political consensus was achieved—however with only a minimum of the necessary, and in some aspects in contradiction to, proven military advice."[45] The British Defence Committee simply stated, "The hope that the campaign would last only a few days helped to shape a strategy that proved to be flawed."[46]

The assumption that Milošević would quickly give in to NATO demands, the need for Alliance consensus, and the lack of an adequate political strategy should this assumption fail quite clearly had, collectively, a direct impact on the military strategy. As Michael Gordon pointed out in the *New York Times*, "The need for consensus has left an unmistakable imprint on the Alliance's military strategy, causing it to take a gradual approach to the bombing campaign."[47] Brigadier General Lundberg commented on the military strategy behind OAF on the eve of war, "It became obvious to me that there simply was no strategy at the time."[48] Lieutenant General Short asserted, "We had no strategy because three nights of demonstration of resolve does not require strategy."[49] General Kelche agrees: "There was no political direction in the beginning—absent. Gradually the military strategy improved, but in the beginning—it was a mess."[50] During a postwar briefing, Commander-in-Chief Allied Forces Southern Europe, Adm. James Ellis, said that NATO not only lacked a coherent campaign plan and target set but also the staff to generate a detailed plan when it was clear that one was needed: "We called this one absolutely wrong."[51] According to General Clark, almost all military principles of war were violated when OAF started, and the whole campaign thereafter was a continuous process of adaptation, starting out with an initial military effort "driven by political dynamics toward a more effective military campaign oriented on the Principles of War."[52]

However, General Stöckmann says Lieutenant General Short was wrong in declaring that there was no military strategy. Stöckmann agrees, however, that the strategy was based on vaguely defined political guidance and had significant flaws, with "extremely strong political constraints, which did not provide sufficient room to maneuver and operate. We were not free to act as strategically as we could have done, and had too often only to react on a low level."[53] This perception was backed by the British Defence Committee: "The over-riding need to maintain Alliance unity resulted in strong political control being exerted over the conduct of the campaign, both in NATO and amongst the individual nations."[54] The report continues, "The failure of the North Atlantic Council to reach an early consensus on its policy on recourse to military means, and the inhibitions within NATO on military contingency planning which might have assisted the process of reaching that consensus, undoubtedly hobbled the Alliance during its early attempts to develop a strategy for addressing the crisis in Kosovo."[55]

Still, General Clark argues, he had to move the air campaign along some general paths; he called the factors shaping the events "measures of merit." There were three "measures of merit." The first was not to lose aircraft, or at least minimize the loss of aircraft. The second was to impact FRY military and police activities on the ground: "We had to attack and disrupt—destroy if possible—the actual elements doing the ethnic cleansing," while protecting NATO forces. The third, political, measure of merit was to retain Alliance solidarity and the full support of the regional partners. In addition came the need to isolate the theater of operations and prepare for providing humanitarian assistance. According to General Clark: "Together these were the lines of effort that guided us, day by day, and with very little modification, through the entire campaign."[56] What should be noted is General Clark's second measure of merit, which would represent not only a very difficult tactical task for the air force conducting the campaign but would also generate significant friction within the chain of command, particularly among the airmen actually executing the operation, who felt that this focus prevented strategic results. Instead, the airmen wanted to strike strategic targets in and around Belgrade.

One factor that significantly reduced NATO's political room to maneuver was the lack of UN authorization of force—particularly among European countries. This dilemma was outlined by former Swedish prime minister Ingvar Carlson and former secretary-general of the Commonwealth Shridath Ramphal in an article in the *International Herald Tribune:* "NATO countries are understandably frustrated in their efforts for peace, and rightly indignant at the humanitarian wrongs committed by the Serbian regime." Still, "temptation to assume police powers on the basis of righteousness and military strength is dangerous for world order and world peace." They point out that the UN Charter is every country's superior law and therefore conclude: "NATO air strikes against Yugoslavia have not been authorized by the United Nations. . . . They are therefore acts of aggression against a sovereign nation. They strike at the heart of the rule of international law and the authority of the United Nations."[57] Boris Yeltsin, then president of the Russian Federation, has echoed this theme in his memoirs: "After the bombing of Belgrade, all the rules that had been established by the UN during the long post-war decades collapsed."[58] This logic was deeply rooted, particularly in European nations, and it greatly influenced the domestic democratic governments' views as to how far militarily they could go without significant political consequences.

Others, like General Naumann, argued that OAF was fought on the principle that human rights needed to be protected and that as such it was perhaps the first war in European history that denied the validity of territorial integrity, which had dominated international law since the Peace of Westphalia in 1648.[59] This debate was so fierce and influenced the political perspectives to such a degree that General Clark was convinced that "if he had gone after Belgrade heavily in the first night or two, as he and others had originally wanted to do, the political outcry in Europe might have been so great that the air campaign could have ended then and there. He and Short would have been seen as the butchers of Belgrade; they, rather than Milošević, would have become the principal architects of evil."[60]

Due to the lack of consensus authorizing detailed contingency planning in NATO, the U.S. did almost all the planning for the two NATO air campaigns authorized in the fall of 1998—the "Limited Air Operations Plan" and the "Phased Air Operations Plan"—of which, according to Daalder and O'Hanlon, the latter "in large measure" following a three-stage plan developed in the fall of 1998.[61] The Limited Air Operations Plan relied "predominantly on [a limited number of] cruise missiles to strike selected targets throughout the Federal Republic of Yugoslavia, [and] was developed as a stand-alone option. As originally planned, it was intended to be a short-notice, limited air response, to a serious, but limited incident in Kosovo, with the aim of preventing a further deterioration of the situation."[62]

The Phased Air Operations Plan, which most people came to regard as NATO's air campaign plan, consisted of three executing (excluding the deployment and redeployment phases) phases of gradual escalation. Phase One aimed at establishing air superiority over Kosovo (creating a no-fly zone south of a latitude of forty-four degrees north) and degrading the command and control and IADS of the FRY, as well as the forces deployed in Kosovo. Phase Two authorized military targets in Kosovo and FRY forces south of a latitude of forty-four degrees north. Phase Three expanded the air operations "against a wide range of high-value military and security force targets throughout the FRY."[63] Thus, the Phased Air Operations Plan was devised to increase the pressure gradually on the FRY. However, it thereby also gradually increased the political cost for the NATO nations conducting the air campaign. A system was set up to make sure that the politicians would control the escalation; NATO authorized only Phase One when OAF started, and the military was not to move into Phase Two or Three unless authorized to do so by the NAC (see figure 2).

When OAF started, very few people outside the U.S. chain of command were aware of a third air campaign being executed against the FRY—Joint Task Force Noble Anvil. This operation was based on the previous Joint Task Force Flexible Anvil and Joint Task Force Sky Anvil, activated between

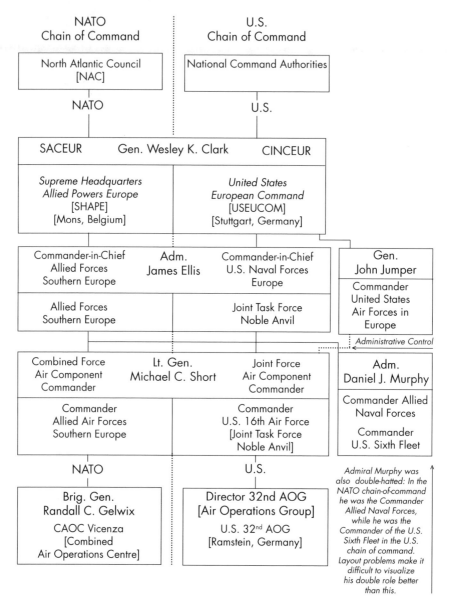

Figure 2. NATO and U.S. organizations during Operation Allied Force

August and December 1998. JTF Noble Anvil was activated in January 1999 and deactivated in July 1999.[64] It was largely a U.S.-only endeavor—presumably only supported by some very limited parts of the British intelligence community. JTF Noble Anvil included such U.S. strategic resources as B-1, B-2, B-52, F-117, E-3, and U-2 aircraft and cruise missiles.[65] The astonishing feature of this air campaign was that the United States did not inform its allies that it was to conduct a completely separate air campaign in the middle of NATO's effort to coerce Milošević to comply with NATO demands. Very few knew of its existence. According to Lambeth, "The Pentagon withheld from the allies mission specifics for literally hundreds of sorties that entailed the use of F-117s, B-2s, and cruise missiles, to ensure strict U.S. control over those U.S.-only assets and to maintain a firewall against leaks from any allies who might compromise those operations."[66]

The U.S. operation was planned by the U.S. European Command (USEUCOM) and involved separate aircraft, targeting teams, air tasking orders—in other words, a unilateral operation in the midst of the NATO operation.[67] The chief of defense of the second-largest contributor to OAF, France, General Kelche, later said that he had been completely unaware of the U.S. operation; he received a phone call from one of his officers at the Combined Air Operations Center (CAOC) in Vicenza, Italy, after OAF had started, telling him that there seemed to be a U.S. air campaign paralleling the NATO effort. The body language of General Kelche when admitting he had been uninformed of JTF Noble Anvil was unmistakable, and his darkened eyes underlined his point when he recalled, "It was just incredible. It was quite foolish, because the whole of NATO shared a political responsibility and accountability—and for the U.S. to start a separate air campaign has been a very strong incentive for some European countries to make up for their military shortcomings in order to avoid such a situation in the future."[68] General Kelche, on behalf of France, demanded to see the U.S. target lists for JTF Noble Anvil as well as for the formal NATO operation, in order to evaluate the air strikes for which France shared the political responsibility.

The chief of staff at SHAPE, General Stöckmann, was also not informed of the U.S. air campaign and was furious that he had been kept out of the information loop. Leaving no doubt of his feelings regarding this issue during the day I spent with him at his home outside Bonn, General Stöckmann simply observed that from the Alliance's point of view it was not acceptable that there was a separate—and unintegrated—U.S. air campaign unfolding, adding "Due to the lack of consistent U.S. information from the outset, we never succeeded in coordinating the two operations until the very end of the campaign."[69] General Stöckmann says the U.S. air operation had separate phases, different code names, and different targeting than NATO's phased air operation—repeatedly creating confusion in efforts to coordinate the two to create maximum effect.[70]

In fact, due to the lack of coordination, on numerous occasions allied forces ended up striking the same targets. Not surprisingly, this created frustration among the airmen involved, who naturally found it hard to see the logic of striking a target that had already been hit. General Short explains another practical example of the confusion during OAF that resulted from the two air operations executing two parallel tasking orders: "On the first night of the war, as the F-117 force was forming up in Hungary with its escort, a foreign national was screaming from a NATO AWACS [Airborne Warning and Control System], asking the CAOC 'What were those airplanes doing in Hungary?'"[71]

One can only imagine what it felt like at the very beginning of the operation to be the chief of staff at SHAPE and not be given detailed information by SACEUR on the U.S.-only air campaign. Gradually, General Stöckmann and the deputy SACEUR, General Smith, were allowed to participate in the U.S. VTCs and so received greater insight into the American operation. General Smith says that he was informed through "the British net cooperating with the Americans" but thinks this campaign was regrettable in the light of Alliance relations and politics: "The whole business of the command arrangements only aggravated the sense of being used. In the sense of an alliance—I think it was fundamentally wrong."[72] Later commenting on the U.S. unilateral operation, Lieutenant General Short admitted:

If we are to be a team, we can't just be a team on paper. We need to be a coalition command structure. We should never again, never again, run a U.S.-only command structure inside of a NATO alliance. We should not try to run that rabbit up our allies' legs and pull it out of their hat ever again. . . . We inserted in the middle of that staff a U.S.-only operation whose commander was a Navy admiral. . . . We called it a joint task force, and they were given operational level responsibility for running a NATO war. We can never do that again to our allies, or we will not have allies.[73]

Below is the command structure showing the "double-hatted" U.S. commanders in their U.S. and NATO chains of command—an arrangement that places JTF Noble Anvil in the U.S.-only hierarchy, with Admiral Ellis as commander of the operation (see figure 3).

When OAF started, as he later admitted, the only military objective Lieutenant General Short was ordered to achieve was loosely defined as a campaign "to show NATO resolve."[74] According to a U.S. Department of

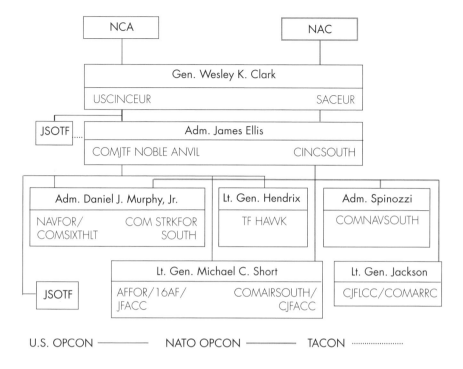

U.S. OPCON ———— NATO OPCON ———— TACON ·····················

NOTE: This figure does not include Joint Task Force Shining Hope

Figure 3. Command structure for the U.S. air operation JTF Noble Anvil, January–July 1999

Defense report after the war, SACEUR had ordered a new option as the peace talks at Rambouillet broke down—a two-day strike option to convince Milošević to withdraw his forces and cease hostilities.[75] Referring to what must be regarded as an inadequate strategy, Lieutenant General Short later acknowledged, "We were prepared to fly a few sorties and bomb them for a couple of nights. Here are your targets; don't think, just execute."[76] The same message was conveyed to the targeting cell at CAOC Vicenza, which was told—less than forty-eight hours before the operation started—to "select three nights of good targets," since it was almost certain that the international community would stop the bombing by the third day. The targeting cell at CAOC Vicenza had received little or no strategic guidance concerning objectives, other than that of showing resolve.[77] This notion is supported by Lambeth, who claims that the frequent hesitation and indecision exhibited by NATO's political leaders led uninformed critics to label its selection process as "ad hoc targeting."[78] Lieutenant General Short admits that the expectation of a short air victory directly contributed to an inadequate targeting organization: "I fault myself for waiting four weeks to stand up the STRAT/GAT [Strategy/Guidance, Apportionment and Targeting] cell. It made an incredible difference. I should've realized that is what's needed in the beginning."[79] At one briefing in the early stages of OAF, one of Lieutenant General Short's subordinates stood up and stated, "It seems to me that what we are doing is randomly bombing military targets with no coherent strategy, sir"—to which Short replied, "You're absolutely right."[80] The British Defence Committee later simply observed, "Political uncertainty may have been the cause of an absence of clarity and coherence of purpose that was sometimes apparent in NATO's choice of targets."[81] In fact, the application of airpower in the perceived absence of either a strategy or focused targeting was so incongruous that the air leadership at CAOC Vicenza was sure that a deal had already been struck with Milošević and that the somewhat "token" bombing had taken place only in order to enable Milošević to restore his domestic power base while giving way to NATO's demands—publicly saying it would be a waste of lives resisting the mighty NATO alliance and wiser to opt for a peaceful solution.[82]

Attempting to sum up the lack of adequate strategy and, consequently, what appeared to be a somewhat random targeting effort, I asked several individuals whether the initial NATO strategy had been reduced to a target list of varying length and quality, from which high-level military officers, ambassadors, and politicians had chosen their targets. In addition, I mentioned the following points: the target list had been produced with limited or no strategic guidance; the targets had often been picked (vetoed, denied, or chosen) by people with limited military experience (ambassadors, bureaucrats, and politicians); the targeting procedure during OAF had been very cumbersome and had been heavily influenced by the fear of collateral damage, loss of domestic political support, loss of alliance cohesion, and the different domestic political agendas in the region. As the very nature of targeting is such that if certain targets are vetoed others cannot be struck the same night, because of sequenced targeting, available forces, planning, risk to aircrew, and so on, it is tempting to say that the initial vague NATO strategy of showing resolve and thereby getting Milošević back to the Rambouillet negotiations was reduced to selecting targets for the following day or night from a list of largely randomly selected targets to achieve loosely focused objectives. The chief of the targeting cell at CAOC Vicenza simply answered, "You are spot on"—adding that because of the lack of strategic guidance, after about a week of the campaign the targeting cell came up with its own objectives for the targeting effort. "Not until much later in the air campaign was a proper strategy to link target sets to strategic objectives put in place, and by then we felt it was much too late."[83] Wing Commander Corbett says that the only guidance received was from media briefs by the NATO military spokesman, which they saw on TV. Thus they tried to piece together a targeting strategy accordingly.

With that, the irony of NATO's lack of preparedness seems to have come full circle: the targeting cell received guidance from watching the Alliance's military spokesman on CNN—a military spokesman who had to explain NATO's choice of targets to journalists, unaware that the targeting cell, which was about to generate new targets for him to comment upon, was watching in order to get some kind of guidance on which to base their choice of targets.

General Stöckmann has confirmed that the operational targeting level continuously warned SACEUR that there were too few substantial high-value targets, but he points out that political constraints were the reason for this lack. "Military execution on the tactical level was not only dictated by striving for effectiveness, but increasingly more by the rules to (1) avoid own losses, (2) avoid collateral damage, and (3) avoid conflicts with humanitarian organizations—in order to maintain NATO cohesion."[84] A NATO air campaign planner during OAF, Col. Chris Lorraine, claims that from the outset he could find no coherent strategy: "The amazingly small target list at the beginning of the campaign caused a lot of sorties to be wasted on insignificant targets."[85] After the war, General Naumann stated that one of the important lessons learned from OAF was that "we have to go after those targets which really hit the opponent and force him to accept our will," which was not done initially in OAF.[86] Asked whether the initial NATO strategy of showing NATO resolve had been reduced as suggested above, the vice chairman of the U.S. Joint Chiefs of Staff, Gen. Joseph Ralston, said he believed that to be correct for the first few days of the air campaign. Ralston added that the perception that little or no strategic guidance was given to the targeting cell was "probably correct" and also that he did not believe the targeting community was well prepared. Furthermore, he argued with Wesley Clark on strategy and the initial Phase One of NATO's phased air operation: "Bombing surface-to-air missile sites—why the hell would Milošević care about something like that? That was not going to cause him to review or change, and that was basically what was on the target list for the first three days—it was defensive systems."[87]

The statement is interesting for several reasons. It indicates the inherent contradiction of aiming to coerce Milošević to accept NATO demands within a few days while largely targeting only the IADS—without identifying Milošević's centers of gravity or factors that would be critical in altering his thinking. Furthermore, it largely confirms the overriding assumption that Milošević would give way within three days and that all that was needed was a show of NATO resolve. So, attacking the IADS these three initial days would not only be standard air force doctrine but it would show resolve, while undergoing minimum risk of collateral damage while targeting military systems only. It would be, politically perceived, a win-win situation—maximum effect with minimum risk. It would be a strategy the former U.S. chairman of the Joint Chiefs of Staff, Gen. Colin Powell, called "a strategy based on the 'hope to win' and not on a certainty that, in the end, the Alliance would prevail."[88] As it turned out, it was a gross miscalculation—a gamble—that jeopardized NATO's credibility.

OAF started with the authorization of Phase One of NATO's Phased Air Operations Plan and the limited air operation.[89] If Milošević did not back down as assumed, NATO would gradually increase the pressure, moving through Phase Two and Phase Three attacks on military and strategic targets throughout Serbia, including Belgrade. Asked what would happen then, after one week of bombing, one senior official admitted, "There is no phase 4."[90] According to Daalder and O'Hanlon, U.S. and NATO officials expected Phase One strikes to change the mindset of Milošević, and that is why at the outset "NATO only had three days worth of targets—about 90 in total."[91] The first night involved some fifty-one selected targets, "directed at Serb air defenses, airfields, and communications."[92] Wesley Clark recalls the first few days of OAF: "The first night we didn't get a knockout blow on the Serb air defense—it didn't come up. The second night, they also didn't bring up the air defense, so we began to realize we had trouble. Third night there was bad weather. The fourth night was a Saturday night and we lost a F-117 and all missions got scrapped. So it was pretty clear by Sunday and Monday that we weren't going to get a knockout blow."[93]

Maj. James Hardin, U.S. Air Force, recalls the initial phase: "All the target sets that were given had been hit, so there weren't any approved targets to go and hit any more unless we went out there and struck the same targets again, which in fact was what we did."[94] General Short comments, "I do remember on the third night cancelling the second wave of F-117s because we were out of targets. Of the 91 that we had been given, we had struck that target set."[95]

The targeting procedures had not been established before the air campaign started, and because of the very limited list of targets authorized for Phase One, by day three NATO and the United States were striking targets already struck, because they had no more targets to strike. General Clark pointed out that on day two of the campaign, "we had to establish a routine and work it [the targeting process] consistently every single day."[96] Without an initial coherent military strategy for selecting targets specifically designed to affect the FRY leadership, NATO was initially left to strike whatever targets were available. Thus one of the key issues became the target approval process. General Clark says, "At first we were able to restrict detailed target approvals to the U.S. channel, but others then sought detailed access, and the process continued to open. . . . The original plans had presumed that the SACEUR would have the authority to strike targets within overall categories specified by NATO political leaders, but Washington had introduced a target-by-target approval requirement."[97]

In addition, the United Kingdom and France were soon demanding greater input into the operation. As previously noted, France was surprised to find that the United States was striking targets in a unilateral air operation, and it demanded to know all targets being struck. General Kelche eventually gained access to the target lists during the first week, and after that the lists and proposed targets were received in Paris before 8 PM each evening. In fact, from then on, according to Kelche, General Clark and the defense chiefs in the United States, the United Kingdom, and France discussed military strategy and targeting regularly.[98] Dana Priest of the *Washington Post* says it was a myth that OAF was run by a nineteen-nation committee: "It was clear that the important choices—such as whether to bomb targets that had a largely civilian character—were made by the leaders of three countries: the United States, Britain and France."[99] Germany became involved later. (It has not been possible to obtain a German explanation at the political level for its initial absence from this forum.) In fact, the rumors within the Alliance of a "black committee" making decisions on military strategy prompted the only collective meeting of all chiefs of defense, which took place at a later stage of the operation.[100] The Norwegian representative on NATO's Military Committee, Lt. Gen. Per Bøthun, said that the Military Committee largely felt bypassed from the outset and that events were driven largely by the strategic side at SHAPE, and by the United States.[101]

With the strategy largely being reduced to bombing according to the following night's target list, influence on authorization of targets became of paramount significance in terms of influence on the operation itself. The targeting process continued to be a source of friction within the Alliance for the days to come. As General Clark characterizes it, "The targeting issue had become the favourite 'whipping boy' within the Pentagon."[102] By the end of the week (General Ralston was not quite sure but believed it was day five or six of OAF), triggered by constant complaints that some European nations were vetoing proposed targets, General Ralston wrote a one-page document providing targeting guidance for Wesley Clark. The proposal, which was almost immediately accepted by France, Britain, Germany, and Italy, said that General Clark had automatic approval to take out any tactical target (field forces, tanks—that is, troops on the ground in Kosovo). The authority came with the following restrictions upon the air campaign (the following is a summary of General Ralston's main terms, not a direct quotation from the document):

1. Don't bomb anything in Montenegro. Because this is a political decision—we are trying to keep Montenegro out of the fight. Even then a caveat said, if an airplane is threatened by a system in Montenegro, you are automatically cleared to take that out. If they put an SA-3 [surface-to-air missile] or a MiG [fighter aircraft] in Montenegro, you can bomb that if you need to, but as a general policy, don't bomb in Montenegro.

2. Don't bomb inside five nautical miles of downtown Belgrade without coming back to the NATO capitals for approval. Now, you can argue about whether that was too much political interference or not, but it was necessary to get agreement from everyone. It didn't say that one *couldn't* bomb within five nautical miles—and we did bomb within five nautical miles—but if you were going to do that, the heads of state wanted to know what it was they were bombing.

3. For every target, we had "what were the predicted casualties and what about unintended casualties—civilian casualties?" If there was a number greater than X—and I am not going to talk about X here—you needed to get political approval. And it was a pretty sizable number.

4. The electrical grid—don't bomb it without political agreement. This turned out to be a legal question more than a strategic one. There were people who said "Take out the electrical grid, because the people in Serbia will get all upset and put pressure on Milošević, and that will help force him to withdraw." If you do that, though, it will be a war crime. If you bomb the electrical grid because it is supplying the electricity to the surface-to-air missile sites, that is a legal target. So that restriction was put on there for legal reasons.

General Ralston added, "Those are not many restrictions. My own view is—in retrospect—that we should have done that prior to the start of the conflict. But we didn't. Once that was done, it solved a lot of the problems."[103] When later asked why this targeting guidance hadn't been provided before the campaign started, General Clark answered, "People weren't smart enough to establish all the basic targeting guidelines up front. It was an interactive process with the political leaders."[104] What should be noted is that the targeting guidance provided by General Ralston was not guidance in terms of what to target in order to achieve the desired effect but rather what *not* to target—most probably indicating the focus and sensitivity of the air campaign. As General Clark makes clear many times in his memoirs, military strategy, the air campaign, and the targeting process were generated, adapted, and modified as the air campaign evolved; they were not chiseled out as a substantial part of the decision to go to war: "It is always preferable, though not always possible, to have agreed on the strategy for full success before the first aircraft is moved or the first shot fired. The corollary, however, is that even in the absence of an agreed strategy, it is sometimes possible to succeed through adapting during war."[105]

Later commenting on the lack of initial adequate coherent strategy, one of the most significant airpower theorists, John A. Warden III, said, "There is a problem with this—namely, the impossibility of creating a coherent attack campaign to meet shifting objectives. Every bomb in today's world that you drop ought to be directly connected to the underlying grand strategy, the essence of going to war. The allied war against Yugoslavia did not meet that standard."[106]

As previously noted, the phased air operation has generally been seen as NATO's air campaign plan for OAF. It was created with three separate phases to allow the politicians to control the escalation of the campaign. One would evaluate the results of one phase and move to another based on consensus in the NAC. Clearly, the military wanted more room to maneuver, but the phases were designed with targeting and geographical limitations to provide political control of the operation. The campaign was initially marked by political sensitivity and the very limited number of authorized targets when OAF started; on the second day Secretary-General Solana asked General Clark how soon he would ask to move to Phase Two of the operation, to which General Clark answered that he would like to move as soon as possible.[107] By day three, however, General Clark admits, NATO was not even close to accomplishing the Phase One objective of destroying the Serb IADS—and NATO was already departing from the original concept of the phased air operation by moving beyond Phase One targets before the Serb IADS had been broken.[108] Wesley Clark was already pushing for Phase Three targets to be authorized. On 28 March (day five), the NAC formally authorized Phase Two targets.[109]

In a special NAC meeting on 30 March, NATO moved to something commonly referred to as Phase Two Plus—a fairly creative solution to a pragmatic problem. Several NATO nations were reluctant to move to Phase Three of NATO's Phased Air Operations Plan, so NATO adopted Phase Two Plus instead. This gave Secretary-General Solana the role of approving or disapproving specific targets that technically were in Phase Three—but informally consulting countries with particular concerns before making decisions.[110] According to Lambeth, Phase Three targets (Phase Two Plus) commenced de facto on day nine of OAF (two days after the NAC meeting).

Seemingly due to the limited preparations, lack of authorized targets, the constant evolution and adaptation of the campaign, and the evidently faulty assumption that Milošević would immediately fold once threatened with force, the phased air operation did not develop as had been politically intended. There were no distinct phases—with clearly defined beginnings and ends—to be evaluated before moving on to another, escalating step that would provide a collective political authorization of each phase. Rather the distinction between the phases was blurred, and the air campaign seemingly became one long process of gradually increasing escalation. It moved from Phase One to Phase Two, and even arguing for Phase Three, with the objective of Phase One clearly not having been achieved. Lambeth argues: "To all intents and purposes, the difference between Phase Two and Phase One was indistinguishable as far as the intensity of NATO's air attacks was concerned. The commencement of Phase Two was characterized as more of an evolution than a sharp change of direction."[111]

General Naumann tells a very interesting story of the transition to the creative Phase Two Plus arrangement. Formally, the phased air operation had geographical limitations. With the exception of the IADS, there was generally no targeting of FRY forces or facilities north of forty-four degrees north until Phase Three. On the first day of OAF, the Greek military representative on the Military Committee objected to targets that had been struck in Serbia proper the preceding night, pointing out that this was not in accordance with what the NAC had authorized (Phase One only). General Naumann replied that NATO had de facto authorized two air operations and that the limited air operation had no geographical restrictions. Therefore striking targets in Serbia proper was authorized. This was clearly a breach of the whole concept of the Phased Air Operations Plan, and I asked General Naumann if the design of the two air campaigns had been specifically devised to provide the political leverage needed to strike outside the formally authorized phases of the Phased Air Operations Plan. He answered: "It was intended, we wanted to have the options open—and we used this option at the time."[112] When it became clear that the campaign was heading toward Phase Three, it became obvious to General Naumann and Secretary-General Solana that it would be impossible for the NAC to reach the necessary consensus to authorize such a step. General Naumann explains, "You need to understand: had we lost the political cohesion, we would have lost the strategic level of war. In order to win strategically, we had to accept tactical and operational limitations.

It was a bitter pill to swallow, but there was no other way after we had started the campaign."[113]

General Naumann admits he was responsible for the Phase Two Plus "trick." Knowing that the military wanted to strike harder to achieve a solution, he was equally aware that Phase Three was likely never to be authorized. Naumann describes how in his summary after the debate in the NAC, before the decision was taken, Secretary-General Solana stated that he intended to authorize expanded targeting in Serbia proper. Solana would personally authorize these targets and in that way reassure the NAC of his personal attention to the process. Naumann believed that the NAC would be "just a little bit tired and less alert after hours of debate," and he—after informally discussing the matter with some members of the NAC—assured Solana that there would be no objections to his authorizing targets exceeding Phase Two but without formally going to Phase Three of the operation. As General Naumann admitted, "That was the secret behind authorizing Phase Two Plus."[114]

When I asked the Norwegian minister of defense, Eldbjørg Løwer, how she perceived political control regarding the transition from one phase to another, she said, "It was not evident when one moved from one phase to another. It was clear that the dynamics of events once the campaign started made it difficult to distinguish the phases."[115] Norwegian foreign minister Knut Vollebæk confirmed the perception of the defense minister: "The transition from one phase to another was not entirely clear—the dynamics of war influenced the process."[116] The Fourteenth Report of the British Defence Committee simply states, "The air campaign was divided conceptually into three phases, though these were very compressed and overlapped . . . however, our informal discussions would suggest that the formal decision to move to strategic bombing of Serbia (Phase Three) was never put directly, in quite those terms, to the NAC."[117]

Col. Morten Klever at CAOC Vicenza said that due to the limited target list and the speed of operations, "the air campaign became de facto one long phase."[118] This is notable, because evidence suggests that the French in particular were somewhat taken by surprise at the Phase Two Plus enlargement of the target base. The attack on the Yugoslav Interior Ministry—that is, providing that Lambeth's information that attacking Phase Two Plus targets commenced de facto on day nine of OAF is correct—happened just two days later. According to a French diplomat, "The first time President Chirac of France realized how fast and far the air campaign had moved from its original, modest size was when he watched the Yugoslav Interior Ministry erupt into a fireball on April 3, day 11 of the war." According to the diplomat, "Paris was shocked," and Chirac made an urgent call to President Clinton to discuss strategy.[119] The NATO targeting cell was not informed that the alliance had moved to Phase Two Plus until it heard NATO's military press spokesman say so in a press conference on TV. As Wing Commander Corbett admits: "Again, that was the first we had heard of this."[120]

After the first week of OAF, NATO was on its way to Phase Two Plus without a clear military strategy, with its targeting cell watching NATO's military press spokesman on TV for strategic guidance, and a military leadership questioning both objectives and the "end-state" of the operation. According to the *Washington Post*, the perspective in Washington was clear after the first week: "By the start of the second week, Clinton administration officials acknowledged that Operation Allied Force had failed to meet its declared goal of halting Serbian violence against the ethnic Albanians."[121] Milošević had not altered his behavior. The gamble that he would do so within a few days had failed. Now it was all about adapting, prevailing, fighting—and not losing NATO's credibility.

Gradually the strategy, planning, and performance improved, but the initial phase—performing what the strongest military alliance in mankind had threatened to do for a year—was an epic underachievement. The rest of this book is dedicated to finding the origins of and reasons for this level of unpreparedness.

NATO's secretary-general, Dr. Javier Solana. Picture taken during a press statement by the NATO secretary-general concerning the crisis in Kosovo, 23 March 1999, the day before Operation Allied Force commenced. (NATO photo)

The chairman of the NATO Military Committee, Gen. Klaus Naumann. Press conference at the close of the Military Committee meetings at chiefs of staff level, 5–6 May 1998. (NATO photo)

NATO's Supreme Allied Commander Europe (SACEUR), Gen. Wesley K. Clark. Photo shows General Clark giving a television interview in Studio Ismay at NATO Headquarters Brussels, 31 March 1999. (NATO photo)

Gen. Jean-Pierre Kelche, chief of defense, France, during NATO defense ministers meetings, 7 June 2001. Left to right: General Kelche talking to Mr. Alain Richard, French minister of defense. (NATO photo)

Gen. John Jumper (left), Commander, U.S. Air Forces Europe, was in charge of the American planning effort in Ramstein, Germany, and thus in effect led the planning effort of both the U.S.-only air operation and the initial planning of the two NATO air campaigns (limited and phased air operations). Here, General Jumper passes the command colors to Lt. Gen. Richard Bethurem, USAF, while Lt. Gen. Michael C. Short, commander of NATO's Air Forces Southern Europe, looks on. (Department of Defense photo / Tech. Sgt. James D. Green)

NATO spokesmen when OAF commenced. Left to right: Air Commodore David Wilby (SHAPE Policy Requirements Division) and Jamie Shea. Air Commodore Wilby was later replaced, according to General Clark, when Secretary-General Solana ordered him to do so due to NATO mistakes in public affairs. (NATO photo)

Vice chairman of the U.S. Joint Chiefs of Staff, Gen. Joseph Ralston. General Ralston was the senior American airman during OAF and wrote the targeting guidance of OAF five or six days after OAF had started. Pictured: Press conference after the change of command ceremony at SHAPE headquarters, on 3 May 2000, when General Ralston replaced General Clark as SACEUR. (NATO photo)

Lt. Gen. Michael C. Short, commander of NATO's Air Forces Southern Europe. Lieutenant General Short says NATO prepared inadequately before OAF: "We were prepared to fly a few sorties and bomb them for a couple of nights. Here are your targets; don't think, just execute." (Department of Defense photo/Master Sgt. John McDowell)

The chief of staff at the Supreme Headquarters Allied Powers Europe (SHAPE), Gen. Dieter Stöckmann. General Stöckmann says that from the military's point of view, it was not acceptable that there was a separate—and not integrated—American air campaign unfolding at the same time: "Due to the lack of consistent U.S. information from the outset, we never succeeded in coordinating the two operations properly until the very end of the campaign." (Copyright Gen. Dieter Stöckmann)

Operation Allied Force commenced 24 March 1999. The air campaign would last seventy-eight days. It was the first time a theater war of the size of OAF had been fought predominantly by airpower. (NATO photo)

Part II
Prelude to War: Setting the Stage for Operation Allied Force

Britain has no permanent friends, only permanent interests. And so it has been for all nations and alliances.

—Lord Palmerston

Chapter 2
THE AIRPOWER DEBATE AND OAF

Airpower is an unusually seductive form of military strength, in part because, like modern courtship, it appears to offer gratification without commitment.

—Eliot A. Cohen[1]

When the first NATO missiles entered FRY airspace on 24 March 1999, the influence of the U.S. Air Force (USAF) on Operation Allied Force could hardly have been overestimated. The planning for the operation was largely done unilaterally by Air Force general John Jumper's staff at the U.S. European Command at Ramstein Air Base in Germany. The U.S. Air Force held the key positions in the chain of command at the Combined Air Operations Center (CAOC) Vicenza, and the target-generation process was largely a U.S.-only endeavor. The Air Force contributed significantly more aircraft to OAF than the other allies combined, and the United States dropped more than 80 percent of the total number of munitions expended. Since their allies could not gather, process, and distribute intelligence in real time, the United States had to provide this capacity. Thus, an American postwar analysis rightly concluded that the United States "provided most of the aircraft, flew most of the sorties, and directed much of the conduct of the operation."[2]

With the U.S. Air Force so influential in the planning and execution of Operation Allied Force and airpower being the key element in NATO's coercive diplomacy—it becomes of particular interest to analyze the Air Force's conceptual thinking on *how* airpower should be used in the unique political context of the Kosovo crisis. How was NATO going to use airpower to coerce the Federal Republic of Yugoslavia to accede to NATO demands?

By the time the Kosovo crisis surfaced, the strategic use of conventional airpower had achieved the status of official doctrine in the Air Force. With its intellectual roots in the interwar period of the 1920–30s, its institutionalized focus for the better part of the twentieth century had lain in fighting high-intensity wars. To the airmen approaching Kosovo, the strategic use of airpower in the 1991 Gulf War had shown that rapid escalation and overwhelming force aimed at the enemy's leadership constituted the preferable way to apply airpower. It was what they had been taught at air campaign courses at Maxwell Air Force Base.

This approach did not fit the political nature of the Kosovo crisis. The Air Force's doctrinaire focus on decisive force and high-intensity warfare proved to be an institutionalized hindrance in terms of crafting a strategy based on the political realities in Belgrade—or on the perspectives, limitations, and political maneuvering room of the various governments within the NATO alliance. As a result, the U.S. Air Force was unprepared for the coercive diplomacy it was intended to support.

The goal of this chapter is to provide an understanding of the historical experiences and lines of thought that formed the Air Force's perspective on airpower. Bringing this perspective to the Kosovo crisis, the service would contribute to shaping the broader international diplomacy, which relied on airpower as the key coercive instrument.

I have chosen to emphasize the teachings and influence of Col. John A. Warden III and the theories of political scientist Robert A. Pape. One should be careful not to overestimate Warden's influence within the U.S. Air Force, but his ideas on the strategic use of conventional airpower, together with the more general experiences and perceived success of the 1991 Gulf War, generated a renaissance in American airpower thinking that demands a particular focus. In the same way, with his book *Bombing to Win: Air Power and Coercion in War,* Robert A. Pape provided a comprehensive study on the coercive effects of airpower and subsequently generated a vigorous debate on how best to employ airpower. Both the timing (*Bombing to Win* was published in 1996) of the debate and the focus on coercive airpower make it a natural focus in terms of evaluating how one envisaged the use of airpower in the Kosovo crisis.

It has been my purpose to outline the key arguments of the airpower debate and provide an understanding of the immense complexities of translating airpower into political effect. It has proven to be a story of inadequate thinking, fighting for institutionalized independence, and friction between the political and military leadership in war. Operation Allied Force would prove no different.

When OAF started, the issue of how best to apply airpower had been debated for almost a century. The dominating focus had been how to win high-intensity wars. Two schools of thought dominated this airpower debate. First, in contrast to the horrors of the trench warfare of World War I, the airplane offered the ability to reach the enemy heartland without confronting land and naval forces. Advocates of this school of thought generally argued that airpower should be applied primarily against the enemy's will and industrial capacity to fight, less against its ability to do so at the front. By analyzing the strengths and weaknesses of the enemy society, one could identify critical elements that if struck would reduce his will or strategic ability to wage war—be it the will of the people, vital infrastructure, key industrial nodes, or the leadership. This perspective has traditionally focused on airpower's ability to win wars, the ability to do so more quickly and cost-effectively than ground and naval forces, and the need for institutionalized independence for the air forces.

The second school of thought generally saw the airplane as yet another technological way to support the more traditional concepts of land and naval warfare. Airpower should be used primarily against the enemy's fielded forces and thus support the land forces winning the battle on the ground. By contributing to the military victory on the battlefield, the enemy's ability to wage war was eliminated, and so was his ability to oppose the attacker's will. This perspective has traditionally been rooted within the army and navy, who generally argue that while air superiority *is* important, a closer organizational and doctrinal relationship with an air force in a supporting role is preferable.[3]

The intellectual roots and often well-reasoned focus on winning high-intensity wars have been in contrast to the far weaker focus directed toward crisis management, how to use airpower in conflicts of the lower band of the intensity spectrum, and coercion to support diplomacy. The general tendency has been to assume uncritically that a capability to fight a big war implies an equal ability to handle smaller conflicts. Thus, with the general notion that fighting high-intensity wars vital to national interest is a premise for the application of airpower, the U.S. Air Force has tended to focus on war-winning strategies and technology, and strategic bombing of the enemy heartland has generally been the center of attention. From this perspective, war has less need for diplomatic sensitivity in ongoing operations. For instance, Germany and Japan were to be defeated in World War II. Period. Less thought was invested in analyzing the effect of airpower throughout the intensity spectrum. Within the Air Force, the tendency throughout the twentieth century was that the general belief in the effect of strategic application of airpower exceeded its intellectual capacity to deliver such effect.

A significant theorist, among the first to recognize the potential of airpower, was the Italian general Giulio Douhet. Impressed by the performance of the airplane, Douhet asserted in 1910 that "the skies are about to become a battlefield as important as the land and sea. . . . only by gaining the command of the air shall we be able to derive the fullest benefit from the advantage which can only be fully exploited when the enemy is compelled to be earth bound."[4] Douhet perceived that the ultimate objective of wars had never been the defeat of the enemy armed forces but rather the destruction of the adversary's will or capability to resist one's will: "Although the enemy armies and navies had been the primary targets in all the centuries that had passed, they no longer were barriers blocking the route to the really vital targets of the enemy heartland."[5] Airpower historian Phillip S. Meilinger argues that Douhet probably was the first to realize that the key to airpower was targeting and to emphasize that one had to identify the most vital areas of a modern country to be targeted.[6] Douhet identified five basic target systems as the vital centers of a modern country: industry, transportation infrastructure, communication nodes, government buildings, and the will of the people—arguing that the will of the people was the most important. One could attack it most effectively by urban bombing, which would terrorize the population; a mixture of high-explosive, incendiary, and gas or biological bombs was preferable.[7] Thus the term "terror bombing" was conceived. By killing and terrorizing the civilian population an attacker could force the enemy nation to accede to its demands, the argument went.

The degree to which Douhet influenced American perspectives on airpower is debated. Airpower historian Gian P. Gentile claims that most scholars "would agree that Douhet's collective works gave a literary comprehensiveness to the ideas that shaped the American conceptual approach to strategic bombing."[8] Where Douhet was quite explicit on focusing on the *will* of the people, the American approach was initially less inclined to accept the logic of terror bombing, instead developing an indirect approach—affecting the enemy nation's *will* by attacking its *capacity* to wage war.

The American approach to strategic bombing was significantly influenced by the airpower community associated with the Air Corps Tactical School (ACTS) in Maxwell, Alabama. The ACTS—represented by Robert Webster and Muir S. Fairchild in the middle and later 1930s—focused on destroying or paralyzing "national organic systems on which many factories and numerous people depended."[9] These ideas became known as the "Industrial Web Theory." The premise was that bombing carefully selected key industrial nodes could produce social collapse of an opponent: "the assumption was that an industrial state's economy was fragile, and if certain critical industry nodes were hit, the entire economic system would collapse. Economic disintegration, in turn, would render the enemy incapable of sustaining military operations, and thus incite the civilian population to put pressure on the government to stop the war."[10]

Along the lines of the Industrial Web Theory, bombardment of key economic, industrial, and societal nodes became U.S. doctrine. This line of thought was embodied in the first U.S. strategic air campaign plan, *Air War*

Planning Document-1 (AWPD-1)—presented by the Air War Plans Division (AWPD) staff in August 1941. By carefully selecting targets that would disrupt or neutralize the German war-making capability, it envisioned that a significant decline could be induced in the operational effectiveness of the German army before an Allied invasion of the European continent—even "bring the German nation to terms."[11] When developing the AWPD-1, the chief of the Air Corps Operations Planning Branch, Gen. Haywood S. Hansell, described how one attempted to identify "service systems, i.e., systems which motivated or connected industries, rather than industries themselves. Electric power, for example, was vital to all industries."[12] This reference to the enemy state and its economy as a "system," and the emphasis on electric power, should be kept in mind, as it would surface during OAF.

General Hansell recognized the problems of selective targeting of industrial systems. In fall 1944, as the commander of U.S. XXI Bomber Command in the Mariana Islands in the Pacific, he stated that it was "exceedingly difficult to measure and evaluate the results of selective target bombing"—adding that statistics of bombs dropped and sorties flown were more measurable. Hansell interestingly noted, "Photographs of burned-out cities also speak for themselves."[13] According to historian William W. Ralph, the focus on area firebombing against the cities of Japan in the latter part of World War II "represented a stunning departure" from the daylight, high-altitude "precision" bombing developed at the ACTS (i.e., the Industrial Web Theory). By early 1945, the perception of the chief of the U.S. Army Air Forces, Gen. Henry "Hap" Arnold, was that "precision" bombing of selected targets did not work, bringing into question air force influence in the Pacific and threatening the prestigious B-29 program—a combination that could "jeopardize the USAAF's long-sought goal of institutional autonomy from the army."[14] With analyses showing Japanese war production intermingled with urban housing because of the widespread practice of subcontracting production of war materials to small workshops, the focus gradually shifted toward area fire-bombing. In addition, some argued that such attacks would cause a psychological collapse in Japan. Cdr. William M. McGovern of the Office of Strategic Studies argued that "after a few major fire attacks, the Japanese would demand that their government surrender."[15] It was a concept that resembled the terror bombing of Giulio Douhet—and another promise of a quick end to a war through strategic airpower. Driven by the need for results and determined to achieve "institutional independence" for the air force, General Arnold ordered Maj. Gen. Curtis LeMay to replace Hansell in January 1945—and to get results.[16] The subsequent campaign against Japan, deemed "blind reliance on destruction" by Ralph, "took on a momentum of its own." Ralph argues that "the campaign stemmed directly from the immediate need to prove strategic bombing's usefulness." On the night of 9 March 1945, 325 B-29s attacked residential Tokyo—creating a firestorm killing some hundred thousand people, "mostly women, children, and the elderly." According to the U.S. Strategic Bombing Survey after the war, it was "the greatest disaster ever visited upon any city."[17]

By spring 1945, the high echelons of the U.S. Army Air Forces had recognized that it was difficult to measure and evaluate the effects of selective targeting of industrial systems. As Dr. John A. Olsen points out:

> The Industrial Web Theory became a popular concept among airmen, but its limitations were obvious: it assumed that war could be treated in a scientific manner, it believed in high-technological solutions to complex matters on the ground, it assumed that the enemy was a passive system and it underestimated the strength of the population. Advocates of strategic bombardment believed society could be viewed as a mechanical piece of clockwork that would stop if certain physical elements were eliminated, not appreciating the resilient nature of the German economy and society.[18]

Not only was the conceptual foundation of the Industrial Web Theory questionable, but in the Pacific theater the United States had shifted its strategy to the even more questionable methodology of terror bombing, because the former strategy appeared not to work. Major General LeMay felt he had to make changes in the application of airpower. "I am working on several very radical methods of employment of the force," LeMay told the chief of staff of the Twentieth Air Force, Gen. Lauris Norstad, in a letter less than a week before the infamous attack on Tokyo. Thus, LeMay admitted shortly before the most devastating conventional strategic bombing attack in history that he "had to do something."[19] Both the methodology and intellectual foundation of strategic bombing were still in the early stages.

The atomic bombing of Hiroshima and Nagasaki and the subsequent capitulation of Japan were to change the conceptual thinking of airpower. With the atomic bomb and the Cold War came the strategic logic of *deterrence,* with the "Massive Retaliation" doctrine—later replaced by "Flexible Response." Airpower historian Carl H. Builder holds that the invention and use of the atomic bomb were to validate beyond question the potential effectiveness of strategic bombing, as well as providing the means to institutional independence for the future U.S. Air Force. The atomic bomb would not only confirm the importance of strategic bombing but also required the Air Force to prevent its delivery on the United States by an enemy. Thus the Air Force viewed itself as the first line of defense of the United States as well as the main deterrent to any aggressor.

And so, the concept of a nuclear-armed bomber force on alert emerged just months after the first atomic bomb had been dropped. The outlines of the Strategic Air Command (SAC) emerged about one year after World War II—before the Air Force had gained its independence. Still, the voices in favor of integrating airpower with ground forces were influential, and the Army wanted its own separate tactical air arm. According to Jeffrey Record, the arguments for an independent air force after World War II rested largely on the proposition that airpower—particularly strategic bombing—could provide a quick and relatively cheap means of winning wars independently of surface forces.[20] The U.S. Air Force was formed in 1947 and consisted of the Strategic Air Command and the Tactical Air Command (TAC). Importantly, Builder notes:

[SAC] would dominate the Air Force and strategic thinking for almost two decades, worldwide. LeMay's SAC would own the Air Force; SAC was the Air Force; and SAC was the world's most awesome and respected military force. . . . At the same time, the leadership of the Air Force was steadily shifting to the more numerous aviators who were not so much airpower theorists as they were [World War II] fliers and operators. These were people who had come into the war as aviation enthusiasts and for whom airpower theory was accepted as proven background, not to be questioned and without any need for development.[21]

Thus for the years to come, the U.S. Air Force was to envisage fighting either a strategic campaign with nuclear weapons or providing airpower in support of ground forces. Therefore, when it became involved in the Vietnam War, the use of *conventional strategic* airpower had neither been trained for nor significantly debated since World War II.

The Vietnam War was not only important in terms of the development of airpower theory but would shape the perspectives of the American officers constituting the top leadership of both the 1991 Gulf War and the 1999 air campaign in Kosovo. The military leadership of the 1991 Gulf War—the chief of the Joint Chiefs of Staff (CJCS), Gen. Colin Powell; the overall commander, Gen. H. Norman Schwarzkopf; and the air commander, Lt. Gen. Charles A. Horner—all served in Vietnam. General Schwarzkopf said that he measured everything in life against the experience of Vietnam. Lieutenant General Horner described his own Vietnam experience:

They [Washington] came up with strategies almost on a day-to-day basis. . . . our generals were bad news. . . . I hated my own generals because they covered up their own gutless inability to stand up to the political masters in Washington. . . . I learned that you cannot trust America[;] . . . the result was that we were living a lie and had lost our pride. . . . We had become a communist nation within the very organization that was to protect our nation from the threat of communism.[22]

Wow!

They both vowed that *this* time, the 1991 Gulf War, they would do it right. The underlying notion was that the overall strategy of the Vietnam War had been inadequate and that the subsequent employment of military force had not been designed to generate the desired effect. An interesting comment was made by General Powell in his memoirs: "We were deluded by technology. The enemy was primitive, and we were the most technologically advanced nation on earth. It therefore should be no contest."[23] Even though Powell's comment was more general, it were applicable to the Air Force focus on technology and means rather than on developing targeting strategies to generate effect through the application of airpower.

In effect, the Air Force turned to the perceived proven strategies of World War II. The Rolling Thunder air campaign (1965–68) was initially proposed to be a fast and hard-hitting campaign of short duration (twenty-eight days) with a limited number (ninety-four) of selected targets. The plan was never implemented, and instead of achieving its objectives within weeks, the air campaign gradually increased in scope and intensity to a three-and-a-half-year "ad hoc programme with hundreds of thousands of bombs dropped and close to 900 aircraft lost."[24]

In his book *The Limits of Air Power: The American Bombing of North Vietnam*, Mark Clodfelter argues that the military planning for Rolling Thunder drew upon the teachings of the Air Corps Tactical School and the development of AWPD-1—in other words, largely, the Industrial Web Theory. Later denounced for its gradual escalation, lack of intensity, and choice of targets, the air campaign envisaged taking out the North Vietnamese war-making capability and disrupting the nation's social fabric. Still, as Clodfelter argues, "as Rolling Thunder would demonstrate, the doctrine deemed appropriate for general war with the Soviet Union was ill suited for a limited conflict with an enemy waging guerrilla war."[25]

Although innovative and intellectually interesting, the continued influence of the teachings of the Air Corps Tactical School and the conceptual foundation of the Industrial Web Theory are no more fascinating than the apparent acceptance of its universal validity. When asked whether the United

States could have won in Vietnam, the then-retired General LeMay answered, "In any two-week period you want to mention."[26] Airpower, according to LeMay, seemingly had the capacity of winning the war literally within days, had the politicians not interfered and put limitations on the effort. Little emphasis appears to have been given to the particular circumstances of this unique war. As General Powell noted: "The enemy actually was taking horrendous casualties. But it made little difference. . . . As long as your enemy was willing to pay that price, body counts meant nothing. This enemy was obviously prepared to pay, and unsportingly refused to play the game of our scorekeeping."[27] The belief in strategic bombing's universal applicability seemingly ran too deep to grasp this reality. Professor Dennis Drew, who was one of the principal authors of the Air Force's basic doctrine manual in 1992, argues that "American airmen have remained 'doers' rather than introspective 'thinkers.' . . . [N]owhere was that more evident than in the US Air Force approach to the problem of protracted revolutionary warfare. . . . American airmen virtually ignored the problem of insurgent warfare until they entered the Vietnam War."[28] Builder points out that "the Army Air Force leadership came out of the Second World War with the air power theory intact, despite considerable evidence that it was flawed and incomplete."[29] With ACTS still providing the conceptual foundation of the application of airpower and conventional strategic use of airpower not having been debated in the two decades leading up to the Vietnam War, the service was doctrinally unprepared for the war that ensued.

The Vietnam War would also have an impact on the military leadership of the Kosovo War in 1999. The CJCS, Gen. Henry H. Shelton; the overall commander, Gen. Wesley K. Clark; and the air commander, Lt. Gen. Michael C. Short, had all served in Vietnam. General Clark—who had fought and had been wounded in Vietnam—drew *his* lessons from the Vietnam War: "Many of us in the United States and the Armed Forces had seen early on the fallacies of gradualism. It was, after all, the thinking that lay behind the early, unsuccessful years of the deepening American involvement in the Vietnam War."[30] Clark studied Rolling Thunder for his master's degree in military art and science at the U.S. Army Command and General Staff College. Interestingly, for his later role as SACEUR during OAF, his research was related to "operations in unanticipated areas that had political aims less sweeping than unconditional surrender." Clark asserts that the U.S. effort to halt North Vietnamese support of the fighting in South Vietnam by signaling resolve through carefully constrained, gradually escalating, politically designed bombing—without seeking decisive military impact—had been a failure. Clark says the reason for the failure seems to have been that North

Vietnamese willpower, determination, and ability to build up resistance and repair damage were greater than the pace and intensity of the air campaign. Greater force had to be applied more rapidly, with greater intensity—and directed at achieving significant military ends: "Only when the targeted state realizes that its military effort cannot succeed will it be 'compelled' to consider alternatives."[31]

Clark argues that political leaders of modern democracies were usually hesitant and imposed severe constraints on military action, whereas military leaders were not bold enough to push for real muscle to achieve significant objectives. The results, says Clark, were extended campaigns that could leave democratic governments vulnerable to domestic opinion; if losses and mistakes accumulated due to the self-imposed political constraints, the policy would appear incompetent in application and foolish in design,

> and that was part of what happened to the United States in Vietnam. Once fighting had begun, you had to escalate rapidly and achieve "escalation dominance" over an adversary, if you were to succeed. And you had to go after meaningful military objectives. I came out of the study convinced that the United States would again find itself engaged in problems of not only deterrence but also "compellence." Little did I suspect that I would be in the middle of the action as SACEUR when it occurred.[32]

Subsequently, preparing for OAF, Clark reportedly applied his Vietnam lesson to Kosovo during a video teleconference: "I don't want to get into something like the Rolling Thunder campaign, pecking away indefinitely."[33] Lieutenant General Short was also very clear that the Vietnam War had influenced him significantly: "It was on my mind all the time, because of the lessons that my generation learned from Vietnam. The major lesson we learned was that if you take the country to war, if the country is going to risk its young men and women, send them into harm's way, then you get it done as quickly as you can . . . so when the decision is made to use force, then we need to go in with overwhelming force."[34] In a congressional hearing after the Kosovo War, Lieutenant General Short said, "I recognize the political limitations that kept us from going downtown the first night. I'm a child of Vietnam, Senator. . . . Classmates died, classmates in the Hanoi Hilton, because of a philosophy driven by incrementalism, and 'let's try a little bit of this today and see how he likes it, and try a little bit tomorrow and see how he likes that.'" He added that he would go to his grave believing that Milošević should have been hit hard the first night.[35]

To many, the Vietnam War was a vindication of the use of airpower in support of ground forces, and the influential role within the Air Force gradually shifted to TAC. After the Vietnam War, TAC and the U.S. Army Training and Doctrine Command (TRADOC) started to share experiences and knowledge from Vietnam—a relationship described as a "relationship that matured from dialogue to a partnership."[36] Basing its view on perceived technological gains by the Soviet Union in tactical weaponry and the numerical strength of the Warsaw Pact in Europe, TRADOC emphasized the need for "extending the battlefield" and "intelligence preparation of the battlefield" in order to focus on offensive attacks against the second and third echelons of the enemy's force. By attacking the depth of enemy formations, tactical advantage could be exploited on the front; in this way, airpower should be employed in close coordination with ground forces to enable victory. The need for close interaction between all air and ground capabilities led to the development of the AirLand Battle doctrine, published in 1982.[37] AirLand Battle favored the traditional TAC perspective on airpower, and from the Vietnam War through AirLand Battle and the ensuing years, the ideas of tactical application of airpower became dominant. By the mid-1980s, offensive and independent strategic use of conventional airpower had not been thoroughly analyzed since World War II.[38] Benjamin S. Lambeth points out that through most of the Cold War, "virtually no consideration was given in U.S. defense planning to the potential ability of conventional airpower to achieve strategic effects independently of ground action that might, in and of themselves, determine the course and outcome of a campaign or war."[39] Clodfelter argues that the advocates of strategic bombing have created "a modern vision of air power that focuses on the lethality of its weaponry rather than on that weaponry's effectiveness as a political instrument. American civilian and military leaders entered Vietnam convinced that bombing's lethality assured political results. They never fully realized that airpower's political efficacy varies according to many diverse elements, and that no specific formula guarantees success."[40]

Conventional strategic airpower was not only neglected; in fact, by the late 1980s the whole concept of conventional strategic airpower, as well as the Air Force as an independent institution, was being questioned. In the autumn of 1989 some Air Staff officers wrote an unpublished paper called "A View of the Air Force Today" that directly criticized the Air Force leadership. They asserted that it was widely believed by other services that the Air Force should be abolished as a separate institution and that airpower was neither decisive nor influential in battle. The paper further asserted that the U.S. Air Force had lost its identity and was being run by pilots who gave priority to their love of aircraft and technology at the expense of a holistic concept — "the US Air Force was created to honour a false premise that should have been discredited long ago; that premise is the efficacy of airpower as an independent war-winning doctrine."[41] In 1990, Dr. Jeffrey Record echoed the same theme in his article, "Into the Wild Blue Yonder: Should We Abolish the Air Force?"[42]

Col. John Ashley Warden III and the strategic Instant Thunder plan of the 1991 Gulf War would significantly challenge this perception. Because John Warden and his teachings were to have a remarkable impact on how professional airmen approached the Kosovo War, a thorough evaluation of this airpower theorist is warranted.

John Warden was a forward air controller in the Vietnam War, flying some 266 combat missions — including targeting the Ho Chi Minh Trail. This experience caused Warden to question seriously the overall strategy, procedures, and limitations imposed on airpower. He vowed that should he ever go to war again, he would not accept such an ill-defined strategy. Warden believed the West generally failed in integrating military and political affairs into a grand strategy and argued that decision making and development of strategies should focus to a much greater degree on the desired end-state. He denounced the concept of limited wars: "The indispensable need for a sound coalition to find a long term grand strategy which looks beyond the war to the peace which will inevitably follow it. . . . If you weren't prepared to expend the effort that was going to assure victory, then you shouldn't play."[43] During his year at the U.S. National War College in Washington 1985–86, Warden started on a thesis, which he later published (1988), called *The Air Campaign: Planning for Combat.* Warden's book is still today generally perceived as one of the most influential contemporary works on modern airpower theory.

In his book, Warden emphasizes the term *center of gravity.* Based on Clausewitz's concept and defined as "the hub of all power and movement," it "describes that point where the enemy is most vulnerable and the point where an attack will have the best chance of being decisive."[44] Warden further asserts that airpower is inherently an offensive weapon and that establishing air superiority is crucial for any air campaign. Destroying equipment at or close to its source is more efficient than destroying it directly at the front; thus, interdiction[45] seems to be the best solution. By providing a conceptual framework for planning and executing an air campaign, Warden argued against linking airpower solely to land warfare and the ground commander. The book became a classic text within airpower theory, and some noticed its strengths right away. The deputy chief of staff for plans and operations, Lt. Gen. Michael J. Dugan, issued copies of the book to all his subordinates.

By mid-1988 Warden had become the director for War-Fighting Concepts Developments (XOXW), developing Air Force strategies, doctrines, and long-range planning. The XOXW organization consisted of six divisions, of which one—simply referred to as "Checkmate"—dealt with war gaming and simulation. Because of its physical layout, Checkmate became the central location when planning started for the air campaign against Iraq in the first Gulf War. Since then, the overall XOXW has been referred to as the "Checkmate team." One individual from the Checkmate team should be mentioned for his later influence, then major David A. Deptula. Deptula was working in the Doctrine Division of XOXW when Warden was assigned as director, and his first assignment was to review, comment, and provide edits on the manuscript of Warden's *The Air Campaign,* as well as to write a paper on how best to use airpower at the operational level of war. According to Olsen, Warden became Deptula's mentor in terms of airpower strategy, and they shared a common view of strategic airpower. In the period between 1988 and 1990, based largely on Warden's ideas in his book and an unpublished paper he wrote called "Centers of Gravity—The Key to Success in War," describing the enemy state as a system—Warden and the Checkmate team produced the "Five Rings Model" (see figure 4) .

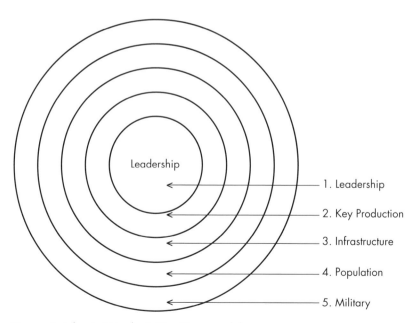

Figure 4. John A. Warden's Five Rings model.

Warden published the ideas of this model in 1992,[46] refining and publishing it in 1995 in *Airpower Journal* titled "The Enemy as a System."[47] Warden envisaged an enemy state as a system composed of numerous subsystems that could be influenced to attain different objectives. He argues that the outcome of a conflict is a combination of physical factors and morale (Physical x Morale = Outcome) and that since the physical elements are far more knowable and predictable than morale—and human beings are so different from each other—one should seek to influence the physical factors. That would render this side of the equation close to zero, at which no morale in the world could produce a high number on the outcome side of the equation. Causing changes to one or more parts of the enemy's physical system would either cause the enemy to alter his behavior in accordance with the opponent's will, or create a *strategic paralysis* in which it becomes physically impossible for the targeted state to oppose the attacker. By analyzing the elements critical for a state's functioning, one is able to prioritize operations and focus on the most critical factors—or rings, in Warden's model.

The most critical ring is the command ring, because it is the civilian (heads of state, leadership) or military commander that "is the only element of the enemy that can make concessions, that can make the very complex decisions that are necessary to keep the country on a particular course, or that can direct a country at war." The point is to make the command structure make concessions (by overthrowing government, killing the leader, or forcing them to give up), or to make the leadership incapable of leading—the latter achieved by targeting command communications.

The second ring—and the next most critical ring, one that exerts pressure on the leadership if targeted—contains organic essentials. On a state level, this means mostly electricity and petroleum products. If these essentials are destroyed, both daily life and military capacity are greatly hampered; further damage to organic essentials could lead to the collapse of the enemy system, make it physically difficult or impossible to maintain a certain policy or to fight, or cause political or economic repercussions too costly to bear. Warden points out that even large states have a reasonably small number of organic-essential targets, "and each of the targets in subsystems such as power production and petroleum refining is fragile."

The third most critical ring is infrastructure. "For both military and civilian purposes, it is necessary to move goods, services, and information from one point to another. If this movement becomes impossible, the state system quickly moves to a lower energy level, and thus to lesser ability to resist the demands of its enemy." This includes rail lines, airlines, highways, bridges, airfields, ports, and similar systems.

The fourth most critical ring is the population. Warden asserts that it is difficult to target the population *directly* but points out that the North Vietnamese *indirect* targeting of the American population during the Vietnam War may be especially effective if the targeted country has a relatively low interest in the outcome of the war.

The fifth critical ring comprises fielded military forces. Warden believes the majority of classic writing and thinking on warfare has been done by continental soldiers "who had no choice but to contend with enemy armies." New technology and airpower have made it possible to see the fielded forces as something protecting the targeted states' vital rings, not in themselves of vital importance—they are means and not ends. Warden argues that all subsystems can be divided using the same model and can be used at all levels of war (strategic, operational, and tactical). In this way the model can prove a useful tool for analyzing courses of action.

All actions should be focused on the mind of the enemy command or against the enemy system as a whole. Thus, an attack against industry or infrastructure is not primarily conducted because of the effect it might or might not have on fielded forces. Rather, it is undertaken for its direct effect on the enemy as a system, including its effect on national leaders and commanders, who must assess the cost of rebuilding, the effect on the state's economic position in the postwar period, the internal political implications for their own survival, and whether the cost is worth the potential gain from continuing the war.[48]

It is not my purpose to evaluate the validity of Warden's teachings but rather to examine the influence they had on the U.S. Air Force as an institution and the officers assigned to plan and execute Operation Allied Force in 1999. It should be noted, however, that Warden appears to contradict his previous emphasis on the *physical* factors, since the "mind of the enemy command" now becomes essential to "assess the cost of rebuilding" and analyze "whether the cost is worth the potential gain from continuing the war."

Instead of carrying out *serial* attacks against the enemy, which has been the historical way of war, new technology has now provided the opportunity to conduct *parallel* and "near simultaneous attacks on every strategic- and operational-level vulnerability of the enemy." The technological revolution, utilizing unprecedented precision, enabled the U.S.-led coalition in 1991 to carry out parallel attacks against all rings of the Iraqi regime in a way not previously possible. It enabled airpower to attack the enemy as a system to a much larger degree than ever before, potentially causing strategic paralysis or altering behavior in the targeted state. Warden concludes that one should focus on what one wants the enemy state to be like after the war: "Fighting is not the essence of war, nor even a desirable part of it. The real essence is doing what is necessary to make the enemy accept our objectives as his objectives."[49]

Thus, adhering to his airpower principles, Warden commented shortly after OAF that "Operation Allied Force foundered at the outset, conducting serial attacks on Yugoslavian targets that allowed Milošević's regime to readjust and bring power, communications, and other systems back on-line after short black-outs." He added that the Kosovo air campaign did not conduct parallel attacks as in Desert Storm and hit key targets only at the end of the war.[50]

In later discussions, Warden emphasized that the Five Rings Model is part of a strategy-development process and that since everything happens in the context of a system, the model helps to analyze the complex system of the adversary (and oneself). Once the Five Rings Model methodology has discovered the centers of gravity of the enemy system, one should conduct quick and parallel attacks to increase the probability of success. Interestingly, Warden says of his Five Rings Model methodology, "I am not aware of another good approach usable in the real world that allows you to understand the enemy as a system and find practical centers of gravity to address. When a better methodology comes along, we should use it, but as far as I know, one does not exist now."[51]

By late 1988, Deptula had left the Checkmate team to work for a policy group chaired by secretary of the Air Force, Donald B. Rice. Rice had observed that—unlike officers in the Army and Navy, who were often debating military strategy—airmen generally discussed nothing but aircraft, and he wanted to change that. On 28 March 1990, Rice sent an information memorandum called "The Potential of the Air" to Secretary of Defense Richard Cheney. The memorandum was drafted by Deptula, and soon he became the principal author of the white paper *Global Reach—Global Power: Reshaping for the Future.* The paper asserted that one should focus on airpower's inherent strengths—speed, range, flexibility, precision, and lethality—and that among other things, airpower should include the ability to "inflict strategic and operational paralysis on any adversary by striking key nodes in his war-making potential."[52] The paper came as a reaction to voices questioning the role and future of the Air Force; it asserted that if airpower were applied correctly, the Air Force would not be only one of four services but the dominating one.

According to Dr. Olsen, a few days after the Iraqi invasion of Kuwait in August 1990 Warden and Deptula met and started planning for what would become the Instant Thunder plan—a concept founded on the Five Rings

Model and the policy of *Global Reach—Global Power*. Warden was sure that a military response would be founded in the AirLand Battle doctrine, in which TAC would support the army by focusing on the enemy armed forces, not in the offensive strategic manner Warden favored. Thus Warden, without higher authorization, started planning for an alternative use of airpower to attack the Iraqi regime. Interestingly, with regard to the relative immaturity of conventional strategic airpower thought, the commander of U.S. Central Command (CENTCOM), General Schwarzkopf, and the CJCS, General Powell, agreed to ask the Air Staff what airpower could achieve in Iraq. On 8 August—less than a week after the Iraqi invasion of Kuwait—General Schwarzkopf called the Air Staff and reportedly asked to talk to "whoever was in charge." During a ten-minute conversation with Gen. John Loh, Schwarzkopf said he needed to develop a broader set of targets, a task in which he needed a quick and decisive response: "We are doing a good job on AirLand Battle—on tactical application—but I need a broader set of targets, a broader air campaign; and I need it fast because if he [Saddam Hussein] attacks with chemicals or nuclears, I have got to be able to hit him where it hurts right away, and that is a strategic air campaign. . . . I have got to hit him at his heart. . . . I need it kind of fast because I may have to attack those kinds of targets deep, that have value to him as a leader."[53]

General Schwarzkopf had in effect asked for a conventional strategic air campaign plan. The Checkmate team had prepared for a conventional strategic air campaign like this for two years, had planned explicitly for Iraq two days before Schwarzkopf made the call, and thus within twenty-four hours Warden was able to provide a fairly comprehensive presentation on the issue. Targets for Instant Thunder were selected in accordance with the Five Rings Model. They were aimed at affecting the Iraqi national leadership by precision air strikes against the political-military leadership organs of Hussein's regime and its command and control—the central nervous system of the Iraqi regime. This system as a whole was the political center of gravity; Instant Thunder sought to isolate the Iraqi leadership and in essence to be a *war-winning* rather than *war-fighting* air campaign. The plan envisaged victory within six to nine days and would represent a key airpower perspective after World War I—that one should largely disregard the ground forces and go straight for the opposing regime's decision-making body. Warden wanted to eliminate Saddam Hussein because Hussein was perceived to be the root of the problem. Eliminating Hussein would provide the circumstances needed to overthrow the regime. Thus, the Iraqi leadership was at the heart of the targeting effort—though Warden assumed killing Hussein would be very difficult and therefore aimed at first isolating the leader from his population and armed forces. Interestingly, Warden assumed that there would be a coup of some sort within a week of the air campaign; according to Olsen, "War-den believed that attacks on the Iraqi regime's instruments of political con-trol, combined with a major psychological warfare campaign, were certain to make someone overthrow the Iraqi leader somehow." Electrical power supplies were perceived to have a particularly significant impact on the popu-lation and the regime. It was important to convey that it was Hussein and the regime that were being targeted—not the Iraqi population—and that the desired end-state would be a new Iraqi leadership with good relations with Washington.[54]

What is of particular interest is the assumption that victory would be reached within six to nine days. Throughout history, advocates of strategic airpower—perhaps in line with the prewar rhetoric of the services involved—have tended to describe it as decisive, short, and swift. A few years later, it was believed that OAF would be over within two to four days.

Warden and his Checkmate team represented a more radical approach to conventional airpower—more in line with the traditional thinking of Douhet, ACTS, and the Industrial Web Theory. The second school of thought was represented by the TAC, which saw airpower largely as a tool to be used in support of the Army. According to the American historian and journalist David Halberstam, "They had a much more conventional view of the order of battle and believed that airpower was there to support the army on the ground and to interdict enemy forces. They despised Warden and his ideas, a hostility that never lessened. . . . To the TAC people the air force was for pilots, and pilots flew, and if you did not fly, if you wrote or planned, you were not really an air force man."[55]

These sentiments are significant from a historical point of view, because several sources have pointed to the Air Force's institutional lack of conven-tional strategic thought after World War II—with airmen generally being aviation enthusiasts, focusing mostly on the aircraft, technology, and tactics. As Builder asserts, "Not only was airpower theory neglected, the people who were now [after the Vietnam War] running the Air Force had no roots in the theory."[56] Airmen were regarded as military craftsmen, with generally little intellectual interest and education in conceptual and theoretical analyses of how to apply airpower. On the contrary, authority within the community has (arguably) often been derived from tactical skills flying the aircraft. Those more academically than tactically inclined were regarded as anomalous; air-men generally perceive academic analyses as something elevated and theo-retical and not particularly relevant to the everyday practice of war fighting. Certainly Warden's airpower perspective and his proposed Instant Thunder plan had their strengths and weaknesses, but the seemingly institutionalized denunciation of his plan and of himself as a military leader are of interest.

As a Vietnam veteran who had flown the F-105 over Hanoi and a TAC officer himself, General Horner commented when he first saw Warden's Instant Thunder plan, "How can a person in an Ivory Tower far from the front, not knowing what needs to be done, write such a message? Will wonders never cease?" He later quipped that the term *centers of gravity* was a "college boy term." When Warden presented the plan to him in Riyadh, Saudi Arabia, on 20 August 1990, he stated: "You took and made an academic study. Now I have to turn that into reality. What you've essentially brought me, for all intents and purposes, is a target list, and I thank you for your efforts for doing that. Now I need to turn it into an executable plan."[57] Importantly, though Horner admitted that Warden's plan contained elements of brilliance, he noted during the briefing, "I have trouble with the basic premise, severing the head from the body"—referring to Warden's focus on removing Saddam Hussein, going straight for the opposing regime's decision-making body, and largely disregarding the ground forces. This figurative rhetoric of a nation's political leadership as "the head" and the rest of the society as "the body" should be kept in mind, as it would surface during OAF and represent an increasingly powerful argument and philosophy within the service for years to come.

Warden's initial Instant Thunder plan was modified, but it would make up the core of Phase I of the final air campaign plan for Operation Desert Storm. Warden was sent home by Horner and was not formally allowed on the team developing the final air campaign plan for Desert Storm. This was a disappointment for Warden, but he was in regular informal contact with the secret planning group chaired by Brig. Gen. Buster C. Glosson. This cell included Warden's former colleague from the Checkmate team, David Deptula, now a lieutenant colonel.

According to Olsen, the preparations for the air campaign for Operation Desert Storm became a clash between the radical airpower ideas of Warden and his Checkmate team, on one hand, and the more conventional thinking of the TAC, on the other. Even though Warden focused more on strategic effects and regime targets than industrial and economic centers, Olsen argues, Warden's theories represented less a revolution than an evolution from the early theories of Douhet, Mitchell, and the Industrial Web Theory of the ACTS. He also claims that even though Warden focused on rapid and intense bombing rather than gradual escalation, he was influenced by the targeting theories of Thomas Schelling. To what extent Warden influenced the air campaign of Operation Desert Storm is open to debate, but it seems fair to argue that the offensive strategic use of airpower—particularly in Phase I—would have been awarded less prominence by the political and military leadership had it not been for the ideas, perspectives, and determination of John Warden and his Checkmate team.[58]

In his memoirs, General Powell wrote: "The Air Force staff quickly came up with an air campaign, the brainchild of Col. John Warden, a brilliant, brash fighter pilot and a leading Air Force intellectual on the use of airpower. . . . Warden's original plan would undergo numerous modifications and there would be much debate over targets, but his original concept remained the heart of the Desert Storm air war."[59]

Operation Desert Storm was generally considered as an overwhelming success of U.S. military power in general—and U.S. airpower in particular. The thirty-eight-day air campaign left the ground campaign with limited fighting, lasting only a hundred hours. The precision, firepower, and effect of the air campaign were generally considered the decisive factors of the war, and airpower advocates were quick to claim that the potential of strategic airpower had finally been proven. The war fortified the beliefs that airpower could be decisive in battle and that conventional strategic airpower was the proper use of this military tool in limited wars, and it largely restored the prestige of the Air Force.

The high-profile effect of strategic airpower after Operation Desert Storm also influenced politicians, who by the early 1990s were increasingly inclined to use this seemingly proven tool to coerce international opponents—particularly in the Balkans. The mounting crises in Bosnia increasingly threatened American supremacy as the sole remaining superpower after the Cold War. As Robert Pape asserts, "People's views on the future of coercive airpower are likely to be determined by their interpretation of the Persian Gulf War. The many televised films of modern precision-guided weapons making deadly accurate strikes on all types of targets have fed a perception that a technological revolution has made it possible to win wars with airpower alone."[60]

In fact, according to Peter Kellner in a *New York Times* article during OAF, "The overwhelming display of risk-free American airpower in the Persian Gulf handicaps President Clinton in any debate on using ground troops."[61] Referring to Kosovo, National Security Adviser Samuel "Sandy" Berger asserted that airpower "was where the West's great advantage lay—an advantage of perhaps one thousand to one in airpower, whereas if it was a struggle with ground troops in terrible terrain, the advantage dropped to seven to one and the terms began to favor Milošević."[62] Similarly, Professor Colin McInnes points out that Western aerospace technology represented an advantage that provided a comparatively low risk for own casualties and thus became attractive to policy makers.[63] Byman and Waxman claim American policy makers in the 1990s viewed airpower as particularly attractive in limited wars because they allow the coercer to escalate the conflict without becoming irrevocably involved. Airpower offers the flexibility to influence the whole spectrum from coercion to brute force, as well as the ability to escalate, while at the same time allowing policy makers to vary and—to a degree—control the amount of damage inflicted in accordance with their needs. This includes the level of pain inflicted on the enemy, as well as the domestic political cost (financial and human) of an intervention.[64] As Eliot A. Cohen wrote in *Foreign Affairs:* "Airpower is an unusually seductive form of military strength, in part because, like modern courtship, it appears to offer gratification without commitment."[65] When interviewed during OAF, the U.S. director of offensive planning during Desert Storm, General Glosson, argued that one should do in Belgrade what had been done in Baghdad eight years earlier: he would have gone downtown Belgrade and "taken out the television station, part of the electricity and certainly some of the locations of his political stalwarts."[66]

Since the 1991 Gulf War to many officers provided a near-perfect example of how airpower should be employed against Serbia in 1999, a few factors should be mentioned when comparing the two operations. First, the invasion of Kuwait represented an attack on a core interest (oil) of the United States, and the political thrust and credibility invested in it significantly exceeded that in Kosovo some eight years later. To forestall the Vietnam Syndrome, a ground force of more than six hundred thousand troops was gathered before going to war. This not only sent a very strong political signal of determination but also provided significant tactical and operational leverage for airpower to exploit, with Iraqi forces being forced to organize to counter a ground attack from the U.S.-led coalition. In OAF, ground troops were initially not a part of the military effort at all. The UN Security Council Resolution 678 (29 November 1990) authorized the use of force to drive Iraqi troops out of Kuwait; no such authorization was provided before OAF. This significantly reduced the political leverage of NATO. Iraq had invaded another country; Serbia was oppressing its own citizens inside its own territory, which in terms of international law was an entirely different case.

In addition to considering aspects such as the differences in terms of terrain, weather, and the emotional reluctance to bomb in the heart of Europe, the Desert Storm forces trained for months before the campaign commenced. The lack of NATO authorization for detailed planning before OAF largely precluded such training. Significantly, on 8 August 1990, President George H. W. Bush provided clear objectives for military planners to achieve.[67] Clear objectives had not yet been provided when OAF commenced in 1999, and they were not formulated until several weeks into the campaign. The number of aircraft and level of resources allocated to Operation Desert Storm were significantly greater than in OAF. Finally, American leadership of the coalition fighting Operation Desert Storm was never contested; nations chose to participate in a U.S.-led coalition, not in an alliance. In OAF one had to fight within the framework and protocol of NATO—a consensus alliance of sovereign nations with different perspectives and agendas leading up to the air campaign, and sometimes facing overwhelming domestic opposition to the operation.

One should therefore be careful when comparing the two air campaigns in terms of effectiveness. President Clinton's national security adviser, Anthony Lake, comments on the difference between the 1991 Gulf War and airpower as a coercive instrument as it was used in Bosnia and Kosovo: "If you are trying to see airpower as a coercive instrument you have to put it in the context of a diplomatic policy; the objective is not only simply to defeat an enemy militarily. Thus, the parallel to the 1991 Gulf War is a bad one, because in the Gulf War airpower was being used to fight a war, and part of a broader military effort to defeat an enemy."[68]

These differences should be mentioned because Operation Desert Storm would influence the way politicians and airmen approached the Kosovo crisis. With airpower peaking in perceived effectiveness after Desert Storm, it seemed that politicians had not adequately understood the combinations of factors that made airpower so effective against Saddam Hussein's regime. The lesson they learned—or chose to learn—was simply that airpower was very effective. Seemingly, airpower was much more politically cost-effective, with a low risk of own casualties and significantly reduced potential of collateral damage. Pictures of an overconfident General Schwarzkopf boasting about precision-guided munitions during the 1991 Gulf War created an image of "surgical bombing," one that was fortified by strategic airpower advocates who wanted the Air Force to be the dominant service and believed airpower had not yet reached its full potential. Governor Clinton, running for president in summer 1992, argued airpower should be used against the Bosnian Serbs; once the Clinton administration took office in January 1993, UN ambassador Madeleine Albright's and Vice President Al Gore's rhetoric of using airpower against the Serbs grew louder.

What should be noted is that between World War II and Warden, U.S. airpower had predominantly operated within a nuclear context (SAC) or in tactical support of ground forces (TAC)—both approaches having intellectual and professional roots in the Cold War. With the Cold War ending and airpower in Desert Storm seen as enormously effective, the *political* expectations exceeded conceptual and intellectual competence to meet them. Warden "was certain to make someone overthrow the Iraqi leader somehow" after about a week of his Instant Thunder plan; this statement's lack of precision on how this would happen probably reflected his lack of knowledge of the subject.

John Warden and the success of Operation Desert Storm were to influence significantly Air Force perspectives and education. In March 1992, the service published the *Basic Aerospace Doctrine of the United States Air Force* (AF Manual 1-1)—a document the then chief of staff, Gen. Merrill A. McPeak, called "one of the most important documents ever published by the United States Air Force. . . . It is what history has taught us works in war, as well as what does not."[69] The document reflects the debate concerning the role of the Air Force and the growing awareness of conventional strategic airpower. The document points out the decisive potential of airpower: "Aerospace forces directly assigned to surface forces have surface support mission priorities that limit their ability to exploit the full scope of aerospace operations. . . . [I]n contrast, only the Air Force is charged with preparing aerospace forces that are organized, trained, and equipped to exploit fully aerospace power's flexibility and potential decisiveness."[70]

Growing awareness of the *Global Reach—Global Power* concept, largely written by Deptula, could (arguably) be seen: "The capabilities of being able to concentrate rapidly at any point on or above the globe and of being able to attack any segment of the enemy's war-making capability must be preserved and exploited through the procurement of appropriate equipment."[71] The focus on potential decisiveness, global reach, and strategic effect were debated within the Air Force team set to write the doctrine. Professor Dennis Drew, who was one of the principal authors of the 1992 basic doctrine manual, says the early drafts included extensive information on the nature of protracted revolutionary warfare, but that it was deleted at the general-officer level. Seemingly challenging the doctrinaire focus on attacking leadership, electricity, and communication lines, Air Force Manual 2-11 argues that, unlike an industrialized enemy, insurgents "have no heartland, no fixed industrial facilities, and few interdictable lines of communications."[72] When Drew wanted to insert this sentence in the 1992 doctrine (AFM 1-1), it was again stricken at the general-officer level over Drew's objections; instead the drafters inserted the sentence, "Any enemy with the capacity to be a threat is likely to have strategic vulnerabilities susceptible to air attack."[73] The influence of Warden appears significant.

Arguably capturing the sentiments of many airmen, Maj. Jason B. Barlow wrote in 1993 that the 1991 Gulf War marked airpower's "coming of age." He argued that "strategic paralysis calls for attacking or threatening national-level targets that most directly support the enemy's war-making efforts and will to continue the conflict, this strategy holds promise for changing the enemy's behavior at a relatively low cost to both sides. Airpower is the primary weapon of this strategy because only it can provide the access, mass, persistence, and simultaneity of attack needed to induce paralysis."[74] Barlow added, "strategic paralysis is suited for the US military, which prefers to fight wars as quickly, inexpensively, and bloodlessly (on both sides) as possible. Strategic paralysis has come of age."[75]

David A. Deptula later commented that the 1991 Gulf War introduced significant changes to the planning and conduct of warfare: "The results were dramatic in that they changed the expectations of modern warfare." Deptula explains, "The first night of the Gulf War air campaign demonstrated that the conduct of war had changed. . . . The Gulf War began with more targets in one day's attack plan than the total number of targets hit by the entire Eighth Air Force in all of 1942 and 1943."[76] Deptula says simultaneous application of force—in time and space—describes parallel warfare, adding, "However, the crucial principles defining parallel warfare are how time and space are exploited in terms of what effects are desired, and for what purpose, at each level of war—the essence of effects-based operations."[77] Despite the fact that most advocates of strategic airpower throughout the twentieth century have focused on how operations produce effects,[78] the term "Effects-Based Operations" (EBO)[79] became associated with the 1991 Gulf War and continued to shape Air Force thinking for the years to come.

With a publication by the National Defense University called *Shock and Awe: Achieving Rapid Dominance,* another term within the defense community surfaced in 1996. The document states, "The military posture and capability of the United States of America are, today, dominant. Simply put, there is no external adversary in the world that can successfully challenge the extraordinary power of the American military in either regional conflict or in 'conventional' war as we know it once the United States makes the commitment to take whatever action may be needed." The document further states that the United States "has adopted the doctrine of employing 'decisive or overwhelming force'" and that "perhaps for the first time in years, the confluence of strategy, technology, and the genuine quest for innovation has the potential for revolutionary change. We envisage Rapid Dominance as the possible military expression, vanguard, and extension of this potential for revolutionary change."[80]

> The aim of Rapid Dominance is to affect the will, perception, and understanding of the adversary to fit or respond to our strategic policy ends through imposing a regime of Shock and Awe. Clearly, the traditional military aim of destroying, defeating, or neutralizing the adversary's military capability is a fundamental and necessary component of Rapid Dominance. Our intent, however, is to field a range of capabilities to induce sufficient Shock and Awe to render

the adversary impotent. This means that physical and psychological effects must be obtained.[81]

A member of the team producing this document was Charles A. Horner—the air commander during Desert Storm. Airpower theorist Robert Pape argues that the "shock and awe" concept was a variation of strategic bombing and service thinking on airpower that largely came out of the Washington civilian defense community—including, for instance, the National Defense University. Representatives from this community would come to Maxwell—together with representatives from the U.S. Army and Navy—to talk to John Warden, take "nuggets" of his ideas, and turn them into their own concepts.[82] Pape denounced this concept as old news: "Shock and Awe is what air forces have been doing since World War I—that is always the plan. This is the 'same old.' We want to believe it is something new, because we want to believe we're always bigger and better. But the fact is, if there are new twists and turns, this won't be it."[83] In *Air Force Magazine,* John T. Correll similarly commented, that "Strategic airpower, Effects-Based Operations and Parallel Warfare have characteristics in common with Shock and Awe, but they are far from synonymous with it."[84]

The term or doctrine of *shock and awe* did not officially enter Air Force doctrine, but the concept resurfaced in 1998, when the same authors produced *Rapid Dominance: A Force for All Seasons,* published by the Royal United Services Institute for Defence Studies. In order to enable the concept of shock and awe to alter the behavior of an opponent, they recognized, it "would have to be sufficiently powerful, frightening, intimidating and threatening to convince, compel or scare an adversary into accepting the imposed strategic, political, or operational aims and objectives."[85] A plan for further developing the Rapid Dominance concept was included in 1999 in a plan entitled *Rapid Dominance: A Strategic Roadmap for Fielding and Testing an Experimental Rapid Dominance Force.* In a comment during Operation Allied Force in 1999, former secretary of defense Donald Rumsfeld made a statement to CNN denouncing the air campaign for not being forceful enough: "There is always a risk in gradualism. . . . It pacifies the hesitant and the tentative. What it doesn't do is shock, and awe, and alter the calculations of the people you're dealing with."[86] Even though the phrase "shock and awe" was never explicitly mentioned in doctrine, its conceptual content could be found in classic conventional strategic airpower thinking. Perhaps more importantly; it arguably signified a wider belief in overwhelming force and a high-intensity warfare approach to conflicts.

In 1997, the Air Force published a new basic doctrine, "to promulgate the Air Force perspective on the employment of air and space power."[87]

In the foreword, the then chief of staff, Gen. Michael E. Ryan, reflects the growing self-confidence as an independent decisive military force: "Together, the principles, tenets, and core competencies describe air and space power as a force distinct from surface forces and the air arms of other services. The United States Air Force, through operations in the air, space, and information environments, is a global strategic power that can protect national interests and achieve national objectives by rapidly projecting potent air, space, or joint force land power anywhere on earth."[88]

Interestingly, chapter 1 of this overarching doctrinal publication starts with a quotation by Col. Edward C. Mann III praising the decisive role of airpower in Operation Desert Storm against the regime of Saddam Hussein in 1991. The doctrine emphasizes the qualities of airpower that distinguish it from the roles of the other services—flexibility and potential decisiveness: "All military Services provide strike capabilities, but the ability of the Air Force to attack rapidly and persistently with a wide range of munitions anywhere on the globe at any time is unique. . . . When combined with our inherent strategic perspective, Air Force operations can be both the theater's first and potentially most decisive force in demonstrating the nation's will to counter an adversary's aggression."[89]

It further states: "Air and space forces are inherently manoeuvre forces with unmatched organic lethal and nonlethal 'firepower.' These forces have the capability to orchestrate maneuver on a global scale and directly achieve strategic objectives." The publication quotes Giulio Douhet on the same theme: "Both the army and navy will possess aerial means to aid their respective military and naval operations; but that does not preclude the possibility, the practicability, even the necessity, of having an air force capable of accomplishing war missions solely with its own means."[90] To some degree the debut of the B-2 Spirit bomber during the Kosovo War would realize the service's quest for *Global Reach—Global Power.* Commenting on this issue after OAF, Lieutenant General Short said the B-2/Joint Direct Attack Munition combination was the "absolute ultimate" in *Global Reach—Global Power,* adding: "Villains around the world should now think less about where the nearest carrier group is and instead count takeoffs from Whitman AFB [Air Force Base]."[91]

What is particularly significant is that by now the strategic use of airpower was official doctrine and that in the years between Operation Desert Storm and Operation Allied Force airmen were taught that airpower was a potentially decisive force and that strategic use of airpower was the preferable way to use it.

After Operation Desert Storm, John Warden became commandant of the Air Command and Staff College at Maxwell Air Force Base, remaining until he retired in 1995. His perspectives on airpower immediately influenced the education of Air Force officers. Warden admits that his theoretical approach was influenced by earlier airpower theorists:

> Especially, Douhet and Mitchell were important because they had opened the whole idea of using airpower to accomplish things that had previously been impossible. Their influence was general. As far as ACTS and the Industrial Web Theory, there were many good ideas that flowed out of this very fine work and they helped me enormously in developing a concept that I believe was a significant step forward.[92]

In fact, after taking the post, Warden almost immediately initiated an Air Campaign Course "to recapture the enthusiasm and concept-building atmosphere embodied in the Air Corps Tactical School (ACTS) prior to World War II while avoiding its failings." It was primarily "to educate and develop officers who will represent airpower as advisors to a war-fighting commander in chief and who one day will lead, maintain, and continue to provide our nation with the most effective air force on the globe."[93]

According to Professor Muller, a member of the ACSC faculty before, during, and after the Warden era, Warden's contribution to the education of Air Force officers is all-important:

> Most people will remember John Warden for his contribution to air power theory, and those are substantial. But to me, his most lasting impact was on air force education, with its potential to shape the thinking of generations of officers. For the first time in a long time, curriculum content, the quality of the faculty, and intellectual rigor were the top priorities. Perhaps most importantly, he made certain that ACSC focused on the business at hand—educating people about air power at the operational level of war. It was not perfect. In the years after Warden, the curriculum continued to develop, and the overall quality of the program improved tremendously. Yet, it was Warden who started the school down that path. Those were exciting times and it was a privilege to be part of it.[94]

Commenting on Warden's influence, Professor Dennis Drew asserts; "As one of the architects of the air campaign against Iraq in the Gulf War and subsequently as the commandant of Air Command and Staff College at Maxwell AFB, his stature as an authority on airpower theory has grown significantly, and his influence over an entire generation of Air Force officers is enormous."[95]

It seems fair to assume that these generations of officers taking classes at Maxwell during the following years were thoroughly introduced to Warden's Five Rings Model philosophy, its use in the 1991 Gulf War, and the concept of *strategic parallel attacks* with *overwhelming force* aimed at the adversary's *leadership* in order to alter its behavior or create *strategic paralysis.*

Commenting in retrospect on the Kosovo War, the commander of the Allied Air Forces Southern Europe, Lieutenant General Short, said his generation learned that "you take the fight to the enemy. You go after the head of the snake, put a dagger in the heart of the adversary, and you bring to bear all the force that you have at your command."[96] The focus on the adversary's "head of the snake" should be noted, as the metaphor apparently focuses on the enemy leadership and resembles Warden's metaphor of killing or isolating the brain—after which "the body is no longer a human being, or a strategic entity."[97] According to Short, NATO should have conducted strategic attacks on centers of gravity in the Balkans—not tactical attacks on troops and tanks. The leadership of Serbia—Milošević—should have been in focus.[98] In no uncertain terms, Short provides his vision for the air campaign: "On the first day or the first night of the war, you attack the enemy with incredible speed and incredible violence. Violence that he could never have imagined. . . . You should use every bit of technology that you have to shock him into inaction until he is paralysed. . . . That was how I thought airpower should be used in Serbia."[99]

Short's perspective represented the essence of the Air Force thinking that had evolved through the preceding decade. It was the largely institutionalized strategic airpower perspective of "decisive" or "overwhelming force," "strategic paralysis," and "shock and awe," all in one sentence. Annoyingly, politicians precluded such an approach: "I think we were constrained in this particular conflict to an extraordinary degree and were prevented from conducting an air campaign as professional airmen would have wanted to conduct it." Short reveals the origins of this perspective: "It was not just apparent at the three-star level that we weren't following the classic air campaign that we'd all learned at Maxwell[;] . . . airpower [was] not being used as well as it could be and the way you have been taught to use it."[100]

The challenge in the Kosovo War, however, was *not* to fight a high-intensity war but to find a way to incorporate airpower in a politically constrained strategy of coercive diplomacy. In this scenario, for all practical purposes, the use of overwhelming, decisive force—inconceivable violence—from the outset was politically unacceptable.

An article in *Aerospace Power Journal* by Lt. Col. Paul C. Strickland, USAF, pointed out that OAF was influenced by the Air Force's doctrinal focus on decisive force: "Allied Force highlighted a significant doctrinal imbalance between decisive and coercive airpower. US Air Force aerospace-power doctrine focuses almost exclusively on the idea that airpower is decisive in a major theater war scenario. Consequently, it minimizes discussion regarding the coercive application of airpower in nontraditional types of conflicts like Kosovo."[101] Strickland further asserted that the Air Force's doctrinal quest for decisiveness influences the leadership of air leaders in air operations: "The result is a doctrinal void of guidance in the education of future Air Force leaders to understand the complexities and truly coercive nature of airpower."[102]

One individual who focused on airpower and coercion was Robert Pape. His *Bombing to Win* almost immediately generated an intense airpower debate.[103] In it Dr. Pape performed quantitative analysis of thirty-three strategic air campaigns of the twentieth century, as well as detailed case studies of what he considered the five most important instances: Japan 1945, Germany 1945, Korea 1953, Vietnam 1965–68 and 1972, and Iraq 1991. Pape concluded that strategic bombing does *not* work, asserting instead that history shows coercion is most likely to work if focused on denying the enemy victory on the battlefield. Pape argued that tactical airpower is more cost-effective than strategic airpower and that theater airpower in combination with ground forces is more likely to coerce an adversary to change his behavior. To some extent Pape's arguments are the antithesis of those of John A. Warden, who asserted that the enemy's fielded forces had little influence on the battle and that airpower should be effect based and directed against the enemy's leadership. Consequently, the book was disliked in parts of the Air Force, with some, according to Pape, even arguing that it represented the greatest threat to the service at the time.[104] (It should be noted that Pape had worked at the School of Advanced Airpower Studies at Maxwell for three years and had discussed airpower theory with Warden.)

Pape asserts that major national security threats to the United States and other Western powers were reduced when the Cold War ended, while the number of failed states, ethnic conflicts, and bids for regional hegemony have increased since. According to Pape the problem of the Cold War was *deterrence,* while the problem of the post–Cold War era is *coercion.*[105] With the impressive U.S. victory in the Gulf War in 1991, Pape said, strategic bombing gained more popularity than at any time since the Vietnam War: "Proponents claim not only that strategic bombing was the decisive factor but also that the Gulf War heralds a new age in which strategic bombing will be the strongest form of military power, dramatically enhancing America's coercive capability and options"—a notion Pape claims is largely a flawed perception.[106]

It is useful to pay particular attention to the combination of factors outlined by Pape and the timing of events. The somewhat steady and predictable security policy regime resulting from the Cold War largely adhered to the logic of deterrence. The end of the Cold War increased the number of conflicts faced by the United States and Western powers. The need to address these issues without recourse to full military victory increased as the number of international disputes increased, and coercion—or *coercive diplomacy*—became the preferred policy in the United States. This was true particularly of issues not considered vital national interests. Shortly after the Cold War ended, the Gulf War proved to many the spectacular new technology and potential of airpower. A nearly bloodless victory in Desert Storm showed the potential of rapid escalation and low political risk—meaning low risk of own casualties and collateral damage when the tolerance of such in Western societies was declining.

Pape's starting point for his analysis is that some states change their behavior when threatened with military consequences but other states do not. There are several ways to coerce an enemy (economically, diplomatically, or by other forms of nonmilitary coercion), but in terms of airpower, Pape says, there are four distinct coercive air strategies: *punishment,* which attempts to inflict enough pain on enemy civilians to overwhelm their territorial interest in the dispute and to cause either the government to give way or the population to revolt against the government; *risk,* which seeks to raise the risk of civilian damage slowly, compelling the opponent to fold in order to avoid suffering future costs; *denial,* which seeks to thwart the enemy's

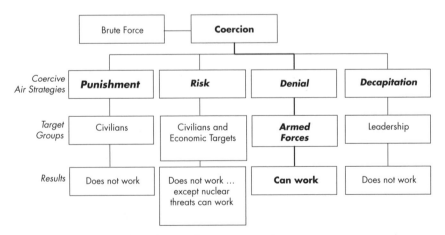

Figure 5. Robert A. Pape's Theory of Coercive Air Strategies.

military strategy from taking or holding its territorial objectives, compelling concessions to avoid futile expenditure of further resources; and *decapitation,* which aims at key leadership and telecommunication facilities to cause a system collapse ("the whole house of cards comes down") when the leadership is eliminated.[107] The four coercive air strategies and their (general) target groups are shown in figure 5.

Pape says punishment was the first coercive strategy to be used in the early evolution of airpower, when Gotha bombers and Zeppelins were used against British population centers in the German air offensive of 1917. Punishment can be used directly against the population, or it can influence them indirectly by targeting the civilian economy, electric power grids, oil refineries, water and sewer systems, or domestic transportation systems, reducing a nation's ability to distribute and refrigerate food, purify water, heat homes, and so on. Pape claims the Industrial Web Theory contained elements of both punishment and denial but that the punitive elements were dominant. Punishment strategies have thus been at the core of conventional strategic airpower for close to a century. Instead of a gradual approach, punishment seeks to inflict as much harm as possible, as fast as possible, to maximize the shock effect. Overwhelmed by the precision and firepower, the government becomes pressured to alter its behavior. However, Pape argues that punishment does not work: "Modern nation states have extremely high pain thresholds when important interests are at stake, which conventional munitions cannot overcome. Low to moderate levels of punishment inspire more anger than fear; heavy bombardment produces apathy, not rebellion."[108]

The nuclear revolution after World War II triggered considerable attention to military coercion—with the Massive Retaliation doctrines of the 1950s exemplifying the manipulation of risk theories that became dominant. Pape argues that the idea of manipulating the risk of punishment for political purposes has largely come to be identified with Thomas Schelling's book *Arms and Influence.* Like Douhet, Schelling focuses on population and economic targets. But where Douhet and the classic perception of punishment call for the greatest possible damage in the shortest possible time, Schelling and risk strategy focus on not throwing a devastating first strike but rather assert that coercive leverage comes from the *anticipation* of *future* damage and hence that military action must spare vital interests in order to threaten further destruction.[109] As Schelling points out: "It is the expectation of more violence that gets the wanted behaviour, if the power to hurt can get it at all. . . . To exploit a capacity for hurting and inflicting damage one needs to know what an adversary treasures and what scares him and one needs the adversary to understand what behaviour of his will cause the violence to be inflicted and what will cause it to be withheld."[110]

According to this theory, the usefulness of punishment is reduced because *sunk costs* do not influence decisions, and thus massive damage reduces the coercer's leverage. Consequently, Schelling argues for gradualism, even bombing pauses, to let the adversary assess the situation. Pape argues that the strategy of risk does not work, asserting that risk is merely a weaker form of punishment: "Although they [risk strategies] depend on credibility, their credibility is often low because they have usually been employed by governments that were domestically constrained from unleashing full-scale punishment. Nuclear coercion is the exception; the prospect of nuclear devastation is so horrible that even threats with low credibility can coerce."[111]

In addition, Pape argues that denial strategies *can* work, that they entail smashing the enemy military forces, "weakening them to the point where friendly ground forces can seize disputed territories without suffering unacceptable losses." Thus denial strategies focus on targeting supply lines and arms manufacturing and on wearing down field forces. According to Pape, however, strategic bombing is not the best way to achieve success. No strategic bombing campaign has ever yielded decisive results; theater airpower is more cost-effective. Since the condition of fielded forces is the factor most likely to force an opponent to alter his behaviour, strategic bombing of high-value targets will not influence the theater of operations until considerable time has elapsed. Thus strategic bombing can only matter in wars of attrition. "Strategic airpower cannot be decisive. The most it can do is to reduce the costs that friendly land and theater air forces have to pay to defeat enemy forces on the battlefield."[112] In fact, contrary to the popular belief that Operation Desert Storm showed the supremacy of strategic airpower, Pape says, it was the denial strategy of targeting the Iraqi field forces that was decisive. "Airpower did succeed in coercing Iraq to withdraw from Kuwait, but it did so by undermining its ability to defend against the coalition's ground threat. . . . Iraq's willingness to abandon Kuwait grew as airpower crippled its military strategy for holding the seized territory."[113]

Decapitation strategies pursue a combination of punishment and denial effects simultaneously, and can be divided into three main categories: *leadership* decapitation, seeking to kill specific leaders on the assumption that they are the driving force behind the war and that eliminating them will lead to peace, either because their successors are not as committed to the objectives of the war or because they fear that they will also become targets in turn; *political* decapitation, "the use of airpower to create the circumstances in which domestic opposition groups overthrow the government and replace it with one more amenable to concessions"; and *military* decapitation, seeking to isolate the leadership from its units in the field. by attacking command and communications networks, so they cannot provide strategic direction or respond to enemy moves. Pape argues decapitation strategies do not work, because individual leaders are hard to kill, governments are harder to overthrow, and even if the coercer can overthrow the opponent's government, he can rarely guarantee that its replacement will be more forthcoming. "Military decapitation is ineffective because airpower cannot isolate national leaders from control over battlefield forces for long, and short disruptions do not matter unless other instruments are poised to exploit them immediately."[114]

Two factors are of particular interest when comparing the coercive diplomacy of the Kosovo crisis to the theories of Dr. Pape: political pragmatism—rather than conscious military choice—favored the strategy of denial; the French perspective on airpower in Kosovo seems to be more in line with Pape's risk strategy. Both would be sources of friction during OAF.

With the majority of the population in some European NATO nations opposed to bombing the Federal Republic of Yugoslavia, it was clear to most politicians and diplomats possessing even a minimum of political sensitivity that a strategy of immediate overwhelming parallel attacks against the political and military leadership in Belgrade could undermine several European governments. In addition it would most likely destroy allied cohesion—and thereby exclude NATO from exercising the military and political pressure that was the rationale for going to war in the first place. In fact, the political sensitivity was such that for quite a long time NATO opted not to approve serious military planning, out of fear of propelling itself into a war it was not politically ready to handle. According to the chief of staff at SHAPE, General Stöckmann, the planning was "tolerated but not approved by NATO out of fear of 'self fulfilling prophecy' as a driving factor for unintended escalation."[115] As previously noted in chapter 1, the moral objective of preventing a humanitarian disaster in Kosovo dominated the political rhetoric for engaging NATO militarily. The limited political and military room to maneuver was then reduced by the lack of a UN Security Council resolution authorizing the use of force. Political pragmatism dictated that overwhelming use of force against a sovereign state in the middle of Europe without prior UN authorization would further reduce room to maneuver—even though attacking the actual perpetrators of ethnic cleansing in Kosovo was morally acceptable to most people. Thus, a strategy of attacking *these* forces made far more political sense—even though from a purely military point of view it was very difficult. Attacking field forces in Kosovo—more in line, although probably unconsciously, with Pape's denial strategy—was by many simply perceived as a political necessity. In retrospect, they were probably right.

Another interesting source of friction within NATO's chain of command during OAF was the French perspective on airpower. After the

Kosovo War, many within the United States criticized France for vetoing too many of the proposed targets and therefore reducing the efficiency of the air campaign. In a congressional hearing after the war, Lieutenant General Short stated that targeting became a problem, "and as you know, the red card (veto) was played by France, in particular, on many occasions."[116] Also General Naumann confirmed the tendency of France to veto targets.[117]

In his description of risk strategy—the classic approach during the Cold War, and eloquently described by Thomas Schelling—Pape points out that it was based on gradualism, to manipulate the risk of punishment for political purposes. But since coercive leverage, according to Schelling, comes from the anticipation of future damage, the key is *not* to destroy the entire target set "in one fell swoop." In fact, since it is the anticipation of future violence that is the key, sunk cost in terms of targets struck is counterproductive in terms of creating the political leverage that represents the objective of the strategy.[118] As such, the risk strategy is rather the antithesis of the decisive, immediate, overwhelming, parallel attacks of the USAF. To some, the risk strategy bore some resemblance to the gradualism of the Vietnam War. When trying to describe the French attitude, Wesley Clark says, "France seemed to have a different view, however—to limit the strikes at the lowest possible level and to leave implicit the threat of more destructive strikes. As one French officer explained, 'We believe we must save the best targets, so that Milošević will know that he has more to lose in the future than he has lost thus far.'"[119]

As such, the French perspective had clear elements of the risk theory described by Schelling and Pape. It would largely explain some of the friction between Short and the airmen at Vicenza and France. It was a matter of perspective and differing conclusions of what would coerce Milošević to give in—and what would not. General Kelche explained how the differing perspective surfaced during a discussion between him and Wesley Clark during the campaign. General Clark wanted to strike five of Milošević's residences, to send a strong coercive signal to him personally; Clark told Kelche he wanted to take out all five locations on the same night. Kelche disagreed, asserting that it was highly unlikely that Milošević would be living in any of these locations. Therefore killing him in the strike was unlikely. Attacking all five locations would not send as powerful a message as bombing one location at a time—signaling that the different locations of personal value to Milošević were known and would continue to be bombed—one at a time—until he changed his mind (this information has not been verified by General Clark). In the end, according to Kelche, the British agreed with the French view in this particular matter; he added: "It is surprising that American generals do not fully appreciate this approach in a coercive context like OAF."[120] The different perspectives go right to the heart of the airpower debate how best to apply airpower to achieve the desired effect.

When the Kosovo crisis emerged in early March 1998, Lieutenant General Short was the director of operations at the headquarters of the U.S. Air Forces Europe, at Ramstein Air Base in Germany. A few months later he became the commander of Allied Air Forces Southern Europe, as well as the U.S. Sixteenth Air Force—in charge of the air forces that would be the key element of the coercive diplomacy chosen to handle the crisis.

Michael C. Short felt he knew how airpower should be used. An experienced officer marked by the gradualism and political interference in Vietnam and impressed by the hard-hitting strategic application of airpower in the 1991 Gulf War, he had a perspective that was shared by many. One of Short's battle staff directors at CAOC Vicenza, Col. Tom Johansen, said that even though some politicians and diplomats perceived Short as a bit of a bully, he was regarded by his colleagues at CAOC Vicenza as a very strong commander, dead serious, experienced, smart, and with a genuine concern for his troops. Moreover, the overwhelming majority agreed with his view on the application of airpower.[121]

The problem was that the Kosovo crisis was a different war than either the Vietnam War or the Gulf War. The perspectives and advice on airpower offered to the politicians by the professional airmen to enable the crafting of a coercive diplomatic approach to handle the situation were rooted in a philosophy nurtured by conflicts at the high end of the intensity spectrum. As we shall see, it precluded a creative opportunity to focus on integrating airpower in a broader political strategy to coerce the FRY leadership.

As it happened, Short's perspectives would reflect sentiments in a larger foreign policy debate in the United States—between the U.S. State Department and the Pentagon—that would have strong influence on the political handling of the Kosovo crisis.

Chapter 3

FROM VIETNAM TO KOSOVO
U.S. Foreign Policy and the Use of Force

The renaissance of strategic conventional airpower in the 1990s coincided with a broader domestic U.S. foreign policy debate on *when* and *how* to use force. One school of thought asserted that only vital American interests were worth fighting for, and that once vital interest was threatened, one should apply decisive force to attain clear political objectives. The other school of thought argued that there were reasons other than vital interest that could trigger a military response—like humanitarian interventions—and that on occasion, limited use of force could produce favorable results. In many ways it was a continuation of a long U.S. foreign policy debate of protecting and advancing one's own interests versus a perceived moral responsibility to use its political and military might to assist people less fortunate. It was a debate that in the Clinton presidency would reach a crescendo during the Bosnian War—leaving the first Clinton administration almost paralyzed in its handling of the conflict. It would also be a debate that significantly shaped the approach to the Kosovo crisis a few years later.

A natural starting point for this debate and its implications for Kosovo is the American involvement in the Vietnam War. Even though the roots of this debate are far deeper, the Vietnam War had immense consequences on a number of domestic structures, perhaps particularly in terms of U.S. foreign policy and the military. The first defeat in the history of America,[1] it is described by one of the most respected American diplomats, George Kennan, as "the most disastrous of all America's undertakings over the whole two hundred years of its history."[2] It was a war that brought into question the belief in America's exceptionalism, its military invincibility, and people's trust in their military and political leaders.

According to Professor Daniel Bell of Harvard, the roots of the American intervention in Vietnam had been planted and nurtured by "America's concept of its own 'exceptionalism.'"[3] According to Stanley Karnow, a traditional view held by many Americans was that of the United States as a beacon of democracy, with a "manifest destiny" that resulted in a feeling of being obliged to export its benefits to less privileged civilizations abroad. The traditional rhetoric of American presidents echoed this theme.[4] Abraham Lincoln told Congress in December 1862 that America was a nation that could not escape history, because it was "the last best hope of earth."[5] In 1968, when Robert Kennedy announced his presidential candidacy, Theodore Sorenson wrote in his announcement speech, "At stake is not simply the leadership of our party, and even our own country, it is our right to the moral leadership of this planet."[6] Hence, both the government and the public leading up to the Vietnam War generally shared these assumptions of moral global responsibility.[7] The strategic debates after World War II were focused on *means* rather than *aims;* it was less a question of whether the United States was entitled to—or had any moral right to—project its world views and values onto other societies and cultures, than of *how.* This was, of course, not only an American way of thinking. The British writer Rudyard Kipling explained British expansionism with the infamous "white man's burden" philosophy; the French had their similar *"mission civilisatrice."* Therefore, it can be argued that this notion probably had its roots in the thinking of Western civilization in general rather than being a specific American phenomenon. Still, few Americans questioned the decision to send U.S. troops to Vietnam to "rescue" South Vietnam from the communist North Vietnam, to fight for democracy and freedom. Polls showed overwhelming public support for President Lyndon B. Johnson's deployment of troops in Vietnam.[8]

The Vietnam War would change all this. What started out with overwhelming public support for President Johnson's deployment of troops in Vietnam gradually split the country as the war went on. Slowly, the rosy reports of the government were contradicted by war correspondents in Vietnam, and the public gradually got to see daily reports of the horror and suffering. This largely eroded the public's faith in official statements and thereby decreased the government's credibility.[9] As Harvard Sitikoff writes, "The United States [also] paid a political cost for the Vietnam War. It weakened public faith in government, and in the honesty and competence of its leaders."[10] Arguably reflecting the feelings of many Americans, the mayor of Bardstown—a small city in Kentucky that had one of the highest casualty rates relative to its population during the Vietnam War—said, "We believed that the first thing that you did for your country was to defend it. You didn't question that. But I think we realized as we went along—maybe later than we should have—that the government was pulling a bit of a flimflam. We weren't getting the truth. The Vietnam War was being misrepresented to the people—the way it was conducted, its ultimate purpose. Though I am still a patriot, I ended up very disillusioned."[11]

This notion—known as the "Vietnam Syndrome"—would discourage American presidents from intervening abroad for years to come, and in that way it significantly influenced U.S. foreign policy. As Stanley Karnow eloquently put it, "In a larger sense they [the names on the Vietnam Memorial in Washington] symbolize a faded hope—or perhaps the birth of a new awareness. They bear witness to the end of America's absolute confidence in its moral exclusivity, its military invincibility, its manifest destiny. They are the price, paid in blood and sorrow, for America's awakening to maturity, to the recognition of its limitations."[12]

The U.S. Army and the Pentagon suffered the gravest immediate impact of the war. With public resentment against the war in Vietnam gaining strength in the late 1960s and early 1970s, and with antiwar protests televised all over the globe, these sentiments also spread to the U.S. Army in Vietnam. According to the last American commander in Vietnam—Gen. Fred Weyand—the growing public disaffection for the war, fueled by the press, demoralized the American forces in the field. He claimed, "The American Army is really a people's army in the sense that it belongs to the American people—when the army is committed the American people are committed; when the American people lose their commitment, it is futile to try to keep the army committed."[13] So by the early 1970s, the U.S. Army had largely disintegrated, and as Stanley Karnow points out, "nobody wanted to be the last to die for a cause that had lost its meaning, and for those awaiting withdrawal only survival counted." Troops wore peace symbols and refused to go into combat, race relations increasingly became an issue as the sense of purpose evaporated, and by 1971 an official report estimated that a third or more of the troops were addicted to drugs. Not only did the number of cases in which soldiers disobeyed their superiors rise, but in a number of cases soldiers murdered their superiors with fragmentation grenades, a practice referred to as "fragging."[14] According to Secretary of the Army (2001–3) Thomas White, the service had basically been destroyed by the Vietnam War; he added, "The non-commissioned officer leadership had vanished, indiscipline rates were way, way up—we needed just a complete rebuilding of the force from the bottom to the top, and that was precisely what we engaged ourselves in for the next 20 years or so."[15]

According to Spiller there was a remarkable unanimity that by 1973 the United States Army was an institutional wreck.[16] The defeat by what Henry Kissinger called "a fourth-rate power" caused a loss of pride and self-confidence to many in the United States who liked to think of the nation as invincible; and the military was largely discredited for years.[17] The Pentagon was harassed by demonstrations and blood thrown at its entrance, and around Washington many military personnel seldom wore their uniform, in order to avoid problems and hostility.[18] Not only was morale very low, but the expenditure of the Vietnam War had created inflation. This skyrocketed during the 1973 oil crisis, when the Middle East producers stopped the flow of oil and later quadrupled its price—in turn leading to lower defense expenditures than before the Vietnam War. The antiwar movement had generally strong support on college campuses, a factor that significantly reduced the recruitment potential of the young and clever who were to lead the new army and its sophisticated technology. By the middle seventies, 40 percent of the Army's soldiers had not graduated from high school.[19] Therefore the armed forces—perhaps particularly the U.S. Army—needed to be rebuilt, and as Deputy Secretary of Defense (1975–77) Robert Ellsworth commented, "Of course, when we left we all felt that we had a lot of unfinished business to attend to. People like Colin Powell who stayed in the military, undertook to do that unfinished business—and they did it very well."[20] Still, such an endeavor would need time to succeed, and in 1980 the Army chief of staff, Gen. Edward C. Meyer, warned the Congress that he was [still] presiding over a "hollow force"—short of personnel, experience, and equipment.[21]

After the Vietnam War the military establishment's view was largely the feeling of "no more Vietnams," in terms of intervening far away in distant countries without being provided with clear objectives, decisive force, or adequate political will to see it through. The deeply rooted feeling was that bureaucratic and political limitations imposed on the military had precluded victory. The military had been left to fight "with one hand tied behind its back." In his memoirs the U.S. commander in Vietnam (1965–68), Gen. William C. Westmoreland, claimed that restraints imposed on him had precluded his effectiveness and blamed President Johnson for escalating the war too slowly, restricting him from attacking enemy bases in Laos and Cambodia, providing inadequate equipment to South Vietnamese allies, and not leveling with the American public in order to ensure support for the U.S. armed forces in Vietnam. The politicians were micromanaging the military effort to such a degree that President Johnson himself was selecting bombing targets in North Vietnam. The president even had a sand-table model of Khe Sanh (1968) built in the basement situation room of the White House in order to be able to follow the battle as it progressed.[22] A recently aired TV documentary addressing the Pentagon frustration after the Vietnam War points out that "Vietnam had cast a long shadow over the Pentagon. It was their bleakest time. Throughout the building, they had their memories of old battles between the military and the civilian leadership[;] . . . the army was broken—it simply could not function effectively. And they believed it was the civilians who had broken it—micromanaging every detail, even picking bombing targets from the White House. They vowed to take more control."[23]

The U.S. military in Vietnam went through years of hard postwar self-examination, and fundamental reforms in training and doctrines—particularly within the Army—paid off. Slowly and systematically, the Army gradually regained its strength, and its vindication would come in the 1991 Gulf War, Operation Desert Storm.

The Vietnam War also had a profound impact on American foreign-policy makers. Gen. Maxwell Taylor[24] later admitted that Vietnam was both a blunder and a lesson, asserting that the United States did not then know either itself, its allies, or the enemy. Its leaders thought they were going to fight another Korean War. As General Taylor pointed out: "So, until we know the enemy and know our allies and ourselves we'd better keep out of this kind of dirty business. It's very dangerous."[25] Robert McNamara—the secretary of defense under both Kennedy and Johnson—echoed the same sentiment when he later admitted, "We were wrong, terribly wrong."[26] General Westmoreland asserted, "A lesson to be learned, is that young men should never be sent into battles unless the country is going to support them."[27] For the years to come, U.S. policy makers listened to the lessons from Vietnam, and the appetite to engage abroad with military forces decreased. According to Dr. Jeffrey Record, post–Vietnam War presidents have been more careful in picking overseas fights. They have picked relatively easy wins like Grenada, Panama, Iraq, and Serbia, and they have been more willing to cut American losses in dead-end interventions like Lebanon and Somalia.[28]

Rooted in the experience of Vietnam—and largely triggered by a car bomb killing 241 U.S. marines in Beirut, Lebanon, on 23 October 1983—the secretary of defense in the Ronald Reagan administration, Caspar Weinberger, presented in an address to the National Press Club on 28 November 1984 six tests for weighing the use of U.S. combat forces abroad.[29] Jeffrey Record believes that Weinberger's speech—called "The Uses of Military Power"—"remains probably the single most influential contribution to the post–Vietnam War debate on the use of force."[30] According to Jim Mokhiber and Rick Young, the speech was "immensely influential within military circles."[31]

The *Washington Post* referred to the six tests, or tenets, as the "Weinberger Doctrine." The tests were:

1. Commit only if our or our allies' vital interests are at stake.

2. If we commit, do so with all the resources necessary to win.
3. Go in only with clear political and military objectives.
4. Be ready to change the commitment if the objectives change, since wars rarely stand still.
5. Only take on commitments that can gain the support of the American people and the Congress.
6. Commit U.S. forces only as a last resort.[32]

Weinberger argued that military involvement had to be a last resort, launched only after every attempt to gain a diplomatic solution had been explored. America should avoid armed conflicts unless it could count on the unwavering support of the public. According to Karnow, who was present, the message from Weinberger was clear: "No more Vietnams."[33] In his speech Weinberger warned against those who advocated limited force, thinking that American forces of any size would solve problems, and he decried the use of force or threatened force as a means of political coercion—"As a tool of coercive diplomacy, force had obviously failed against North Vietnam, and its failure was followed by a real war."[34] Weinberger rejected force as a companion of diplomacy, seeing it rather as a tool to be used when diplomacy failed. Weinberger's speech was a warning against "what Weinberger believed was a penchant of some policy makers, most notably his rival, Secretary of State George Shultz, for casual military intervention."[35]

It is worth noting the difference in perspective between the Department of Defense and the State Department when it came to the use of force. According to Mokhiber and Young, "In the United States, this debate—which frequently pits the military versus the 'civilian' arms of the government, including the State Department and the White House—has resurfaced with each major conflict and intervention since the second World War."[36] Hence, while the Weinberger Doctrine was embraced in military circles, the doctrine was challenged by diplomats—including Secretary Shultz—who was "worried that American diplomacy, not backed up by credible threats of force, would be hamstrung by the military's supposed reluctance to become involved in 'limited' wars."[37]

Weinberger's military assistant was Colin Powell—the Vietnam veteran who had stayed to rebuild the U.S. military and would later rise to become the chairman of the Joint Chiefs of Staff (CJCS). Together with the administration, Powell saw the draft of the Weinberger Doctrine before it was made public and summarized, "In short, is the national interest at stake? If the answer is yes, go in, and go in to win. Otherwise, stay out. Clausewitz would have applauded. And in the future, when it became my responsibility to advise presidents on committing our forces to combat, Weinberger's rules turned out to be a practical guide."[38]

Responsibility for advising presidents came just a few years later, when Powell became CJCS in 1989—the Gulf War in 1991 was to be the arena in which the lessons of Vietnam and his adopted rules of the Weinberger Doctrine were tested. Powell asserted regarding foreign interventions: "Many of my generation, the career captains, majors, and lieutenant colonels seasoned in that war, vowed that when our turn came to call the shots, we would not quietly acquiesce in half-hearted warfare for half-baked reasons that the American people could not understand or support."[39]

Another key lesson Powell drew from his Vietnam experience was the Joint Chiefs' inability to confront the civilian leadership in government with the flaws of their strategy. "Our senior officers knew the war was going badly. Yet they bowed to groupthink pressure and kept up pretenses, the phony measure of body counts, the comforting illusion of secure hamlets, the inflated progress reports. As a corporate entity, the military failed to talk straight to its political superiors or to itself. The top leadership never went to the Secretary of Defense or the president and said, 'This war is unwinnable the way we are fighting it.'"[40]

Powell's chance to call the shots came when Iraq invaded Kuwait in 1990. The Persian Gulf would preoccupy General Powell immediately after his taking office as CJCS. Powell explains, "Since the free flow of oil from the Persian Gulf was as crucial to us as blood pumping through an artery, Iraqi and Iranian threats to Kuwaiti oil tankers would be met."[41] But how to respond if Kuwaiti oil supplies to the United States were threatened was another matter. The American public was still wary from the Vietnam War and was skeptical about intervening militarily abroad. Polls taken in the late fall before the first Gulf War said that 53 percent of Americans felt that rather than resort to war, President George H. W. Bush should continue sanctions against Iraq "no matter how long it takes." According to a poll in the *Washington Post* published one week before the first Gulf War, 44 percent of the public were willing to accept a thousand American dead, and only 35 percent favored a war if the casualty numbers reached ten thousand.[42]

The United States went to war (17 January 1991) after Iraq had invaded Kuwait (2 August 1990), thus intervening to secure the oil deemed by Colin Powell so crucial to the American economy. The effect of Vietnam was explicit, in the refusal of gradualism and the use of decisive force.[43] As General Clark explains, "Certainly the work General Powell did leading up to the Gulf War and the Powell Doctrine of decisive force was a wholehearted refutation of the failed gradualism of Vietnam."[44] When President Bush went to war, he had gathered a force of more than six hundred thousand troops—more than the number of U.S. troops in Vietnam at its peak. According to John Olsen, the much heralded strategic air campaign during Operation Desert Storm was named Instant Thunder, as an antithesis to the gradual approach of Vietnam's Rolling Thunder. John Warden explained that Instant Thunder was a "focused, intense air campaign designed to incapacitate Iraqi leadership and destroy key Iraqi military capability, in a short period of time," not a "graduated, long-term campaign plan designed to provide escalation options to counter Iraqi moves."[45] Warden, Powell, and the military establishment who had long blamed President Johnson for his incremental approach in Vietnam intended not to make the same mistake.

When the American offensive started in January 1991, President Bush not only felt it necessary to underline to the American public that "this will not be another Vietnam" but pointed out that this would not be a conflict in which troops were "asked to fight with one hand tied behind their back."[46] The air campaign was generally perceived as an overwhelming success; in just six weeks of fighting and only four days of ground warfare the United States liberated Kuwait and captured more than a hundred thousand Iraqi troops at a cost of some two hundred U.S. casualties. This prompted President Bush to claim in the moment of triumph, "By God, we've kicked the Vietnam Syndrome once and for all."[47]

This victory was important not only in political terms— to many officers it signified the restoration of the U.S. armed forces. This referred not only to the impressive and spectacularly successful use of airpower but also, perhaps particularly, to the Army, which had suffered the most after the Vietnam War. Operation Desert Storm exponentially raised the profile of the U.S. military—most notably through General Powell and General Schwarzkopf, who dominated the press conferences. In a somewhat "larger than life" performance, General Powell rather impressively stated, "Our strategy to go after this army is very, very simple: first we're going to cut it off, and then we are going to kill it."[48] General Schwarzkopf showed pictures of the tremendous accuracy of the air campaign, and with a confident grin he boasted about "the luckiest man in Iraq"—an Iraqi who drove across a bridge that was destroyed immediately after and could be seen collapsing "in his rear view mirror."[49]

This high-profile performance was seen by many at the Pentagon as a restoration of military influence after the Vietnam War, and the influence of the chairman was significant. According to the author James Mann, "What you regularly see is Colin Powell physically imposing, in uniform, very confident, talking about what the U.S. is going to do—he is really the center of the press conferences. The usual picture is Powell at the podium, Cheney kind of behind him. It is a reminder of just how powerful the Chairman of the Joint Chiefs of Staff is, and how powerful Powell was."[50]

In fact, General Powell's influence on the Gulf War of 1991—adhering to the Weinberger Doctrine of overwhelming force—led commentators to start using the term "Weinberger-Powell Doctrine."[51] According to Halberstam, "The Gulf War had showed that the American military had recovered from the malaise of the Vietnam debacle and was once again the envy of the rest of the world[;] . . . the troops who fought in the Gulf War were honored as the troops who had fought in Vietnam were not. Colin Powell and Norman Schwarzkopf, the presiding generals of the war, were celebrated as William Westmoreland had never been."[52]

To many in the Pentagon the Gulf War in 1991 proved that the U.S. military had recuperated from the experience in Vietnam, and that their influence was somewhat restored.[53] Perhaps a remark by Lt. Gen. Paul Van Riper (U.S. Marine Corps) captured the feeling in the Pentagon: "At the end of the Gulf War, if there's one word that would describe how most of us felt, it was *vindicated.* Vindicated in the sense that we had got it right between Vietnam and the Gulf War, and we got out on the battlefield and proved it."[54]

However, as Jeffrey Record points out, the Vietnam Syndrome had *not* been "kicked" in the Gulf War of 1991 as President Bush had proclaimed.[55] Former secretary of state Henry Kissinger warned that the success of Operation Desert Storm should not imply that the United States could deal with every issue simultaneously. He also warned that America had to be selective and cautious with its resources and credibility.[56]

Colin Powell remained in office as the CJCS, and in 1992 he wrote an article in *Foreign Affairs* called "U.S. Forces: Challenges Ahead" that described his view of the world and of the utility of U.S. forces.[57] Powell asserted that with the end of the Cold War and with the United States established as the sole remaining superpower, the strategy should move from global war-fighting to regional contingencies. The United States should be able to fight two major regional conflicts (MRCs)—notably in the Persian Gulf and in the Pacific (North Korea)—at the same time. Powell explained that two schools of thought were dominant in the American debate concerning the use of force: the *limited war* school and the *all-out war* school. However, Powell argued, *all* wars are limited, and they are limited by "the territory on which they are fought (like Korea and Vietnam)," "the means used to fight them (no nuclear weapons in Korea; no massive mobilization in Vietnam)," and "by the objectives for which they are fought—the most significant limitation in political terms and therefore the limitation that is most often discussed and debated." According to Powell, when a crisis emerges, you should evaluate the circumstances and ask questions like, "Is the political objective we seek to achieve important, clearly defined and understood? Have all other non-violent policy means failed? Will military force achieve the objective? At what cost? Have the gains and risks been analysed? How might the situation that we seek to alter, once it is altered by force, develop further and what might be the consequences?"[58]

Powell particularly emphasizes that the political objectives must be important, clearly defined, and understood, and that clear and unambiguous objectives must be given to the armed forces. These objectives must be firmly linked to the political objectives. Doing that would preclude mistakes like the Bay of Pigs, Vietnam, and the Beirut bombings.

In his article, Powell warned of the limited war school, "We should always be sceptical when so-called experts suggest that all a particular crisis calls for is a little surgical bombing or a limited attack. When the 'surgery' is over and the desired results are not obtained, a new set of experts then comes forward with talk of just a little escalation—more bombs, more men and women, more force. History has not been kind to this approach to war making."[59] This caution was reminiscent of the warnings Caspar Weinberger had formulated in his "Uses of Military Power" speech, which suggested that his State Department counterpart treated military intervention too lightly.[60] Rather, Powell explains, when one does use force one "should win and win decisively."[61] This notion—expressed so clearly in Powell's 1992 article in *Foreign Affairs*—has since been referred to as "the Powell Doctrine."

When the Balkans and the issue of Yugoslavia came to the attention of the Bush administration, the Vietnam Syndrome was still active. President Bush chose to stay out of Bosnia, which was perceived as a brutal civil war in a place of relatively little strategic significance to the United States. The Bush administration was slow to react to Yugoslavia for two main reasons: "The first and more obvious was the ghosts of Vietnam, the immense resistance of the Pentagon to direct military involvement, the great fear of being sucked into a Balkan quagmire"; and secondly, exhaustion from the Gulf War, the end of the Cold War, the future of Eastern Europe, and its relation with Russia.[62] It was questionable whether conventional U.S. military power would work against the unconventional, elusive, irregular forces that were responsible for much of the killing. The president himself told the *New York Times,* "I do not want to see the United States bogged down in any way into some guerrilla warfare [in Bosnia]. We've lived through that once already."[63] By summer 1992, according to the last U.S. ambassador to Yugoslavia (1989–92), Warren Zimmermann, there was no debate within the government regarding giving Milošević the blame for the havoc in Bosnia. The issue at stake was whether Bosnia and the former Yugoslavia involved such American interests that it warranted military intervention. In the summer of 1992 it was considered not to be of such vital importance.[64]

There are many and complex reasons why the Americans regarded the Balkans this way. Richard Holbrooke points out that when the former Yugoslavia collapsed, the Americans were divided between those who called for intervention, for either moral or strategic reasons, and those who feared that an intervention would turn into a Vietnam-like quagmire.[65] When Warren Zimmermann confronted Secretary of State (1992–93) Lawrence Eagleburger about the lack of a comprehensive strategy for dealing with the Serb aggression, Eagleburger admitted that he was heavily influenced by the U.S. involvement in Vietnam. Then came the experience in Beirut of October 1983. U.S. troops were sent to Lebanon largely as a show of force, and the operation ended with 241 Americans being killed in a car bomb, a loss that triggered a withdrawal. Eagleburger also pointed out that the tremendous success of the Gulf War had vindicated the views of General Powell, whose *Foreign Affairs* article spelled out clear criteria for achieving results by military means—criteria that could hardly be met by the complex Bosnian Crisis. This was why Colin Powell consistently opposed military intervention in Bosnia.[66]

Eagleburger believed the greatest change at the highest levels of the Washington power structure was how, some two decades after Vietnam, both the State Department and the Pentagon differed. Previously, "the Pentagon had tended to be gung ho about military involvement and brought a can-do attitude to all its endeavors, while State tended to be cautious. Vietnam had changed that—the army had gone in there and paid a high price both in blood and in its psyche. Now the roles were reversed. State had a number of activists among its younger officials, many of whom had come along after the Vietnam experience."[67]

According to President Bush's National Security Adviser, Gen. Brent Scowcroft, the prevailing view in the Bush administration by summer and fall 1992 was that getting involved in Bosnia would ultimately jeopardize American credibility and that in order to avoid that Washington had to do whatever was necessary to prevail—even if it involved the use of ground forces. Since no one was prepared to wage a ground war, the administration opted not to use force at all.[68] In other words, Bosnia was not considered a vital interest, and the political objective was not important enough to use decisive force. A limited response, however, was strongly opposed by Colin Powell, the military establishment, and others. Zimmermann explains how "the Vietnam Syndrome and the Powell Doctrine proved to be powerful dampers on action by the Bush administration, particularly in an election year."[69] Reflecting on the lack of resolve of the Bush administration in preventing the atrocities in Bosnia, Eagleburger later admitted: "Every day when I look at myself in the mirror when I shave, I question myself on what happened there. Should we have done more, should I have expressed my doubts harder with the President?"[70]

George H. W. Bush lost the election in 1992, and on 20 January 1993 the Clinton administration took office. The new secretary of state, Warren Christopher, made public a policy review on 10 February, stating, among other things, that "under no circumstances short of a comprehensive peace settlement that was voluntarily accepted by all the parties would U.S. ground troops be deployed to Bosnia."[71] According to the new national security adviser, Anthony Lake, the argument in favor of this decision was the same as that of the previous administration: "President Clinton refused to engage our troops in a ground war in Bosnia because he knew that no outside power could force peace on the parties. To do so would have risked a Vietnam-like quagmire."[72] This view was widely shared by the Department of Defense. Halberstam points out that "Powell and others in the Pentagon believed that if we got entangled with the Serbs in some way, it might become like Vietnam, a distant, peripheral war for our people and politicians, but an all encompassing blood war of survival for the Serb people and politicians."[73]

In other words, the use of decisive force was effectively taken off the table.

Colin Powell was to continue as CJCS under Clinton until the fall of 1993. Almost immediately, the two schools Powell had referred to in his *Foreign Affairs* article were evident in the high echelons of the Clinton administration. The difference between the limited war school and the all-out war school was largely the same as the division in how to approach the conflict in Bosnia, described, as we have seen, by Richard Holbrooke as between those who thought the United States should intervene for either moral or strategic reasons and those who feared that an intervention would turn into a Vietnam-like quagmire.[74] At the head of these schools were, respectively, two members of the administration's inner circle—called the Principals Committee—the newly appointed U.S. ambassador to the United Nations, Madeleine K. Albright, and the CJCS, General Powell.

Born in Europe (Prague, Czechoslovakia) just before World War II, Madeleine Albright points out in her memoirs that she was influenced by her family's experience during and after World War II and by the great powers' approach to the German Third Reich. Here she was referring to her diplomat father, Josef Korbel, who could never forget the lessons of Munich. He told her: "Unspeakable tragedies ensue when great countries appease evil, make decisions over the heads of smaller powers, and do not pay attention to what is happening in faraway places."[75] When President Clinton named Albright as the new secretary of state, he said that she had watched her world fall apart (during World War II and later during the pro-Moscow communist coup d'etat in 1948) and ever since had dedicated her life to spreading the freedom and tolerance she found in the United States to the rest of the world.[76] Albright comments on this issue in her memoirs: "When I was still a little girl, my family was driven from its home twice, first by Fascists, then by Communists. While in office I was able to fight against ethnic cleansing in Yugoslavia, a country where I had lived as a child. . . . Once in office I was able to help the newly democratic nations of Central and East Europe, including the land of my birth, Czechoslovakia, become full partners of the free world."[77]

Together with her candid admission of being a person with strong opinions and "born with a tendency to express them"[78]—this legacy could have contributed to her forceful approach to the destruction of Yugoslavia and the suffering in Bosnia. According to Henry Kissinger's former aide and editor of *Foreign Affairs,* William G. Hyland, Madeleine Albright—together with President Clinton and other administration officials like Warren Christopher, Tony Lake, and Strobe Talbott—thought that the end of the Cold War allowed the United States to shift focus "from primarily an interest-based foreign policy to one that rested more on such values as democracy, market economics, humanitarian relief, and genocide suppression."[79] To some degree echoing this theme in her own memoirs, Albright underlines her pragmatic approach when summing up her foreign policy lessons; she hoped she "never again [had] to hear foreign policy described as a debate between Wilsonian idealists and geopolitical realists. In our era, no president or Secretary of State could manage events without combining the two."[80]

Madeleine Albright was described by the *Washington Post* as one of the Clinton administration's leading advocates of the use of force in Bosnia, and by Ivo H. Daalder as "the administration's leading hawk on the issue of Bosnia."[81] She felt that, if planned carefully, the lessons from Vietnam could be learned *too* well, that limited force *could* be effective in achieving limited objectives.[82] The president's representative for the Dayton implementation in Bosnia, Robert Gelbard, said, "I believe Madeleine Albright handled the situation in Bosnia better than anybody in the administration at the time. She understood that getting through to Milošević demanded more than diplomacy, and that force sometimes is needed—and she deserves credit for that."[83] The commander of the United Nations Protection Force (UNPROFOR) in Bosnia (1994–95) when Albright was ambassador to the UN, General Smith, said that Albright "saw a series of principles being abandoned, because nobody was prepared to fight for them. Her view was that there were certain principles at stake here, which should be defended by force."[84]

Warren Zimmermann shared Madeleine Albright's view on the use of limited force, arguing that there had to be a middle ground between *no* involvement and *total* involvement and that if the United States would not intervene until absolutely sure of winning it would keep American power on the sideline in most future events.[85] Secretary of Defense Les Aspin similarly rejected the Powell Doctrine and argued for more limited objectives, seeking a less restrictive rule for committing troops to combat—including the use of airpower to send political signals to an adversary.[86] Arguing along the same lines, Jeffrey Record held that the Weinberger and Powell Doctrines—prompted by the lessons from Vietnam—were inadequate as foreign policy tools. How do you define vital interest? Who defines them? What does winning mean? How are assured public and congressional support to be gained in advance and maintained throughout the conflict? Drawing a historical parallel, Dr. Record argued that none of the conservative doctrine's criteria would likely have been met when approaching Germany in Munich in 1938 and so would presumably have indicated the appeasement policy so criticized in the aftermath.[87] Author and U.S. Army major H. R. McMaster argued that there is nothing inherently wrong in limiting the use of force as long as the means employed are connected with strategic goals and objectives. In fact, all warfare is limited to some degree, McMaster argues, but he adds that once departing from a limited force strategy, senior military advisers and commanders should first develop a military strategy to achieve the strategic goals described, and *then* determine the level of force to carry out the strategy chosen. The reverse happened in Vietnam, when President Johnson started by determining the level of military force that was politically palatable and then asked the military to do the best it could with that.[88]

Madeleine Albright believed in the use of limited force, and she wanted limited force to generate political leverage to address issues that were not confined to vital national interest only. In the Balkans, she wanted to address the human rights issues involved and the moral responsibility of assisting the weaker Bosnian Muslims against the stronger and more brutal Bosnian Serbs. During the administration's first months in 1993, the "lift and strike" policy—lifting the weapons embargo to allow weapons to the Bosnian Muslims and sending air strikes against the Bosnian Serbs—was debated within the administration. Vice President Al Gore and Ambassador Albright strongly favored air strikes against the Bosnian Serbs, with Albright even arguing for unilateral American air strikes if necessary.[89] As secretary of state, Albright often sat next to Gore during meetings and compared notes on policy and personalities. Albright describes Gore as influential within the administration. He was treated as a full partner in policy discussions by the president, and he "cared passionately about issues of justice and human rights."[90]

Representing the other school of thought, which argued for clear objectives and decisive force as described in Powell's *Foreign Affairs* article, was the military establishment. Pentagon officials like General Powell and General Shalikashvili, who was then working as SACEUR, argued that a substantial ground force would be necessary to provide the desired outcome in Bosnia.[91] According to Ivo H. Daalder, Powell's doctrinal preference to use decisive force to attain clear and attainable objectives dominated Pentagon thinking at the time.[92] However, debating the use of force with General Powell was difficult for the—by comparison—somewhat inexperienced Albright, who admitted that "the sight of Powell walking into meetings with his charts and briefing papers was impressive. During the Gulf War Powell had seemed a larger-than-life hero, expressing American determination in a period of widely celebrated, if incomplete, triumph."[93] Albright candidly noted that "in the face of all his medals and prestige, I found it hard to argue with Powell about the proper way to employ American force."[94] In his memoirs, General Powell recalls one debate with Madeleine Albright in which she stated, "What's the point of having this superb military that you're always talking about if we can't use it?"—at which General Powell thought he would have an aneurysm. He had to explain *patiently* to Albright that if one wanted to use military force one needed clear political goals and that the military commitment should match those very goals.[95] Powell explains his view of the almost continuous friction between the Pentagon/Defense Department and the State Department back in the 1980s: "I was developing a strong distaste for the antiseptic phrases coined by the State Department officials for foreign interventions which usually had bloody consequences for the military, words like 'presence,' 'symbol,' 'signal,' 'option on the table,' 'establishment of credibility.' Their use was fine if beneath them lay a solid mission. But too often these words were used to give the appearance of clarity to mud."[96]

In fact, as General Powell recalls, "My constant, unwelcome message at all the meetings on Bosnia was simply that we should not commit military forces until we had a clear political objective." Anthony Lake—who had resigned his job as an assistant to Henry Kissinger in protest over the Nixon administration's invasion of Cambodia during the Vietnam War—added, "You know, Madeleine, the kinds of questions Colin is asking about goals are exactly the ones the military never asked during Vietnam."[97] In her memoirs, Albright shoots back at Lake: "Tony Lake, who had come in charged up by the robust rhetoric of the Clinton campaign, soon had the Vietnam bug humming in his ear."[98]

Commenting on the lessons of Vietnam and the perspectives of General Powell and the Pentagon, Tony Lake nuanced the perspectives of both; he did not share Eagleburger's perception that the Pentagon became more reluctant to get involved in engagements abroad after the Vietnam War. He pointed out that the Pentagon had become more reluctant to engage in Indochina to assist the French in 1954 and in Laos in 1961:

What I learned in Vietnam was that it is very dangerous for civilian leadership to make assumptions of what the military can do, and then ask the military to go off on a mission impossible, and then watch as our society blames them for the mistakes that were actually made by the civilian leadership for sending them on the mission in the first place. Thus, the lesson of the military was not "we shouldn't be in favor of going in"—it was "we're going in, but make damn sure that you're giving us what we need to win."[99]

Similarly, Lake asserts that General Powell was not so much adhering to the so-called Powell Doctrine when debating military engagement in Bosnia as arguing that if one opted to use airpower, one should make sure not to send it on a "mission impossible," but make sure it achieved whatever effect one wanted it to achieve:

My position was that even while I supported the use of force, Powell was right to be questioning the sort of automatic assumption that one could coerce the Bosnian Serbs into doing most things through airpower. Powell described the problem by rhetorically questioning how a twenty-three-year-old in the cockpit of an aircraft flying at five hundred miles an hour could locate and take out a mortar that was being kept in a garage somewhere and then taken out to fire a few rounds and then hidden back in the garage. It just wasn't so easy as we civilians might think.[100]

Lake says the administration's debates were not only confined to the doctrinaire terms of the Powell Doctrine versus the limited-force advocates, although that perhaps was at the back of people's minds: "We were discussing specific issues of how to push the Bosnian Serbs back from Sarajevo."[101] Even so, according to Halberstam, Powell, shaking his head, would tell his friends after meetings with Albright that "Madeleine's at it again"; Halberstam adds that some observers felt she had such a perceived relaxed perspective on using force because she was the principal least affected by Vietnam.[102]

The friction between the proponents of limited force versus decisive force would continue, but—as the hopeless situation in Bosnia continued—the advocates of limited force slowly gained ground.

General Powell left office as CJCS in fall 1993 and was replaced by Gen. John M. Shalikashvili. According to Halberstam, the Pentagon had favored Gen. Joe Hoar as chairman because "he was thought to be stronger, if need be, in standing up for the Pentagon's traditional sense of its territory in any conflict with the civilians."[103] However, Shalikashvili was chosen for the job. He agreed with much of the Powell Doctrine but said he wanted to change the Weinberger Doctrine, claiming that only *vital* interests of the United States would signify military involvement and opening the possibility of a more flexible way of using force. This put him somewhat at odds with the largely conservative Pentagon establishment.[104] Even though Powell had left office, his perception of the use of force was well rooted within the Pentagon and, to some extent, among policy makers in the administration. The televised disaster of Somalia once again proved to some in the Pentagon that limited force was the wrong way to get involved in faraway conflicts. Halberstam says that even though Powell had retired just before the debacle in Mogadishu, "the Powell Doctrine lived on—and Somalia was ammo for it."[105]

The Somalia debacle strengthened the arguments of General Powell and hurt those of Madeleine Albright. According to Halberstam, Albright had advocated involvement in Somalia. She had written articles in the *New York Times* about nation building in Somalia and the need for democracy, and she had argued in favor of standing up to Aidid in order to protect UN credibility. After the failure of Somalia, this would hurt her politically: "In Washington, her speech and op-ed pieces on nation building in Somalia clung to her like a cloak after that disaster."[106]

The suffering in Bosnia, however, put pressure on the administration to do something, and during the summer of 1993 television pictures of the horrible conditions in Sarajevo and surrounding areas made an impact in Washington. The president ordered a new review of political and military options, during which Tony Lake and his staff adopted a strategy of linking the threat of air strikes directly to diplomacy.[107] It was the first time in the Clinton administration that this combination had been thoroughly explored. According to Daalder, the people in the Clinton administration who believed that fighting the Serbs with airpower would not necessarily result in a quagmire were Madeleine Albright, Alexander Vershbow (Tony Lake's director for European affairs on the NSC staff), and Richard Holbrooke—with Al Gore, Tony Lake, and William Perry largely sharing their views but not consistently or with equal determination pushing such a case.[108] According to Halberstam, "Sandy" Vershbow—who had come over from the State Department to be Tony Lake's top deputy on Balkan policy—was one of the most vocal hawks in the upper bureaucracy.[109]

One additional name should be mentioned—Wesley K. Clark. He had worked with General Powell back in May 1983 and shared his denigration of the gradual approach of the Vietnam years.[110] When OAF later commenced, General Clark asserted, "The U.S. military, and especially the Army, was deeply affected by the Vietnam War and its aftermath."[111] In August 1994, Clark, then director for strategic plans and policies (J-5) on the Pentagon's Joint Staff and a major general, visited Allied Forces Southern Europe (AFSOUTH) to consult with the NATO regional command about Bosnia and the perceived effect of airpower. The chief of staff of AFSOUTH, Lt. Gen. Marv Covault, pointed out, "There aren't enough targets, and they don't represent any kind of a centre of gravity. With five days of good weather we could take them all out, and then we would find that the Serbs would just keep on doing whatever they were doing. Air strikes just won't be decisive."[112] General Clark noted the reply. In a November 1994 conversation with Richard Holbrooke regarding the use of air strikes in Bosnia—Holbrooke advocating such use—Clark criticized him for placing too much credence in the belief that air strikes would convince the Serbs to give up their aims in Bosnia. He felt obliged to go through the limits of airpower for him. For his part, Holbrooke felt a certain irony in being an airpower hawk in Bosnia, since he had believed that dependence on airpower in Vietnam had been a serious mistake, but airpower had gone through a quantum change in precision and effectiveness, he believed, and Bosnia was a different war.[113]

What is significant is that Wesley Clark came to alter his perception of the need for decisive force in foreign policy issues. In mid-August 1995, with American diplomacy on the offensive, Richard Holbrooke went to Europe with the U.S. peace plan and started shuttle diplomacy to end the war in Bosnia. The United States was finally committed; on his team Holbrooke had Sandy Vershbow from the NSC Staff and the Pentagon J-5, Major General Clark. In his memoirs, Wesley Clark recalls, "Holbrooke had a clear sense for using military force to back diplomacy. It was a view that, as I travelled with him, I came to share."[114] This is particularly interesting, because Richard Holbrooke had long favored limited force by using air strikes even though a political strategy had not been forged in Bosnia, and—as we have seen—such a military approach was perceived by the regional NATO commanders who were to execute the air strikes as unlikely to have any significant effect.

Even by the time Major General Clark joined the negotiating team, both Clark and Holbrooke point out, the diplomatic endeavor—which air strikes were supposed to back up—had no fixed schedule but rather was improvised in order to end the war and secure the peace.[115] It seemed to be the opposite of the Powell Doctrine and what most of the military establishment viewed as the proper application of power. With Holbrooke admitting that events in Bosnia were sometimes moving too fast for coherent policy review[116] and adopting a "We're inventing peace as we go" stance[117] there could hardly be any clear objectives. With the option of using ground troops still off the table, the argument for the use of decisive force was rather difficult to make.

Commenting on General Clark's position change, Robert Gelbard said that Clark was generally more in line with the State Department's perception than with that of the Pentagon, at least in terms of limited force—though it did depend upon circumstances.[118]

For many members of the limited-war school in the Clinton administration, the air campaign against the Bosnian Serbs in September 1995—Operation Deliberate Force—was to prove that they were right. In their view, it finally unleashed the potential of airpower on the Bosnian Serbs, who quickly sued for peace. It was regarded as a lesson to be learned. Wesley Clark writes in his memoirs that the interagency team dealing with the Bosnian issue during the air campaign leading to the Dayton Peace Accords brought together a wide perspective on the issues, adding: "Together we would help end one war. And I would learn how to fight another."[119] Later he added that even though it happened in conjunction with a powerful Croat ground offensive, it was the air campaign that had made the difference in Bosnia: "Precision strike capped off the limited air strikes that helped us secure the Dayton Agreement in Bosnia."[120] In her memoirs, Madeleine Albright points out the lessons she learned from the crisis in Bosnia: "It showed that the limited use of force—even airpower alone—could make a decisive difference."[121]

After the Dayton Peace Accords, the Pentagon continued to resist having U.S. troops on the ground in Bosnia. It feared that participation in the Implementation Force (IFOR) would gradually mean more tasks and that it would gradually become sucked into something initially not intended—popularly called "mission creep."[122] As Richard Holbrooke described the mood in the Pentagon when debating IFOR: "Two less pleasant memories still hung like dark clouds over the Pentagon. Phrases like 'slippery slope' and 'mission creep' were code for specific events that had traumatized the military and the nation: Mogadishu which hung over our deliberations like a dark cloud; and Vietnam, which lay further back, in the inner recesses of our minds."[123]

When the administration decided to extend the American presence in Bosnia by eighteen months (IFOR renamed SFOR—Stabilization Forces), Secretary of Defense William S. Cohen opposed the Clinton administration policy in Bosnia and wanted the American forces in SFOR withdrawn.[124] In other words, the Pentagon wanted to keep the mission in Bosnia as limited as possible and preferably to withdraw as many troops as possible—a policy labeled "the Pentagon's Bosnia Exit Strategy" by General Clark.[125]

Madeleine Albright was sworn in as the sixty-fourth secretary of state on 23 January 1997. Later that year, General Clark replaced Gen. George Joulwan as SACEUR. According to Halberstam, "Some of the civilians who had watched the difficult Dayton negotiations regarded Clark as one of the quiet heroes of Dayton[;] . . . he had to know that almost no one in the Pentagon was behind him and many senior people were against any peacekeeping role. He had, they thought, put himself at risk with his own institution."[126]

And so Clark came to be at odds with the Pentagon—a rift that would eventually lead to the end of his military career after the Kosovo War. According to Halberstam, the other chiefs of the JCS felt General Clark believed too much in airpower. They believed he was pushing too hard and was too confident on the issue. Clark, however, felt "it showed that the Chiefs were much too cautious, too affected by the Vietnam Syndrome."[127]

The reliance on airpower did not adhere to the doctrine of decisive force, and at the time it was a hot topic at the Pentagon. The need for a restructuring of the services to meet the demands of the limited-force advocates met significant opposition within the Pentagon, and according to Halberstam, General Shelton was not "eager to adjust the army to more flexible missions that fell outside the guidelines of the Powell Doctrine."[128] Interestingly, Robert Gelbard explains this reluctance largely with the "use of force debate": "This all goes back to the so-called Powell Doctrine of using overwhelming force. And the military—particularly CJCS Shelton and Secretary Cohen—were very reluctant to get involved in something in Kosovo, as the military had been in Bosnia.[129] In fact, according to Halberstam, by summer 1997 General Clark received warnings from Cohen and Shelton that he should be careful to talk to the civilians in the White House: "to be very specific, Berger, Albright, and eventually Holbrooke."[130]

General Clark's contact with the State Department was well known. This, combined with his perspectives on limited force, earned him few friends in the military establishment. General Clark explained his perspectives on the two schools of thought; in his view, the two schools are not necessarily in conflict. Both are preceded by diplomacy (unless there exists an urgent requirement to preempt), and both precede an all-out effort, ultimately, to win decisively. In other words, "If you choose to use force and start killing people, it represents a threshold you cannot back away from, and you need to see it through and be willing to do whatever is necessary to succeed." Interestingly, General Clark added the use of limited force and the notion that once you start, you see it through: "Of course, sometimes it doesn't work out that way, but those cases are usually judged to be failures."[131]

Another issue influenced the Pentagon's reluctance to get involved in the Balkans. The focus on the two major-regional-conflicts (two-MRCs) strategy—as outlined by General Powell in his *Foreign Affairs* article—meant that if events occurred outside these two theaters, they would divert resources from what were defined as the areas vital to U.S. interest. When the Clinton administration took office in 1993, it had vowed to cut the defense budget.

By the time Kosovo became an international issue, according to General Clark, the armed forces had been told to cope with a painful 30–40 percent contraction in resources and capabilities, which made the Pentagon struggle to protect its own programs and priorities.[132] So the military found itself having to downsize significantly at the same time the Bosnian (and later Kosovo) crises emerged outside the MRC-strategy—both of them diverting resources from the wars for which the services had been trained and equipped to fight. Commenting on this particular issue after the Kosovo War, the U.S. *OAF After-Action Report* to the Congress explicitly considered OAF's impact on U.S. strategy: "In considering the implications of OAF for U.S. defense strategy, two important questions arise: what would be the impact of OAF on our ability to execute a single major theater war (MTW), and did the participation of U.S. forces jeopardize our ability to execute the most demanding requirement of the defense strategy, namely the ability to fight and win two nearly simultaneous major theater wars?"[133]

The Pentagon had been reluctant to engage in the Balkans for nearly a decade when the Kosovo crisis surfaced. Needless to say, allocating resources to Kosovo was not particularly popular. Secretary Cohen later candidly admitted, when asked why he had not wanted to put peacekeepers on the ground in Kosovo in the fall of 1998, "Understandably, we had cut the size of our force by nearly a third. We had cut our procurement by two-thirds, and we are now in the process of trying to rebuild that back up. But I did not want to add additional strains."[134]

Also the Congress was wary of military involvement in the Balkans. Without clear objectives vital to American interests and a defined exit strategy, Congress was not inclined to put U.S. troops in harm's way in faraway countries. When approaching the situation in Bosnia, according to Zimmermann, Congress did not want direct U.S. military involvement. Many wanted to help the Bosnian Muslims by lifting the arms embargo, but not military involvement in a region characterized by centuries of ethnic violence.[135] The fear of intervention and getting entangled abroad in conflicts not vital to the United States reappeared in the public debate when the Clinton administration sent troops to Somalia in fall 1993[136]—troops that were quickly withdrawn when the televised pictures of enraged Somalis dragging a dead American through the streets of Mogadishu went around the world.[137] According to Richard Holbrooke, "The scars from that disaster would deeply affect our Bosnia policy. Combined with Vietnam, they had left what might be called a 'Vietmalia Syndrome' in Washington."[138] Halberstam says, "To people on the Hill, what had happened in Somalia smacked of everything that could possibly go wrong. It was a war in a distant country in which we had no vital interest."[139] According to Jeffrey Record, the Somalia experience torpedoed the U.S. intervention in Rwanda, "and it came close to crippling the U.S. will to use force in the former Yugoslavia."[140] General Clark says, "The failed raid on Mogadishu, Somalia, in 1993, in which eighteen elite U.S. Army soldiers were killed, was especially significant in shaping Americans' attitudes toward casualties."[141] In April 1994—just six months after the Clinton administration's withdrawal from Somalia—the slaughter in Rwanda started, leaving some eight hundred thousand dead in about a hundred days.[142] Reflecting on the matter, President Clinton later admitted that his focus on Bosnia, the memory of Somalia, and "opposition in Congress to military deployments in faraway places not vital to our national interest" all influenced his decision not to intervene (a decision he now deems one of the greatest regrets of his presidency).[143]

Later reflecting on the mood he encountered when he argued for American peacekeepers on the ground in Bosnia after the Dayton Agreement had been fixed, President Clinton would recall, "Everybody said, oh, it was going to be just like Vietnam. It was going to be a bloody quagmire, even though there was a peace agreement."[144] In fact, according to Albright, the reluctance in Congress and in the Pentagon for involvement in Bosnia after Dayton was such that the administration publicly stated an exit strategy for the IFOR in 1996, one "designed to reassure Congress and the Pentagon that Bosnia would not become another Vietnam."[145] So when approaching the growing conflict in Kosovo, Congress was perceived by the administration as opposed to putting "boots on the ground." Albright concedes that the senators on Capitol Hill were reluctant, and some questioned the legal basis for the operation.[146] According to Record, congressional support for air strikes in the former Yugoslavia was always problematic, "and Capitol Hill was resolutely opposed to putting U.S. ground troops in harm's way in the Balkans."[147]

The perspectives of both the Pentagon and the Congress would influence President Clinton. Criticized for his lack of foreign policy experience by the Republicans during his election campaign, Clinton knew he had to face up to the foreign policy challenges that would come.

Clinton was the first president born after World War II, the first president since Franklin D. Roosevelt who had never performed personal military service, and the first president to take office after the end of the Cold War.[148] Halberstam asserts that both Clinton and Berger had been against the Vietnam War but that it did not mark their perspectives as it had for Lake, Holbrooke, Powell, and others.[149] Clinton wanted to focus on domestic politics rather than foreign affairs.[150] With his election slogan, "It's the economy, stupid," and his promise to "focus on the economy as like a laser beam," it was domestic politics that were closest to his heart.

According to Halberstam, Clinton's perspective on foreign policy differed significantly from that of his predecessor, George H. W. Bush: "For Bush, foreign policy had been his raison d'être. For Clinton, it was an inconvenience, something that might pull him away from his primary job at hand—domestic issues, above all economy."[151] Clinton came to office as the former governor of Arkansas and therefore without any significant foreign policy experience to prepare him for the presidency. One of his first decisions on Bosnia came only a fortnight after taking office, when Secretary Christopher made public the administration's policy review on 10 February 1993. This review stated that ground forces would not be deployed in Bosnia unless a peace settlement had already been accepted by the parties. The experience in Somalia made Clinton even more wary of intervening with ground troops,[152] to the degree that he opted not to intervene at all in Rwanda.[153] Commenting on the atmosphere in the White House, Robert Gelbard says, "It was very clear that the White House was nervous, they were very tentative, they were unsure of themselves—and there was an enormous amount of criticism from the Republicans about these kinds of interventions."[154] In fact, Gelbard says, it is still something of a mystery why President Clinton chose a Republican—William S. Cohen—as the new secretary of defense in late 1996; Gelbard is confident, however, that it was because Clinton "wanted to have some cover with the Republicans,"[155] in order to soften their criticism.

Clinton had opted not to send in ground forces in the Balkans other than as peacekeepers enforcing a peace agreement, and as previously noted, when considering war against Serbia both the Clinton administration and the military establishment viewed the deployment of ground troops into combat as "a Rubicon not to be crossed under any circumstances."[156] In fact, the Clinton administration thought neither the Congress, the American public, nor allies would support a ground presence, and Secretary Cohen argued along those lines in a Senate hearing after OAF. Cohen said that the lack of allied cohesion on this issue, the need for significant funding, and the demand for an expressed number of troops, duration, and exit strategy would have caused the Senate to say no.[157]

However, this perception may have been flawed, because the United States would not have had to deploy forces unilaterally. The United Kingdom and one other (unnamed) European nation had already volunteered to contribute to a ground presence in Kosovo. The United States and the United Kingdom would have made a powerful case for such a mission, which in turn could have pushed NATO in favor of a ground presence. In interviews with allied officials, Daalder and O'Hanlon found that France, Germany, and others "might well have been prepared to send troops to help implement and enforce any agreement Holbrooke could reach in his talks with Milošević."

Furthermore, the Clinton administration had never gone to Capitol Hill to get authorization for deploying troops abroad before, so there was no reason for that now. The administration could well have made a case for deploying troops to Kosovo and then asked for congressional support. Finally, the need for an exit strategy and the need to define the size and duration of the force required in Kosovo would be almost the same as for any process leading to the deployment of troops. Daalder and O'Hanlon point out that "indeed, one would have hoped that these questions would have been asked and answered by the administration before going to the Hill to ask Congress for its support."[158]

When Kosovo became an issue during spring 1998, the Pentagon had been reluctant to engage on the ground in the former Yugoslavia for the better part of a decade. The Pentagon opposed sending ground troops to Bosnia, reluctantly gave them to the IFOR after Dayton, and kept insisting that the deadline for SFOR and the withdrawal of U.S. troops by summer 1998 should be held. As Halberstam rightly observed when the Pentagon approached Kosovo, "[the] Pentagon had its foot on the brake just as it had on exactly the same issue for exactly the same reason six years earlier."[159] When the argument for limited force and an air campaign in Kosovo was made, it met resistance in the Pentagon. According to Bradley Graham of the *Washington Post,* "From the outset, the Chiefs reportedly were sceptical of the rationale for American military involvement in Kosovo. Having struggled for the past few years to get out of a NATO-led peacekeeping operation in Bosnia, the commanders were reluctant to get involved in yet another ethnic conflict in the Balkans."[160]

Furthermore, the Pentagon's focus on decisive force and clear objectives should be noted when evaluating the Air Force's and Lieutenant General Short's focus on strategic conventional bombing, "decisive" and "overwhelming" force, and "strategic paralysis." The Pentagon's focus was on the big, traditional wars at the high end of the intensity spectrum—to win America's wars to secure vital U.S. interests. Their MRC strategy pointed explicitly toward North Korea (the Pacific) and the Persian Gulf. Strategy, training, and education largely pointed toward these types of scenarios and not toward politically constrained coercive diplomacy, with eighteen additional sovereign nations demanding influence on operations. Accordingly, the Air Force's and Short's perspective of winning the war against the FRY with decisive and overwhelming force was to a significant degree a product of an institutionalized focus within the American defense community rather than the view of a single service or officer.

Finally, the limited-war school prevailed. Key individuals believed in the coercive effect of combining diplomacy and airpower and had advocated its use in Bosnia for years. When the United States, as the sole remaining super-power in the international arena, was debating how to deal with the ethnic violence in Kosovo, the limited-force advocates held the key positions: Al Gore was still the vice president of the United States, Madeleine Albright had risen to become secretary of state, Sandy Vershbow had been appointed U.S. ambassador to NATO, and Wesley K. Clark had become the Supreme Allied Commander Europe. The man who was about to be trusted to negotiate a solution was once again Richard Holbrooke—the man to whom Madeleine Albright had felt so close in these matters that she stated, "We used to say we were joined at the hip on Bosnia Policy."[161]

Chapter 4
LESSONS FROM BOSNIA

The real problem is that too many of our world leaders think that Dayton on Bosnia was a result of NATO air strikes. That is complete nonsense. If you can't get them to re-think that particular issue, they are going to continue making mistakes.
— Lord David Owen[1]

Kosovo had been on the radar screen of the international community for more than a decade when the Kosovo crisis commenced, and the preludes were to be the disintegration of Yugoslavia and the war in Bosnia (1992–95)—both of which provided numerous lessons for the international community. For many actors on the international stage, the lessons from Bosnia would shape their approach to the escalating violence in Kosovo. To some, the lessons appear to have been learned *too* well—the foundations of their lessons were sometimes wrong, frequently questionable, their relevance to Kosovo often exaggerated. Even so, in understanding the international handling of the Kosovo crisis, the general importance of the Bosnian War should not be underestimated.

The end of the Cold War and the subsequent changes on the world stage were to have immediate consequences for NATO. Founded as a defense organization in 1949, and molded by decades of the predictable security structures of the Cold War, it now found itself in a rapidly changing security environment. Perhaps capturing the atmosphere in the Alliance at the time, NATO wrote on its Internet site in 1990, "The breathless pace of change does not stop."[2] With its raison d'être largely swept away by the fall of the Soviet Union, a key question for NATO and the Alliance members was how to deal with this new reality. In the midst of this process of re-orientation, the Yugoslavian crisis emerged.

According to Warren Zimmermann, the American ambassador in Yugoslavia at the time, when the cities of Vukovar and Dubrovnik were shelled by the Yugoslav People's Army in 1991, no one in the international community called for the intervention of NATO.[3] In June 1992, the foreign ministers of NATO's member nations met in Oslo to discuss the role and future of the Alliance. Thorvald Stoltenberg—who was the Norwegian foreign minister at the time—tells an interesting story from this session. At the end of the meeting the ministers tried to agree on whether or not NATO should make forces available in peacekeeping operations. The discussion went on, but finally it was agreed that NATO could make forces available for peacekeeping operations under the Conference for Security and Co-operation in Europe (CSCE). Someone then asked whether they should consider making the forces available to the United Nations as well, but he was "immediately cut down and simply told one had to take one thing at a time."[4] So by summer 1992, getting involved in UN operations was generally considered to be a step too far for the member nations of the Alliance. This is interesting, in light of the new role for NATO that was in the making and the lack of a working relationship experience between NATO and the UN when the Bosnian War started. The NATO website adds that "soon after" this foreign ministers meeting, it was decided to extend the support to include UN operations: "In a short space of time, a number of further actions are undertaken by NATO to implement decisions of the UN Security Council relating to the Yugoslav conflict."[5] A few months later, NATO was involved in the (by then) biggest operation in the history of the United Nations.

The general perspective among Western leaders at the outset of the Yugoslav crisis was that the conflict had limited strategic significance and was therefore of limited interest to their nations. The resources and political will available to stop the war reflected this perception. From the outset, the United States felt the situation in the Balkans was a European issue, one that was to be dealt with by the Europeans—a notion shared by many of the European leaders themselves.[6] Richard Holbrooke believes this was a miscalculation by both sides. Secretary of State James Baker thought it was time for the Europeans to face up to their post–Cold War responsibilities and felt that the crisis in Yugoslavia was as good an opportunity as any; as Holbrooke points out, however, this was not a good test at all. Certainly the Europeans needed to play a larger role in this crisis, but for half a century the Europeans had not been able to act as a unified power, and any belief that they should be able to do that now could not have been adequately thought through. An equal miscalculation was made by the Europeans—maybe exemplified by Luxembourg's foreign minister, Jacque Poos, who then held the rotating presidency of the European Community. He articulated Europe's role in the Yugoslav crisis rather ambitiously: "The hour of Europe has dawned."[7] As Carl Bildt points out, for Europe to assume leadership was optimistic because at this point the European Community hardly had anything that could be described as a common security and foreign policy, and its decision-making processes were driven more by domestic agendas and calculations than by a common EC strategy.[8] Still, as the former chairman of the Joint Chiefs of Staff, Gen. John Shalikashvili, has pointed out:

> We forget this now, but everywhere you went in Europe in 1991 and 1992 there was this enormous optimism about what the new Europe could do, and this idealistic belief in the possibilities for the new positive forces about to be unleashed. The Europeans would handle this one, they were saying, and the Americans, who had just finished the Gulf War and were playing out their role as the overseer in the end of the Soviet empire, were only too glad to accommodate them.[9]

The president's special envoy to Bosnia and Kosovo, James Dobbins, later commented, "I think the biggest lessons-learned was that it was foolish and naïve of the United States to believe that Europe at its then state of development was going to be capable of dealing with the crisis in Yugoslavia, and that the United States should have been more willing at an earlier date to engage itself in those efforts, and that a stronger U.S. engagement in the early '90s might actually have prevented the conflict from beginning in the first place."[10]

The Norwegian foreign minister and UN peace negotiator in the former Yugoslavia, Thorvald Stoltenberg, was very clear about the significance of the United States during the Yugoslavian crisis. To him, the crisis showed there was only one superpower left in the world, and he regretted that it had not been forcefully involved from the very start.[11] Richard Holbrooke says that the 1991 Gulf War and the simultaneous death throes of the Soviet Union had exhausted Washington. Since the presidential election was only a year away and policy makers did not want to get involved in Yugoslavia—partly because senior officials did not believe they could prevent the situation from deteriorating further—the administration was divided and opted to wait out its term.[12] Christopher Hill, the principal American aide to the Dayton Peace Accord process (1995) and office director of the U.S. State Department's Bureau of European Affairs (1995–96), feels that the George H. W. Bush administration's decision to do nothing and just wait out its term was a little naïve.[13]

Thorvald Stoltenberg claims it was not entirely true that the United States actually left the handling of the Yugoslav crisis to the Europeans: "We honestly felt it was a fair deal that the Europeans were left to deal with the Yugoslav issue, but then the US should have left the arena, and left it to us to deal with it. But they didn't. They stayed on the sideline influencing the game, so to speak, and that created problems for the Europeans. In fact, it would have been better if the Americans either joined the negotiations [best solution] or stayed out of it entirely."[14]

So the crisis was influenced by the Western powers on both sides of the Atlantic, and their perspectives on the cause and nature of the conflict were to differ substantially. According to Professor Susan L. Woodward, their disagreements over the cause of the conflict fell into two opposing views. The first was that the conflict was related to Serb aggression toward legitimate governments of sovereign members of the UN—starting with the wars in Slovenia and Croatia, and later that in Bosnia. Led by Slobodan Milošević, the Serbs, in alliance with the Federal Army of Yugoslavia, wanted to create a Greater Serbia. This Serbian expansionist aggression would break out in areas as military opportunity arose, independent of other national projects in the area; hence the Serbian military machine would erupt into Macedonia and Kosovo once the war in Bosnia was over. The U.S. government and portions of its political and intellectual elite represented this view. This view fell into a post–Cold War American pattern of denouncing opposing political leaders in "rough states" as international pariahs, to be politically and diplomatically isolated and threatened with airpower in order to protect civilized norms and innocent civilians.[15] The second view—more commonly held by Europeans, Canadians, and some elements in the United States—claimed that the fighting constituted a civil war, not a conflict between internationally recognized nations. Communism having repressed local ethnic identities and freedoms for years, the conflict now emerging was based on the revival of ethnic conflict made possible by its fall. With freedom now restored, ethnic hatred and tension resulted in revenge, violence, and atrocities. Hence, the conflict between Serbia and Croatia—and later Bosnia—was an ethnic conflict, which had to be resolved through a political settlement of their territorial claims. One problem was, of course, that nations and borders did not coincide, and just as Serbian claims entangled Serbia, Croatia, and Bosnia, the Albanian question involved Serbia (Kosovo), Montenegro, Macedonia, Albania, and potentially Greece. This view favored a policy of containment, to prevent the Bosnian War from spreading, and a negotiated settlement, whereas the first view saw international mediation and a cease-fire as rewarding military aggression by the Serbs.[16]

These perspectives would go to the heart of what was to evolve to be a significant crisis in the transatlantic relationship. The Americans felt that the Europeans were playing into the hands of the Bosnian Serbs—the aggressors—by refusing to use force to respond to the atrocities committed. Richard Holbrooke states his perspective in no uncertain terms: "The international response to this catastrophe was at best uncertain and at worst appalling. While both the United States and the European Union initially viewed the Balkan wars as a European problem, the Europeans chose not to take a strong stand, restricting themselves to dispatching UN 'peacekeepers' to a country where there was no peace to keep, and withholding from them the means and the authority to stop the fighting."[17]

Dr. Brendan Simms argues along the same lines, saying the British government had known about the Serb concentration camps and mass rapes but opted not to intervene. He claims, in fact, that for years Britain worked to wreck any military initiative on behalf of the Bosnian government, charging that the president of the European Commission, Jacques Delors, and the leader of the American Republican Party, Senator Robert J. ("Bob") Dole, "came to identify Britain as the greatest obstacle to collective action on Bosnia." Simms asserts that the key to understanding the British foreign policy toward Bosnia in the early 1990s was "the profound philosophical realism of its practitioners"—exemplified by the rhetoric of Malcolm Rifkind, who in his first speech on becoming foreign secretary in 1995 said that "the furtherance of British interests ought to be the sole object of a British foreign secretary." According to Simms, the handling of the Bosnian conflict was "Britain's unfinest hour since 1938."[18] The ever-increasing evidence of Serb camps and atrocities that was emerging by summer and fall 1992 would largely be withheld from the public; as David Halberstam noted, "What senior Western diplomats were learning from their intelligence sources and from representatives of nongovernmental organizations, they were quite content to keep secret because of the enormous disparity between the horrors that were being committed and the impotence of their response."[19]

As outlined in the previous chapter, the United States had its own internal debate regarding foreign policy, the use of force, and how to handle the Bosnian conflict. The Pentagon and Colin Powell were reluctant to get involved, and according to Halberstam, so were Secretary Baker and President Bush. In contrast, at the lower levels of the State Department "almost everyone wanted a more aggressive policy towards Yugoslavia."[20]

One person who spoke publicly on the need to take a more forceful approach to the deteriorating situation in Bosnia was the Democrats' candidate for the presidency—William J. ("Bill") Clinton. By summer 1992, during his election campaign, Clinton was saying that he wanted NATO air strikes and U.S. involvement in Bosnia, arguing that the Serbs had overwhelming firepower in the region, that the Bosnian Muslims were being subjected to ethnic cleansing, and a weapons embargo would favor the Serbs, who already had enough weapons and ammunition to fight for years.[21] Bill Clinton won the presidential election in 1992, but just before he took office the Bush administration issued a letter to Milošević in which President Bush—in his so-called Christmas warning—warned that "in the event of conflict in Kosovo caused by Serbian action, the United States will be prepared to employ force against the Serbs in Kosovo and in Serbia proper."[22] The "Christmas warning" was reiterated by the Clinton administration within a month of taking office in January 1993, when the new secretary of state, Warren Christopher, stated, "We remain prepared to respond against the Serbians in the event of conflict in Kosovo caused by Serb action."[23] Though the Clinton administration reiterated the warning, its resolve was wavering, and according to Ivo H. Daalder, it failed to back up its campaign rhetoric of producing either a military or political commitment to end the conflict in Bosnia.[24]

The U.S. foreign policy team advised threatening air strikes and ending the arms embargo on arms shipments to Sarajevo—the "lift and strike" policy—in order to let the Bosnians defend themselves and to "send a message to the Serbs that they should refrain from further aggression."[25] The European allies publicly opposed such a policy, largely because they—unlike the United States—had UN peacekeepers on the ground, who could be subjected to retaliation. They further argued that arming the Bosnians would violate the neutrality that UN forces needed to provide humanitarian aid, and that it would introduce more guns into the area, thereby escalating the conflict rather than containing it—in direct contradiction of the key element of the European strategy.[26]

To persuade their allies the United States needed to provide firm leadership combined with an all-out diplomatic campaign—but such a campaign would put the credibility of the Clinton administration on the line, a risk the administration was not ready to take in the spring of 1993. Reflecting back on this issue, Madeleine Albright admits, "We couldn't hope to persuade others if we had not at least persuaded ourselves. At this stage, with a new President, a wary Secretary of State, a negative Pentagon, nervous allies, and crises in Somalia, then Rwanda and Haiti blowing up, we weren't prepared to run the risks of leadership on Bosnia. And thereby invited even greater risks."[27]

This notion is backed by Halberstam, who points out that the newly installed Clinton administration could not find an agreed policy on Bosnia and the former Yugoslavia. They were searching for answers they did not find, and "with frustration mounting, the administration was inclined to blame others, the Allies, and, of course, the fates."[28] In essence, as Daalder points out, the allies said they would accept the use of force—notably airpower—if the United States committed ground troops that would share their risk of retaliation, a risk the Clinton administration was not willing to take. When the lift-and-strike policy was debated within the administration in spring 1993, Vice President Gore and Ambassador Albright strongly favored air strikes against the Bosnian Serbs, with Albright even arguing for American unilateral air strikes if necessary.[29] According to Halberstam, Al Gore had significantly contributed to putting Bosnia on the agenda for Clinton during his election campaign, and he was considered a hawk on the issue — while "Madeleine Albright was a champion of the use of force."[30] When asked whether Washington — represented by Albright and Gore — perceived air strikes as perhaps more effective than could actually be the case without a coherent political strategy, Gen. Sir Rupert Smith replied that "they saw the use of air strikes as a relatively — I am not putting words in their mouths, one must be careful — but as a relatively simple act of short duration which could directly support the diplomacy, without actually understanding the context of doing this."[31]

The key senior foreign-policy advisers of the Clinton administration met as the Principals Committee on 28 January 1993. Those participating at this meeting — and subsequent ones — were National Security Adviser Tony Lake, Secretary of State Warren Christopher, Secretary of Defense Les Aspin, CIA director James Woolsey, the chairman of the Joint Chiefs of Staff, Colin Powell, and Ambassador Albright.[32] Thus Madeleine Albright — the strongest advocate for the use of airpower — had a voice in the Principals Committee from the very start.

It should also be noted that during spring 1993 the Principals Committee seemed to waver somewhat in their search for U.S. foreign policy. The committee's meetings were described by Daalder as "group therapy — an existential debate over what is the role of America."[33] General Powell — who had joined sessions like these in both the Reagan and Bush administrations — has described the meetings rather patronizingly: "the discussions continued to meander like graduate-student bull sessions or the think-tank seminars in which many of my new colleagues had spent the last twelve years while their Party was out of power."[34] The Clinton administration apparently searched for its foreign policy footing during the spring of 1993 and consequently lacked an agreed and consistent approach to Bosnia in this period.

After dismissing the Vance-Owen Peace Plan in spring 1993, President Clinton finally decided on the lift-and-strike policy. Secretary Christopher traveled to Europe to make the case for such an approach but did not find support. According to Brendan Simms, the United Kingdom was "the single most virulent opponent of the American strategy of 'lift and strike.'"[35] David Halberstam claims the British prime minister, John Major, told Secretary Christopher, with regard to his lift-and-strike proposal, that with no support either in the cabinet or Parliament, his government might fall if it backed escalation in Bosnia.[36] Arguably, U.S. policy making concerning Bosnia at the time could be summed up by what one top American policy maker stated on the matter: "The basic strategy was, this thing is a no-winner, it's going to be a quagmire. Let's not make it our quagmire. That's what lift the arms embargo, and the limited air strikes, was about."[37] Still, the American rhetoric of limited air strikes would continue.

After this failed political endeavor, the United States changed policy and opted to support the European perspective, which by now favored defending six Muslim enclaves, which were declared "safe areas" by the UN on 6 May (see map 2).

Map 2. UN safe areas in Bosnia

The UN "safe areas" deserve a closer look, because they were to become the saddest example of the international community's lack of resolve in dealing with the Balkan crisis. In his book *The Utility of Force,* the commander of the UN forces in Bosnia, General Smith, says, "It seems to me that the most coherent imperative was the need to be seen to be doing something—'something must be done' was a catchphrase of the times, used exhaustively by politicians, diplomats and media as much as by the UN." He argues that UNPROFOR was "not intended to create the conditions for peace but rather to 'ameliorate' the situation." This would be evident when establishing the UN "safe areas": "The UN worked hard to draft a SCR [Security Council resolution] that would appear strong and decisive, while at the same time avoid exposing their own national troops at risk. One has only to read the 'constructive ambiguities' of SCR 819 of 16 April and 836 of 4 June to see how well they did." Smith refers to the undersecretary of state for peacekeeping operations, Shashi Tharoor, who said the resolutions "required the parties to treat them as 'safe,' imposed no obligation on their inhabitants and defenders, deployed UN troops in them but expected their mere presence to 'deter attacks,' carefully avoided asking the peacekeepers to 'defend' or 'protect' these areas, but authorized them to call in airpower 'in self defense'—a masterpiece of diplomatic drafting but largely unimplementable as an operational directive."[38]

General Smith points out what would be a key dynamic in the international community's involvement in Bosnia: "There was no strategic direction, there was no strategic military goal to achieve, there was no military campaign, there were no theatre-level military objectives: all were tactical":

> Each major decision [in Bosnia] was triggered by the TV coverage of some gross incident, such as a larger than usual number of deaths by shell fire in Sarajevo, the bombing of refugees or the evidence of a massacre. The visual image and the ensuing questions of the commentators to politicians provided the stimulus for capitals to engage again. This usually resulted in imposing on the UN another task for which it was promised forces and resources that arrived late, if at all. . . . There is nothing wrong with that—but for the fact that in reacting to each event without the logic of a strategy and a context, the operation was and became increasingly incoherent.[39]

During summer 1993, television images of the horrible conditions in Sarajevo and surrounding areas made an impact in Washington, and the president ordered a new review of political and military options, during which Tony Lake and his staff adopted a strategy of linking the threat of air strikes directly to diplomacy. This was the first time in the Clinton administration this combination had been thoroughly explored, and in the years to come it would develop into a key thought process for dealing with both Bosnia and Kosovo. By July 1993, although lacking allied consensus, the United States had decided that it would enforce the UN "safe areas" unilaterally if necessary, and Lake traveled to Europe with a more decisive diplomatic approach—

returning with Britain in support of such an approach, while France was more reluctant.[40] In a sixteen-hour NAC meeting on 2 August—described by an American official as "as bitter and rancorous a discussion as has ever taken place in the Alliance"[41]—the allies agreed on the "dual key" system for authorizing air strikes. It meant that the UN and NATO had separate keys which—if both decided to use them—could authorize air strikes. The dominant roles in UNPROFOR of France and the United Kingdom gave them an opportunity to veto or restrict the NATO air strikes that the United States was continuously arguing for. According to Owen, several countries contributing UN forces in Bosnia were worried by the U.S. advocacy of the use of airpower in Bosnia and feared a unilateral American air campaign that could threaten their lightly armed and dispersed servicemen. The U.S. ambassador to NATO, Robert E. Hunter, and Richard Holbrooke confirmed that several countries wanted to create an arrangement for "controlling the holders of that weapon [airpower]."[42] General Smith, who attended the NAC meeting establishing the "dual key" system, later recalled, "We had created—for reasons one could understand and explain, but nevertheless—a military stupidity. We had two groups of forces answering to two different political masters operating in and over the same space; how else do you key them together without a dual key?"[43]

With the implementation of the "dual key" system, the transatlantic stalemate was fortified in a kind of "catch-22" situation. The United States blamed Milošević and Serb aggression for the havoc in Bosnia and were unwilling to support a negotiated solution based on territorial compromises that, the Americans felt, would reward the unacceptable behavior of the Bosnian Serbs. In general, they were sympathetic to the suffering of the Bosnian Muslims, but they did not accept the political risk of a potential military quagmire—and opted not to participate in UNPROFOR. The only remaining military option, if they were not to appear politically impotent with respect to Bosnia, seemed to be the threat of airpower, and so they frequently threatened it—though not as part of a broad coherent political or military strategy to end the war in Bosnia. Thus, by late 1993 the Bosnian Muslims—supported by the United States—rejected the Owen-Stoltenberg peace plan. Subsequently, at a meeting in Paris in early 1994, the French foreign minister, Alain Juppé, argued that either the United States should contribute ground troops to force a negotiated solution in Bosnia or exert political pressure on the Bosnian Muslims to accept a deal less favorable than they hoped for. According to Daalder, Paris had pointed out the fundamental contradiction in U.S. policy at the time—that the United States supported the Bosnian Muslim notion that nothing less than the status quo and the reversal of Serb war gains was acceptable but was unwilling to take the military risk necessary to achieve such an outcome.[44]

The Europeans were also afraid of being sucked into a region marked by centuries of ethnic hatred and not deemed vital to their national interests. Consequently, they argued this was an ethnic conflict, which had to be addressed with a political settlement of territorial claims. Despite evidence that Bosnian Serb aggression was the predominant source of the atrocities in Bosnia, their rhetoric often implied that all parties involved was more or less responsible for the havoc. In 1999, the UN secretary-general, Kofi Annan, released a report on the Srebrenica massacre in 1995. In this report Annan criticized the "prism of 'amoral equivalency' through which the conflict was seen [by] international observers and actors"—adding that for too long there had been a "general tendency to assume that the parties were equally responsible for the transgressions that occurred." According to Annan, neither humanitarian assistance nor a peacekeeping force could solve a problem "which cried out for a political-military solution."[45] According to Brendan Simms, Britain tended to relativize and "humanitarianize" the conflict. By continuously referring to the "sides," "parties," or "factions," it sought to portray the situation as less clear than it was, in order to weaken the call for a more forceful approach than the situation might actually warrant. Instead, they argued that a more forceful approach would jeopardize the humanitarian aid effort and put the men under UN command at risk.[46] So, when the United States argued for the lifting of the arms embargo and threatening airpower against the Serbs, the Europeans replied that the idea necessarily threatened the lives of their countrymen on the ground in Bosnia and that until the Americans got involved on the ground themselves and thereby became vulnerable to the potential consequences of their own statements they should have the decency to stop issuing threats.

In an article in the German magazine *Der Spiegel* on 17 January 1994, the Belgian General Francis Briquemont—commander of the UN forces in Bosnia in 1993–94—publicly denounced the notion that air strikes could do the trick in Bosnia. Dividing the parties in Bosnia into "good guys" and "bad guys" was an oversimplified notion that did not fit in the complex weave of causes and effects, and those who were not familiar with the situation on the ground should be careful of arguing for air strikes.[47] The transatlantic relationship, which had been under pressure for some time, continued its downward spiral. According to Susan Woodward, the ongoing debate about the role of NATO as a transatlantic security organization was the defining issue that ultimately led the Americans to admit that this conflict was of strategic significance to them and in the spring of 1994 to assume leadership. Even this produced only momentary commitments, and the deteriorating relationship between the United States and its European allies continued for the rest of 1994.[48] In a later conversation, Christopher Hill pointed out that even though there surely were human rights dimensions in the US policy toward the handling of the Balkans, there was a very strong alliance issue there as well, and the United States did not want the Balkans to become a further source of alliance problems.[49] As Richard Holbrooke articulated it, "Dealing with the Europeans was delicate and nettlesome throughout the Bosnia crisis, and put an unprecedented strain on NATO and the Atlantic Alliance."[50]

According to Woodward, a psychological shift happened in February and March 1994. For years the major powers had had competing interests and commitments, had been unable to unite on the parameters of a permissible outcome of the conflict or how to achieve it, and had therefore given contradictory signals to the warring parties.[51] After the shelling of the Sarajevo market on 5 February 1994, however, for the first time the UN and NATO authorized air strikes against the Bosnian Serbs if they did not move their heavy artillery surrounding the city. On 28 February, the first military action in the history of NATO took place, when four Serb aircraft were shot down by NATO jets.[52] On 18 March, Alija Izetbegović and Franjo Tudjman signed an agreement in the White House creating a federation between the Bosnian Muslims and Croats, thus isolating the Bosnian Serbs at the negotiating table.

In late 1994, fighting erupted in the UN "safe area" of Bihać. The United States argued for NATO air strikes against the Bosnian and Croatian Serbs, but the UN authorized only limited strikes. The Bosnian Serbs responded by blockading some two hundred UN peacekeepers, detaining fifty Canadian troops, and stopping the movement of UN military observers throughout Bosnia. The Bosnian Serb leader, Radovan Karadžić, warned the UN and NATO forces, "If a NATO attack happens, it will mean that further relations between yourself and our side will be rendered impossible because we would have to treat you as our enemies. All United Nations Protection Force personnel as well as NATO personnel would be treated as our enemies."[53]

The Americans were outraged by the lack of Western resolve in the matter and continued to argue for the use of airpower. The Europeans were irritated by what they perceived as a double standard. The Americans should either contribute forces to deal with the Serbs on the ground or let the UN forces continue their humanitarian effort without arguing for air strikes that would endanger them. The Spanish foreign minister, Javier Solana, stated, "The unity of the alliance has been broken because a member of the alliance has broken it."[54] The British defense minister, Rifkind, said that "those who call for action by the world must match words [with] deeds, and that doesn't require just a few aircraft."[55] The Europeans threatened to limit their activities to protecting humanitarian agencies and supplies or to pull out altogether if the United States continued air strikes without contributing troops on the ground.[56] Lord David Owen said the Bihać incident represented "the nadir in UN-NATO and US-EU relations"; Brendan Simms asserted that "the resulting crisis was to be the most serious test of Anglo-American relations and NATO yet."[57] According to Daalder, Bihać would trigger the worst crisis within the alliance since the Suez Crisis of 1956: "The impact of the Balkan conflict on NATO's credibility and even its continued viability had become too great. The issue dominated every NATO meeting[;] . . . over time, NATO's failure to end a brutal war on its doorstep had a profound impact on both the alliance's viability and the credibility of the United States."[58]

As we have seen, according to Woodward, the Western leaders had not initially perceived this conflict as of particular national interest or strategic significance, but by 1994 this conflict had become "the most challenging threat to existing norms and institutions that Western leaders faced."[59]

In fact, not only NATO's credibility was on the line—so was that of the United Nations. According to Carl Bildt, General Smith explained the UN situation in 1995 in this way. The UN, he claimed, was in the middle of a civil war; it was in retreat and did not seem to have a cohesive strategy. The Bosnian government gradually paid less attention to the UN, and the Serbs played their usual game. UN forces needed to be concentrated in order to protect themselves and to create room for maneuver, but when they asked whether they should start maneuvering to achieve what the UN resolutions ordered them to achieve, the answer was no. The situation was worsening, and the UN had effectively become part of the problem instead of the solution.[60] According to Halberstam, the UN in Bosnia was outnumbered, under-armed, and focused on protecting its impartiality: "Again and again, they were damned if they did and damned if they didn't. In all, UNPROFOR turned out to be a horror, representing not so much the weakness of the United Nations, though the UN command had little to be proud of in the Balkans, but the weakness and indecisiveness of the member nations."[61] The British journalist and author Misha Glenny wrote in similar terms about UNPROFOR: "Outgunned, demoralized, and subject to the most inflexible bureaucracy in military history, this force became a convenient scapegoat for everybody. But the real responsibility lay with the governments of the great powers. . . . The British and the French at least had the decency to contribute a large force to UNPROFOR. The Americans carped from the sidelines."[62] According to Woodward, "Frequent amendments to the mandate aimed to quell dissatisfaction with actual results and the failure to achieve peace and disagreements among major powers played out around the table of the Security Council. But this only increased the contradictions in the UN mandate, leading to ever greater difficulties of implementation and need for more troops."[63]

This notion was backed by Thorvald Stoltenberg, who points out that the nations constituting the UN Security Council make decisions they often do not back up with resources. The Americans and others (Europeans) often criticized the UN for not fulfilling its mandate. However, their own lack of funding contributions significantly exacerbated the lack of equipment and manpower, which made it extremely difficult to enforce the mandate they themselves had designed.[64]

The conflict among the major powers should not be seen solely as related to what had caused the conflict, how to put an end to it, and how to obtain peace. Woodward points out that the disagreements revealed the lack of leadership after the Cold War and the question of what security regime should replace the division of those years—a question that touched upon the survival and purpose of NATO. What would the role of the sole remaining superpower, the United States, be? What would the relationship between the United States and its European allies in a "new" Europe be like? And what role would Russia assume after the Cold War?[65]

By now, Tony Lake felt, the administration's constant shifting response on Bosnia was hurting Clinton's foreign policy as a whole. In a memo Lake recalled, "The administration's weak, muddle-through strategy in Bosnia was becoming a cancer on Clinton's entire foreign policy—spreading and eating away at its credibility."[66] According to Carl Bildt, who met Richard Holbrooke on 1 May 1995 in Washington, Holbrooke perceived the situation in Bosnia as something close to a catastrophe and feared that if the situation did not improve, it might well cause the fall of the Clinton administration.[67] However, events from May onward would trigger the response that ended the war in Bosnia.

In May 1995, Bosnian Serbs seized artillery in a containment depot within the Sarajevo heavy weapons–exclusion zone, an event triggering NATO air strikes. This in turn prompted the Bosnian Serbs to take hundreds of UN troops hostage. The newly elected French president, Jacques Chirac, was reportedly furious: "I will not accept this. You can kill French soldiers! You can wound them! But you cannot humiliate them! That will end today! France will not accept that! We will change the rules of the game!"[68] General Smith, who ordered the use of force in May, says the incident showed that the safety of the UN force was more important than achieving its mandate, handing the Bosnian Serb commander Mladić a victory. After the bombing, General Smith received explicit orders from the UN headquarters in New

York: "The execution of the mandate is secondary to the security of UN personnel. The intention being to avoid loss of life defending positions for their own sake and unnecessary vulnerability to hostage taking."[69]

By June, the United States was still "muddling through" in Bosnia, as Lake had pointed out in his memo. In her memoirs Albright says that during a foreign policy meeting in late June, she argued that their foreign policy made President Clinton look weak. President Chirac had publicly stated, "The position of leader of the Free World is vacant"—a comment that Madeleine Albright would recall chilled her heart for weeks afterward.[70]

Daalder argues that by early August 1995 the Clinton administration was boxed in by an unworkable diplomatic strategy in a situation defined by a tendency to substitute Milošević for the Bosnian Serbs; American refusal to put U.S. troops on the ground; allied resistance to using force as long as allied forces could be subject to hostage taking; UN insistence upon "traditional peacekeeping principles"; a Republican-dominated Congress bent on taking the moral high ground but not responsibility for the consequences of doing so; and an election the following year in which President Clinton hoped to be reelected.[71] In other words, a new policy was needed.

Tony Lake was at the helm of forging a new U.S. political strategy toward Bosnia called "the endgame strategy."[72] Working on the issue throughout the summer of 1995, the decisive meetings in early August would set the stage for the diplomatic endeavor leading to the Dayton Agreement. Preparing for these meetings, Madeleine Albright argued in a paper: first, Bosnia's future and the credibility of U.S. foreign policy were linked, and so the United States should take the lead to settle the issue of Bosnia in 1995; second, the U.S. policy of opposing the withdrawal of UNPROFOR should be abandoned, because the allies were withdrawing their forces, and if U.S. forces were to be deployed sooner or later, they should be deployed on American terms—not those set by the UN or allies. Third, "the essence of any new strategy for Bosnia must recognize the one truth of this sad story. Our only successes have come when the Bosnian Serbs have faced a credible threat of military force. Hence, we must base our plan on using military pressure to convince the Bosnian Serbs to negotiate a suitable peace settlement."[73]

At a meeting of the Principals Committee on 7 August, President Clinton stated that although not agreeing with all her prescriptions, he agreed with Albright's paper as a whole. The "endgame strategy" was further refined over the next two days, and then Tony Lake went to Europe to communicate the new U.S. strategy. According to Daalder, the Europeans—although not agreeing on every aspect of the strategy—were pleased to see the United States engaged and willing to take the lead. After some debate in Washington, it was decided to send Richard Holbrooke to secure a deal with the parties and to negotiate a solution to the Bosnian crisis. Richard Holbrooke went to Europe with the U.S. peace plan in mid-August and started shuttle diplomacy to end the war in Bosnia. The United States was finally committed. In his small team traveling to Europe Holbrooke had the Pentagon's J-5, Maj. Gen. Wesley Clark.

The shift of policy in Washington toward a stronger involvement during the summer of 1995 immediately had ramifications in the Balkans. By late July, as the U.S. political commitment grew, Washington was offering twenty-five thousand troops for a NATO force to enforce a territorial division between the federation (Croats and Bosnians) and the Bosnian Serbs. If the Serbs did not agree, they would be subjected to air strikes. Providing military equipment and training to the federation was discussed in Washington, and both Major General Clark and National Security Adviser Lake argued favorably for such an option, claiming this would balance the power in the region.[74] At the previously mentioned meeting in the White House after Srebrenica, President Clinton had declared, "We must commit to a unified Bosnia. And if we can't get that at the bargaining table, we have to help the Bosnians on the battlefield."[75] Shortly afterward, in the beginning of August 1995, the Croatian army—backed by the United States—drove out some 170,000 Serbs from the Krajina region in Croatia in only three days (Operation Storm).[76] In a meeting on 22 July—a meeting Ivo H. Daalder says Washington may have engineered[77]—Tudjman and Izetbegović met in Split and agreed to defend jointly the Bihać pocket. According to Robert C. Owen, the nearly hundred-thousand-strong, well-equipped Croatian army was joined in a "hammer and anvil" attack on the Croatian and Bosnian Serbs by the Bosnian Muslim forces, which had prepared for a summer offensive.[78]

In February 1995, the Croatian minister of defense, Goyko Susak, had come to the United States and the Pentagon to gather U.S. support for a military campaign designed to regain Krajina by force.[79] In July 1995, Defense Minister Susak went to Washington once more to make the case for a Croatian offensive.[80] By then President Clinton had authorized a private company to use retired U.S. military personnel to improve and train the Croatian army, and as he candidly admits in his memoirs, "I was rooting for the Croatians. So was Helmut Kohl, who knew, as I did, that diplomacy could not succeed until the Serbs had sustained some serious losses on the ground."[81] So when a high-level Croat military official came up to the American diplomat Bob Frasure during the London Conference in July and unveiled a detailed plan for the invasion of Krajina, Frasure looked at the map for some time, smiled, and, according to Halberstam, said, "Well, do be careful."[82]

The offensive started 4 August. The U.S. backing for this operation was intended to shift the power balance in the favor of the federation, give the Krajina and Bosnian Serbs a military, political, and psychological defeat, and make a significant contribution to the U.S. diplomatic offensive President Clinton had initiated.[83] According to Tim Judah, other Western countries mumbled their disapproval but did not act to prevent the offensive. "Unspoken but ever-present was the feeling that if there were no more Serbs in Croatia, then, in future, there would be no more problems either."[84]

On 27 August, Richard Holbrooke appeared on the television news program *Meet the Press* threatening the Bosnian Serbs with a six-to-twelve-month air campaign if they did not lay down their weapons. Later he further prophesied: "If the Bosnian Serbs don't want to negotiate, then the game will basically just be to wait for the trigger for air strikes."[85] The trigger came the very next day, when two mortar shells fell in a Sarajevo marketplace and killed thirty-seven people and wounded another eighty-five. Who had fired the mortar shells was not quite clear, but UNPROFOR announced shortly afterward that it had confirmed "beyond reasonable doubt" that the shells had come from a Serb-held area. Two days later, on 30 August, NATO's air campaign, Operation Deliberate Force—backed by the United Nations (Rupert Smith had turned the UN "key")—began pounding Bosnian Serb targets.[86] The air campaign was halted on 1 September to allow negotiations, but it resumed on 5 September and lasted until 14 September. Holbrooke had met the Bosnian Serb leadership in Belgrade the previous day, and Karadzić and Mladić had agreed to the NATO and UN demands. The operation was suspended for seventy-two hours and was then suspended for an additional seventy-two hours when Bosnian Serb compliance became evident. This led to a statement on 20 September that the Bosnian Serbs had fully complied with the demands of NATO and the UN and that there was no need to resume the air strikes. By then, Operation Deliberate Force was the largest NATO military action in the history of the Alliance.[87] The Bosnian Serbs and Milošević were ready to negotiate, and with the United States leading the negotiations, the pressure on the parties increased significantly. On 5 October Holbrooke managed a cease-fire in Bosnia, and on 31 October the three presidents, Milošević, Tudjman, and Izetbegović met at Wright-Patterson Air Force Base, outside Dayton, Ohio, and the peace negotiations that would lead to the Dayton Accords began.

The United States had criticized others for negotiating with Milošević in the years leading up to the Dayton negotiations and had demanded that he be isolated. It had also refused to partition Bosnia, which it said would reward Bosnian Serb aggression. Now Milošević was the key to the U.S. effort to end the conflict in Bosnia, and the Bosnian Serbs got their Republika Srpska. Still, the settlement was a major accomplishment.

The Dayton Peace Accords were concluded on 21 November and formally signed in Paris 14 December 1995. The war in Bosnia was over.

The disintegration of Yugoslavia in general, and the war in Bosnia in particular, provided numerous lessons for the international community. These were lessons that would influence the future handling of the emerging crisis in Kosovo some two and a half years later. As Anthony Cordesman rightly points out, "In retrospect, Bosnia was a natural prelude to Kosovo."[88]

During the Dayton negotiations, an attempt was made to integrate lessons from UNPROFOR in the mandate for NATO's Implementation Force (IFOR). In his memoirs, General Clark summed up the UNPROFOR experience with the assessment that while UNPROFOR's obligations had been almost unlimited, in terms of protecting civilians, assisting aid deliveries, securing safe zones, and so on, the commander on the ground had lacked the authority to use force in order to fulfil them. As early as the fall of 1994 the United States was trying to find a way to strengthen UNPROFOR, fearing that it could be completely compromised or forced out, and plans were laid for extracting UNPROFOR if needed. This problem was corrected when IFOR received a more robust mandate—described as the "silver-bullet clause" in the Dayton Accords: "IFOR has the right and is authorized to (a) compel from any location in Bosnia Herzegovina the removal, withdrawal, or relocation of forces or weapons and (b) compel the cessation of any activities that IFOR deems a threat or potential threat to itself or its mission, or to another Party. Forces resisting IFOR action in these regards shall be subject to the use of necessary force by IFOR."[89]

Having in mind the denunciations of the UN-NATO "dual key" system of authorizing air strikes for its ineffectiveness in Bosnia and the (particularly) American critique of the UN and its handling of Bosnia, General Clark was quite explicit in stating that the NATO command and control structures of IFOR were constructed on the basis of the experiences of UNPROFOR. No one wanted to repeat that structure when establishing IFOR during the Dayton negotiations in 1995.[90]

In a letter to President Clinton in 1996, Richard Holbrooke summed up the international community's influence in the former Yugoslavia: "Of the many organizations in the former Yugoslavia in the last 5 years, only NATO—that is, the United States—has been respected."[91] Damning the European nations and the Contact Group (discussed below) for inability to forge a common foreign policy and internal squabbling over procedures, Holbrooke called the U.S.-generated NATO bombing a historic development in post–Cold War relations between Europe and the United States; the United States, he said, once again had provided leadership for the Europeans. Holbrooke characterized the efforts of the UN and the EU as tortured half-measures that had proved inadequate, and he pointed out that the role of the UN and the European Union was now largely financial and political reconstruction of the former Yugoslavia.[92]

These events significantly contributed to Secretary Albright and others' favoring NATO when dealing with Kosovo a few years later, and they are why she and others in the Rambouillet negotiations insisted that NATO lead the proposed peacekeeping mission in Kosovo, with NATO command-and-control structures, to ensure the effectiveness of the mission.[93] According to Holbrooke, "The dual-key arrangement [was] an unmitigated disaster that placed the UN and NATO in a stressful and improper relationship of overlapping responsibility and friction."[94] Not only were the failed "dual key" relationship and the UNPROFOR model to be avoided, but the whole crisis was to be managed by NATO. As Daalder and O'Hanlon point out, "Unlike Bosnia, this time the alliance would be involved from the start."[95]

Contributing also to the U.S.-driven decision to let NATO handle the Kosovo crisis was probably the lack of consensus and unity among the international actors in Bosnia. By spring 1994 Russia had become a major player in Balkan diplomacy, and it had contributed largely to the creation of the new international body for dealing with the former Yugoslavia, the Contact Group. But its perceived constant refusal to allow air strikes put it at odds with the Americans. Neither the UN nor the Contact Group was perceived to have the unity necessary to provide international leadership. Both President Clinton and Secretary Albright argued in their memoirs that American leadership had been necessary to end the war in Bosnia. [96]

By the second Contact Group meeting (held on 25 March 1998 in Bonn) after the crisis had emerged in Kosovo, the lack of progress in the meeting had convinced Secretary Albright that it was not the right body to counter Milošević. The United States had to provide leadership, Milošević needed to be persuaded by the threat of force, and NATO was the institution to carry out the threat.[97] Robert Gelbard, asked later whether he believed that transatlantic bickering, the experiences of UNPROFOR, and the "dual key" arrangement for authorizing air strikes had been what triggered the U.S. insistence on NATO crisis management and allied insistence on NATO supervision on the ground of a negotiated settlement in the Rambouillet negotiations—he immediately answered, "Yes, of course."[98]

Another factor influencing the approach to the Kosovo crisis was the sense of collective guilt or moral failure after Bosnia. Daalder argues that the breakup of Yugoslavia was the first post–Cold War test of the United States and Europe—and that they all failed miserably.[99] Warren Zimmermann asserted that "the refusal of the Bush Administration to commit American power early was our greatest mistake of the entire Yugoslav crisis. It made an unjust outcome inevitable and wasted the opportunity to save over a hundred thousand lives."[100] He added: "Western diplomacy was reduced to a kind of cynical theater, a pretence of useful activity, a way of disguising a lack of will. Diplomacy without force became an unloaded weapon, impotent and ridiculous."[101]

For years the international community had known about the atrocities being committed in Bosnia and had had the power to intervene. It had opted not to. It should be noted, of course, that none of the great powers either started the war or perpetrated the atrocities reported. It is up to each government to decide how to use its resources. Also, UNPROFOR did help thousands of people with food and medicine they would otherwise have been denied. Still, the international community failed to stop some of the worst atrocities since World War II, committed in the midst of Europe. To their credit, Albright, Gore, and others pointed out the moral responsibility early on, but the resources to back up these sentiments were never adequately provided. It is highly questionable whether the great powers would have themselves risked an endeavor like the Croatian/Bosnian ground offensive in summer 1995. In particular, the "safe areas" that the UN—which for all practical purposes means the great powers—had vowed to defend, represent a tragic chapter for the international community. Silber and Little rightly say, "The fall of Srebrenica was the darkest moment in international involvement in Bosnia."[102] In a White House meeting in July 1995, Vice President Gore mentioned that his twenty-one-year-old daughter had asked him about a *Washington Post* article describing a young Srebrenica rape victim who had hanged herself at the UN air base in Tuzla, and what the United States was doing about it. "What am I supposed to tell her? Why is this happening and we're not doing anything? . . . My daughter is surprised the world is allowing this to happen . . . [and] I am too."[103] Madeleine Albright points out that the Serbs had overreached in the Srebrenica massacre, that the atrocity made President Clinton's "frustration boil over" and significantly contributed to ending the Bosnian War.[104]

But it had taken an incident like Srebrenica to galvanize resolve, and the term "safe areas" had been shown to be deeply ironic. The resources needed to protect the "safe areas" were not provided, and Srebrenica stands as a reminder of what happens when words and actions do not go hand in hand, even though the Bosnian Serbs must bear the responsibility for this barbaric and inhuman act.[105] Carl Bildt was quite clear on this point: though it was Gen. Ratko Mladić who massacred the men in Srebrenica, it was the nations of the UN Security Council that made it possible, by promising "safe areas" that did not exist.[106]

As a fourth key lesson from Bosnia, Madeleine Albright has pointed out the moral obligation of the United States and its allies to intervene in Bosnia.[107] This factor should be noted in connection with Kosovo. When that crisis emerged in 1998, Madeleine Albright stated in the first Contact Group meeting, "We are not going to stand by and watch the Serbian authorities do in Kosovo what they can no longer get away with in Bosnia." Albright recalled that in that very room (in Lancaster House in London) numerous fruitless meetings had been held on the issue of Bosnia and that earlier in the decade the international community had ignored the first signs of ethnic cleansing in the Balkans. "History," she declared, "is watching us."[108] Kosovo, then, should not be seen as just another crisis emerging on the world stage but as a continuation of the disintegration of Yugoslavia, and particularly as a product of the lessons of the war in Bosnia. Knut Vollebæk, the Norwegian foreign minister and chairman-in-office of the Organization for Security and Co-operation in Europe (OSCE), believes Srebrenica significantly influenced Western politicians in the period leading up to Operation Allied Force: not only did they fear that something like Srebrenica could happen in Kosovo, but the fact that the international community had failed to face the challenge of Srebrenica influenced their handling of the Kosovo issue.[109]

The most important lessons from Bosnia for the future war in Kosovo were arguably the (particularly) U.S. belief that the only language the Serbs would respect was force, and that airpower would provide the force needed to achieve political goals. In particular, to many policy makers the two weeks of air strikes—Operation Deliberate Force—preceding the cease-fire in Bosnia and the Dayton negotiations proved that a similar approach could achieve a similar negotiated settlement in Kosovo. Secretary of Defense William Perry commented on the influence of airpower in Bosnia: "Deliberate Force was the absolute critical step in bringing the warring parties to the negotiating table at Dayton, leading to the peace agreement."[110] Tim Judah feels that Holbrooke ultimately succeeded where the Europeans had failed "because he could back up his threats with real military might."[111]

During a dinner in Belgrade before the signing of the Dayton Accords in Paris in late 1995, Slobodan Milošević told General Clark, "It was your NATO, your bombs and missiles, your high technology that defeated us."[112] According to Clark's memoirs, Milošević's fear of NATO and perception of his own military limitations was a memory Clark took with him and would recall in the lead-up to OAF.[113] Asked later about the significance of Deliberate Force in terms of fortifying belief in limited force, coercive diplomacy, and airpower, General Clark said the experience was "very important."[114] After

OAF had started in 1999, David Rhode wrote in the *New York Times:*

> One perception driving the Clinton administration's strategy of car-
> rying out punishing NATO airstrikes against Slobodan Milošević is
> the idea that the only language he understands is force. In 1995, this
> view goes, a NATO bombing campaign compelled Milošević and his
> Bosnian Serb allies to end the three-year war in Bosnia. Another round
> of airstrikes might therefore break the will of the Yugoslav leadership
> and force Milošević to halt his attacks on Kosovo Albanians.[115]

In a *PBS Frontline* interview, Secretary Albright pointed out that "he
[Milošević] didn't see the light in Bosnia until the NATO bombing, and then
he agreed to the Dayton Accords."[116] The notion seems to be that Deliberate
Force provided a rational and well-founded empirical example that paved the
way for a similar approach in Kosovo. The Serbs only understand the language of force, and Bosnia showed that when NATO airpower was allowed
to unleash its capacity, the Serbs would quickly sue for peace. The prevailing
view was that a similar approach in Kosovo would achieve similar results
within a few days.[117]

This assumption was flawed. It was a substantial exaggeration of the
role of airpower and failed to recognize that a combination of factors contributed to ending the Bosnian War—not airpower alone. It had taken until
late summer 1995 to put in place the conditions and context to exploit the
coercive potential of airpower. This is of particular significance, because for
years key individuals in the Clinton administration had argued for air strikes
when the conditions and context were *not* conducive to releasing the full
coercive potential of airpower. This should have been the lesson that policy
makers brought with them to the deteriorating situation in Kosovo; instead,
an unsound belief that NATO airpower would somehow do the trick in
Kosovo, as it had done in Bosnia, appears to have been imprinted on their
consciousness.

The following six factors were of particular importance in creating the
conditions for airpower to succeed in August–September 1995.

The first was the *economic embargo on the Federal Republic of Yugoslavia.* On 30 May 1992, following the atrocities committed by Serb paramilitary units in Bosnia after its proclaimed independence in spring 1992, an
economic embargo on Serbia and Montenegro was passed by the UN Security
Council.[118] The economy in Serbia had been a domestic source of friction in
the 1980s; a decade of declining economic conditions and reduced living stan-
dards not only contributed significantly to the downward spiral of nationalism and the disintegration of Yugoslavia—but also corroded the social fabric

and the rights and securities that individuals and families had come to rely on.[119] The UN-imposed economic embargo forced the already declining Serb economy—which for years had been intertwined with the other republics of Yugoslavia—to cope with new limitations. The expenditures of the ongoing wars in Croatia and Bosnia had their effects, and an ever-increasing number of Serb refugees moving into Serbia proper from Croatia and Bosnia brought additional strain.

Gradually, the increasingly poor Serb living conditions—now significantly deepened by the imposed UN embargo—became a threat to the power base of Slobodan Milošević. This was the one thing Milošević was least inclined to accept. Milošević sought to remove the embargo, and the obstacle became the Bosnian Serb leadership, which by its conduct in Bosnia made sure the international community would continue to uphold the embargo. This entangled Milošević in a power struggle with the Bosnian Serb leader Radovan Karadžić. According to Susan L. Woodward, Milošević started a coordinated strategy to replace Karadžić by spring 1994.[120] In the summer of 1995, when the Krajina Serbs were driven out of the Krajina region, Milošević did not assist them. As David Rohde points out: "Milošević, who had urged Serbs in Croatia to rise up and declare their own state in 1991, now did nothing to aid them. With his economy ruined by UN economic sanctions, Milošević was focused on cooperating with the West, ending the war, getting UN economic sanctions lifted and shoring up his own power base in Serbia."[121] This notion was shared by analysts interviewed by Owen after Deliberate Force; they felt Milošević's move to act as a peace broker even before the Croatian offensive in Krajina took place was triggered by the growing strength of non-Serb military forces in the region and by the worsening economic conditions in his country, brought on by UN sanctions.[122]

So, when Richard Holbrooke in August initiated a diplomatic endeavor to end the war in Bosnia, Milošević almost immediately (16 August) approved the 1994 Contact Group peace plan as a basis for further negotiations with Holbrooke.[123] According to Silber and Little, "By then [summer 1995], Milošević was ready to accept almost anything on offer. For him the overriding priority was the lifting of sanctions."[124] The fact that Milošević was ready to negotiate on the foundations of the Contact Group peace plan and signaled this to Holbrooke is significant because it indicates that Milošević was ready to negotiate with the United States *before* NATO air strikes commenced on 30 August. According to Daalder and O'Hanlon, as well as David Rohde, Milošević told Holbrooke that he would take the negotiations from Bosnian Serb hands—some ten days before Operation Deliberate Force commenced—and "secure the Bosnian Serb leadership's acquiescence in his taking the lead role in negotiating a Bosnian peace," shortly before Deliberate Force started.[125] This was a few days before an artillery shell landed in the Sarajevo marketplace (28 August)—which triggered Operation Deliberate Force—and thus somewhat lessens the significance of Deliberate Force as the decisive factor in making Milošević concede to allied demands. According to Silber and Little,

> Years of waging war in Croatia and Bosnia, as well as the sanctions imposed by the UN, had taken a huge toll on Yugoslavia. Milošević paid for the war by inflationary funding, printing money that was not backed by real state resources. He unleashed a hyperinflationary spiral that won for his country the dubious honor of holding the world-record inflation rate—313 million per cent per month—surpassing previous record holders Weimar Germany and Hungary in 1946.[126]

This series of events should be noted when analyzing why the cease-fire was endorsed so quickly. The domestic situation in Serbia and the threat to the one thing Milošević could not compromise—his power base—produced a political climate that inclined him to put domestic pressure on the Bosnian Serbs and resume negotiations to end the war in Bosnia.

The second major factor was the *parties' war exhaustion.* Adding to the domestic Serb inclination to end the war was the toll that years of fighting had taken in terms of casualties, violence, and material devastation. With increased pressure from both Milošević and the international community, the future looked bleak for the Bosnian Serbs. According to author Tim Judah, after the Dayton Accords parts of the U.S. and European establishments argued that "all sides" of the Bosnian War were "exhausted," contributing to the Bosnian Serbs' lack of significant opposition at the end of the war.[127] Commenting on the Serb battle fatigue by the time the Croatian and Muslim forces started the ground offensive, the United States became politically involved, and the NATO air campaign started, Robert Gelbard says, "I think the Serb forces were exhausted by that time, to a very large degree."[128]

What is significant here is that when the Rambouillet Conference started outside Paris in February 1998 to find a negotiated settlement to the mounting crisis in Kosovo, such fatigue was not a factor. Peace negotiations are most likely to *end* fighting that has already occurred. In Kosovo, peace negotiations started *before* significant fighting had occurred, and hence one factor often contributing to a negotiated peace—that the parties have experienced war and want the devastation and suffering to end—was largely absent.

The third was *the relative strength of the federation forces and their ground offensive.* On 18 March 1994, Alija Izetbegović and Franjo Tudjman signed an agreement in the White House that created a federation between the Bosnian Muslims and the Bosnian Croats. The United States had long wanted to shift the power balance in the region against the Bosnian Serbs and had secretly allowed the Croatian and Bosnian Muslim governments to violate the UN arms embargo and import crucial equipment like tanks and heavy artillery.[129] During each passing week the Croatian and Bosnian Muslim armies grew stronger. Retired U.S. officers were training the Croatian army in NATO tactics,[130] and by June 1995 General Smith considered that the Serbs wanted to conclude the fighting by 1995 because their strength compared to that of the Croatian and Bosnian Muslim armies was declining by the week.[131] This notion was shared by analysts interviewed by Owen after Operation Deliberate Force; they felt Milošević's decision to act as a peace broker before the Croatian offensive in Krajina took place was triggered by the growing strength of non-Serb military forces in the region and the worsening economic conditions in Serbia proper.[132]

The federation's previously noted ground offensive consolidated their momentum and pushed the Serbs onto the defensive. The U.S. diplomatic offensive was at full speed, controlling both the air campaign and the ground offensive. During the offensive Richard Holbrooke sent a memo to Secretary of State Christopher stating that "the map negotiations . . . are taking place right now on the battle field, and so far, in a manner beneficial to the map. In only a few weeks, the famous 70 percent–30 percent division of the country has gone to around 50-50, obviously making our task easier."[133] Holbrooke was in constant dialogue with Tudjman and Izetbegović during the offensive and signaled his support for the operation in order to achieve a favorable situation during negotiations later. He admits saying to the parties, "Speed is important. We can't say so publicly, but please take Sanski Most, Prijedor, and Bosanski Novi. And do it quickly, before the Serbs regroup."[134] Hence, by 19 September, the Croatian and Bosnian Muslims had captured some three thousand square kilometres, or some 21 percent of the ground previously held by the Bosnian Serbs.[135] According to Ivo Daalder, by early October the offensive had gained its strategic purpose, and further fighting would be counterproductive. President Clinton proclaimed the cease-fire in the White House on 5 October.[136] (See map 3.)

A key factor in the success of the ground campaign was that it was very difficult for the Bosnian Serbs to send troops when and where they were needed. This was largely because concentrating maneuver elements to achieve the firepower needed to counter the ground offensive made them vulnerable to the NATO air campaign. In addition, the ground campaign largely denied

Front lines mid-July 1995

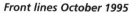

Front lines October 1995

Serb controlled areas

Muslim and Croat controlled areas

Map 3. Bosnian front lines by mid-July 1995 (top) and October 1995 (bottom)

the Bosnian Serbs the possibility of dispersing and waiting until the air campaign lost momentum, because it forced them to get out of their hiding places and counter the attack. Hence, Christopher Hill asserted that "the federation offensive in western Bosnia would not have been as successful without the air campaign," and, as Owen points out, due to the air campaign the federation "capitalized on the BSA's [Bosnian Serb army's] difficulty in bringing its forces to bear when and where they were needed."[137] Adm. Leighton Smith, commanding AFSOUTH at the time, assessed that "the Federation ground offensive in the west helped the air campaign's effectiveness 'dramatically,'" and Richard Holbrooke felt the ground offensive was "extremely important" in influencing the Bosnian Serbs.[138]

The ground offensive surely decreased the leverage of Milošević and the Bosnian Serbs at the negotiating table in Dayton. President Clinton says in his memoirs, "Our efforts were immeasurably helped by the Croatian and Bosnian military gains on the ground."[139] Adhering to his advocacy of the coercive denial strategy, Pape asserts that the NATO bombing in 1995 succeeded because it was backed by a credible threat from ground troops.[140] Robert Gelbard simply points out, "I think there has generally been an under-recognition in the West of how much that Croatian (and Bosnian Muslim) ground operation really contributed."[141]

The fourth major factor favoring the settlement was the *U.S. political and diplomatic offensive by August 1995.* Evidence suggests there were several reasons why the Clinton administration assumed leadership by the summer of 1995 (Srebrenica, European pressure, domestic criticism). Not the least of these was that the administration perceived it as paramount to the upcoming election campaign. It did not want Bosnia to continue to be the Achilles' heel of its foreign policy—or, as Daalder put it: "Given the high stakes of the election campaign, Clinton's political fortunes could not be held hostage to events in the Balkans."[142] So by summer 1995, the Clinton administration took the initiative, agreed on the "endgame strategy," and sent Richard Holbrooke to the Balkans to end the war in Bosnia. The United States put its credibility on the line, and with that its political might. The political, military, and economic influence of the United States can hardly be overestimated, and this shift by Washington is considered by Thorvald Stoltenberg to be the decisive factor in terms of ending the war. Certainly the federation's military offensive changed the power balance in Bosnia, and there is no doubt the NATO air campaign generated devastation and reduced the leverage of General Mladić and his forces. However, Stoltenberg asserts, the decisive factor was that the United States assumed leadership and committed itself to a negotiated strategy to end the war.[143]

With the other Western powers rallying behind U.S. leadership and its political/diplomatic offensive to end the war in Bosnia, the Bosnian Serb ability to manipulate international divisions largely ended. According to the former ambassador to NATO, Robert Hunter, by summer 1995 the Bosnian Serb leadership realized that its only leverage lay in trying to manipulate the internal divisions within the international community in such a way as to preclude the possibility of decisive action against them by either the UN or NATO, or both. So when the London Conference transferred the authority to the UN commander on the ground and both NATO and the UN expressed commitment and (in the NAC) unanimity in their support for air strikes, the Bosnian Serb leverage had decreased to a level at which the benefits of compliance outweighed those of continued resistance.[144]

When the Cold War ended, the United States had become the sole superpower in the world, and by summer 1995 it had decided to use this overwhelming influence in Bosnia. In his memoirs, President Clinton asserts that American leadership was one of four key factors ending the war in Bosnia[145]—a notion shared by Madeleine Albright who, in her memoirs, says three factors ended the war in Bosnia, of which the "third factor was Bill Clinton's willingness to lead."[146]

The fifth major predisposing factor was the *Republika Srpska and the relative importance of Bosnia.* Evidence suggests Bosnia was not nearly as important to Milošević as Kosovo. David Rohde has pointed out in the *New York Times* that Kosovo "represents far more to Milošević than the Serb-controlled chunks of Bosnia and Croatia did. When some of those lands were lost in 1995, Milošević had little to fear from opponents in his power base in Serbia proper, where few people were prepared to die or suffer on behalf of Bosnian or Croatian Serbs."[147] The American envoy to the Balkans at the time, Robert Gelbard, says flatly that Milošević's support for the Serbs in Krajina, Eastern Slavonia, and Bosnia was negligible. They "were games to him—they were throwaways."[148]

So when Milošević pressured the Bosnian Serbs into the Dayton negotiations, not only was Bosnia of relatively limited strategic interest, but he had every reason to believe that the Bosnian Serbs would keep a significant chunk of Bosnia as their "Republika Srpska." When he persuaded the Bosnian Serbs to give him the authority to negotiate, they held a disproportionately large percentage of Bosnia—close to 70 percent—which would be an excellent starting point for Milošević in the negotiations. The Bosnian Serbs were confident that a negotiated solution would let them keep their self-proclaimed Republika Srpska. With their ambition of an "ethnically clean"

Bosnian Serb territory largely fulfilled—and the ground situation increasingly against them—a negotiated solution would be acceptable.

The sixth factor was Operation Deliberate Force, and although one of the most important factors, it was not the only one—as many policy makers seemed to believe. On 30 August, Deliberate Force began pounding Bosnian Serb targets in an air campaign that would end on 20 September. Deliberate Force included some 220 fighter aircraft and seventy support aircraft, plus the naval air assets on the aircraft carrier *Theodore Roosevelt.* In total some 3,535 sorties were flown, delivering 1,026 high-explosive ammunitions against 338 aim points on forty-eight Bosnian Serb targets.[149] By then, as we have seen, Deliberate Force had become the largest NATO military action in the history of the NATO Alliance.[150]

By late summer 1995, Operation Deliberate Force had undoubtedly added to the overall pressure against the Serbs. It destroyed communication centers, communication lines, and military equipment, and it had weakened the Bosnian Serb military leader Mladić and his forces. It is widely regarded as a significant contribution to ending the war in Bosnia.[151] As noted above, President Clinton asserted in his memoirs that NATO's aggressiveness was one of four factors ending the war in Bosnia.[152] Madeleine Albright believed that Bosnia showed that limited force—even airpower alone—could make a decisive impact.[153] Richard Holbrooke asserted that while the federation's ground offensive was "extremely important," the air campaign remained "the most important single factor influencing the Serbs."[154] However, according to Daalder and O'Hanlon, it was the Croatian ground offensive in August 1995 that brought Milošević to the negotiating table, with the artillery fire and the NATO air campaign only reinforcing the pressure for a diplomatic solution.[155] The Balkan analyst Norman Cigar goes even further, claiming the ground offensive showed the Bosnian Serbs that they were losing control of the military situation on the ground and thus had a profound impact on their diplomatic calculation, while "the air campaign had minimal direct effect on the Serbs' military capabilities and consequently had little impact on their diplomacy."[156]

However, it seems unreasonable to believe that the involvement of the most powerful military alliance in the history of mankind did not influence the Bosnian Serb leadership significantly. In fact, Owen points out, "Every diplomat and senior commander interviewed believed that the air campaign distinctly affected the moral resistance of the Serb leaders and, consequently, the pace of negotiations."[157] In this regard, the ten-thousand-strong Rapid Reaction Force (RRF) that was deployed in early July should be mentioned. It both contributed firepower and served as a signal of international determination. As with the notion that the signal of resolve among the international community was most important, Richard Holbrooke believed the actual targets struck in Deliberate Force "were less important to the effect on Bosnian Serb leaders than the fact that the NATO campaign was sustained, effective and selective."[158]

A certain element of irony with regard to the international community's handling of the Bosnian crisis and the use of airpower must be noted. According to General Smith, when he turned the UN "key" that started Operation Deliberate Force, he did so with no idea of what was to be its political outcome, let alone how to get there. With no strategic direction or strategic military goal, General Smith wanted to use force for tactical achievements—breaking the siege of Sarajevo. As he points out: "This was the first real use of force, and it had no previous or planned context." Before Deliberate Force commenced, General Smith called Richard Holbrooke to inform him of the imminent use of force, because he thought Holbrooke "would want to provide some political input, since I was sure what we were about to do would affect his negotiations. To my surprise he saw the intended action as a separate and disconnected activity and apparently of no consequences to him." Still, the impact of the air strikes would of course have an effect on the negotiations, and "it was not long before Richard Holbrooke was in almost daily contact, now seeking to exploit the impact of our military actions in his negotiations."[159] In his memoirs, Holbrooke confirms these circumstances: "History is often made of seemingly disparate events whose true relationship to one another becomes apparent only after the fact. This was true of the last two weeks of August." Holbrooke says almost everyone believed that the bombing had been part of a master plan, "but in fact in none of the discussions prior to our mission had we considered bombing as part of a negotiating strategy." To use airpower to bomb the Bosnian Serbs in combination with diplomacy "would not have been a bad idea . . . but it simply did not happen that way. It took an outrageous Bosnian Serb action to trigger Operation Deliberate Force. But once launched, it made a huge difference."[160]

Neither General Smith nor Richard Holbrooke, then, had any strategic guidance in terms of what the employment of airpower should achieve. Smith admits that the air campaign was not linked explicitly to a political strategy to end the war in Bosnia. After the bombing in May 1995 he came to the conclusion that he "had to understand the use of force in a different way, that it had to be applied to alter the decision maker's mind, and that this understanding must affect my choice of targets."[161] Thus, Smith touched upon a key element in the airpower debate—the importance of targets. Col. Phillip S. Meilinger wrote as the fourth proposition in his article *Ten Propositions Emerging from Airpower*, "In essence, airpower is targeting; targeting is intelligence; and intelligence is analyzing the effects of air operations."[162] Still, as we have seen, General Smith, who was involved in selecting targets for Operation Deliberate Force, "had no idea of what was to be the political outcome, let alone how to get there"—and the man in charge of the diplomatic endeavor to end the war apparently did not have airpower in the diplomatic equation to do so.

Even so, from the Serb perspective at the time, the link between force and diplomacy must have seemed part of a coherent effort. By now the coercive potential of airpower had been released. The threat of force was finally credible, and the Bosnian Serbs had every reason to anticipate further damage should they not alter their behavior and start negotiations. It was not an option to hunker down and wait out the air campaign—because, as we have seen, the ground offensive was forcing them to counter the threat. Negotiations that would lead to their own ethnically homogeneous territory appeared far preferable to facing stronger opponents. This would arguably be a classic example of coercive diplomacy. Owen concludes: "Since the Federation potentially offered them one of their dearest objectives—a degree of political autonomy—it seems reasonable to think that it lowered their willingness to fight on in the face of simultaneous NATO air attacks and ground offensives by their regional enemies."[163]

While it seems fair to argue that the air campaign did have a significant effect, it seems equally fair to question why the air campaign was perceived by many as the most critical factor influencing the Serbs; it is an arguably more rational conclusion that the interaction of several key factors in combination made the Bosnian Serbs accept an end to the war in Bosnia.

Comparing the international approach in Kosovo with the lessons from Bosnia, Tim Judah argues: "The fact that the Serbs had sued for peace immediately the bombs had started falling in Bosnia inevitably influenced calculations—or more accurately speculations—about how they would react two and a half years later."[164] Elaine M. Grossman, in *Inside the Pentagon*, asserted during OAF, "While political leaders in Washington may have been confident Milošević would fold, based on his ultimate acquiescence in November 1995 to an accord over Bosnia, senior military officials at NATO headquarters in Brussels feared otherwise."[165] Daalder said: "There was a widespread conviction on the part of civilian and military leaders that bombing would either get Milošević to back off, or get him to the table. That was the lesson we thought we had learned from Bosnia."[166] Tony Blinken (a member of the National Security Council) similarly asserted, "I think if you look at what happened in Bosnia, there was certainly reason to believe that faced with NATO airplanes, he would quickly calculate that his interest lay in making peace."[167]

To believe that airpower alone proved decisive in bringing about the Serb position to negotiate an end to the war in Bosnia is simply wrong. Whether these arguments were politically motivated or rooted in a flawed conviction of the superior potential of airpower independent of circumstances is not clear. Discussing the matter later, Robert Gelbard said: "I think there has generally been an under-recognition in the West of how much that Croatian ground operation really contributed. . . . I think the air operation in Bosnia had a big effect, but I believe there were a number of factors that contributed to the impact of bringing the Serbs to the negotiating table at Dayton."[168] David Rohde asserted during OAF in 1999, "Bosnia and Kosovo are very different. And it was not NATO bombing alone, but a mix of politics, diplomacy and military pressure that brought Milošević to the negotiation table over Bosnia."[169] In the same article, Anthony Cordesman pointed out, "What was going on in Bosnia was completely different politically, historically and emotionally from what is going on in Kosovo." Tony Lake felt it was a combination of the successes of the federation on the ground, air attacks, and the diplomatic unity between the Americans, the Europeans, and the Russians that ultimately ended the war in Bosnia.[170] Misha Glenny asserted, "The illusion that he had crumpled after a short sharp bombing campaign would lead to unreasonable expectations, on the part of statesmen who should have known better, four years later in Kosovo."[171]

A BBC documentary about the war in Kosovo pointed out that "somehow after all the bluff and talking, NATO and Yugoslavia had stumbled into war. In Washington the prevailing view was that Milošević was a cowardly bully! A few days of feeling the sharp end of the NATO stick, and he would back down. That was the gamble as the war began."[172] A few weeks into the air campaign over Kosovo, David Owen was interviewed by the BBC and asked to comment on the lack of progress in the initial phase of the air campaign; Lord Owen replied, "I mean, the real problem is that too many of our world leaders think that Dayton on Bosnia was a result of NATO air strikes. That is complete nonsense. If you can't get them to re-think that particular issue, they are going to continue making mistakes. . . . Their bluff was called by Milošević. That's what happened."[173]

Commenting on Bosnia's importance in terms of shaping the U.S. approach to Kosovo, Ivo Daalder says the Clinton administration saw Kosovo through the lens of Bosnia, adding: "The Administration's experience in Bosnia was the single most defining element in how it approached the pending crisis in Kosovo."[174]

Airpower theorist Col. John A. Warden. Warden was one of the key architects of the strategic application of airpower in the 1991 Gulf War, and his thinking has since significantly influenced the U.S. Air Force. Picture taken in mid-August 1990. The Instant Thunder plan is laid out in front of him. (Copyright John A. Warden)

The Powell Doctrine. Secretary of Defense Richard B. Cheney and chairman of the Joint Chiefs of Staff, Gen. Colin Powell. General Powell adhered to his doctrine of clear objectives and decisive force and recommended that ground troops not be deployed in Bosnia without such political commitment. Picture from the defense ministers meeting in Brussels, 28 May 1991. (NATO photo)

NATO's foreign ministers meeting in Oslo, Norway, 4–5 June 1992. During the meeting the foreign ministers felt that making forces available to UN peacekeeping operations was a step too far . A few months later, NATO was involved in the biggest operation in the history of the UN. Front: Norwegian foreign minister Thorvald Stoltenberg and Lawrence S. Eagleburger (who became secretary of state in December 1992). (NATO photo)

Secretary of State Warren Christopher (left) with NATO secretary-general Manfred Wörner (right) on 6 May to discuss the situation in Bosnia. After Christopher's failed political endeavor to persuade the Europeans of the American "lift and strike" policy, the United States changed policy and opted to support the European perspective of defending six Muslim enclaves in Bosnia, declared "safe areas" by the UN. (NATO photo)

National Security Adviser Anthony Lake (left) with President Bill Clinton (right) in 1994. Tony Lake was one of the principal architects behind the "endgame strategy," which paved the way for the Dayton Accords, ending the war in Bosnia. (Corbis photo)

French UN forces at the Sarejevo airport, 1993. Gen. Sir Rupert Smith argues that UNPROFOR was "not intended to create the conditions for peace but rather to 'ameliorate' the situation." Richard Holbrooke says, "The Europeans chose not to take a strong stand, restricting themselves to dispatching UN 'peacekeepers' to a country where there was no peace to keep." (Corbis photo)

Left: Bosnian Serb leader Radovan Karadžić; middle: the chief of staff of the Bosnian Serb army, Gen. Ratko Mladić. Karadžić and Mladić bear particular responsibility for the Srebrenica massacre—a crime that galvanized the diplomatic effort to end the war in Bosnia. Picture taken 6 August 1993. (Corbis photo)

Assistant Secretary of State for European Affairs Richard Holbrooke and General Clark. Holbrooke and Clark worked together in the U.S.-driven diplomatic effort to end the war in Bosnia and would re-create a similar diplomatic effort during OAF. Picture taken after a briefing of the NATO Council on the situation in Bosnia on 2 September 1995. (NATO photo)

The U.S. ambassador to the United Nations, Madeleine Albright, and Alexander "Sandy" Vershbow of the State Department. Both Albright and Vershbow argued for the use of airpower during the war in Bosnia. Albright would become secretary of state, Vershbow the American ambassador to NATO. Picture taken during OAF, at the extraordinary meeting of the North Atlantic Council at foreign ministers level, 12 April 1999. (NATO photo)

Serbian president Slobodan Milošević, Croat president Franjo Tudjman, and Bosnian president Alija Izetbegović sign multiple copies of the Dayton Peace Agreement in the Palais de l'Elysee. To many the Dayton Accords was largely a product of the coercive effects of airpower—a perspective that failed to acknowledge the combination of factors that combined ended the war in Bosnia. It was a flawed perception that would mark the international handling of the Kosovo crisis a few years later. (Corbis photo)

Part III
The International Handling of the Kosovo Crisis

I regret to say, but it is obvious that Milošević only responds to force or the absolute credible threat of the use of force. This was clear in Bosnia, and it was clear in Kosovo.

—Richard Holbrooke

Chapter 5
THE CRISIS EMERGES
NATO Becomes Responsible for Crisis Management

It was a big mistake to permanently transfer the crisis management responsibility to NATO in the spring of 1998.

– Gen. Klaus Naumann[1]

When Kosovo—the southernmost province of Serbia—was stripped of its autonomy in March 1989, it was barely noticed by Western diplomats. Ten years later, the situation in Kosovo would propel NATO into its first war.

Kosovo's loss of its autonomous status and the Serb reimposition of rule from Belgrade enraged the Albanians, who had enjoyed a significant degree of self-rule since 1974. Even so, war did not break out in Kosovo, unlike in Croatia and Bosnia, largely due to the nonviolent strategy chosen by the Albanian leadership. In Elida Café in Priština in December 1989—about half a year after Kosovo had lost its official autonomous status—twenty-three individuals met to form a political foundation in Kosovo. The Democratic League of Kosovo (LDK) was founded on 23 December 1989, and it chose Ibrahim Rugova as its leader. One key issue regarding Rugova and the LDK was that for centuries, more often than not, the Serbs and Kosovar Albanians had resorted to violence, though with varying degrees of intensity, as the preferred mode of political expression in crises like these. As a historical experiment and break with tradition, they now chose a nonviolent political strategy.[2] This strategy and the subsequent Kosovar Albanian politics until 1997 derived from the following notions. First, the Serbs were so overwhelmingly militarily superior that a violent insurrection could have catastrophic results for the Albanian population, as was later shown in the wars in Croatia and Bosnia. Second, and paradoxically, it was argued that Milošević had laid the groundwork for future Albanian claims when he tried to tie Serb enclaves in Croatia and Bosnia into a Greater Serbia, wanting to alter borders for ethnic purposes. If this were to be accepted in a future international conference—for instance, that the Krajina Serbs and Bosnian Serbs could not live in Croatia and Bosnia but had to secede to Serbia and consequently borders were altered to achieve this—it would be hard for the international community to object to Albanians asking for the same. Thirdly, if they adopted a nonviolent strategy and it was self-evident that the vast majority of Albanians wanted independence in a future international conference, the international community would grant them their independence as a reward for their nonviolent approach and "good behavior." Fourthly, some argued, the key was democratic institutions and a parliament, since such institutions would—in the long run—grant the Kosovar Albanians their independence. Such institutions carried out the will of the people, and the Kosovar will for independence was clear. This was also later influenced by experience in the wake of international recognition of Slovenia, Croatia, Bosnia, and Macedonia in 1992, because this recognition was largely based on the legal opinion that these republics had the attributes of statehood and could therefore be recognized. Therefore building legitimacy for "the Republic of Kosovo" became important.[3]

Consequently, it became a vital part of the Kosovar Albanian strategy to avoid an open conflict with the Serbs and to build their own separate democratic institutions. In effect, Rugova and LDK de facto pacified the province between 1989 and 1997. The benefit from the Kosovar Albanian point of view would be that Kosovo remained stable and would avoid the ethnic cleansing witnessed in Croatia and Bosnia; the flip side was to be that Kosovo did not get the international focus the Kosovar Albanians wanted in order to achieve their goal of independence.[4] As the nonviolent strategy of Rugova failed to have the desired effect of gaining Kosovo independence, the more radical elements slowly gained ground. Two factors were particularly important in bolstering the growth of the radical forces.

First, the Dayton Accords ending the war in Bosnia became significant to the Kosovar Albanians, because they "confirmed to them in the most dramatic and humiliating way that Rugova's policy of passive resistance had failed. And not only that, but that his idea that they would be rewarded for their 'good behavior' by Western countries had been just plain wrong."[5] The Dayton Accords had rewarded the violent approach of the Bosnian Serbs and their genocide in Bosnia, and the Kosovars believed that the Serb and Croat parts would sooner or later secede to join the respective "motherlands." After Dayton, the EU recognized the Federal Republic of Yugoslavia (FRY), which consisted of Serbia, Montenegro, and, of course, Kosovo. This came as a shock to the Kosovars and played right into the hands of the radical nationalists, who for years had claimed that this would happen.[6]

According to Misha Glenny, the killings by the Kosovo Liberation Army (KLA) started on Monday, 22 April 1996, when three Serbs in a café in Dečani in western Kosovo were killed by the KLA. Within an hour three other attacks in Kosovo left two additional Serbs dead. The attacks came a few months after the Dayton signing, indicating that Rugova's nonviolent strategy had not worked out and that violence was the only thing that would make the international community listen. "After five years of vicious conflict in the former Yugoslavia, the West had tired of the Balkan tragedy. The death of a few Serbs in Kosovo barely registered in diplomatic cables and no government was interested in pursuing the matter. The peace in Bosnia depended on the goodwill and cooperation of Slobodan Milošević. This was not the time, Western politicians thought, to open a Pandora's box like Kosovo."[7]

Hashim Thaci, the KLA representative at the Rambouillet negotiations in 1998, later commented on the situation in the mid-1990s: "We felt the international community was ignoring us. We had to force them to pay attention to Kosovo. But at that time, we didn't have a lot of weapons."[8]

The second important factor for the growth of the radical elements in Kosovo was the disintegration of Albania, triggered by the collapse of a nationwide pyramid investment scheme in the spring of 1997, which caused the Albanian economy to plummet and sent the country into chaos. The Albanian government lost control, the army dissolved, the police fled, and, perhaps most importantly with regard to Kosovo, the arms depots were thrown open and hundreds of thousands of Kalashnikovs and ammunition were suddenly available for virtually nothing. With no functional Albanian government to prevent the smuggling of these arms into Kosovo, one of the greatest obstacles to an armed uprising—how to get enough weapons into Kosovo—was largely eliminated.

It is important to note, however, that even though radical extremists had existed in this area for a long time, evidence suggests that as late as early 1997 the number of active KLA activists was only about 150, according to Tim Judah.[9] That number hardly constitutes a popular uprising. Even when the war began in Kosovo in spring 1998, very few had even heard about the KLA.[10] In fact, the Serbian commander of the Yugoslav Third Army in Kosovo, General Nebojsa Pavkovic, later said he first heard of the KLA as an organized army in the first half of 1998: "Until then, there were some isolated, sporadic actions, mainly directed against the units of MUP [Serbian Interior Ministry Police], as well as state security units and Serbian people."[11]

By fall 1997, the radical sentiments within the Kosovar community were on the rise. On 1 October 1997, some twenty thousand Kosovar Albanian students were involved in a violent clash with the police in Kosovo. Some weeks later, reports indicate, thirteen thousand people attended the funeral of the first KLA member to die in uniform (Adrian Krasniqi). When an Albanian teacher (Halit Gecaj) was later killed by a stray bullet in a KLA attack on a Serbian police patrol, some twenty thousand people attended his funeral. Uniformed KLA men took off their masks during the funeral, one of them making a speech: "Serbia is massacring Albanians. The KLA is the only force which is fighting for the liberation and national unity of Kosovo. We shall continue to fight." Reportedly the crowd chanted, "KLA! KLA! KLA!"[12] With the radical elements gaining momentum, a tense atmosphere was evident in Kosovo by early 1998. On 22 January 1998, the police tried to arrest the longtime hard-liner Adem Jashari, but according to his father (Shaban) the attempt did not succeed because friends of Adem came to his aid.[13] The Serbian police would try again some weeks later. This event would have very significant ramifications for the future of Kosovo.

With the United States seemingly a little uncertain about how to proceed diplomatically, the U.S. special envoy to the Balkans, Robert Gelbard, visited both Belgrade and Priština in late February. Gelbard reports from his meeting with Milošević in Belgrade:

> What I told Milošević was the following: I had just presented to him a modest package of positive incentives as a small movement forward as a result of his newfound cooperation on pressing the Bosnian Serbs to implement the Dayton Agreement. However, this moment coincided with the beginning of the Serb military (VJ) and police (MUP) aggressive new actions in Kosovo—but before the first massacres. I met alone with Milošević and told him that he was at a crossroads. He had just been presented with some rewards, albeit modest ones, but he could get much more *if* he continued to help with progress in Bosnia *and* the situation in Kosovo *not only* did not worsen, but moved in a new and positive direction. In dark terms, I said that he was at a crossroads and could make the choice of taking Serbia into the light of progress and out of the mess it was in, or down into a spiral of destruction and darkness.[14]

In Priština on 23 February 1998, Gelbard publicly declared that the violence in Kosovo was very dangerous and denounced the violence by the Serb police. He also took a forceful stand against the KLA: "We condemn very strongly terrorist actions in Kosovo. The UÇK (KLA) is, without any question, a terrorist group."[15] Although saying what many felt at that point (particularly the Europeans) and what was explicitly expressed in UN Resolution 1160 a little more than a month later,[16] the statement was to have consequences.

As Tim Judah points out, "If the KLA were a terrorist group and the most powerful nation on earth said so, then there could be no objection to the Serbian police moving in to finish it off"—so the comment did not earn any friends in Kosovo.[17]

The American ambassador to Macedonia and later part of the troika leading the Rambouillet negotiations, Christopher Hill, said the comment by Gelbard was not well thought through because—even though it was not intended—it probably created the notion in the Balkans that there was a green light for Milošević to deal with the KLA. In an attempt to correct the issue, Gelbard might have overreached in the other direction, providing signals that could be equally misinterpreted as sympathetic toward the Albanian side.[18] Not only did the comments not earn many friends in the Balkans, but, evidence suggests, Gelbard was somewhat out of tune with Washington as well. According to Marcia Christoff Kurop of the *Wall Street Journal Europe*, by the end of February the United States had removed the KLA from the State Department's terrorism list, in order to improve relations with the organization.[19] Confronted in early March with his previous comments, Gelbard apparently felt he had to modify his statement. According to the *New York Times*, "Questioned by lawmakers today on whether he still considered the group a terrorist organization, Mr. Gelbard said that while it has committed 'terrorist acts,' it had 'not been classified legally by the U.S. Government as a terrorist organization.'"[20]

Milošević's reply to Gelbard's suggestion to accept the incentives of the international community rather than to go "down into a spiral of destruction and darkness" came shortly after their conversation. According to Tim Judah, a firefight broke out between KLA and a Serb police patrol in a small village (Likošane, see map 4) in Kosovo on 28 February, leaving four dead Serb policemen (two died at the scene, and two died later from injuries) and injuring several others. The KLA men escaped, one of them Adem Jashari. Although what happened is not quite clear, the Serb police killed some thirteen Albanians in the nearby household—eleven of them being lined up and executed. Later the same day, Serb police forces attacked the neighboring village of Ćirez, and at the end of the day twenty-six Albanians were dead. Fifteen thousand people attended their funerals. However, the KLA men had escaped, and the police decided to move in on Adem Jashari and his family.[21]

A longtime radical hard-liner in the Drenica Valley, "Jashari had decided the KLA needed martyrs, and he and his family were going to provide them."[22] According to a BBC2 television documentary,[23] Adem Demaci (KLA) had tried to warn Adem Jashari, but Jashari would not listen to him, replying, "I hear what you are saying, but if I escape, it will hurt our cause. We stay here

Map 4. Kosovo

and resist to the last man." According to Hashim Thaçi, Adem Jashari had been quite clear: "I do not leave the house, and I am not sending away my family." Goran Radosavljević, a major in the Serb Interior Ministry police, reported that Adem Jashari "used women, children and elderly as hostages. For several days the police advised them through megaphones to release the hostages and lay down their weapons. Every time we tried to enter we risked more policemen being killed. Therefore we were forced to use artillery fire." In the event, Adem Jashari and forty-five others died—among them twelve women and eleven children.[24]

The significance of this event should not be underestimated. The KLA had gained a martyr, and the deaths of the Jashari family left Kosovo reeling. As Tim Judah describes it, "Years of accumulated frustration boiled over and demonstrations were held across the province. Within weeks everything began to change, the status quo that had held since 1990 began to collapse and everyone was shocked by what was happening—no one more so than the KLA men themselves." According to Pleurat Sejdiu (of the KLA), the plan was to start a war in 1999 by bombing depots and such, but events in Albania (access to weapons) speeded things up. The killings of the Jashari family further accelerated the process, and in the Drenica Valley people began to say that now was the time to fight the Serbs. Across Drenica the Serb police began digging in and constructing fortified bunkers and checkpoints.[25]

With this incident the level of violence in Kosovo reached a critical threshold, one that demanded international attention. Unless stopped by a third party, the Serbs and the Kosovar Albanians were heading for war.

By now, though Ibrahim Rugova still argued for a nonviolent strategy, people seemed not to see the contradiction between supporting both Rugova *and* the KLA—arguing that the KLA was their army and Rugova their president. Still, as Veton Surroi argued, to define the KLA was hard, because it was still a somewhat splintered group of resistance fighters without one supreme commander giving orders. Some village groups just called themselves KLA because that was what everyone else was doing.[26] Some were only fighting for Kosovo independence, while other KLA commanders made no secret that their ambition was to carve out a Greater Albania. In a conversation with Richard Holbrooke a KLA commander noted, "This is the army which is liberating people," adding, "our job is to free the whole of Kosovo, the Albanians of Macedonia and Montenegro too."[27]

On 5 March, Gelbard reiterated the "Christmas warning" to Belgrade, speaking so forcefully to Milošević that the latter took a dislike to him and later refused to see him.[28] The same day the NAC issued the first of many statements on the crisis, expressing its concern with the situation and urging Belgrade and the Kosovar Albanian community to find a political solution. Interestingly, it included a condemnation of "terrorist acts to achieve political goals."[29]

The United States and NATO ruled out the use of force the first months of 1998, but, determined to use the lessons from Bosnia, Madeleine Albright took the lead to push the Europeans and the United States to act in concert. The first Contact Group meeting on the issue of Kosovo convened 9 March. Before the meeting, Secretary Albright stated in public, "We are not going to stand by and watch the Serbian authorities do in Kosovo what they can no longer get away with in Bosnia."[30] President Clinton similarly noted, "We do not want the Balkans to have more pictures like we've seen in the last few days so reminiscent of what Bosnia endured."[31] During the meeting Albright pointed out numerous fruitless meetings had been held on the issue of Bosnia and the international community had ignored the first signs of ethnic cleansing in the Balkans. "History is watching us," she asserted, arguing that this time they had to learn from past mistakes.[32] Secretary Albright further argued that concrete measures were what had brought Milošević to Dayton, and that they were the only language Milošević would respond to. The British foreign minister, Robin Cook, shared her views, but according to Albright, the French foreign minister, Hubert Védrine, wanted a delay in sanctions, a clearer condemnation of the KLA, and an explicit statement of opposition to independence for Kosovo. The Italian foreign minister, Lamberto Dini, wanted to halt the arms smuggling to the KLA and feared that sanctions on Milošević might result in less rather than more cooperation from him. The Russian envoy (Foreign Minister Yevgeny Primakov did not attend the meeting) had explicit orders to oppose any punitive measures against Belgrade.[33] As the debate grew heated, Secretary Albright famously remarked, when James Rubin of the U.S. State Department urged her to compromise on a particular issue, "Jamie, do you think we're in Munich?" The Contact Group meeting concluded by stating, "Our condemnation of the actions of the Serbian police should not in any way be mistaken for an endorsement of terrorism. Our position on this is clear. We wholly condemn terrorist actions by the Kosovo Liberation Army or any other group or individual."[34] It demanded that Milošević agree to cease all action by Serb security forces against the civilian population, withdraw Serb special police units from the territory within ten days, allow humanitarian groups to enter Kosovo, and commence an unconditional dialogue with the Albanian community. Failure to meet these demands would lead to imposition of an arms embargo, denial of travel visas for senior Yugoslav and Serb officials, a moratorium on export credits, and a freeze on funds held abroad.[35] Variations on the same theme came when the Permanent Council of the Organization for Security and Cooperation in Europe (OSCE) convened on 11 March, stressing "the unacceptability of any terrorist action" and "recognizing that the crisis in Kosovo is not solely an internal affair of the Federal Republic of Yugoslavia because of violations of the principles and commitments of the Organisation for Security and Cooperation in Europe on human rights and because it has a significant impact on the security of a region."[36]

A second Contact Group meeting was held on 25 March 1998 in Bonn, chaired by the German foreign minister, Klaus Kinkel, but lack of progress at the meeting convinced Secretary Albright that the Contact Group was not the right body to counter Milošević.[37] Albright claims that as Russia was reluctant to oppose its Slav brethren, France and Germany were reluctant to confront Moscow, and the Italians did a lot of business with the Serbs and disliked sanctions, it would be too easy for Milošević to immobilize these countries with reassuring gestures and empty words. The United States would not be content to follow a consensus on Kosovo. It had to provide leadership, Milošević needed to be persuaded by the threat of force, and NATO was the institution that would carry out the threat.[38]

Commenting later on her frustration at the time, Secretary Albright said, "It seemed that we were meeting for the sake of meeting, rather than resolving something. The real problem came down to the fact that there were, among the Europeans, those who were prepared to use force. But the force question was wrapped up in legalisms, as to whether there needed to be a Security Council resolution, authorizing the use of force."[39] It should be noted that her conclusion was largely the same as her conclusion after Bosnia—it all came down to "the only language Milošević understood," the threat or use of force. It evidently took her only a few weeks and two meetings in the Contact Group to draw this conclusion in public. Daalder says Albright had been "perhaps the most forceful advocate for strong forceful opposition to the kinds of policies that Milošević conducted, in Croatia, then in Bosnia, and by February, 1998, inside Kosovo. . . . She has a particular knack for putting this in highly rhetorical and forceful language."[40] Commenting on the situation later, she said: "I believe in learning lessons, and I felt, at the time, that we were much too slow in responding to what Milošević was doing in Bosnia. It is not often that you get a second chance."[41]

She had learned her lesson well, and now was her second chance. Her close aide from Bosnia, Richard Holbrooke, shared her view: "I regret to say, but it is obvious that Milošević only responds to force or the absolute credible threat of the use of force. This was clear in Bosnia, and it was clear in Kosovo."[42] However, the Clinton administration was divided on the issue, and the Pentagon was weary of her statements of resolve.[43]

The United States and Europe had been concerned about the situation in Kosovo but had not actively and forcefully pursued a policy that prevented the province from sliding into bloodshed. The attacks on the Jashari family in March put the issue of Kosovo on the international agenda, and according to Daalder/O'Hanlon, the governments within the Contact Group shared some key assumptions based on the handling of Bosnia with regard to approaching the growing conflict in Kosovo. They needed to react quickly, and unity of effort was essential. In Bosnia, Europe and the United States had been so divided that it had put an unprecedented strain on NATO and the transatlantic cooperation; this too was to be avoided. American leadership was needed to provide a viable strategy. In Bosnia, the United States had handed the issue of Yugoslavia over to the Europeans, but without the military, financial, and political backing of the United States, their negotiations had failed.

Concerted pressure on Milošević was needed to reach a settlement. In November 1997, the European Union had offered to help Milošević improve FRY's diplomatic and trade relations and to support Belgrade's reentry into international institutions in return for accepting a negotiating process on the Kosovo issue. Just before the Jashari situation in March, the Americans had lifted a number of sanctions as a reward for Milošević's assistance in moderating the Bosnian Serb leadership, but the policy of carrots had failed, and Milošević went on an offensive in Kosovo, prompting Madeleine Albright to claim that "by his actions in Kosovo, Slobodan Milošević has made it clear that he is spurning incentives that the United States and others have offered him in recent weeks—unfortunately the only thing he truly understands is decisive and firm action."[44] A solution short of Kosovo's independence would have to be found. There were several reasons for this, but arguably one of the most imminent reasons was that due to the large Albanian minority in Macedonia, disturbing the fragile interethnic consensus could generate a desire to join Kosovo to a Greater Albania. Kosovo independence could also have ramifications in Bosnia, because both the Bosnian Serbs and the Croats wanted either independence or to merge with their neighboring states. No one wanted to risk destabilizing Bosnia.

Daalder and O'Hanlon point out three contradictions with regard to these assumptions: the desire to act quickly and decisively versus the perceived need to forge a consensus policy with NATO and Russia; the belief that the solution to the Kosovo crisis lay in pressing Milošević versus needing him for a political solution, leaving the question of who had leverage over whom; and pressing Milošević to end violence versus not encouraging the Albanians in their quest for independence. "Rather than making these choices, however, the United States and its European partners sought to defer making difficult decisions, preferring instead to muddle through in the hope that somehow and someway a solution would present itself that would at once end the violence, provide a firm political basis for a settlement, and avoid confronting the international community with the need to use massive force."[45]

UN Resolution 1160 (1998) was issued on 31 March. The resolution condemned "the use of excessive force by Serbian police forces against civilians and peaceful demonstrators in Kosovo, as well as all acts of terrorism by the Kosovo Liberation Army."[46] It is interesting to note the explicit link between terrorism and the KLA, which was also apparent (if not so explicit) in the NAC statements of 5 March and 30 April, the OSCE statement on 11 March, and that of the Contact Group 9 March. General Naumann said afterward that these references to the KLA as terrorists later came back to haunt NATO when it tried to influence the KLA. As several NATO nations for a long time had vowed never to speak to terrorists, for fear of creating a precedent, NATO was denied the option to talk to the KLA and hence had little leverage over it.[47]

Thus far, in late March and early April, NATO had not issued any threats of military force. Gelbard had reiterated the Christmas warning, but that was a unilateral American threat, which, interestingly, stood in contrast to Secretary Cohen's belief that the United States could not afford to act unilaterally without NATO consensus and support. The National Security Adviser, Sandy Berger, shared the notion that the United States could not act unilaterally, saying that the Americans by now were "beginning to work with our NATO Allies to try and gain a consensus for NATO to issue something called the 'Act Toward,' which is essentially the readiness of NATO to use military force."[48] The least-common-denominator approach of the Contact Group made the United States threaten to abandon this forum in favor of using NATO as the coercive tool by threatening air strikes in order to avoid the lack of concerted resolve so apparent in Bosnia.[49]

NATO's role would change rapidly during the next two months. Meanwhile, according to Tim Judah, on 24 March, Milošević's SPS party entered a coalition with the Yugoslav United Left (JUL), led by his wife Mira Marković, and the Serbian Radical Party, led by the extreme nationalist Vojislav Šešelj. There were at least two reasons for this. First, Milošević needed to strengthen his position in the Serbian parliament, and with tension in Kosovo rising, having the nationalist hard-liners on board would be useful. Second, by inviting Šešelj into the government, Milošević sent a signal to the Western leaders: You might not like me, but you might want to consider the alternative.[50]

In the spring of 1998, tension had again risen in Iraq, when Iraqi authorities barred U.S.-led weapons inspection teams from conducting inspections at several sensitive sites. This led to "intense diplomacy and a continuing buildup of U.S. forces in the Persian Gulf region."[51] With the Clinton administration recovering from this round of threatening force, the appetite for further threats of force in the Balkans was not rising—an issue of which Sandy Berger was particularly wary.[52] By now, according to Halberstam, Albright was convinced Milošević was the problem. She detested Milošević and was convinced that he was the villain of the Balkan problems; "Albright was absolutely sure that Kosovo was a repeat of Bosnia and that the United States would, sooner or later, have to take military action against Belgrade."[53]

On 23 April, Berger had a meeting with Albright, Gelbard, and Strobe Talbott. Gelbard and Secretary Albright felt it necessary to again raise the issue of bombing, at which Berger became somewhat irritated and said, "You can't just talk about bombing in the middle of Europe. What targets would you want to hit? What would you do the day after? It's irresponsible to keep making threatening statements outside of some coherent plan. The way you people at the State Department talk about bombing, you sound like lunatics."[54] At the meeting, Gelbard pointed out that General Clark had developed a list of targets that if struck could convince Milošević to find a solution to the issue of Kosovo.[55] It is interesting to note this comment by Gelbard, because after OAF, several key players pointed out the link between SACEUR (an expressed belief that a short air campaign could convince Milošević to find a negotiated settlement) and Secretary Albright (whose firm belief was that a forceful approach—bombing—would produce leverage over Milošević) as the driving political force that made OAF possible in March 1999.

Gelbard adds some interesting perspectives to this meeting and its lead-up. As the American envoy in the Balkans with responsibility for the Dayton implementation, he formed a close working relationship with Clark, claiming they were the "leading hawks on Kosovo."[56] This notion is backed by Halberstam, who says Clark, just like Albright, by early 1998 believed Kosovo was a replay of Bosnia, Milošević was at the heart of the problem, and only force would work.[57] When violence erupted in Kosovo, both Gelbard and Clark very early perceived that Milošević was unable to make a negotiated diplomatic deal on Kosovo—because of his growing domestic political weakness and the fact that he had used Kosovo as a vehicle to gain power in Serbia. They realized that limited but credible force was necessary in order to create the political leverage to make a negotiated deal possible. So when the meeting started, Gelbard argued that the United States had to reiterate the Christmas warning and proposed that Milošević needed to be warned again—using the same warning. Second, if Milošević did not withdraw his troops within a specified number of days, he should be warned that the threat was not a bluff and that NATO was prepared to act against him. Third, if Milošević still did not withdraw, Gelbard argued that they should deploy Tomahawk missiles, attack the Ministry of Defense and the Ministry of the Interior in Belgrade in the middle of the night and destroy them, and, fourth, go back to Milošević the next morning and say: "Look, we were serious. We warned you. You now have X amount of days—very short—to withdraw your troops, or we will dramatically escalate against you." Gelbard says Sandy Berger got furious during the meeting and believes his frustration was largely triggered by domestic pressure from the Republicans, who were criticizing foreign policy in Bosnia and now Kosovo. Also significant was the growing frustration and criticism surrounding the Monica Lewinsky affair, which became public in January 1998. Gelbard later said: "Berger was very, very unwilling to use air strikes at that time, and I am sure this goes back to his concern about the need to protect Clinton when the Republicans were all over Clinton due to the Lewinsky business."[58]

What is of further relevance is that Gelbard's proposal was backed by General Clark. Gelbard's reference to the target list that Clark had developed reveals that they had been exchanging notes on the matter. Just as Albright had concluded in March that the only thing Milošević truly understood was decisive and firm action, both Gelbard and Clark felt it was "crystal clear that Milošević was intending to kill more and more people in Kosovo" and wanted to use force in order to stop his actions before many more Kosovar Albanians were killed.[59] In fact, just as Albright had learned her lesson from Bosnia, so had General Clark. According to Lieutenant General Short, who was director of operations for the U.S. Air Force in Europe at the time, in February 1998 General Clark asked for a military plan to handle the mounting crisis in Kosovo. Within a few days, Short and his planners came up with a limited air option, which included bombing targets south of a latitude of forty-four degrees north and establishing a no-fly zone south of this line.[60] The limited air option Clark signaled to Washington before the meeting between Albright, Gelbard, Talbott, and Berger is likely to have been the plan Short had developed.

Another reason for Berger to be reluctant to use force was that he believed the Christmas warning had been overtaken by events (even though Gelbard had restated it to Milošević in March). The United States no longer wanted to threaten a unilateral endeavor. NATO had become the principal instrument for exerting military pressure and influence in the region, and as Berger recalled, "We wanted to avoid the empty rhetoric as we tried to multilateralize the threat of force."[61] Another aspect was the fact that many European allies still had forces in neighboring Bosnia, and as one U.S. official stated, "the idea of us using force over the objection of allies who have troops on the ground, subject to retaliation, is fantasy-land. Allies do not do that to each other."[62] The United States now turned to NATO instead of the Contact Group, and in late spring 1998 it urged the Alliance to start planning for several possibilities, like air strikes, a peace implementation force, and preventive deployments to Macedonia and Albania.[63]

In late spring 1998, a key issue was raised. Robin Cook circulated a draft for a UN Security Council resolution authorizing the use of force, arguing that it was a legal requirement before NATO could act on Kosovo. This was a huge issue in a number of countries in Europe, and many probably felt like the Norwegian minister of defense, who described as "very difficult" the criticism from domestic political opposition and parts of the general public for not having a UN Security Council resolution before bombing the former Republic of Yugoslavia.[64] Secretary Cohen said later that by summer 1998, "the overwhelming majority [of NATO's defense ministers] said they couldn't take any action without a UN Security Council resolution."[65] The United States had a more pragmatic view of the matter, with Secretary Cohen later stating with regard to a UN authorization: "The United States does not feel it's imperative. It's desirable, not imperative."[66] In the same vein, Secretary Albright pointed out that if a precedent were established that NATO required a UN Security Council resolution in order to act, Russia and China would have a veto over NATO. As Secretary Albright later pointed out to the Russian foreign minister, Igor Ivanov, in Moscow in January 1999:

> We don't want war in Kosovo]. There has to be a political settlement. But the Albanians won't lay down their arms unless NATO is there to protect them. And Milošević will never allow NATO in unless we threaten force. The Europeans are worried about your reaction if NATO tries to act without going to the Security Council, but I can't entrust this to the Council, because Milošević knows you will veto force, which means our threats won't be credible, which means there will be no political settlement, which means war in Kosovo. This is a real "Catch 22."[67]

With the situation on the ground in Kosovo deteriorating, the NATO foreign ministers met in Luxembourg 28–29 May and announced that "in order to have options available for possible later decisions and to confirm our willingness to take further steps if necessary, we have [also] commissioned military advice on support for UN and OSCE monitoring activity as well as on NATO preventive deployments in Albania and the former Yugoslav Republic of Macedonia." NATO outlined two objectives on the matter: to help achieve a peaceful resolution of the crisis by contributing to the response of the international community; and to promote stability and security in neighboring countries (Albania and the former Yugoslav Republic of Macedonia). Also, a number of Partnership for Peace (PfP) activities were to be conducted to promote security and stability.[68] Secretary-General Solana further underlined that NATO "will consider further deterrent measures, if the violence continues. Let me stress, nothing is excluded."[69]

During the NATO foreign ministers meeting Robin Cook initiated a conversation with General Clark, in which he asked whether the threat of airpower could halt the increased Serb repression of the Kosovar Albanians. Clark answered along the lines he had indicated to the White House a month earlier, saying it probably would.[70] This is particularly important, because at both the White House meeting and in conversation with the British foreign minister, the advice to the politicians from one of the most influential military officials in Europe—the Supreme Allied Commander Europe—was that limited use of airpower would most likely provide significant political leverage over Milošević.

By early June a Richard Holbrooke–led U.S. diplomatic endeavor was in the making, and General Clark wanted to use airpower to back up the diplomacy, as in Bosnia in 1995. Clark subsequently briefed the CJCS, General Shelton, Secretary Cohen, Sandy Berger, and Strobe Talbott on his strategy.[71] It should be noted that General Clark's strategy not only was a blueprint of the diplomacy used by Richard Holbrooke in 1995 but was similar to what Secretary Albright had argued for since the second Contact Group meeting on 25 March—that NATO airpower should be threatened to provide political leverage over Milošević.[72]

In the Pentagon the strategy was received with a significant amount of skepticism, and Gen. Joseph Ralston called General Clark and asked him what would be the case if the threats did not work. Clark replied that he thought they would work, claiming, "I know Milošević; he doesn't want to get bombed." In case airpower did not have the desired effect, General Clark felt, the West had to make good upon the threats and ultimately see it through—perhaps with a ground option in Kosovo.[73] This is an important distinction. Clark believed limited force would ultimately evolve to decisive force once applied, if the use of limited force did not provide the desired results. There is little evidence to suggest this perception of limited force was shared by other advocates of limited force. It should be noted that even though Clark says in his memoirs that airpower did not guarantee a result; the notion that the threat of air strikes ultimately could mean escalating the conflict to a ground campaign came only after being pushed hard by General Ralston. But the impression Clark conveyed in Washington—particularly at the State Department and the NSC—was that airpower was likely to provide the political leverage sought to handle the issue of Kosovo.[74]

The reluctance to emphasize the possible need to escalate if the air campaign failed might have derived from the political sensitivity to a ground option—to Pentagon reluctance to use limited force in general, and ground troops in the Balkans in particular. General Ralston later said the Pentagon was very skeptical about the notion that a few days of bombing would be sufficient to coerce Milošević to concede and that Ralston, General Shelton, and Secretary Cohen simply did not believe that this was going to be over quickly.[75] For his part, General Clark deems the lack of support from the Pentagon "military conservatism," due to their commitment to the national strategy, which left the Balkans with a mounting crisis in Kosovo and the Pentagon reluctant to contribute.[76]

[handwritten margin note: "HOW IS THIS A NATO ISSUE?"]

The escalation of violence in early June prompted NATO to act on its previous threats. The defense ministers met on 11 June and directed alliance military authorities to undertake planning for "a full range of options with the mission, based on the relevant legal basis, of halting or disrupting a systematic campaign of violent repression and expulsion in Kosovo."[77] Interestingly, the word "terrorism" was not used. The emphasis was now on violence by Serb security forces; the level of threats was rising, and the legal issue was included in the text—reflecting the debate in many NATO countries with regard to legality if force were to be applied in this matter. Secretary-General Solana made a statement to the press after the meeting explicitly pointing out that "President Milošević has gone beyond the limits of tolerable behaviour. So NATO must prepare to go further if required."

He also announced that NATO would immediately conduct an air exercise "which will demonstrate NATO's capability to rapidly project power into the region." Solana told the press that the defense ministers had instructed NATO's military authorities to see how the full range of NATO's military capabilities could be used to achieve three objectives: to halt the systematic campaign of violent repression and expulsions that had been seen recently in Kosovo; to support international efforts to secure a cessation of violence and the disengagement of armed forces; and to help to create the conditions for serious negotiations that could achieve a lasting political settlement.[78]

Two important factors should be noted from this defense ministers meeting. By now, the focus on airpower was mounting, and the experience in Bosnia was the dominating rationale for the presumed effect of this military tool. Second, management of the crisis in Kosovo was—as Albright, Gelbard, and others had wanted since the second Contact Group meeting in late March—gradually transferred to NATO, and the defense ministers meeting somewhat fortified this notion.[79]

In a later conversation, General Naumann made some very interesting remarks. Naumann believes it was a mistake to transfer permanently the crisis management responsibility to NATO in the spring of 1998. The foreign ministers' meeting in Luxembourg of 28–29 May had started issuing threats toward Milošević, and a couple of weeks later the defense ministers had somehow felt they needed to top this by adding even more steps to the ladder of escalation.[80] The growing escalation Naumann refers to was a "slippery slope" toward war, as Tim Judah describes it: "When, by March 1999, and many more threats later, there was still no compromise, there was also no way back—and, short of a humiliating climb down, force had to be used."[81] NATO had threatened itself into a corner.

General Smith later commented that he believed NATO was pushed into this crisis management by American diplomacy. The United States had been threatening the use of NATO airpower without properly consulting NATO, and then suddenly NATO found itself having to make good threats that had already been made; many countries in NATO did not like that but felt obliged to go along out of solidarity and consideration of realpolitik.[82] Daalder and O'Hanlon say that during spring 1998 the Europeans were less inclined to use NATO to handle the crisis in Kosovo than Washington; "without a concerted effort by Washington to persuade them, it is almost certain that the Allies would not have supported the threat—or use—of force."[83]

In London on 12 June, the Contact Group issued a statement calling for a cease-fire, effective international monitoring in Kosovo, and access for United Nations High Commissioner for Refugees (UNHCR) and nongovernmental organizations. Also included were issues of refugee return and serious dialogue between Belgrade and the Kosovo Albanians, with international mediation. The Contact Group further "condemned Belgrade's massive and disproportionate use of force" but also said it would "expect the Kosovo Albanian leadership to make clear its rejection of violence and acts of terrorism."[84]

On 15 June, NATO began an air exercise called Determined Falcon. Eighty aircraft from thirteen NATO countries taking off from fifteen bases across Europe and from carriers in the Adriatic Sea flew over Albania and Macedonia in a NATO show of force announced by Secretary-General Solana on 11 June. Tim Judah described the effort as a "limp gesture because it proved nothing more than the fact that NATO had planes in the region which could fly very fast."[85] General Naumann later admitted that the order to plan and conduct an air exercise to show NATO's capability to project power rapidly into the region was ridiculous, because Milošević could see that NATO would not be able to strike within the next forty-eight hours. That was one of the first lessons Naumann learned in this conflict—never threaten something if you cannot execute it the next day or so.[86] In a Senate hearing, Naumann noted that Milošević "rightly concluded that the NATO threat was a bluff . . . and finished his summer offensive."[87]

By now, according to Daalder/O'Hanlon, there were three main obstacles in terms of developing an allied consensus on how to handle the issue of Kosovo. Some feared that the KLA would benefit from a NATO intervention against Serb forces, those who supported an intervention disagreed on how to best proceed, and "with Russia threatening a veto of any UN resolution authorizing NATO's use of force, there was considerable disagreement on what, if anything, would constitute the legal basis of a NATO decision."[88]

By June 1998, the key lessons from Bosnia had been implemented. U.S. leadership had immediately been provided, and NATO had been put in charge of the crisis management. The UN played no significant role other than providing the legal basis for the use of force. Airpower was to be the coercive instrument for altering the behavior of Milošević. The moral failures to act in Bosnia were used rhetorically to avoid a similar fate in Kosovo. Although incentives were offered Milošević to find a negotiated solution to the issue of Kosovo, the emphasis was put on the cost of not doing so. Albright, Gelbard, and Clark were all convinced that Milošević could not be persuaded to alter his behavior—thus leaving airpower as the key instrument in their coercive diplomacy.

What should be noted is Gelbard's plan to coerce Milošević, which in principle (reportedly) was supported by Albright and Clark. The notion of hitting the Ministry of Defence and the Ministry of the Interior in Belgrade—with subsequent threats to escalate dramatically—was not merely overly simplistic. It significantly exceeded the available political room to maneuver and thereby weakened the very credibility needed to coerce Milošević. There was no appetite in Washington for a unilateral U.S. endeavor, and the Europeans were certainly in no mood either to bomb governmental bodies in Belgrade or subsequently escalate dramatically. Washington, Europe, and—probably—Belgrade all knew this, and Milošević would very likely have exploited the deaths of numerous civilian and military employees to influence Western public opinion in his favor. Still, the answer according to Albright, Gelbard, and Clark lay in "sending a message" with cruise missiles and threatening with the "big stick."

To many, NATO had proven the lack of credibility with Operation Determined Falcon and its subsequent empty threats. On the world stage, the United States would prove twice in the ensuing six months that airpower and coercive diplomacy in conflicts at the lower end of the intensity spectrum did not produce the results sought. Furthermore, by late spring 1998 the United States decided to make a change in its policy toward the KLA.

Chapter 6
SHIFT IN U.S. POLICY TOWARD THE KLA— AND THE SUMMER OFFENSIVE

I may have suggested to Mahmuti [of the KLA] right away that that [Kosovo independence within three to five years] was a possibility if they handled themselves correctly.
—Richard Holbrooke [1]

In May/June 1998, a major shift of U.S. policy seems to have occurred. The KLA had been regarded more or less explicitly as terrorists by both the Contact Group and NATO during the spring of 1998—even as late as 13 June by the Contact Group—but the United States now shifted its strategy toward negotiating with the KLA.[2] Secretary Albright claims that Washington sought to strengthen the Albanian moderates by signaling only the restoring of Kosovo's autonomy and discouraging international support for the KLA, and her memoirs provide a very eloquent (official) account of why the United States could not support Kosovo independence. Still, Secretary Albright admits she had a mixed view of the fighters (KLA) and that she "sympathized with their opposition to Milošević, understood their desire for independence, and accepted that force was sometimes necessary for a just cause to prevail." By mid-June 1998 she had assessed that a political settlement without the rebels would not be possible and sent Richard Holbrooke, Christopher Hill, Robert Gelbard, and other diplomats to talk to the KLA.[3] By then, Holbrooke admits to having met KLA representatives secretly for weeks.[4]

A BBC2 television series aired in January 2003 tells an interesting story of this diplomatic endeavor.[5] The United States reportedly did not know much about the KLA at the time, so in June 1998 Ambassadors Richard Holbrooke and Christopher Hill went to Kosovo and stopped in a local village to talk to the chief. While sitting in a room with the local villagers, a man in uniform with a gun squeezed himself down beside Holbrooke, and a picture was taken. Soon the picture was in the news (*New York Times,* 26 June 1998) and provided useful publicity for the KLA, who knew that U.S. support was critical to their cause; the photograph was signaling that the United States was changing its position and was now in dialogue with the KLA. Described by the United States as an unintended mistake and manipulation by the KLA,[6] what happened one week later could hardly meet such a description. Holbrooke—using a conference as a cover—met the international spokesman of the KLA, Bardhyl Mahmuti, in Switzerland. During the meeting, according to Mahmuti, Holbrooke said that the United States would force Milošević to accept constitutional changes that would provide *independence* for Kosovo within a time frame of three to five years. When asked on camera whether he really signaled Kosovo's independence during the meeting, Holbrooke answered: "I may have suggested to Mahmuti right away that *that* was a possibility if they handled themselves correctly."[7] As the BBC2 commentator remarked, this was great news for the KLA, who after this very meeting— according to Xhavit Haliti (of the KLA)—decided to get rid of all symbols that could be associated with communism, shave off their beards, and start saluting with an open hand like the Americans, in order to become even more attractive to the Western powers. When asked later whether he believed the reason for the rather uncompromising attitude of the Kosovars (KLA) in 1998–99 was that the Kosovars had been told that their goal of independence was within reach, Knut Vollebæk, then Norwegian foreign minister and chairman in office of the OSCE, said he had the impression that signals like this were provided to the Kosovars by "an influential nation." When asked which nation he was talking about, he declined to answer, but with a barely noticeable grin stated that it was "pretty obvious who it was."[8]

When Ambassadors Christopher Hill and James Dobbins were asked the same question, Hill denied that the United States had signaled such support for Kosovo independence but added that there was a certain logic in the Balkans regarding political signals. If the world's greatest superpower did not stamp out the Albanian cause, it must be because the world's greatest superpower wanted the Albanian cause to succeed, and "signals are in the eye of the beholder, so I am sure there were people in the Balkans who believed that we did signal our support."[9] James Dobbins answered that he did not know of any such communication, but added: "Obviously there were debates in the United States, including the Congress, and there were elements within the United States and elsewhere that supported Kosovo independence, but I don't believe that the Clinton administration ever did more than say that they were prepared to act to prevent Kosovo's human rights from being suppressed."[10] However, Gelbard says he knows this promise by Holbrooke to have been given, because he himself met with the KLA leadership in Switzerland about a week *before* Holbrooke went there to talk with Mahmuti—and subsequently spoke to them *after* Holbrooke had met them—but claims the promise of independence was not the adopted U.S. policy but rather Holbrooke acting on his own.[11]

By June, the United States was well into planning for air operations in the FRY, and according to General Clark, at that point the air operations planning was a United States–only endeavor. A few important factors should be pointed out in this regard. First, the intention was to take this plan to NATO at a later stage, but the planning was done by General Jumper's staff (USEUCOM) at Ramstein Air Base, Germany.[12] When the U.S. commanders Admiral Ellis and Lieutenant General Short briefed General Clark on the U.S. developed plan in June, according to Short, Clark said, "Mike, this is a great effort, and I appreciate all that you and your people have done. I am concerned that, if we continue to plan in NATO channels, we will have problems with operation security, and the essence of our planning will end up in Paris or Belgrade papers. So I am going to take this planning effort and put it into U.S. channels only."[13]

Short added that by this the allies were largely excluded from the planning process. Even though the plan was presented to NATO in July 1998, the main planning was done in Ramstein. Second, the intention of General Clark was that this air operation would be (a) *coercive* in nature in the sense that it would coerce Milošević to give in due to his losses; it was (b) intended to strike Serb forces on the ground in order to slow or halt ethnic cleansing; it was (c) intended to deter a wider conflict; and (d) it was following the (coercive) model of Bosnia.[14] Third, when Clark asked Jumper how long it would take to destroy Milošević's air defense system, he pointed out it was hard to tell but indicated that it could take anything from a few days to about a week.[15]

After Milošević gathered the Main Board of his party (the SPS) in Belgrade (10 June), the Serb presence in the Drenica Valley was reduced and the Serbs were no longer on the offensive. Fueled by Western rhetoric and NATO threats, KLA morale was boosted, and a recurring pattern emerged. When the Serbs withdrew, the KLA moved in and filled the vacuum—and provoked new Serb crackdowns. Armed KLA attacks occurred in June and July, which were to have very significant impact on the war in Kosovo. On 23 June one KLA commander seized the Serbian coal mine of Belaćevac, which the Serbs retook after six days. In a similar event on 15 July, the KLA attacked the Trepča mine. By now the situation was being dictated by events on the ground. The Serbs had their revenge when they ambushed some seven hundred men returning from Albania with weapons and ammunition. The second KLA attack of significance happened during the same day the Serbian ambush took place (18 July), when the KLA stormed the town of Orahovac.[16] According to BBC2, during their summer offensive the KLA killed some eighty policemen and sixty civilians.[17] By now, many Europeans and some in the United States were questioning the policy of backing what many regarded as a band of armed thugs in Kosovo and publicly stated that they did not want NATO to become the air force of the KLA.[18]

The town of Orahovac was back in Serbian hands after four days, but by now a Serbian counteroffensive occurred. Sweeping through Drenica, burning and looting, the Serbs caused thousands of Kosovars to flee their homes. At the end of July, the political directors of the British, Austrian, and German foreign ministries visited both Kosovo and Belgrade. Their travel through Kosovo was not interfered with by Serbian authorities, who allowed the three individuals to see the Serb offensive and its devastation up front. When later visiting Belgrade, Milošević denied that they had seen the real situation, to which the British member (Emyr Jones Parry) replied, "Mr. President, it is either that your people are not telling you of the things we have seen or you are ignoring them. . . . [I]f you carry on like this the British government will take military action against you within six months."[19]

It is interesting to note this statement by Jones Parry, because in a later conversation, General Naumann pointed out that the United Kingdom played a leading European role in terms of dealing forcefully with the issue of Kosovo. The British pushed hard for the humanitarian issue of the conflict—perhaps also due to legal considerations. Without a humanitarian reason, there was no legal basis for employing British forces.[20] Daalder and O'Hanlon say after June 1998 the British government argued strongly for the use of force, believing that the only thing that would change the mind of Milošević was military action in and over Kosovo itself, and suggested that NATO should consider deploying peacekeepers to enforce an agreement once reached with the parties involved.[21] If the Clinton administration was significantly influenced by its Bosnia experience when approaching Kosovo, so was Britain. Perceived as somewhat reactive and reluctant to use force in Bosnia, it now wanted a forceful approach in Kosovo should Milošević continue his heavy-handed treatment of the Kosovars. According to Daalder, Britain wanted to lead the effort in a firm way: "It [Britain] doesn't want to do what it did in Bosnia, in which British policy was to wait, to halt, and to put a brake on any development that might lead [to] increasing use of force. In this case, Britain was committed."[22] This notion was somewhat confirmed by General Smith, who feels it is fair to say that the main line of communication and resolve between the United States and the European allies ran through London.[23]

In July and August, the U.S. air operation plan (Phased Air Operations Plan)—together with ten preventive deployments and four forced intrusions using ground forces—was presented to NATO. The diplomats in Brussels, acting on behalf of and in constant coordination with their various capitals, felt the air operations plan was too large and too threatening. They did not like striking anything close to Belgrade and wanted a more limited approach. The NAC was not particularly interested in the forced-entry (ground force) options but rather encouraged the planners to refine the preventive deployment options as well as the air operation plan. The lack of authorization of the use of force by the UN Security Council contributed to the European reluctance to take this step, and due to this feedback from the allies, it was agreed to plan for a limited air operation as well, an operation without manned aircraft—using cruise missiles only.[24] Many NATO nations did not have any appetite for any forceful approach whatsoever, much less what would probably turn into a bloody forced entry on the ground.

By early August, the Serb heavy-handed counteroffensive generated television pictures of some of the estimated two hundred thousand Kosovars who had fled their homes into the woods and mountains. Although Serbian authorities claimed they now had control of Kosovo, their strategic ambitions were being damaged, because the international television crews had turned the Serb offensive into a complete disaster—the unfavorable publicity was galvanizing Western opinion in favor of doing "something." As Tim Judah metaphorically writes: "Despite having inflicted undoubted reverses on the KLA, they had in fact tumbled, like a lumbering giant, into a vast trap."[25] NATO estimates that the fighting between the KLA and Serbian military and police forces during this period resulted in the deaths of over 1,500 Kosovar Albanians. Rather than suppress the Kosovars, the Serbian attack led to steadily increasing Kosovar support for violent resistance to the Serbian effort, weakening the Kosovar moderates and bolstering the KLA.[26]

Another event with ramifications for the issue of Kosovo took place in August 1998. On 20 August Operation Infinite Reach commenced, sending some seventy-nine cruise missiles from U.S. ships in the Red and Arabian seas toward Sudan and Afghanistan. The attack was a response to the bombing of the American embassies in Kenya and Tanzania on 7 August, which had killed 220 people, of whom twelve were Americans, while injuring almost five thousand Africans and Americans.[27] Besides, perhaps, sending a political signal that the United States could strike at will, the operation was short, limited, and, according to Daalder and O'Hanlon, did not "achieve core U.S. strategic objectives . . . since the Bin Laden network [al-Qaeda] remained intact and, by all accounts, poised to strike again."[28] What should be noted from this incident is the tendency of the Clinton administration to believe in the coercive effect of airpower; the conceptual simplicity of the effort, the lack of political will to pursue the chosen course, and the lack of political result on the matter; the signal this event sent to Belgrade, Iraq, and other defined "rough" states; and that this was in fact a larger operation than envisaged in NATO's limited air operation, which was considered the preferable option in NATO at the time.

The escalating conflict in Kosovo was of grave concern to the international community, particularly the humanitarian consequences and the risk of its spreading to other countries in the region. On 2 September during a Clinton summit meeting with Boris Yeltsin of Russia, Secretary Albright and Russian foreign minister Ivanov issued a joint statement on Kosovo calling for negotiations and an end to the Serb offensive.[29]

What is interesting to note, according to Judah, is that by now it seemed clear that neither the Serbs nor the KLA *wanted*—or believed it possible—to live together, and that hence a negotiated solution was almost impossible.[30] The Serbs felt they were under attack from the terrorist KLA and they had every right (even duty) to suppress the rebellion and search out the insurgents—particularly in Kosovo, which represented the historical foundation of modern Serbia. The Albanians argued that they had lived in Kosovo for centuries and were now the area's overwhelming majority. The province had been stripped of its autonomy in 1989, had been subject to repression for close to a decade, and by fall 1998 was suffering tremendously, due to the disproportionately violent response of Serb authorities to the KLA attacks. These had forced hundreds of thousands to flee their homes and killed hundreds. A solution short of the prospect of independence would not suffice.[31]

The question, according to Tim Judah, was rather how the international community could force the Serbs and Albanians to accept a solution in which both groups lived together in Kosovo.[32] Also, even as the situation on the ground was deteriorating, with civilians suffering and disaster impending, could the international community use force against a sovereign country that had not attacked any of them in an effort to try to end the civilian suffering? Would it be acceptable to use force without a UN Security Council mandate? According to Daalder and O'Hanlon, the NATO members agreed that Kosovo was an integral part of Serbia and should remain so. Hence, independence was not an option. This was also due to the previously mentioned fear of producing a precedent for other violent radical groups in their own countries. A partition of Kosovo into a Serb part and a Kosovar Albanian part was opposed by both the United States and its allies because of the situation in Bosnia. With the Dayton Accords insisting on not partitioning Bosnia—in which case the Republika Srpska would probably join Serbia—a partition of Kosovo would send a terrible signal to the fragile peace in Bosnia. Therefore, the option left was the autonomy of Kosovo, which neither the Serbs nor the Kosovars favored.[33]

Some argued that since the Serb offensive was putting down an armed uprising within Serbia, it was an internal affair and force could not be authorized without a UN mandate. The British government, however, argued that this humanitarian emergency still needed to be addressed, and said, "In the exceptional circumstances of Kosovo . . . a limited use of force was justifiable in support of purposes laid down by the Security Council but without the Council's expressed authorisation when that was the only means to avert an immediate and overwhelming catastrophe."[34] The secretary-general of the UN, Kofi Annan, arguably captured the dilemma using another historical example: "If, in those dark days and hours leading up to the genocide [in Rwanda], a coalition of states had been prepared to act in defense of the Tutsi population, but did not receive prompt Council authorization, should such a coalition have stood aside and allowed the horror to unfold?"[35] The question was really, at which point does a country cross a certain undefined line in its violent handling of a domestic situation, at which the humanitarian situation becomes so grave that it triggers an international response? As Tim Judah points out, no one knew the answer, and the issue was at the core of contemporary debate about the development of international law.[36]

By the end of summer 1998, the United States had sent clear signals of support to the KLA—further distancing itself from Belgrade and Milošević. NATO had continued issuing threats but was reluctant to put any credibility behind them. Fearful of the effect on domestic public opinion, NATO politicians and diplomats focused on the limited air operation, which involved a relatively small number of cruise missiles—even though the effect of such limited military effort was at best highly questionable. The effort could hardly have been further away from the Powell Doctrine and decisive force, and it represented what Powell had developed a strong distaste for—military efforts to send a "signal" to the adversary without a thoroughly agreed strategy as a foundation. Political pragmatism rather than military principles dominated NATO's crisis management, and clear objectives were absent.

Chapter 7
NATO THREATENS WITH AIR STRIKES
Silence before the Storm

We did not have adequate firepower for larger operations, but we could provoke the Serbs by using snipers. Our intention was to get NATO to intervene as fast as possible.
—Remi (KLA commander) [1]

In September, the U.S. resolve to deal with Milošević's heavy-handed treatment of the Kosovar Albanians was hardening. In a meeting with Secretary Cohen in Washington, General Clark argued that the need was urgent to respond to the expulsion of Kosovar Albanians, that NATO was losing credibility by not preventing it, and that the upcoming meeting in Portugal with NATO's defense ministers was the key opportunity to influence the Europeans. Cohen pointed out that he doubted that the Europeans would support a strong threat against Milošević, saying that as far as he was concerned, it was time for the Europeans to make up their minds on this issue. As Clark pointed out, the meeting showed that the transatlantic relationship was already suffering.[2] Secretary Cohen and General Clark discussed the need for an interagency diplomatic team like the one ending the war in Bosnia and the importance of coordinating the diplomatic effort. Secretary Albright was also arguing at this time for a concerted strategy to end Milošević's rule in Belgrade. She understood why for pragmatic reasons Milošević was necessary in the Dayton negotiations but now admits that she never trusted Milošević and thought he should be removed from office in order to help Yugoslavia transfer into a peaceful Europe. Together with continuous murky news reports from Kosovo, her view gained ground, and President Clinton approved a strategy to support alternatives to Milošević by overt public means. The United States decided to push for a clear-cut Alliance decision on Kosovo.[3] According to Secretary Albright, the American strategy at this point was "to compel Milošević to halt his offensive and reduce the number of Serb security forces in Kosovo to the level that existed before the violence began. Milošević also had to agree to negotiate seriously with the Albanians to develop interim arrangements on autonomy. If he did not take these steps, NATO would launch a sustained campaign of strikes against Serb positions in Kosovo and Serbia itself."[4]

Secretary Albright points out that she knew she could not count on the UN Security Council for the explicit authorization of force but wanted an endorsement of the political objectives. On 23 September the Security Council (with China abstaining) passed Resolution 1199, which called for a cease-fire and improvement of the humanitarian situation, urged the parties to enter a dialogue for a political solution to the issue of Kosovo, and demanded that the FRY immediately implement a series of measures. These were a cease-fire, withdrawal of FRY security forces, enablement of effective and continuous international monitoring in Kosovo, return of refugees and the internally displaced, access for NGOs and humanitarian organizations, and rapid progress toward a timetable and dialogue with the Kosovar Albanians in search of a political solution.[5]

The day after the UN resolution, the defense ministers of NATO met in Portugal (Villa Mora) to discuss how they could put force behind it. NATO's secretary-general, Javier Solana, opened the session by arguing for NATO involvement, claiming the Serb actions were mocking the Alliance, and famously stating that Milošević's motto seemed to be, "A village a day keeps NATO away."[6] Gen. Klaus Naumann was the next speaker, followed by General Clark; both argued for NATO resolve. Secretary of Defense Cohen argued along the same lines, calling Serb actions a challenge to NATO's credibility and urging NATO to issue an activation warning (ACTWARN).[7] France was worried about these threats of air strikes, but according to General Naumann, the United Kingdom was quite clear that the UN was not an organization that could put force behind its wishes and argued eloquently and forcefully that NATO could. In this way, according to General Naumann: "The British built a bridge with their arguments on which the rest of the NATO alliance could walk across together."[8] In this context what Richard Holbrooke stated about the international community and its relations is interesting: "On the one hand you have us [the United States] and on the other you have the French. Then you have the Germans who usually go to us, reluctantly. Thus, Britain is often the key to NATO decision making."[9]

The defense ministers agreed on limiting their statement to ACTWARN, and on 24 September, Secretary-General Solana issued a statement that began, "Just a few moments ago, the North Atlantic Council approved the issuing of an ACT WARN (Activation Warning) for both a limited air option and a phased air campaign in Kosovo."[10] NATO had agreed to begin the formal buildup and preparation of forces to conduct air strikes, and Solana now made clear what Milošević needed to do to avoid air strikes: "This Resolution makes it clear what President Milošević must do: he must stop his repressive actions against the population, he must seek a political solution to the Kosovo crisis based on negotiations, as must the Kosovar Albanians, and he must take immediate steps to alleviate the humanitarian situation."[11]

It is interesting to note the timing and content of both the UN resolution and the NATO activation warning, which coincided with the initial U.S. strategy described by Secretary Albright and General Clark in their memoirs. Both indicate the level of political influence the United States possessed in general, and in terms of Kosovo in particular.

In response to the NATO decision, Milošević gathered his Supreme Defense Council. Momčilo Perišić (then army chief of staff) expressed his belief that NATO *would* bomb if UN Resolution 1999 were not obeyed. According to Milo Djukanović (president of Montenegro) who attended the meeting, this tone did not suit Milošević. Neither did he think Milošević actually believed that the international community was ready to put its threats into action. According to Djukanović, Milošević stated at the meeting: "So what? First they bomb, and then peace resumes. They bomb for about 5–7 days, and then the international community mobilizes. NATO is forced to stop their actions, and we become the moral winners."[12] A few weeks later, in November 1998, Momčilo Perišić—who for a long time had been reluctant to be dragged into the Kosovo issue because he felt it to be a police rather than a military job to seek out the KLA, and because he believed fighting the KLA would lead to NATO military action—was replaced by a hard-liner, Gen. Dragoljub Ojdanić.[13]

The comment made by Milošević during the meeting in the Supreme Defense Council is of particular interest. As noted in chapter 2, Thomas C. Schelling has pointed out that the power to hurt is a bargaining power. It is anticipation of more damage to come that coerces the enemy, thus making credibility the pivotal issue. The comment by Milošević shows that at the time he simply did not perceive NATO's threats as credible, thus rendering the key element in NATO's coercive diplomacy largely impotent. It also reveals a significant part of Milošević's strategy. That is, he would play the underdog against the powerful NATO alliance, and, with NATO acting without UN authorization, he knew that European public opinion particularly would question the legality of the operation. Thus, once televised pictures began to appear of NATO bombs causing suffering and casualties, it would be a matter of time before the bombing had to stop. Those arguing for more decisive force apparently did not fully comprehend this logic, which was accessible to anyone who read official newspapers in the various NATO countries. The opposition was significant in most European countries, perhaps most notably in Germany, Italy, and Greece. Everyone in NATO knew that the will to begin a sustained air operation against the FRY would be extremely hard to muster—and so did Milošević.

At the end of September another incident occurred that was to have severe consequences. Fighting broke out near the town of Gornje Obrinje, and at least fourteen Serbian policemen were killed. According to Human Rights Watch, the Serb Special Police Forces retaliated by killing some twenty-one civilians on 26 September. Five of the victims were children between eighteen months and nine years. On the same day, some kilometers away from Gornje Obrinje, some fourteen men were randomly selected from a crowd of several thousand. They were abused for several hours, and later thirteen of them were executed.[14]

The *New York Times* printed a grotesque picture of one of the victims of the massacres at Gornje Obrinje on its front page, and at a subsequent National Security Council meeting in the White House Situation Room on 30 September the picture was lying on the table, reminding everyone of the gravity of the situation. When she looked at the horrible picture, Secretary Albright perceived this to be Milošević's response to the UN and NATO statements made a week earlier. She thought of the several hundred thousand killed in Bosnia and felt that a repetition could not be allowed.[15] According to Daalder and O'Hanlon, National Security Adviser Sandy Berger said the massacre at Gornje Obrinje—with the subsequent pictures and media focus—represented a crossing of the "atrocities threshold."[16]

During this meeting, a recommendation (later approved) was made to President Clinton to send Holbrooke to Belgrade, and a decision to press ahead for NATO action was taken. The day after—on 1 October—NATO's North Atlantic Council issued an activation request (ACTREQ) for both a limited air option and a phased air campaign in Kosovo.[17] Four days later, the UN released a Security Council report on FRY compliance, with the provisions of UNSCRs 1160 and 1199. The report stated:

> In the week following the adoption, on 23 September 1998, of Resolution 1199 (1998), the forces in fact intensified their operations, launching another offensive in the Drenica region and in the Suva Reka–Stimlje-Urosevac triangle. Those operations have reportedly resulted in the displacement of some 20,000 additional people. . . . Fighting continued on 28 and 29 September, contrary to the statement of the Serbian Prime Minister, Mr. Marjanović, on 28 September, that anti-insurgency operations in Kosovo had been completed and that peace reigned in Kosovo.[18]

The very critical report continued, over the signature of Secretary-General Annan, "I am outraged by reports of mass killings of civilians in Kosovo, which recall the atrocities committed in Bosnia and Herzegovina," but it also noted: "While the victims of the conflict are overwhelmingly ethnic Albanians, Kosovo Serbs are suffering as well. There have been a number of reports of the kidnapping and killing of Serbian and Albanian civilians by Kosovo Albanian paramilitary units." The UN secretary-general referred to one of the conclusions of the Contact Group meeting held on 2 October, which stated, "We all concluded that time is running out," and he declared his support of this perception. This report contributed to the American decision to ask NATO to escalate further and push for the activation order (ACTORD) of both a limited air option and a phased air campaign in Kosovo.[19]

By now, with the television pictures of the Serb counteroffensive seen worldwide, the new German chancellor, Gerhard Schröder, somewhat reluctantly told President Clinton that he would support bombing. The French signaled their support on 6 October, when Jacques Chirac stated that "the humanitarian situation constitutes a ground that can justify an exception to the rule . . . and if it appeared that the situation required it, then France would not hesitate to join those who would like to intervene in order to assist those who are in danger."[20]

On 8 October, Secretary Albright attended a meeting in Brussels with representatives from the NATO Alliance in which she energetically argued for the authorization of the use of force. In a statement afterward, she pointed out that "one of the keys to good diplomacy is knowing when diplomacy has reached its limits. And we are rapidly reaching that point now."[21] On the same day, a Contact Group meeting was convened at Heathrow Airport outside London (Secretary Albright came directly from the meeting in Brussels) that was to become one of the most significant events in the international community's resolve to deal with the situation in Kosovo. The foreign ministers discussed the use of force and whether a UN mandate was needed. Britain, France, and Germany wanted one, but the Russian foreign minister, Ivanov, was clear: "If you take it to the UN, we'll veto it." The subject was forcefully debated, but at one point Ivanov, questioned by the German foreign minister, Klaus Kinkel, said, "I just told you, Klaus, we'll veto it. . . . If you don't we'll just make a lot of noise . . . saying it was all foreshadowed. The Russians can't do anything. NATO is the power." According to Tim Judah, "What had just taken place, then, was a watershed. The Russians had, in effect, told NATO that it would do nothing [but make public noise] if it [NATO] were to bomb."[22]

The Contact Group decided to send Richard Holbrooke back to Belgrade to secure an agreement to the requirements of Resolution 1199, and he spent the next days talking to Milošević and the Kosovar Albanians. On the same day, NATO approved a plan for the phased air operation (called OPLAN 10601, Allied Force), and with this plan Holbrooke possessed increased leverage over Milošević. Lieutenant General Short was asked to travel with Holbrooke to Belgrade. During the meeting Milošević said to Short, "So you're the one who will bomb us," to which Short famously replied something he had rehearsed on his way to Belgrade: "I've B-52s in one hand and U-2 surveillance spy planes in the other. It's up to you which I'm going to use." Another observation by General Short is also interesting. During the negotiations with Holbrooke and Milošević, he was asked to join Holbrooke and Milošević separately to discuss the issue of the Serb surface-to-air missile systems (SA-3 and SA-6). NATO aircraft would be allowed to overfly Kosovo and monitor the situation, but Milošević was reluctant to move these missile systems, because, he argued, it would be a logistical nightmare to do so. Lieutenant General Short told Milošević, in explicit terms, that he had watched the Serbs move their SA-6 systems every day for the last six weeks, to which Milošević replied: "You are right. I will move the missiles." The striking part is not so much Milošević's reply but Short's conclusion about Milošević: "If you hit that man hard, slapped him upside the head, he'd pay attention."[23] This general perception of Milošević as a man who would quickly buckle if posed with a threat would be a decisive factor in shaping the OAF air campaign a few months later.

Holbrooke continued his negotiations with Milošević during the next few days. Both Germany and Italy changed governments during the fall of 1998, and the new governments were more inclined to support NATO. Holbrooke asked NATO in a late-night NAC meeting to move toward an activation order to provide even more diplomatic leverage.[24] On 13 October NATO issued the formal activation order to maintain pressure on Milošević. Secretary-General Solana stated,

> Ambassador Holbrooke reported that there has been progress. He stressed that the process was largely due to the pressure of the Alliance in the last few days and that we have to maintain this pressure in order to ensure that the process continues. In response, just a few moments ago, the North Atlantic Council decided to issue activation orders—ACTORDs—for both limited air strikes and a phased air campaign in Yugoslavia, execution of which will begin in approximately 96 hours.[25]

The statement ended simply: "The responsibility is on President Milošević's shoulders. He knows what he has to do."[26] What should be noted is that SACEUR was ordered not to execute the limited air operation for ninety-six hours and that further suspension would have to be voted by the NAC. A few hours after the NATO activation order was issued, Holbrooke announced that he and Milošević had a deal. The deal included a two-thousand-man OSCE ground verification presence (Kosovo Verification Mission [KVM]) and a NATO air surveillance mission to monitor FRY compliance with UNSCR 1199 (by which there would be no Serb aircraft in Kosovo airspace when surveillance missions were ongoing, and all air defense systems — except early-warning radars — would be removed from the area or placed in cantonment sites). It also included a commitment to cease attacks on civilians, to withdraw some of the security forces from Kosovo, to grant access for humanitarian relief agencies, and to allow refugees and displaced persons to return to their homes.[27]

In addition, a unilateral statement was issued by Milošević on 13 October that included a number of key principles that could form the framework of a peace settlement, including substantial autonomy, elections, and a local Kosovar police force. A political solution was to be achieved by 2 November, and general agreements on the rules and procedures of elections were to be in place by 9 November (neither of the ambitions were to be achieved, however).[28]

The activation order had its effect, and according to Zoran Lilić (former president of Yugoslavia) Milošević by now was clearly worried that the bombing attacks could be executed in the near future.[29] The agreement on the OSCE's KVM was formally signed on 16 October, endorsed by the UN Security Council (Resolution 1203) on 24 October, and established by the OSCE Permanent Council Decision 263 on 25 October. The primary mission of the KVM was to ensure FRY compliance with UN Security Council Resolutions 1160 and 1199.[30]

Resolution 1203, although concerned with the humanitarian situation in Kosovo, welcomed the air verification mission and the KVM but insisted "that the Kosovo Albanian leadership condemn all terrorist actions, demands that such actions cease immediately and emphasizes that all elements in the Kosovo Albanian community should pursue their goals by peaceful means only."[31]

Immediately after issuing NATO's activation order, a number of high-ranking officials (Secretary-General Solana, Gen. Klaus Naumann, Gen. Wesley Clark, and U.S. envoys Richard Holbrook and Christopher Hill) went to Belgrade to point out the seriousness of the situation, and according to General Clark, the pressure provided by NATO undoubtedly created political leverage over Milošević. In one of these meetings Milošević told Clark and General Naumann: "You know, General Clark, we know how to handle the problems with these Albanian killers. . . . We have done this before [in] Drenica 1946. . . . We kill them, all of them."[32]

By 27 October the NAC found that the FRY compliance was such that execution of the limited air operation and the phased air operation could be suspended. It is important to note, however, that the NAC did not cancel the activation orders. Both air operations would remain in place but would require an explicit NAC decision for execution. Remembering the UN hostage situation in Bosnia in 1995, NATO deployed its first combat troops to the area (the NATO Extraction Force in the former Yugoslav Republic of Macedonia [FYROM]) to extract the KVM should it become necessary.[33]

It is worth noting, in terms of the British role in this conflict, that during the negotiations leading up to the October agreement the United Kingdom (and one other minor European nation) was willing to put ground troops as armed peacekeepers in Kosovo. However, no one else shared this view at that time.[34] Before the October agreement negotiations, Secretary Cohen had explicitly told Holbrooke that the United States and NATO would not provide any peacekeepers in Kosovo, and when the French offered to provide leadership for the two-thousand-troop Extraction Force, the United States insisted on leaving this issue to the Europeans.[35]

The October agreement, according to Secretary Albright, was important in the sense that it allowed hundreds of thousands of people to come home from the hills before winter, reinforced the perception that Kosovo was an international problem, established a set of formal obligations for which Milošević could be held accountable, and, perhaps most importantly, merely suspended, not withdrew, the NATO authorization of force.[36] Holbrooke himself points out that the October agreement was a response to "an emergency inside a crisis"—pointing to the potential military confrontation (emergency) and therefore bringing a solution to the source of the problem (crisis), notably the political issues that caused the tragedy in Kosovo.[37]

The critics of the October agreement, however, say that it revealed the indecisiveness of the international community and showed the nations preferred to push the final reckoning as far into the future as possible, rather than push hard for an immediate and lasting solution to the conflict in Kosovo. Neither did it have a mechanism for dealing with the parties if they did not comply with the agreement. To Robert Gelbard, the October agreement proved what he had perceived since the violence erupted, that Milošević had no intention of negotiating a diplomatic solution to the issue of Kosovo.[38]

The October agreement had at least one additional significant flaw, that it put pressure only on Belgrade—the KLA was never asked to sign on to the cease-fire. As a BBC2 commentator pointed out, the KLA accepted this "gift" from the international community and did not try to hide its intentions. Remi (the commander of the KLA, according to BBC2) explained on camera: "It was even more than we hoped for. Almost no Serb troops left. Then we could go in and conduct operations."[39] It meant that the agreement allowed the KLA to fill the vacuum once the Serb forces withdrew and gave them a chance to reorganize, rearm, and—as they said themselves—prepare for the spring offensive.[40] It was a familiar pattern: it was quite clear that Belgrade was concerned by the activity of the KLA, and given the previously mentioned reports and statements by the UN, NATO, the Contact Group, and OSCE all through 1998, it had good reasons for its concern.

That, therefore, makes it even odder that the KLA was not even included when negotiating the October agreement. Three possible explanations should be mentioned. First, the scope of the agreement, according to Holbrooke, was not to get a political solution but to prevent a military confrontation over the issue of Kosovo. Second, Holbrooke claims there was no concerted Albanian leadership to negotiate with at the time, Third, after the October agreement, according to Braca Grubačić (editor of Belgrade's English-language *VIP* newsletter), Milošević was under the impression that Holbrooke had promised to close the border to Albania to prevent arms smuggling, freeze KLA assets, and make arrangements to terminate KLA influence. When this did not happen, he became angry and felt betrayed by Holbrooke. This was also asserted by Daalder and O'Hanlon, who say that when the KLA moved in and took advantage of the Serb withdrawal, Milošević believed he had been double-crossed by Holbrooke and NATO. This fortified his belief that he had to deal with the KLA on his own and put into effect a plan both to deal with the KLA and to change the ethnic balance of Kosovo.[41]

It should also be noted that the OSCE presence (the KVM) had not initially been discussed with either NATO allies or the OSCE in advance,[42] illustrating the U.S. influence in the matter and the somewhat unconcerted nature of the effort by the international community. In fact, when discussing the matter later, the chairman in office of OSCE at the time, Knut Vollebæk, admitted that he was never informed about the content of Holbrooke's October agreement, despite bringing this issue up with the Americans several times. This became a problem when Vollebæk spoke to Milošević on matters concerning OSCE and KVM, because Milošević would simply say, "No, that was not what I agreed with Mr. Holbrooke."[43]

According to General Clark, when the October agreement was negotiated and Milošević had to pull back, Milošević argued that he was within two weeks of finishing off the KLA.[44] This contributes to the perception that the number of KLA hard-line activists was still relatively limited, indicates the nature of the strategy with which Milošević opted to handle the issue, and could help explain why Milošević decided to challenge NATO in March 1999. He had good reason to believe that the air campaign would not be sustained, considering the U.S. missile operations against Osama Bin Laden during summer 1998, U.S. and British air strikes against Iraq in December 1998, and the well-known reluctance by several NATO countries even to begin limited air strikes in the period leading up to OAF. He might be able to have his "two weeks" to root out the KLA insurgents before a cease-fire was established. In that case he could portray a bombing pause and further negotiations as a victory.

A covert attempt to oust Milošević from power—reportedly authorized by President Clinton in September—was well under way by October. Robert Gelbard says he initiated contact with the Serb opposition in Serbia and Montenegro, and by fall 1998 he had conducted more than half a dozen meetings with Montenegro's President Djukanović and Serbian oppositional leaders like Vuk Drašković and Zoran Gingic in Montenegro, the Hague, and other places. In October, Gelbard met with a high-ranking Serb general—together with Brig. Gen. George Casey—for three hours and tried to make him "start a coup or something" to oust Milošević from power, but he refused to do so. Gelbard points out that because the opposition elements were all fighting each other, the ambition was to develop a common position so they could work together and present a unified front. It turned out not to be possible. What is significant is that some of these meetings were reported in the Serb press and so could have increased Milošević's fear that the United States was planning to oust him from power.[45]

The international community's interaction with the KLA is a particularly interesting saga. According to Remi, the KLA received support from some KVM verifiers: "They gave us their maps. It was just what we needed. Any army has to be able to orient itself in the terrain."[46] Later, according to Jakub Krasniqi (KLA spokesman), the KLA aided NATO in its bombing campaign by assisting their targeting effort.[47] After the war a NATO military official admitted, "We always said NATO would never serve as the KLA's air force, but they [KLA] ended up serving as our surrogate army."[48] In fact, according to the *Washington Post*, the CIA had a close relationship with the KLA, as did other European covert forces, and during the war a secret operations center was set up in the Albanian border town of Kukes. One U.S. official reportedly involved in the cooperation with the KLA stated: "Let's just say there was a growing appreciation for what the KLA could do for us."[49] Kåre

Eltervåg, who was the political adviser to the head of KVM, William Walker, says he was surprised by how the great nations (particularly the United States and the United Kingdom) operated as parties in the conflict under the OSCE's neutral umbrella. Not only did they provide maps to the KLA, but as the KVM left, "some nations" left behind communications equipment that the KLA later used to provide NATO with map references, assisting bombing missions and battle-damage assessment.[50]

The deputy head of mission/chief of staff for the Kosovo Verification Mission, Maj. Gen. Bjørn Nygård, shared Eltervåg's perception.[51] Eltervåg personally witnessed this communication from Macedonia after the war had started, and as he later reflected, "It was like some of the powerful nations had foreseen what was to come, and decided that this was one of few opportunities to get intelligence information out of Kosovo when the war finally started. For all practical purposes, this activity largely reduced the integrity of the OSCE which was needed in order to play a significant role as an international body in Kosovo after the war."[52]

In fact, not only was this a low-level covert intelligence endeavor but high-level KLA officials were seen within NATO's military headquarters (SHAPE) in Belgium;[53] General Smith later admitted that NATO allied itself with the KLA.[54] General Kelche shared this point of view. Kelche pointed out that although the Americans did not like to speak about their cooperation with the KLA, out of fear of publicity and the unmasking of their sources, he felt it was a militarily sound relationship and provided very useful information that was fed into the operations planning.[55]

According to Eltervåg, the KVM mission was difficult, for several reasons. The Serb perspective was that this was not a humanitarian issue or a violation of human rights but an internal fight over territory and should be treated as such. Therefore, the KVM presence represented an unwarranted international presence in the area. The Albanians, however, initially welcomed this international presence, but as time went on, by December 1998–January 1999, something changed in the Albanians' perception. As the crisis deepened, the KVM lost significance and seemed to be left behind by other, more influential international actors. Eltervåg's perception was that the KLA strategy was to provoke the Serbs in order to trigger forcible retaliation, which in turn would provoke the international community and lead to NATO involvement.[56] Major General Nygård later stated that he had exactly the same perception.[57] This view was later confirmed by Remi, who on camera did not conceal the KLA's ultimate goal: "We did not have adequate firepower for larger operations, but we could provoke the Serbs by using snipers. Our intention was to get NATO to intervene as fast as possible."[58]

Between the October agreement and Christmas, a UN report stated that some 150 civilian Serbs had been kidnapped by the KLA, and even Albanian LDK activists were targeted by the KLA.[59] Interestingly, Nygård points out that the international community seemed to have demonized the Serbs as the source of problems for so long that anything the KLA did in this period was perceived as more or less legitimate resistance by the weaker party. According to him, within the KVM in this period the French and German perception of the situation was significantly more objective than that of the United States and Britain.[60] According to the UN, Serb authorities had detained some 1,500–2,000 Albanians between the October agreement and Christmas 1998.[61] Richard Holbrooke later stated that "the KLA was arming, the KLA taking very provocative steps in an effort to draw the west into the crisis. That was ultimately successful, the Serbs were playing right into the KLA's hands by committing atrocity after atrocity, way overreacting, wiping out entire villages, outrageous actions which had to be responded to."[62]

What should be noted in terms of the international diplomatic effort to find a solution to the issue of Kosovo is, first, that during the summer of 1998 the highest-profile diplomat in the Balkans, representing the most powerful nation in the world, Richard Holbrooke, had told the KLA that independence was within reach; second, that the KLA was not included in the October agreement that provided KLA tactical leverage on the ground in Kosovo; and third, that some of the great powers—through their national representatives in OSCE's KVM—were providing maps and communication equipment to the KLA. This signal of support could hardly be missed, and it would be fair to argue that this must have boosted the KLA's morale, speeded up its desire for further international involvement (i.e., by NATO), and deepened its belief that independence was within reach. In other words, the KLA had nothing to lose from the ongoing process.

Another incident happened in December 1998 that was to have impact on the Serb perception of the threat of an allied air campaign. On 31 October 1998, Iraq decided to ban almost all UN inspections, which prompted U.S. and British military planners to prepare for air operations aimed at altering Saddam Hussein's decision. According to the Congressional Research Service, a four-day air operation called Operation Desert Fox, commencing on 16 December, flew 650 sorties, dropped more than six hundred bombs on Iraqi military and logistical facilities, and launched 415 missiles.[63] According to Daalder and O'Hanlon, neither this nor the air strikes aimed at Osama Bin Laden some four months earlier had achieved core U.S. strategic objectives: "These generally unsuccessful attacks did little to enhance the credibility of

United States. They were designed more to punish, and to 'send a message,' than to compel an adversary to change his behavior or directly achieve concrete strategic objectives."[64]

In fact, when OAF commenced in March 1999, these incidents and use of limited Western airpower influenced the Serb expectations as to how severe the NATO attacks would be, should it ever come to that.[65] About one month before OAF commenced, FRY officials went to Baghdad in what the Pentagon believed to be a collaboration between the two nations, in order to provide the FRY with intelligence data on U.S./British air strikes.[66] In conversations with Serb officials before OAF, General Nygård received information that Serbia was not impressed by the bombing of Iraq and because of this did not fear the level of bombing NATO was likely to exert.[67]

In a *New York Times* article, Tim Weiner and Jane Perlez said that it had become a Clinton doctrine to use airpower to try to coerce political change abroad at little or no risk to American soldiers; they deemed it "cruise missile diplomacy." The air attacks on Iraq, they said, "did little or nothing to undermine President Saddam Hussein," and the Sudan/Afghanistan attacks "created mostly disbelief among allies and defiance in the Islamic world."[68] For the second time in four months the Clinton administration had chosen a limited use of airpower in a low-intensity conflict, had not achieved its desired political results, and likely had reduced its credibility in the process. Paralleling the two efforts, NATO threatened and planned for a similar approach. In his Supreme Defense Council meeting, Milošević had signaled he did not believe the NATO threat to be credible, and Operation Desert Fox was likely to bolster his perception.

In November 1998, another incident contributed to Milošević's calculations. French officials said one of their military officers, Maj. Pierre Bunel, had passed secret NATO war plans to Milošević during the October cease-fire in Kosovo. The leaks reportedly included details of which areas NATO planned to bomb if the crisis led to air strikes.[69] The French major was later found guilty of the charges and sentenced to jail for two years but claimed he had been acting under the orders of French intelligence services.[70] NATO was gradually losing its credibility, and the politicians and the military officers in the Alliance knew it.

In mid-December Serb forces killed thirty-one (thirty-six, according to Tim Judah) members of the KLA as they were crossing the border from Albania. A few hours later ethnic Albanians shot six Serb teenagers in a Kosovo bar. Five thousand Serbs attended their funeral, and several thousands rallied in Priština to protest the killings. Two days later a Serb official was found dead on the road to Priština airport.[71] In this period there were provocative acts on both sides. The KLA continued its strategy of provoking the Serbs, and the Serbian Army and Special Police continued to reply with disproportionate force. The fighting flared up again in early 1999.

On 15 January the U.S. Principals Committee met in order to discuss a new strategy in Kosovo, but Albright did not feel the strategy was enough, and she argued (again) for a more forceful approach.[72] Little did she know that the pretext for the forceful approach she had argued for so long was in the making as they spoke, around a small village in Kosovo called Račak.

Chapter 8
RAČAK—AND THE RAMBOUILLET CONFERENCE

I can't believe that Milošević won't sign, when the crunch comes. He always holds out. He has to be leaned on very hard. But he will come around.

—Gen. Wesley K. Clark [1]

On 8 January the KLA ambushed and killed three Serb police officers in Kosovo, near the village of Štimlje.Two days later they killed another two policemen in another village nearby, prompting a Serb police and army buildup in the area.[2] Early on 15 January fighting broke out near the village of Račak. Goran Radosavljević of the Serbian Interior Ministry Police (MUP) explains: "We received reports that a family in the village of Račak was responsible for the killings of three policemen. We received orders from higher echelons to prepare an operation in order to kill the terrorists there."[3] A KVM unit in the area saw Yugoslav Army (VJ) tanks and armored vehicles firing directly into houses near Malopoljce and Petrova and noted houses burning in Račak. Late in the afternoon on 15 January, a KVM patrol got to the village of Račak; it noted one dead Albanian civilian and five injured civilians and received unconfirmed reports of other deaths.[4]

After some fighting, the KLA retreated, and the Serb police entered the village. According to Human Rights Watch, a twelve-year-old boy and thirty men were hiding in a cellar in Račak. The Serbs found the group and separated the boy from the group. "The conscious decision to return him, while later executing the others, suggests that the police had a clear order to kill the adult males of the village."[5] By the next day, forty-five people had been found dead in Račak.[6] When William Walker (head of OSCE's KVM) arrived that day, he immediately accused the FRY authorities of bearing responsibility for the massacre. Still at the scene, he called Richard Holbrooke and described the atrocities committed—adding that he was about to call it a crime against humanity.[7] While Richard Holbrooke says no one should question the decisions of a seasoned diplomat in the field, it seems fair to say Walker had made his conclusion within minutes—with little or no forensic or other formal competence to make such authoritative assessments. Walker's chief of staff called the State Department from Račak and began dictating a report. According to Secretary Albright, William Walker was clear: "It was the Serbian police."[8] Commenting on Albright's response to the somewhat hasty verdict by Walker, Halberstam says, "If there were some people in the Administration who thought that Walker had gone too far, she was not one of them. She picked up the phone and called him: 'Bill, you're doing a great job. You were right on as far as Račak was concerned.'"[9]

During the next few days, suspicions arose that at least one group of dead men might not have been villagers but rather moved there by the KLA to make it look even worse, and that Walker had rushed to condemn the Serb authorities because he wanted to provoke a showdown. The French representative (Gabriel Keller) indicated to French journalists that he believed that there was something odd about Račak. The authorities in Belgrade declared that the KLA had faked a massacre scene and ordered Walker out of the country—a move they later suspended due to international pressure. However, the head of the International Criminal Tribunal for the former Yugoslavia, Louise Arbour, who wanted to find out what had happened, was denied a visa and forced to turn back, which undermined Belgrade's own claim it had nothing to hide.

William Walker's political adviser, Kåre Eltervåg, personally believed the Serbs were responsible—partly because of the events taking place and partly due to the fact that he had experienced the KLA as fairly honest when it came to admitting its own losses. However, he added that the quick response from William Walker felt strange, as if he had received a go-ahead from Washington to stage a press conference even though the situation had not been fully investigated.[10] Maj. Gen. Bjørn Nygård attended Walker's press conference that day and said later that although he certainly regarded it as most likely that the Serbs were responsible for the massacre, he was also well aware that the KLA was fully capable of staging such an event.[11] A Finnish forensic team was later sent to investigate at Račak. According to an article in the German newspaper *Berliner Zeitung,* the final report by the Finnish forensic team found no evidence of any massacre in Račak. However, the leader of the Finnish team, Helena Ranta, delivered a report to the Yugoslavian War Crime Tribunal on 21 June 2000, a report that was immediately marked *secret.*[12]

Later commenting on the issue, Ranta says she "couldn't react to all the nonsense that was said and written on this matter"—referring to the article in *Berliner Zeitung* and other articles and TV documentaries. Ranta believes nothing indicates that the twenty-three men in that infamous ditch had been laid there later; they had not been killed from a long distance, and the bullets found in the bodies had come from a small number of weapons—all indicating that a massacre had taken place. As Ranta asserts: "[The Račak affair is the] best investigated matter in the history of the [Yugoslavia War Crimes] tribunal. . . . I think that we are probably very close to the truth."[13] Human Rights Watch concluded that a massacre had taken place in Račak.[14]

Račak was to change the diplomatic atmosphere and momentum of the Kosovo crisis. British prime minister Tony Blair said Račak came as a shock and called it a pivotal moment for the international community and Kosovo.[15] Halberstam compared the defining incident with Srebrenica: "The last time, in Bosnia, it was Srebrenica that had moved the West to take action. This time, in Kosovo, it was a village called Račak."[16] After Račak, according to Daalder and O'Hanlon, it was obvious to a majority within the Clinton administration that a new and forceful policy was needed.[17] Secretary Cohen felt it was a galvanizing event and a rallying point for the NATO allies;[18] Madeleine Albright also felt Račak was "a galvanizing event. . . . [I]t energized all of us to say that this requires a larger plan, and steady application of military planning for an air campaign."[19]

The State Department developed an approach in which it linked the threat of air strikes to the goal of achieving a political settlement; NATO would *compel* the Serbs to negotiate if they did not negotiate in good faith by themselves.[20] If her plan were implemented, Secretary Albright argued, the negotiations could have three possible outcomes. First, the pressure would force both parties to sign an agreement that would include self-government for the Kosovars, with a NATO peacekeeping force to guarantee security. Second, a Serb no and an Albanian yes would mean NATO bombing until Milošević decided to negotiate. Third, however, if both parties said no, the situation would be "a mess" for which both parties would bear responsibility.[21] According to Daalder, her plan was in fact implemented; Albright was the leading advocate of what became the Rambouillet strategy.[22] Commenting on the mood in Washington after Račak, Christopher Hill says Račak became something of a Srebrenica in miniature:

> I should not say it became hysterical, but the mood turned very anti-Serb immediately. No one asked whether the Serbs had a point, or if we really did know what had happened at Račak. With Walker walking around among the dead bodies, it completely changed my carefully developed autonomy peace plan which sought to provide something to all parties involved—suddenly the agreement became very one-sided against the Serbs.[23]

Hill added that Račak changed the atmosphere in terms of triggering a military threat into the peace agreement. "And I knew that once you put NATO into the peace agreement, you are into a different set of circumstances, and that the Serbs would never agree to it."[24]

Within four hours of the news of the Račak massacre, there was a Washington meeting of the National Security Council's Deputies Committee, in which the representative from the State Department argued for immediate military action using the limited air operations plan that NATO had authorized the previous fall. This proposal was questioned by the Pentagon representatives: "What was the purpose of air strikes? . . . [I]f it was just punishment, what tangible objective would that serve? If it was to end the fighting and persuade Milošević to accept a political settlement, airpower alone might not be able to ensure success. Was the Administration prepared to go in on the ground?"[25] This showed once again the divide between the State Department and the Department of Defense in their perceptions of the application and effect of airpower. Evidently, a more comprehensive strategy was needed.

On 19 January, a high-level U.S. debate started on how to handle the Kosovo issue. During these meetings, according to Secretary Albright, President Clinton authorized the administration to make clear that the United States was prepared to use force and that NATO would be the institution to carry the threat to Milošević.[26] The Pentagon, represented by Secretary Cohen and General Shelton, doubted Secretary Albright's strategy, did not want another American contingent in the Balkans, and did not want to be caught in the middle of a civil war. Albright argued that American leadership was necessary to involve NATO, that NATO was necessary to provide the security needed for the Kosovar guerrillas to disarm, and that NATO was the only thing that would stop Milošević from attacking. Combined with intelligence indicating a Serb operation planned for March/April, which would conceivably displace hundreds of thousands of people in Kosovo, her arguments won ground within the administration. By 23 January, she indicates, she had the administration "more or less on board";[27] the next issue was to get the other international players on board as well. According to Daalder and O'Hanlon, the other allies—with few exceptions—were not ready to take military action, as shown during a NAC meeting two days after Račak, which opted instead to send General Naumann and General Clark to warn Milošević.

According to Daalder and O'Hanlon, there were three main factors precluding allied consensus on the use of force. First, key NATO allies insisted that force should not be threatened just to punish Belgrade for its actions at Račak but rather to promote a distinct political objective, including a notion of how the conflict in Kosovo could be settled. Second, due to the U.S. reluctance to support a ground presence, the allies feared that the United States would not participate in enforcing the peace in the aftermath of an air campaign, leaving this burden to them. Third, the allies feared that the threat tied to a U.S. ultimatum would be directed solely against Belgrade and would thus leave the arena once again to the KLA, which could exploit the situation and try to provoke further Serb retaliation. This would mean a breach in the agreement, and NATO would be obliged to support KLA's military aims. It should be noted that all these factors seemed to derive from the lack of a thorough, long-term political strategy. As Daalder and O'Hanlon point out: "All of these concerns were not only valid but also useful correctives to the inclination of some Clinton administration officials to lash out violently against Milošević without really having thought through the consequences of doing so."[28]

At the same time, Secretary Albright had long preferred NATO to the Contact Group but knew that many Europeans favored the Contact Group (because in it their voices would not be diluted). She also knew that some Europeans would support a NATO operation and air strikes only if they were linked to a high-profile peace conference (this was particularly true of Paris, if the conference were to be held in France). At the same time Russia could become a key player if both international bodies were used (i.e., the Contact Group and the UN). A few days later Albright met Russian foreign minister Ivanov in Moscow. Boris Yeltsin, who articulated his concern about the Kosovo crisis in the book *Midnight Diaries,* says he never supported Milošević. Even so, "once the bombs started falling, the internal political stability in our country would depend on the situation in the Balkans. Already the communists and the nationalists were trying to play the Balkans card in order to destroy the balance of political forces in our society. . . . 'Today Yugoslavia, tomorrow Russia.'"[29]

Ivanov, similarly, stated that NATO air strikes on a sovereign state would be totally unacceptable, but he added, "We do, however, share your desire for a political settlement, and perhaps the threat of force is needed to achieve that. I do not see why we cannot try to work together." It was a response similar to that given in the Contact Group meeting at Heathrow Airport on 8 October 1998, in which Ivanov had said Russia would veto a UN SCR on the matter but otherwise only "just make a lot of noise," thereby—informally—"authorizing" NATO air strikes without a UN mandate. The same night Secretary Albright phoned her foreign-ministerial colleagues and told them that Russia would not prevent them from moving ahead and that all should join in and exert pressure on Milošević.[30]

Secretary-General Solana issued a statement (28 January) indicating that NATO fully supported the early conclusion of a political settlement under the mediation of the Contact Group, that FRY needed to comply with the October agreement, and that all parties (including the Kosovar armed elements) must end their violence and pursue their goals by peaceful means.[31] The same day, the secretary-general of the UN, Kofi Annan, issued a statement to NATO's North Atlantic Council supporting the Contact Group and others in their efforts to get the parties to the negotiating table.[32] The allies and the United States refined the strategy and sought to tie the threat of force to political objectives. The most recent plan by Christopher Hill was to be used as a framework for an interim political settlement. The United States would contribute ground troops to a ground force in Kosovo (KFOR);[33] the United Kingdom, France, and Germany publicly stated that they would be willing to use force if a negotiated settlement to the conflict over Kosovo were not reached.

As a result of this, Secretary Albright resumed working with the Contact Group, which she had previously decided not to use in this matter. The Contact Group met the following day (29 January) in London. The goal was to have both parties accept the peace plan, which was to be negotiated in Rambouillet, France. Both Tony Blair and Jacques Chirac wanted one final attempt to find a political solution and to exert maximum pressure on the parties in order to achieve this. The NAC supported the Contact Group by a statement on 30 January giving full support to the Contact Group's strategy. The NAC further agreed to give Solana authority to authorize air strikes against targets in the territory of the Federal Republic of Yugoslavia. NATO's strategy, it said, was to halt the violence and to support negotiations on an interim political settlement for Kosovo, thus averting a humanitarian catastrophe.[34]

By now, according to Daalder and O'Hanlon, there was a widely shared belief within the Clinton administration that decisive military action was not needed, that a credible threat would suffice to convince Milošević to make a political deal on the issue of Kosovo, and that once Milošević acceded to a political deal the Kosovar Albanians would go along.[35] According to General Clark, the planning for further air operations and targeting was a U.S.-only endeavor, and the targets were being presented to the White House for approval. On the ground in Kosovo, the Serbs were reinforcing their presence with more troops and better equipment. When confronted on the issue, General Ojdanić explained that they were doing this in order to defend themselves from a NATO invasion.[36]

The negotiations commenced 6 February in a fourteenth-century chateau in Rambouillet, southwest of Paris. The day-to-day negotiations were to be coordinated by Christopher Hill (United States), Wolfgang Petritsch (EU), and Boris Mayorski (Russia).[37] The negotiations were held by the Contact Group—a decision described by General Naumann as problematic, because since the previous spring crisis management had been done largely by NATO, and to "change horses midstream" was not a good idea. Besides, the contact group only involved five NATO nations, "but all the others were supposed to carry the risk of executing the threat if necessary, but at the same time they had no say. So we introduced, if I may say so, a first and a second league of NATO nations, and this weakened the cohesion in the Alliance."[38]

Prime Minister Blair and President Chirac were serious about exerting maximum pressure. The Serbs were being told that if they failed to sign the draft proposals they would be bombed, and the Albanians were, in effect, being told that if failure were their fault, they would be left to the tender mercies of the Serbian security forces and paramilitaries—an approach rightly characterized by Tim Judah as "a modern version of gunboat diplomacy."[39] An interesting observation from a British Foreign Office official should be noted. Just before the Rambouillet conference started, the British official pointed out the difference between Dayton and Rambouillet: all parties in the Bosnian conflict had been exhausted after fighting for years and had already turned down three peace plans, whereas Rambouillet was an attempt to impose an agreement before the fighting had really commenced. The conference was also somewhat odd in the sense that from the negotiators' perspective, most of the work on the settlement had already been completed before the parties arrived. As the British foreign secretary, Robin Cook, stated: "In order to complete the work and fill in the remaining 25 percent we have to have the parties together, which is the purpose of this meeting." As Tim Judah points out, with most of the settlement completed before the parties even met and the major players believing they were holding guns to the heads of both the Serbs and the Albanians, "there was a certain amount of theater in what then followed."[40]

Slobodan Milošević remained in Belgrade, which meant that the individual perceived as the de facto Serbian decision maker was absent. According to Daalder and O'Hanlon, his physical presence and full participation in Dayton had proved critical to its success, but this time he did not come.[41] A U.S. special envoy to Kosovo, James Dobbins, believed that the initial level of the delegation and the degree of interaction with the international community at Rambouillet indicated that the Serbs were not seriously trying to reach an agreement.[42]

For the first ten days, the Serbian delegation fell more or less silent and seemed to have very little interest in progress on any issue.[43] Christopher Hill stated later that he believed the Serbs wanted to "string it out, slow it down, put a sort of framework agreement, and try to get off the idea that there should be any NATO role on the ground in Kosovo." Believing that the Russians would help them in this matter, they dragged their feet at Rambouillet.[44] Secretary Albright received reports that the Serb delegation were not taking the negotiations seriously, and the situation became so alarming that on 16 February Christopher Hill went to Belgrade to talk to Milošević. Immediately afterward, the Serbs produced a major document responding to the proposed draft; according to Tim Judah: "Not only was it obvious that the Serb delegates in Rambouillet had no power but it now looked as though the real work on the papers was being done back in Belgrade and not in the château."[45]

On 12 February, President Clinton was acquitted of impeachment charges, and shortly thereafter he announced willingness to put American peacekeepers on the ground in Kosovo. Commenting on the importance of the impeachment on Clinton's political room to maneuver, Halberstam says: "Back in America, Clinton had been impeached by the House of Representatives on December 19, 1998, and he was acquitted of the charges by the Senate on February 12, 1999. The siege of the White House was over."[46]

During the negotiations, General Clark received a call from the deputy secretary of state, Strobe Talbott, in which Clark was asked whether he believed the Serbs would accept the Rambouillet proposals. Clark answered: "I can't believe that Milošević won't sign, when the crunch comes. He always holds out. He has to be leaned on very hard. But he will come around."[47] This is interesting, because it contributes to the pattern of General Clark's perceiving Milošević would buckle once pressed hard, and because it illustrates his close contact with the State Department. Sharing the view of many State Department officials, Clark argued it was unreasonable always to consider worst-case scenarios before committing limited military force to diplomacy; he was convinced that air strikes in Bosnia had proved that limited force could bring results.[48] Therefore, as previously described, Clark's professional advice, as conveyed to the State Department and the Clinton administration ever since before the White House meeting on 23 April 1998, was that limited air operations could be decisive against Milošević.[49] A few days after the telephone conversation with Talbott, Secretary of State Madeleine Albright met Clark in London, in a one-on-one meeting to get his advice regarding Kosovo. As Clark points out, she had been a firm advocate of threatening force to provide political leverage over Milošević, and now she wanted to know if air strikes could work. According to General Clark himself, he pointed out that in the short run air strikes could not prevent Serb forces from attacking civilians but recommended to Secretary Albright that NATO respond in order not to lose credibility. Reflecting on this explicit advice to Secretary Albright, Clark admits he had crossed a line "from forecasting to recommending. I was now responsible for the outcome, in a way I hadn't been before."[50]

It appears that the main strategy of the Serbs in Rambouillet was based on the assumption that the Albanians would reject an agreement because it would not offer them the independence they sought. For a long time the Europeans had rejected the notion of Kosovo independence, and the Serbs had allegedly received information from the Russians that in Contact Group meetings just before Rambouillet the word "referendum" had been deleted from the final proposed text; this had been done because everyone knew the overwhelming majority of Kosovar Albanians in Kosovo would vote in favor of independence if a referendum were held. As a result, the Serbs trusted that the Albanians would have to shoulder the conference's collapse and that the status quo would be somewhat restored. That would be the third and least desirable outcome, the situation previously described by Secretary Albright in January as "a mess for which both sides would bear responsibility."[51]

As the conference went on, the lack of significant progress became clear; particularly the military annex, which had not been dealt with from the start, caused problems. Even before the negotiations started the Western leaders had simply decided that a peace deal without a NATO-led peacekeeping force would not be implemented at all.[52] The reason for this derived from experience in Bosnia, notably the ineffectiveness of the "dual key system" and the lack of authority and resources provided to UNPROFOR—which had led to what General Clark described as the "silver bullet clause" in the Dayton Accords. The clause was there to ensure that the peacekeeping mission was led by NATO, with NATO command and control structures, which enabled the international community to respond more quickly, robustly, and effectively. The Serbs found the military annex unacceptable. The disputed proposed text read: "Together with their vehicles, vessels, aircraft, free and unrestricted passage throughout the FRY including associated airspace and territorial waters. This shall include, but not be limited to, the right of bivouac, manoeuvre, billet, and utilization of any areas or facilities as required for support, training and operations."[53]

The Serb authorities claimed that this was tantamount to an attempt to occupy the whole of Serbia, and it was one of the major reasons they rejected the whole package at the Rambouillet conference. According to General Clark, the military annex used at Dayton was used as a model for Rambouillet.[54] General Smith later described the process as looking at the Dayton military annex and adopting that as a model for what one should demand from the Serbs; in effect, "the Rambouillet draft was almost like the military annex of the Dayton Agreement with the dates changed."[55] The military annex of the Dayton Peace Accords says: "The IFOR shall have complete and unimpeded freedom of movement by ground, air, and water throughout Bosnia and Herzegovina. It shall have the right to bivouac, manoeuvre, billet, and utilize any areas or facilities to carry out its responsibilities as required for its support, training, and operations."[56]

The resemblance of the Rambouillet draft to the Dayton Accords, which had been fully accepted by Milošević and the Bosnian Serbs in Republika Srpska, is, of course, striking, and it would be fair to argue that it at least should have been subject to negotiation. But the Serbs did not even want to discuss it.[57] The problem was, according to Daalder and O'Hanlon, that the Kosovars would not sign an agreement unless a substantial military presence (NATO) guaranteed their safety, and the Serbs were not going to accept an agreement if it required a foreign military presence on their soil.[58]

Later reflecting on the issue, Christopher Hill says the problem was that the Serbs would not engage the question at all, that Milošević wanted to avoid the military element because he felt that the true intention of the force was to eliminate him—or detach Kosovo from Serbia.[59] As we saw in chapter 7, Milošević had every reason to be concerned. Daalder and O'Hanlon argue that it was an error to insist on military access to all of Serbia and that it should have been foreseen that the Serbs would interpret the language wrongly instead of bringing it up as an issue of negotiation. However, this was hardly the decisive factor in Milošević's mind, because the Serbs never raised this issue, instead focusing on the NATO-led peacekeeping force inside Kosovo. If they had, NATO would probably have been flexible; the later KFOR operation showed that NATO did not need access to northern and central Serbia to carry out its mission in Kosovo.[60]

By the end of the scheduled time frame, the negotiators had not produced results. This prompted a three-day extension of the talks. By this time, according to Pleurat Sejdiu (Kosovar delegate at Rambouillet), Secretary Albright was telling the Kosovars that they had to sign, because otherwise NATO could not carry out its threat of a bombing campaign.[61]

The Kosovars did not bend. According to one source present at meetings with Secretary Albright and others, the Kosovars were told, "You'll get NATO to protect your people. Don't mind the small print because you will be running the show and many of the problems in the text will be irrelevant."[62] By now, according to one American official, "the price of saving Rambouillet was to tie ourselves more and more closely to the Albanians."[63] The Kosovar delegation was, however, receiving death threats from the KLA hard-liners back in Kosovo, commanders in the field who would not accept an agreement that did not include independence or that involved disarmament of the KLA.[64] Remi, on camera, admitted, "We called every single delegate and warned them: 'Don't sign!' . . . I said: 'we will not use all our surface-to-air missiles against the Serbs. If you sign, we will save one to shoot down your flight back home."[65]

The negotiators then came up with the following text, which was to be implemented in the final agreement: "Three years after the entry into force of the agreement an international meeting shall be convened to determine a mechanism for a final settlement for Kosovo, on the basis of relevant authorities, each party's efforts regarding the implementation of this Agreement, and the Helsinki Final Act."[66] The wording was constructed to give something to the Serbs as well; because the Helsinki Final Act guarantees the territorial integrity of states, even if a referendum on independence *were* held, no result would have to be honored that did not respect international borders.[67] The Albanians refused to sign the agreement.

According to Secretary Albright, during its last days the conference had discussed the idea of letting the Kosovars not actually sign the agreement but promise to do so, in order to put pressure on the Serbs and let the somewhat nervous Albanian delegation discuss the agreement with the different factions back home.[68] At this point the conference was very confused, and when the deadline arrived, Veton Surroi (editor of the Kosovo newspaper *Koha Ditore*), who understood the gravity of the situation, "saved the day." Claiming that the Kosovar delegation had reached a consensus (which was not true), he stated that the Kosovars accepted the agreement in principle but needed time to consult back home. He then moved to a word processor with an American lawyer (Jim O'Brien) and one of the delegation's translators (Dukagjin Gorani) and began typing a letter stating that the Kosovar delegation would sign the agreement within two weeks after consulting with the political and military institutions of Kosovo.[69] The letter pointed out that NATO deployment was an essential part of the agreement and that "at the end of the interim period of three years, Kosova will hold a referendum to ascertain the will of the people."[70] As previously mentioned, the final agreement included no explicit final settlement for Kosovo, and the letter left the legal question of independence open. However, with James Rubin distracting Thaçi while Surroi finished the letter—and announcing it to the press presumably before either the ink had dried or Thaçi fully understood what had happened—the Albanians had agreed to the agreement and suspended the talks for two weeks for consultation. One American official claimed that Veton Surroi, whom he described as the "voice of reason" in the Kosovar delegation, saved the U.S. government by putting the talks in suspension.

The tension had been significant, however, in the Serb delegation as well. Milošević seems to have had a strategy based on two assumptions: that, as noted, the Albanians would refuse to sign and that the NATO countries possible did not really intend to carry out their threats of a bombing campaign. The problem was, of course, that the Serbs did not know what either the Albanians or the international community would do.

The parties were told to reconvene on 15 March. The Albanian decision was still uncertain, so Secretary Albright sent former Senate majority leader and 1996 Republican presidential candidate Bob Dole to Kosovo. Though a strong supporter of their cause since the first time he had visited Kosovo, in 1990, he conveyed the message that if they did not sign the United States would abandon them.[71] According to Halberstam, Dole's influence on the Albanians was significant and contributed to their decision finally to sign.[72]

When the negotiations resumed in the International Conference Center in Paris, the Serbs handed a new version of the agreement back to the negotiators—having changed about half of it and incorporated a Serb wish list. Even the Russian ambassador was shocked by the obvious lack of interest in further negotiations. Wolfgang Petritsch (EU) recalls that Ratko Marković—the Serb delegation leader—sat silent and appeared embarrassed about the situation.[73] Even so, on 18 March, the Kosovar Albanians signed the agreement. Christopher Hill says the Serbs did not think the Albanians would agree to the accords and that they were "quite shocked when the Albanians did agree," adding, "I must say that the Albanians agreed because we helped them a lot, which I suppose was not fair, but our mediation proved very significant in terms of changing the position of the Albanians."[74] Milošević did not sign the agreement, and according to Braca Grubačić (editor of Belgrade's English-language *VIP* newsletter), one of the reasons was that Milošević thought if he did sign Serbia would lose Kosovo, but if he did not, maybe his grandchildren would get it back.[75]

According to Daalder and O'Hanlon, several factors made the Rambouillet negotiations different from those in Dayton. First, as we have seen, at Dayton the parties had been exhausted by war; this was not the case at Rambouillet, where both the Serbs and the KLA had prepared for a spring offensive for months. Second, Dayton offered a compromise, in the partition of Bosnia. This was not the case at Rambouillet because, among other things, a partition of Kosovo with one part going to Serbia proper would send a potentially catastrophic signal to the Bosnian Serbs and threaten the fragile peace in Bosnia. Third, Milošević's stake in Kosovo—representing his ascent to power and a very significant part of Serb history and culture—was much greater than in Bosnia and thus harder to give up.[76]

Secretary Albright and General Clark had long believed that limited use of force was necessary to alter the behavior of Milošević, and now NATO was heading for war. According to Hirsh and Barry of *Newsweek* magazine, the decision to go to war "was the fruit of a foreign policy carefully nurtured largely by Albright: 'diplomacy backed by force.' For months the Secretary, the Administration's ranking hawk, had labored to unite all 19 NATO members behind Washington. . . . All the Serb dictator had to do was cave, just as he had last October and three years before, at Dayton."[77] Samuel Berger has stated along the same lines: "We needed to demonstrate a real commitment to get a peaceful resolution in order to get the allies to go along with the use of significant force."[78]

On 23 February the Serbs started an offensive west of Vucitrn that displaced some four thousand Kosovars, and on 9 March they attacked the village of Ivaja and villages near Kacanic, burning homes and displacing an additional four thousand Kosovars. By 19 March, the military presence (troops and modern tanks) in Kosovo and the surrounding border area was almost one-third of the FRY's armed forces. According to Cordesman, the Serb offensive rendered the KVM steadily less effective, and the KVM was withdrawn from Kosovo on 19–20 March. The Serb forces followed its departure by intensifying the offensive that had already started. From the way the offensive was executed, it became clear that it must have been planned for months.[79] Knut Vollebæk of the OSCE said that the KVM personnel saw substantially more Serb forces in Kosovo than the October agreement allowed; people were fleeing and houses burning due to the Serb offensive. When Vollebæk called Milošević just before the bombing started on 24 March 1999 and confronted him on the issue, the latter answered as he had done when Ambassador Zimmermann had confronted him with the Serb violence in Bosnia following its independence in April 1992—or when the political directors of the British, Austrian, and German foreign ministries visited Belgrade in late July 1998 and he denied that what they had seen had actually occurred. This time Milošević claimed that "there were no houses burning, the people who were fleeing were actually picnicking and the Serb forces in the area were there to protect Mr. Vollebæk—adding that Mr Vollebæk watched too much CNN."[80]

On 22 March, Richard Holbrooke went to Belgrade to persuade Milošević to accept the Rambouillet Agreement and reduce the military presence in Kosovo, but Milošević refused.[81] The following day, Secretary-General Solana consulted with the NATO allies. When President Clinton received the phone call from Solana, he was clear: "I was in the White House when he called. I felt very strongly that we had to move strongly. We couldn't have another Bosnia."[82]

On the night of 24 March 1999, six U.S. B-52 bomber aircraft fired the first shots in Operation Allied Force when they launched conventional air-launched cruise missiles (AGM-86Cs) against hardened FRY structures. The first hits of the campaign occurred shortly after 8 PM local time in the vicinity of Kosovo's capital, Priština.[83] NATO ended up bombing the FRY for seventy-eight days, with OAF formally ending on 10 June 1999.

Reflecting on the strategic preparedness for what was to ensue after OAF, Gen. Charles Krulak, the commandant of the U.S. Marine Corps and member of the Joint Chiefs of Staff, says he saw very little debate on overall strategy and what was to be accomplished in Kosovo or the Balkans in a longer perspective.[84] Asked whether he believed there was a clear political strategy in terms of what the use of force in OAF should achieve, the vice chairman of the Joint Chiefs of Staff during OAF, Gen. Joseph Ralston, said: "Was there a proper political strategy prior to the bombing? I would agree that there probably was not. People had some vague idea—they wanted to stop the killing and the violence and the brutality—but that is too fuzzy for what you need in terms of coming up with a political strategy and the military strategy we're dealing with. I don't think that had been thought through."[85] Asked whether—on the eve of war—there was any focus on what would happen in Kosovo after the most powerful military alliance in history had won the war, as it presumably would, the chief of staff at SHAPE, Gen. Dieter Stöckmann, said: "From the outset, we were never given a long-term vision for an intended end-state within the Balkans and what the status of Kosovo should be once the war was over. It obviously was not thought through politically when the war started."[86] When answering the same question, Deputy Supreme Allied Commander Europe, Gen. Sir Rupert Smith, gave a big sigh, and said: "Oh, it wasn't in focus at all."[87]

Chapter 9

NATO CRISIS MANAGEMENT IN PERSPECTIVE

The U.S. (and subsequently NATO) response to the Kosovo crisis was shaped significantly more by the history preceding the crisis than the actual events taking place in Kosovo. Secretary Albright, Ambassador Vershbow, General Clark, Robert Gelbard, and Richard Holbrooke all believed Milošević was the source of the problems in Kosovo, that only force would alter his behavior, and that NATO was the institution to handle the crisis. The United States would provide leadership, and airpower was the military tool that would coerce Milošević. This was their shared lesson from Bosnia. Bosnia had been a painful political journey, and Kosovo represented a second chance—and this time they were determined to get it right from the outset.

Pushed into crisis management by, particularly, the State Department and the National Security Council,[1] NATO started issuing threats it was in no political position to fulfill. Once the threats were made, its credibility immediately became an issue, and gradually the fear of losing its credibility became a powerful political force of its own.

While Milošević and the FRY leadership must bear the brunt of the responsibility for the emerging crisis, the KLA must shoulder responsibility for cynically choosing a strategy it knew would cause suffering to the vast majority of the Kosovar Albanians. Killing Serb police officers and innocent civilians, and even attacking moderate Kosovar Albanians, the KLA saw the Kosovar Albanian suffering as means to an end, a way to mobilize the international community against the Serbs. The international community went from heavily criticizing the KLA for their terrorist activities in spring 1998 to gradually reducing its criticism; by the time OAF started, it was becoming a de facto ally of the KLA. This occurred even though everybody knew the

KLA violated the October Agreement and took very provocative steps to deepen the conflict.

This is important, since the nature of coercive diplomacy is to manipulate the *cost* and *benefits* to alter the behavior of the opponent. Tim Judah refers to Braca Grubačić, the editor of Belgrade's English-language *VIP* newsletter, who argues that one of the reasons for Milošević's decision to challenge the West in spring 1999 could be traced to the October Agreement. Milošević was under the impression that Holbrooke had promised to close the border to Albania to prevent arms smuggling, freeze KLA assets, and terminate the KLA influence. When this did not happen, Milošević became angry and felt betrayed by Holbrooke.[2] It has not been possible for the author to verify Grubačić's assessment, but it provides an interesting perspective that fits with the overall picture of the crisis management. The dominating view was that Milošević only responded to the threat—or limited use—of force and that airpower would represent the cost of opposing NATO. Thus, the focus on benefits was very limited. If Grubačić's assessment is correct, it shows that Milošević was willing to respond to the *combination* of cost and benefits introduced by the international community. The KLA was, however, never included in the October Agreement. By then, Holbrooke had told the KLA that its goal of independence was within reach, the Serbian press was reporting Gelbard's covert meeting with the Serb opposition to oust Milošević, and the international community was doing little to stop the KLA from taking advantage of the Serb withdrawal laid out in the October Agreement. As one Western diplomat reportedly acknowledged at the time, "We don't have leverage on the KLA. It is a missing element in our overall strategy."[3] In a crisis involving two main parties, NATO—further propelled by its own fear of losing credibility by not making good on previous threats against Milošević—was reduced to threatening the FRY leadership with extensive use of airpower. Thus, the KLA was barely in the equation of coercive diplomacy.

While any focus on benefits seems to have been largely excluded, the cost of opposing NATO would be a constant—and airpower was perceived as sufficient. How the use of airpower was designed to fit the overall coercive diplomacy is particularly interesting. The evolution of airpower theory, as well as the general focus of NATO and American officers, had been to fight and win high-intensity wars. The institution that would manage the crisis had been founded, educated, trained, and equipped to deter—and if deterrence failed, to fight—the Warsaw Pact in a Cold War scenario. This perspective had been dominant for more than forty years when the Cold War ended. Consequently, only six years before NATO assumed the crisis-management responsibility of the Kosovo crisis, the foreign ministers of NATO felt that making their forces available to the UN in peacekeeping operations was a step too far.

It seems only predictable that the threat of airpower would *not* be calibrated and designed to fit a balanced effort of costs and benefits to alter Milošević's behavior—but instead an inflexible threat of airpower escalating to high-intensity war. The professional airpower community in general, voiced by Lieutenant General Short in particular, wanted instead to avoid a gradual approach and go straight for the extreme intensity, using overwhelming force from the outset. The perspective was this: either Milošević complies with NATO demands or NATO immediately strikes at the heart of the enemy leadership with overwhelming violence that will shock the enemy into compliance. Since this was politically unacceptable, a gradual approach was imposed. As mentioned in my introduction, when I later asked James Dobbins, the special envoy to Bosnia and Kosovo, about the issue of using airpower in OAF, he said the strategy was quite clear: "We'll bomb them a little bit, if that doesn't work, we'll bomb them a little bit more, and if that doesn't work, we'll bomb them a little more, and if that doesn't work—ultimately—we have to consider invading. I don't see anything that lacks clarity in that strategy."[4]

Arguably, Dobbins' oversimplified perception of airpower represents that of many advocates of the limited use of airpower. In a sense, on the eve of OAF the advocates of limited force and the use of airpower in the Clinton administration had come full circle. Their advocacy of airpower in Bosnia was not based on a comprehensive strategy to solve this complex and unique conflict but rather on an oversimplified belief that airpower would somehow influence the Serbs to back off and thereby restore peace in the Balkans. They were either not willing or not able to see that airpower had not been the *sole* decisive instrument in ending the war in Bosnia but had proved effective in combination with other factors that together generated a context in which coercive diplomacy could succeed. In 1998, in Operation Infinite Reach and Operation Desert Fox, they continued the limited use of airpower without achieving core objectives. When going to war over Kosovo, the lack of an adequate strategic context to exploit airpower's coercive potential fully was once again evident. The perspective conveyed by General Clark and others was that Milošević would concede once a credible threat of NATO airpower was made—and if not, a few days of bombing would suffice. This view became the dominant U.S. view leading up to OAF.

What then becomes interesting is the effect this assumption had on the European nations. With the United States providing the political and military leadership of NATO's crisis management, its advice and assessment carried tremendous weight. General Naumann tells an interesting story of his farewell visit to London (ending his tour as chairman of the Military Committee) just prior to OAF. In a meeting with defense secretary George Robertson and the chief of defense, Gen. Charles Guthrie, Secretary Robertson asked General Naumann how long he thought an air campaign against FRY would last. Naumann told him—as he had done in the NAC shortly before—that the only thing he could predict was that "under favourable circumstances it will take us a week or more to win air supremacy and to neutralize the Serb air defense system. That is the only thing I can predict—anything else I can not predict." With a small grin, General Naumann added: "I will never forget the face of Defence Secretary Robertson when I said this." Robertson immediately replied: "Seven days, you say?"—to which General Naumann replied: "Yes, sir, and during those seven days the military needs to do its job without political interference." Robertson then turned to Guthrie and said, "Charles, do you share this view?" Guthrie said: "Yes, I believe the chairman is right." Then Defense Secretary Robertson said, "Then I have to inform the Prime Minister immediately, since he talked to Clinton yesterday, and Clinton told him in two or three days it was over."[5] (It has not been possible for the author to verify this information with Robertson or Guthrie.)

According to Daalder and O'Hanlon, the British Ministry of Defence was so convinced that a bit of bombing would provide the desired outcome "that they proposed restricting the opening salvo to a limited air option, using just twenty to fifty cruise missiles against key targets in Serbia, before pausing to allow Milošević to come back to the negotiating table."[6] This indicates the perception of the air campaign's scope and duration in both the White House and in Downing Street—that is, in the two nations generally considered to be the most active in propelling NATO to war. Many of the smaller nations in Europe—like Norway—perceived both NATO and the United States as cornerstones of their security policy; it seems fair to argue that when NATO decided to start an air campaign many nations felt obliged to join ranks and rally behind the decisions made in Washington and by the bigger European nations. Hence, when Washington and the secretary-general of NATO started calling various capitals for support for an air campaign of short duration they signaled their support immediately, though many nations had significant problems participating in a military campaign without a UN Security Council resolution authorizing such use of force.

One individual particularly contributed to the perspective that Milošević would soon buckle once pressed hard: the Supreme Allied Commander Europe, Gen. Wesley K. Clark. Claiming he probably was unique among twentieth-century commanders in knowing his adversary so well,[7] on numerous occasions General Clark advised politicians and diplomats that airpower was sufficient to coerce Milošević. Some sources have indicated that General Clark perceived Milošević as a personal enemy after three members of the American negotiating team in Bosnia died when an armored personnel carrier fell off the road at Mount Igman—a mountain close to Sarajevo—in August 1995. They had been denied safe air transit to Sarajevo by General Mladić when visiting Milošević in Belgrade and had to drive through Bosnian Serb–held territory. Milošević was perceived to have been fully capable of pressing the Bosnian Serbs on the issue, but he had not. General Clark climbed down to the wreckage to try and save his colleagues, to no avail. The degree to which this incident affected General Clark's perception of Milošević and his objectivity in advising politicians later is probably something he alone can clarify.

According to Halberstam, Clark hated Milošević,[8] and the deputy chief of operations at SHAPE, Brigadier General Lundberg, says on several occasions during planning sessions before OAF Clark showed his personal antipathy toward Milošević, once declaring intensely, "I want Milošević!"[9] The Norwegian representative on NATO's Military Committee, Lt. Gen. Per Bøthun, said that he felt the desire by Clark to get Milošević "sometimes seemed as if it got too personal on behalf of General Clark."[10] It should be noted that both General Ralston and Lieutenant General Short have indicated that perhaps Clark wanted to get NATO involved to stop Milošević's actions in Kosovo. He knew airpower was the only realistic option to get an operation started, and he knew that once started, NATO's credibility would be at stake, which would make it a necessity to finish the campaign successfully. Both generals stress that this is speculation on their part.[11] Whatever his motivation, whenever American or allied politicians asked his opinion, General Clark would say that Milošević would give in once threatened with—or subject to a few days of—airpower.

It would be in accordance with the lessons drawn from Bosnia by himself, Albright, Holbrooke, Vershbow, and Gelbard. It should be noted that Clark also wanted to include ground forces, but the perception he conveyed to politicians was that airpower would suffice. Within the U.S. channels, General Ralston said, Clark's advice was largely more appreciated in the State Department than in the Department of Defense. Ralston added, "When General Clark told Albright that a few days of bombing would suffice—that was attractive to her."[12] General Naumann said he knew for a fact—through personal discussions with General Clark—that initially Clark personally believed that Milošević would accede to the demands of the international community if bombed for a short period of time. General Naumann also perceived that on this matter General Clark's advice had particular impact on both Secretary Albright and President Clinton.[13] General Stöckmann says that he too perceived that Clark had a good relationship with Albright and Clinton, saying both demonstrated undivided confidence in him as a strategic commander, which might have resulted in outsiders' observations that his advice was welcome to a far greater extent within the State Department than within the Pentagon. He also believes that General Clark personally played a significant role in terms of arguing for an air campaign, which Clark believed would convince Milošević to give in to the demands of the international community.[14]

What becomes of paramount importance, although very difficult to assess, was the perspective of the target of NATO's crisis management and subsequent war—the president of the FRY, Slobodan Milošević. More than anything else, evidence suggests Milošević was a political opportunist. He used nationalist sentiments as a vehicle to gain power and influence in the late 1980s and aimed to gain control over Yugoslavia through the existing structures of the Communist Party and the federal government. The power of the Communist Party having been gradually eroded by events and the various republics having pursued their ambitions for independence, his next best solution would be to carve out a "Greater Serbia," including the Serb-dominated enclaves of Croatia and Bosnia-Herzegovina. When that did not work in Croatia, he played the role of peacemaker and helped Cyrus Vance to "take care" of the leader of the Krajina Serbs, Milan Babić—which he publicly did in January 1992. Then the focus turned to Bosnia. Milošević met Franjo Tudjman in March 1991 to discuss possible ways of dividing Bosnia. Several sources provide evidence of the link between Belgrade and the Serb atrocities in Bosnia following its independence in April 1992,[15] but when the goal in Bosnia seemed unattainable to Milošević a few years later, he once again opted to play the peacemaker role and became the dominant figure in securing the peace in the Dayton negotiations.[16]

It seems unlikely that Milošević was a politician with a long-term strategy or a clear, sustained political vision. Rather his focus was power and how he could maneuver to remain in power. He therefore became a brilliant tactician, shifting politically from day to day and week to week.[17] Warren Zimmermann had largely the same perception, asserting that Milošević was an opportunist rather than an ideologue, driven by power rather than nationalism, and not an ethnic exclusivist like Croatia's president Franjo Tudjman or the Bosnian Serb leader Radovan Karadžić.[18] Although admitting that Milošević was a very clever and intelligent man, General Naumann thought Milošević was "a man that does not have the slightest respect for human life. He was a power-oriented man, power meant everything to him."[19] As Tim Judah assessed the situation when violence erupted in 1998, "When trying to comprehend Milošević it is vital to understand that the man has no long-term vision. His main interest is power and keeping it, and what he is best at is manoeuvring from day to day. On occasions, such as the spring of 1998, he lies low, dithers, is uncertain how to react, but finally he decides to pursue a particular course of action—but again is uncertain how it will end."[20] When asked about whether this perception correlated with their own impression of Milošević after their numerous meetings and conversations with him, Robert Gelbard, Thorvald Stoltenberg, General Naumann, and Knut Vollebæk all confirmed it.[21]

If indeed Milošević was a political opportunist without a long-term strategy and one whose overall concern was to stay in power; would it not be logical to deduce that a broader diplomatic spectrum of cost and benefits could influence his behavior? Why conclude then that only military power (airpower) mattered? The answer probably stems from the initial U.S. perspective on the disintegration of Yugoslavia. According to Woodward, the United States generally believed that the conflict was related to Serb aggression in order to create a Greater Serbia. This Serbian expansionist aggression would break out in areas as military opportunity arose. The U.S. government and portions of its political and intellectual elite represented this view, which was part of a post–Cold War pattern of denouncing opposing political leaders as "rogue states" and international pariahs, to be politically and diplomatically isolated and threatened with airpower in order to protect civilized norms and innocent civilians.[22] Thus, when Secretary of State James Baker went to Belgrade 21 June 1991 and gave the American view on the disintegration of Yugoslavia, he singled out Milošević as the main source of the crisis in Yugoslavia, telling him that Serbia would be made an outcast (pariah) if it continued to propel Yugoslavia toward civil war.[23]

This perspective had since dominated U.S. thinking all through the 1990s and had been reinforced by the diplomacy ending the Bosnian War. Although it contains a certain amount of truth, and though the military potential of the United States clearly carried significant weight during the negotiations ending the Bosnian War, the conclusion fails to take account of important nuances. Milošević was more than willing to end the Bosnian War when Holbrooke suggested negotiations in August 1995, because indirectly it threatened his domestic power base in Serbia. It was creating refugees in Serbia proper, the economic embargo was affecting the everyday life of the average Serb, and inflation was skyrocketing. In other words, the situation by autumn 1995 was such that Milošević gained from a negotiated solution to the Bosnian War, and so, following his usual opportunistic pattern, he opted to be the peacemaker at the Dayton negotiations. Would it have been possible to manipulate costs and benefits differently when the Kosovo crisis surfaced in 1998 and put greater emphasis on the potential *benefits* of cooperation with the Western powers and the Kosovar Albanians, rather than immediately focusing to a far greater extent on the potential costs of opposing NATO? Milošević's benefits of a negotiated deal at Dayton seem to be significantly underestimated when summing up the lessons from Bosnia.

One can, of course, argue that the behavior and political record of Milošević dictated that he did not deserve any benefits and should instead be ousted from power, but at Dayton the United States and the rest of the international community had previously shown its pragmatic perspective on this issue. Instead they opted for a negotiated solution to the Kosovo crisis. Two factors made a negotiated deal over Kosovo more difficult to achieve than the one at Dayton: the significance of Kosovo and the domestic political situation of Milošević by late 1997.

By late 1996, Milošević's power was being threatened domestically. Milošević lost the elections held in late 1996 and then annulled the election result, as he did not want to lose his grip on power. According to John Lampe and Dragan Cicic, Milošević's power base had not been more threatened since 1990–91. Unemployment was reaching some 45–50 percent of the work force, and compared to when Milošević came to power in 1987 the GNP and average wages had dropped some 70 percent.[24] According to the British Helsinki Human Rights Group, the power of Milošević continued to be threatened, and during the parliamentary elections on 21 September 1997, Milošević's party (SPS) lost its majority in the Serbian parliament, with the radical party of Vojislav Šešelj (SRS) gaining strength. "The failure of the Serb cause in the Bosnian War and the continuing economic hardships endured by Serbs after Dayton along with the fiasco of local elections in November, 1996, had all weakened the SPS's position."[25]

So by 1997, Milošević was significantly weakened politically in Serbia. Gelbard points out that "due to the electoral losses, the increasing opposition and the threat to his power—Milošević could not afford to negotiate a political settlement to Kosovo in 1998. If he had, he would then have been criticised for giving in by the radicals who had just gained strength in the 1997 elections."[26] According to Gelbard, General Clark shared this analysis, and the argument is logical. It further strengthens the argument that Milošević opted to enter a coalition with the Yugoslav United Left (JUL) and the Serbian Radical Party, led by the extreme nationalist Vojislav Šešelj, on 24 March 1998.[27] Seemingly, Milošević chose to continue to ride the "tiger of nationalism" that had brought him to power in the late 1980s. Still, it does not rule out that a different balance between power and diplomacy could have worked. Being first and foremost a cynical political opportunist, he might have considered a different approach that in sum could have proved more beneficial to him. Furthermore, the simplified perspective that Milošević was the only source of the problem and that he only responded to the use of force gives rise to another significant nuance: How did the KLA fit into this picture, and how could it have influenced the coercive diplomacy in Kosovo?

As previously noted, the KLA aimed for full independence and had adopted a strategy of killing Serb police officers, as well as kidnapping and killing Serb civilians, in order to trigger Serb retaliation—which in turn would engage the international community on their behalf. To many Kosovar Albanians, the establishment of Republika Srpska in Bosnia had rewarded the radical and violent means of the Bosnian Serbs, while not including the issue of Kosovo in the Dayton Accords proved that the nonviolent strategy of Ibrahim Rugova was naïve and a failed enterprise. Bosnia taught radical Kosovar Albanians that violence was needed to get the attention of the Western world—and it worked. All through spring 1998 the United States (Gelbard), the UN, NATO, OSCE, and the Contact Group all condemned the "terrorist actions" of the KLA. After NATO started issuing threats against Belgrade by late May 1998, the condemnation gradually decreased and cooperation gradually increased, until for all practical purposes the KLA was an ally of NATO during OAF, less than a year later. The notion that Milošević was the source of the problem seemingly ran too deep, and the influence of the United States was too strong.

The perspectives should have been more balanced. In Western media, the humanitarian issue of Kosovo was dominant. The focus on the humanitarian issue coincides with the desire for (but not received) a UN authorization of force and the need for domestic support and thereby political leverage to deal with the situation. It therefore suited both the Western powers and the Kosovars to emphasize the humanitarian dimension. Clearly the disproportionately violent retaliation by Serb forces should not be excused, but to a certain extent the humanitarian dimension should be downplayed. Tim Judah argues that the Kosovars managed to portray this conflict as a human rights issue to many Western politicians but argues that it was not. "At the heart of the matter was [instead] a fundamental struggle between two peoples for control of the same piece of land. In our times, however, human rights have become an influential factor in shaping international politics[;] . . . we can see how the question of human rights became another weapon in the arsenal of the Kosovars."[28]

The deputy head of mission/chief of staff for the Kosovo Verification Mission, Maj. Gen. Bjørn Nygård, who experienced the situation on the ground in Kosovo before OAF commenced, admitted the strength of this view, stating, "Even though the conflict from a Western point of view largely was a humanitarian issue, the conflict developed into a classic armed conflict over territory and political and economic power."[29] According to

Susan L. Woodward, "The Serbian government and the Albanian minority both considered the issue to be one of collective political rights of national aspiration rather than one of individual human rights."[30] When Ambassador Zimmermann asked him what the Kosovar Albanian treatment of the Serbs had been like before Milošević rose to power in the late 1980s and the Kosovars somewhat had the upper hand in Kosovo, the Kosovar Albanian leader Ibrahim Rugova answered: "Unfortunately, there were many crimes committed against the Serbs."[31] This answer may add some force to Cordesman's statement that instead of an explicit "good" side or a "bad" side, ethnic wars instead have a "strong" side and a "weak" side, that "it is a grim reality in ethnic conflict that the stronger side often commits atrocities against the weaker side."[32]

Seen from this perspective, the unbalanced focus on Belgrade and strong emphasis on military force appears somewhat prejudiced and predestined rather than based on a balanced and objective analysis of the unique context of Kosovo—particularly by fall 1998. The first political-military plan for a solution in Kosovo did not come until fall 1998,[33] but by then Milošević and Serbia had long been singled out as the targets of coercion. Despite clear evidence that the KLA was the provocateur following the October Agreement, NATO continued its cooperation with the KLA. As General Naumann said after the war, "I think we had a chance to prevent war in the fall of 1998. Milošević honored the October Agreement, but the KLA exploited the withdrawal of FRY forces and took some very provocative steps. They started the conflict then, but NATO had no instrument to influence them. In fact, the failure by NATO to influence the KLA at that time was the biggest deficiency of the diplomatic effort. We had a chance to find a negotiated solution, but we missed it."[34]

James Dobbins later commented that the basic strategy of the KLA seemed to be to provoke Serb retaliation and thereby create a situation that would lead to an international intervention. "There was unhappiness over the fact that the international community was in effect being manoeuvred into this position, but at the same time, there was even less sympathy for the Serb behaviour in Kosovo."[35] Christopher Hill felt that the KLA strategy was ultimately successful: "I mean, NATO ended up in Kosovo, so I would call the KLA strategy a success."[36]

In the end, NATO ended up using airpower the way it had threatened for almost a year. Instead of a few days of bombing, NATO would use more than a thousand aircraft in an effort lasting more than eleven weeks, until Milošević agreed to end the war.

The basis for NATO's intervention and the air campaign, Operation Allied Force, was the humanitarian situation for the Kosovar in Kosovo who were forced to flee their homes into the mountains, woods, or neighboring countries (primarily Macedonia and Albania). Pictured: Kosovo refugees in Macedonia, 1999. (Corbis photo)

In early March 1998, the longtime hard-liner Adem Jashari decided the KLA needed martyrs and that he was going to provide some. Serb forces surrounded the house of the Jashari family and killed forty-five people, among them twelve women and eleven children. The incident meant that the level of violence in Kosovo reached a critical threshold that demanded international attention. Pictured: Serb police tank in front of the ruins of the Jashari family's house in Prekaz, 11 March 1999. (Corbis photo)

Ambassador William Walker, head of the OSCE Kosovo Verification Mission, meets with President Slobodan Milošević on 23 October 1998 to discuss last details to enable the deployment of the mission, which was formally established by the OSCE. (OCSE photo/STR/REUTERS/CONTRAST)

NATO foreign ministers meeting in Luxembourg, 28–29 May 1998. Gradually, according to Deputy SACEUR General Smith, NATO was pushed into crisis management by the United States. NATO started issuing threats after these foreign ministers meetings. Picture shows bilateral meeting between NATO secretary-general Dr. Javier Solana (right) and Secretary of State Madeleine Albright (left) on 28 May 1998. (NATO photo)

Following the threats made during NATO's foreign ministers meeting in Luxembourg, NATO's defense ministers met in Brussels and directed NATO military authorities to undertake planning for "a full range of options." Picture shows Secretary of Defense William Cohen with NATO Secretary-General Solana in the latter's private office, 11 June 1998. (NATO photo)

The Račak Massacre in January 1999, in which forty-five people were killed by Serb forces, would change the diplomatic momentum in the Kosovo crisis. Both Secretary Cohen and Secretary Albright called it a "galvanizing event"; Ambassador Christopher Hill said Račak became a Srebrenica in miniature, adding, "I should not say it became hysterical, but the mood turned very anti-Serb immediately." (Corbis photo)

Middle: American ambassador to Macedonia, and a member of the troika leading the Rambouillet negotiations, Christopher Hill. Left: Kosovar Albanian leader Ibrahim Rugova (leader of the Democratic League of Kosovo [LDK]). Hill says the Serbs did not think the Albanians would agree to the Rambouillet Accords and that they were "quite shocked when the Albanians did agree," adding, "I must say that the Albanians agreed because we helped them a lot, which I suppose was not fair, but our mediation proved very significant in terms of changing the position of the Albanians." (Corbis photo)

Norwegian foreign minister and chairman in office of the OSCE, Knut Vollebæk (left), with Secretary-General Solana (18 May 1999). Vollebæk admitted that he was never informed about the content of Holbrooke's October agreement, despite bringing this issue up with the Americans several times. This became a problem when Vollebæk spoke to Milošević on matters concerning OSCE and KVM, because Milošević would simply say: "No, that was not what I agreed with Mr. Holbrooke." The KVM withdrew from Kosovo shortly before OAF commenced. (NATO photo)

Strategic alliance? General Clark and Secretary Albright shared the belief that airpower would coerce Milošević into resuming negotiations. During the Rambouillet Conference General Clark explicitly advised Secretary Albright to use military force (airpower) in order not to jeopardize NATO's credibility. Reflecting on his advice, Clark admits he crossed a line "from forecasting to recommending. I was now responsible for the outcome, in a way I hadn't been before." Picture taken at a Group of Eight meeting in Cologne during OAF (8 June 1999).(NATO photo)

As in Bosnia, Richard Holbrooke and General Clark cooperated on the diplomatic strategy. Picture taken on 22 March 1999, when Holbrooke came to the NATO Headquarters in Brussels to discuss the deteriorating situation in Kosovo, two days before OAF commenced. (NATO photo)

How to coerce Milošević and the FRY into compliance? Operation Allied Force commenced
24 March 1999 and lasted seventy-eight days. NATO believed Milošević would accede
to their demands within a few days. Milošević, however, knew that allied consensus was
shaky and believed NATO consensus could be broken. Thus, both parties were in a sense
gambling. Tim Judah was probably right when he asserted: "There is no mystery about why
NATO bombed Yugoslavia for seventy-eight days beginning on 24 March. Quite simply,
the leaders of NATO countries thought it would only last a few days, and so did Milošević."
(Corbis photo)

Part IV
Epilogue: Diplomacy and Airpower

It is time to stop pretending that Europeans and Americans share a common view of the world, or even that they occupy the same world. On the all-important question of power—the efficacy of power, the morality of power, the desirability of power—American and European perspectives are diverging.

—Robert Kagan

Chapter 10
DIPLOMACY AND AIRPOWER

We were more worried about how our actions were playing to public opinion in our own capitals rather than analysing the impact on Milošević and his regime.
—NATO ambassador (anonymous)[1]

When the deteriorating situation in Kosovo rose on the international political agenda in early 1998, the link between force and diplomacy immediately became the key ingredient in the international effort to solve the crisis. Commenting on the general relationship between force and diplomacy, President Clinton's national security adviser, Anthony Lake, pointed out, "I think the truth is that there are very, very few cases in which diplomacy divorced from power, or power divorced from diplomacy has ever worked—and it's a false debate: it's got to have both. The question is in which proportions."[2] Coercive diplomacy is the combination of efforts to change the behavior of an opponent by manipulating costs and benefits. It includes the use of threatened force, and at times the limited use of actual force to back up the threat,[3] but the emphasis should be on the total effort to change the opponent's behavior. Both costs and benefits can potentially be distributed in a wide variety of options that, combined, could influence the opponent, and military force is but one available option. The circumstances and context of every crisis or conflict are unique, and the coercive effort to alter the behavior of an opponent should reflect this fundamental notion. In Kosovo it did not.

In retrospect, the basic assumptions and premises for the coercive diplomacy in Kosovo—as well as the evolving transatlantic dialogue on the crisis management—were rooted in differing perspectives of the balance between force and diplomacy. In his book *Of Paradise and Power,* Robert Kagan says Europe and the United States have parted ways when it comes to setting national priorities, determining threats, defining challenges, and fashioning and implementing foreign and defense policies.

It is time to stop pretending that Europeans and Americans share a common view of the world, or even that they occupy the same world. On all-important question of power—the efficacy of power, the morality of power, the desirability of power—American and European perspectives are diverging. Europe is turning away from power[;] . . . the United States remains mired in history, exercising power in an anarchic Hobbesian world where international laws and rules are unreliable, and where true security and the defence and promotion of a liberal order still depend on the possession and use of military might.[4]

Anthony Lake says there is no doubt that the Europeans generally believe more in diplomacy and are more concerned about the application of military force, while the United States believes more in the application of force and is less convinced that diplomacy works without threat.[5] Carl Bildt, who cooperated with Richard Holbrooke as the EU representative in the diplomatic effort to end the war in Bosnia, reflects a similar attitude. He describes a running joke between himself and Richard Holbrooke in which Holbrooke sometimes claimed that Bildt was "too Swedish"—meaning he believed too much in dialogue, compromise, and negotiations. For his part, Carl Bildt sometimes called Holbrooke "too American"—meaning he believed too much in fast and simple solutions based largely on military power.[6] Gen. Klaus Naumann points out, "Grand Strategy is never military alone—it is a combination of all instruments of politics. What is perhaps a real philosophical difference between we Europeans and the Americans is that they have a tendency to believe too much in hard power, and we have a tendency to believe too much in soft power."[7] In his book *Unvanquished: A US-UN Saga*, former UN secretary-general Boutros Boutros-Ghali criticizes the excessive U.S. tendency to use force, and says, "The Roman Empire had no need for diplomacy, nor does the U.S. Diplomacy is perceived by an imperial power as a waste of time and prestige and a sign of weakness."[8] Carl Bildt says while this notion is unfair to both the Roman Empire and the United States, it does highlight some real American tendencies.[9]

Particularly after the 1991 Gulf War, airpower was the preferred military tool of many policy makers in Washington. The conspicuous accuracy of airpower against Iraq promised a lower risk of collateral damage, a lower risk to one's own forces, and the politicians would be in control of events to a much larger degree than they would in a war involving large ground forces.[10] Airpower seemingly provided the political flexibility and room to maneuver that most policy makers were looking for, and the U.S. Air Force had proven its strength.

The service's focus on strategic parallel attacks with overwhelming force embodied the notion that airpower would save the day should an international crisis emerge. Rooted in a tradition of fighting high-intensity wars, the Air Force largely approached Kosovo with a mindset Lieutenant General Short defines as "the classic air campaign that we'd all learned at Maxwell."[11] The former chief of staff of the U.S. Air Force, Gen. Michael E. Ryan, noted by the end of the war that if OAF had been conducted "more in consonance with established Air Force doctrine" and more "massively from the beginning," it would have been even more successful. "The campaign did not begin the way America normally would apply airpower—massively."[12] In a lecture at the Royal Norwegian Air Force Academy after OAF, Lieutenant General Short once again referred to the teachings of airpower:

> I am told that you are studying airpower theory, and have studied airpower history. My hope is that airpower theory has told you that there is a right way to use airpower. At least I believe there is a right way to use airpower, and that is to maximise the potential of our capabilities. That means to me that on the first day or the first night of the war, you attack the enemy with incredible speed and incredible violence. Violence that he could never have imagined. It should be his worst possible nightmare with an incredible level of destruction, relative again, to what he thought was possible. You should use every bit of technology that you have to shock him into inaction until he is paralysed. . . . That was how I thought airpower should be used in Serbia.[13]

In other words, according to Lieutenant General Short there exists "a right way to use airpower." The perception appears to be that the long-debated enigma of how best to use airpower to alter the behavior of an opponent has been solved, leaving a textbook recipe of "incredible speed and incredible violence" in order to "shock him into inaction until he is paralyzed." Attacking the enemy leadership—or "the head of the snake"—had been largely institutionalized in the Air Force after the 1991 Gulf War, and the airmen wanted to attack Belgrade. Sharing this perspective, one of Lieutenant General Short's battle staff directors at the Combined Air Operations Center (CAOC) at Vicenza, Col. Tom Johansen, asserted: "When you design an operation like this, you want to go downtown Belgrade the first night, but we weren't allowed to do that. We [the air leadership at CAOC Vicenza] wanted to go straight for the lion's head, and knock out all its teeth," adding that "the overwhelming majority" of his colleagues at CAOC Vicenza "agreed with his [Short's] perspective on the application of airpower."[14]

David Halberstam says, "Short's view of what we should have been doing represented the purest distillation of air force ideology, untempered by any sympathy for political complexities."[15]

Halberstam's term "air force ideology" deserves additional illumination. Based on the work of the Air Corps Tactical School (ACTS) and the Industrial Web Theory preceding World War II, the first American strategic air campaign plan (known as AWPD-1) envisaged three primary air objectives against Germany: electric power systems, lines of communication, and oil and petroleum systems.[16] As previously noted in chapter 2, John A. Warden admits that the work of ACTS and the Industrial Web Theory helped him "enormously" in developing his own concepts and theories—which were subsequently vindicated by the 1991 Gulf War and largely implemented in the air campaign courses at the Air Command and Staff College at Maxwell Air Force Base.

Open sources on targets struck in OAF during Phase Three—the strategic phase of the OAF air campaign—suggests a striking resemblance to the first U.S. strategic air campaign plan of August 1941; again the emphasis appears to be on electric power, oil and petroleum, and lines of communication. Asked after the war why Milošević caved in after seventy-eight days of bombing, Lieutenant General Short asserted that it was because he "hadn't had [electric] power in his capital for a number of days and wasn't going to have it for a number of days more . . . there was no fuel for his automobiles and his military . . . and communications infrastructure was being systematically destroyed."[17] Airpower's main focus in the strategic phase of OAF in 1999 was apparently the same as the primary air objectives of the first air campaign plan to defeat Hitler in World War II. In a general analysis of the conceptual approach to OAF by the U.S. Air Force, airpower historian Gian P. Gentile says: "The type of targets bombed in Yugoslavia and the attitudes of certain senior airmen toward the air campaign show that the traditional American concept of strategic bombing continues to shape Air Force thinking."[18]

Lieutenant General Short was right that attacking groups of Serb regular or irregular ground forces targeting the Kosovar Albanian population—aside from NATO's fear of collateral damage—clearly represented neither what airpower was most suited for nor what airmen were trained to do. General Naumann later said he agreed with Short that tasking airpower to attack those who carried out the ethnic cleansing was wrong, and on several occasions he told the NAC, "They are asking for the impossible, they want us to stop the individual murderer going with his knife from village to village and carving up some Kosovars; that you cannot do from the air, and I think that is one of the lessons we should learn for the next time."[19] The sentiments of most airmen could arguably be summed up by General Ryan, who pointed out that "airpower could not stop the door-to-door thuggery and ethnic cleansing that were going on, directly. The only way you were going to be able to do that was by taking it to the heart of the matter—in this case, to Belgrade."[20] The problem this time was that using overwhelming force against the FRY leadership was a course of action outside the political room to maneuver. Even though the perspective of the air leadership at Vicenza appears surprisingly in agreement on this issue, some Air Force officers understood this overriding premise. Halberstam points out that "not all his [Short's] colleagues, even senior air force officers, agreed with him completely." "They understood how he felt, sympathized with his rage . . . but they also understood that this mission was something new, that it was a convoluted command, and that the politics of bombing a city in Europe whose citizens had been allies of other European nations were immensely complicated. . . . While what Short said was technically right, they felt that he did not understand the interplay of much larger forces taking place around him."[21]

Quite simply, Lieutenant General Short and the air leadership at Vicenza did not fully appreciate the extraordinary political circumstances of this particular operation and so were at odds with those who had to maneuver within the political context defined by the politicians. General Naumann made a very important distinction: "The aim was to bring Milošević back to the negotiating table. The aim was not to enforce our will on him, and I think this is the difference."[22] General Smith says, "Mike Short saw this whole business in a very simple way, and had no comprehension of the political context either within the Alliance or of the operation as a whole—and he didn't choose to try to understand it."[23] Gen. Jean-Pierre Kelche largely felt the same way, asserting that General Short focused on the more narrow military use of airpower and did not fully comprehend that "we had to use the military tools according to the limitations and constraints outlined by the political management of the crisis."[24]

This put Lieutenant General Short and the air leadership at Vicenza at odds with the military leadership at SHAPE. Attacking the Third Army in Kosovo was not the way Short wanted to use airpower: "I never felt that the Third Army in Kosovo was a center of gravity . . . body bags coming home from Kosovo didn't bother the leadership elite [in Belgrade]."[25] When he received the order from Wesley Clark that the Third Army was to be the primary objective, Michael Short said flatly, "General, that is a high level of effort, high risk and low payoff operation. We will do our best but I do not expect to do very well."[26] In what has become a well-known discussion between Clark and Short regarding targeting the Third Army versus strategic targets in Belgrade, Short recalls finally being allowed to hit the police headquarters in Belgrade: "This is the jewel in the crown." Clark replies: "To me, the jewel in the crown is when those B-52s rumble across Kosovo." Short says: "You and I have known for weeks that we have different jewellers," to which Clark says: "My jeweller outranks yours."[27]

There would be an atmosphere of friction between the two generals all through the war. During video-teleconferences, Lieutenant General Short would regularly voice his firm belief that the strategy was wrong, sometimes sighing in discontent and reportedly displaying a somewhat demonstrative body language, giving a clear signal of his not supporting the chosen strategy.[28] General Stöckmann described the relations between Clark and Short as "determined by a different and repeatedly incongruous operational and strategic approach"; Brigadier General Lundberg has described the atmosphere between the two as "very tense."[29] Seemingly, a different professional perspective surfaced between SHAPE and CAOC Vicenza. General Stöckmann felt that the air leadership at Vicenza unjustifiably discredited SHAPE experts from the outset for not understanding the true nature and potential of airpower, while asserting that they were the ones who understood how this war should have been fought. In that way they simply ignored political guidance and NATO principles. It would remain a source of different views and controversial discussions within the command structure all through the war.[30]

It is the job of a combined force air component commander (CFACC) to provide his professional view of how airpower best should be applied to achieve its objectives. Perhaps Wesley Clark should have spent more time discussing this particular issue with Short before going to war. But there is a fine line between the CFACC signaling his view in an honest, straight-forward, and professional manner, and causing friction over time within the command structure. When asked whether or not he ever considered relieving Short of duty, General Clark says he never did.[31]

The key ingredient in coercive diplomacy is credibility. Since the very nature of coercive diplomacy is the *threat* of force—or the *limited* use of actual force—it implies a limited use of resources to achieve an objective. Thus, if the opponent has no reason to fear either the threat of, or a limited use of, force, the *cost* of opposing the coercer is removed. This renders the dynamics between costs and benefits in the diplomacy largely nonexistent.

General Clark rightly points out that "once the threat surfaces, however, nations or alliances are committed. Following through to preserve credibility becomes a matter of vital interest. Credibility is the ultimate measure of value for states and international institutions."[32] Byman and Waxman make a similar argument, saying that will and credibility often matter more than the overall balance of forces, adding that credibility is necessary to have any chance of successful coercion.[33] Two factors should be noted in this regard. First, NATO had significant problems with its credibility all through its crisis management, and second, the logic of credibility does not only apply to the one being coerced but also to the coercer. Thus, NATO's coercive diplomacy did not only apply to Milošević. In reality, and somewhat ironically, when NATO started issuing threats it did not act upon, it thereby coerced itself into issuing ever more threats in an escalating spiral out of which it was difficult to break.

As noted in chapter 5, Operation Determined Falcon in June 1998 was perceived, even by NATO officials, to be counterproductive in terms of showing credibility. Just by reading public media, one knew that in Greece, Italy, and Germany there was very substantial domestic opposition to military involvement against the FRY. The whole of NATO was aware that some nations' resolve was very shaky, and after a few days of OAF, Italy in fact signaled that it was likely to face a governmental crisis if the bombing were escalated.[34] It is highly unlikely that Milošević was not informed of this lack of resolve or failed to bring it into his calculations. Naumann believes that Milošević was well aware of NATO's intentions until the very start of the campaign. In one of his conversations with Naumann in Belgrade in October 1998, the Serb foreign minister, Milutinović, boasted—long after midnight, after long hours of talks—"We know everything about your NATO Council delegations and their views," and added, "and the British reports are the best."[35] By Christmas in 1998, Milošević seemingly had insight in the internal debates in the North Atlantic Council, had been provided with significant parts of NATO's air campaign plan by a French officer, and had seen in Operation Desert Fox that the United States and the United Kingdom were capable of stopping their bombing short of reaching their objectives. Milošević knew that there was no UN resolution authorizing the use of force by NATO and understood the consequences this had for public opinion in Europe. He felt he had a powerful international ally in Russia, which he believed would continue to block a UN resolution and would put pressure on the international community to stop the bombing if it ever came to that. Also, as shown in chapter 7, he concluded that NATO would only be able to bomb for about a week before being forced to stop. Milošević simply did not believe that the threat was credible, and as Judah rightly asserts: "There is no mystery about why NATO bombed Yugoslavia for 78 days beginning on 24 March. Quite simply, the leaders of NATO countries thought it would only last a few days and so did Milošević."[36] Perhaps indicative of the perception in Belgrade, Milošević's wife, Mira Marković, stated on camera that when OAF commenced she believed the air strikes would last only one night.[37]

The other problem facing NATO was that credibility has its own simple logic: if you threaten something and do not make good upon your threats, your credibility is reduced. This started to haunt NATO through the summer and fall of 1998, and it became a powerful political force in itself. For NATO, losing credibility would have ramifications far exceeding the conflict in Kosovo. As the British Defence Committee's Fourteenth Report says: "Once NATO had threatened the use of force to resolve the crisis, so Milošević's defiance provoked further threats and increasingly it was felt that the Alliance's credibility needed to be defended."[38] Despite what many people recognized as horrific actions by both the KLA and Serb forces by late autumn 1998, the inherent logic of credibility was in Belgrade's disfavor. By the end of the Rambouillet negotiations the U.S.-dominated effort had been largely reduced to having the Kosovar Albanian delegation sign the agreement, which would immediately trigger NATO airpower to bomb the Federal Republic of Yugoslavia.

Finding the balance between force and diplomacy, and between costs and benefits, is a complex and challenging task. Identifying targets that if struck will change the opponent's decision making (behavior) is a difficult, complex, and interactive (that is, with the opponent) endeavor. As Byman and Waxman rightly assert, "Coercion is therefore a two-sided, interactive game in which the situation may change and with it calculations of costs and benefits."[39] One of the key lessons from the Kosovo crisis is that NATO was unable to produce a carefully calibrated strategy that would have been politically acceptable as part of the scheme of crisis management. The U.S. Department of Defense admits the Kosovo crisis would have benefited from more advanced planning:

> Planning focused on air strikes and diplomacy as the primary tools to achieve U.S. and NATO objectives. As it became clear that Milošević intended to outlast the alliance, more attention was paid to other ways of bringing pressure to bear, including economic sanctions and information operations. While ultimately these instruments were put to use with good effect, more advanced planning might have made them more effective at an earlier date. . . . The routine participation of senior officials in rehearsals, gaming, exercises and simulations would strengthen awareness of the broad range of available policy tools.[40]

The British Defence Committee asserted that "Kosovo has, fortunately, dispelled the illusion that NATO is an instrument that can be readily used in a precise and discriminating way to support diplomacy."[41] General Smith argues that "the starting point to understanding all operations in the Balkans in the 1990s, including the NATO bombings of 1995 and 1999, was that they were without strategies."[42] After OAF, General Kelche says, he evaluated the French capacity to develop strategies for low-intensity warfare that could analyze, locate, attack, and assess targets that if struck could produce favorable results as part of the nation's management of the crisis, before the situation had escalated to high-intensity conflict. OAF had shown that France lacked this capacity, and as a result of this evaluation General Kelche established a permanent cell in the operational headquarters to focus on developing various crisis-management strategies that could then be presented as different options to the politicians. "If you do not have options when the politicians ask how to handle a specific situation, you can be sure they will opt to wait or do nothing. We need to improve our capacity to handle limited crises, and be ready at a much earlier stage to be able to provide analyses of what the options are, and what consequences they have."[43] The lessons of Britain, France, and the United States go to the heart of the failure of NATO's crisis management preceding OAF. When politicians said "we have got to do something," the military could not provide an adequate reply, and thus they have to shoulder some part of the lack of preparedness when OAF commenced. It represents a challenge for the military in general and the airpower community in particular to focus more resources and education on the conceptual development of coercive strategies and conflicts in the lower end of the intensity spectrum.

General Smith argues that the character of war has changed and that war as a massive, deciding event in an international dispute no longer exists. He also points out that the ends for which we fight are changing "from the hard absolute objectives of interstate industrial war to more malleable objectives." Smith says modern wars are marked by the relationship between political and military activities, since they will evolve and change together, one impacting the other. "Only when the use of force is analysed in this way will it have utility," he says, arguing that modern war dictates the way the international community approaches confrontations or conflicts: "Military force does not have an absolute utility, other than its basic purpose of killing and destroying. Every confrontation or indeed conflict is different, not only in locations and sides but in nature, especially in our era of humanitarian interventions."[44] Military theorist Martin van Creveld argues that in the future people will probably look back on the twentieth century as a period when vast armies and sophisticated war machines became obsolete, and he stresses the future of war as that of low-intensity warfare.

The demise of conventional war will cause strategy in its traditional, Clausewitzian sense to disappear. . . . The need to concentrate the greatest possible force and deliver a smashing blow at the decisive point will continue to clash with the need to outwit, mislead, deceive, and surprise the enemy. Victory, as always, will go to the side that best understands how to balance these two contradictory require-ments, not just in an abstract but at a specific time, at a specific place and against a specific enemy.[45]

Similarly, the Kosovo crisis seems to have vindicated the perspective of Professor Dennis Drew, who assessed that the dominant NATO contributor of airpower—the U.S. Air Force—to a large extent has preferred to think of low-intensity conflict as just a small version of conventional war, and that it differs fundamentally from conventional war and represents an important void in American airpower theory.[46] General Clark echoes this theme, not-ing that "the 'big battle' philosophy that dominated much of Western mili-tary thought during the twentieth century must be modified."[47] For almost a century airpower theory had focused almost exclusively on winning high-intensity wars and had failed to appreciate simultaneously the need for pro-ducing precise and innovative solutions to complex conflicts and crises in the lower band of the intensity spectrum.

The situation in Kosovo was complicated. The Kosovo crisis was not a classic high-intensity conflict between two parties fighting over territory; it was a humanitarian crisis in the midst of Europe, engaging an alliance formed and educated to counter a completely different set of circumstances. Allied consensus was shaky, and a comprehensive military operation was not an option. At the same time, television pictures of fleeing Kosovar Albanians triggered allied politicians' desire "to do something." General Naumann argues that when politicians were told that the use of airpower in Ko-sovo—like in Bosnia in 1995—was likely to end the hostilities, it was like "the famous swimmer who is about to drown and sees a straw—he grabs it."[48] Secretary Cohen described the operation as "the best of a series of bad options—this was the best option under the circumstances."[49] General Clark explicitly acknowledged that he "was compelled to sacrifice [the] basic logic of warfare to maintain the political cohesion of the Alliance."[50] Politi-cal limitations and sensitivity would have a direct effect on the application of airpower. To a large extent, the targeting effort was focused inward at the domestic public of the various NATO nations rather than outward and on how best to affect Milošević. Fear of losing domestic support or allied consensus and of inflicting collateral damage dominated the effort. As one unnamed NATO ambassador reportedly admitted in a *Washington Post*

article: "We were more worried about how our actions were playing to public opinion in our own capitals rather than analysing the impact on Milošević
and his regime."[51] Similarly, the commander of U.S. air forces in Europe
during OAF, Gen. John Jumper, said planners managed an approved target
list on a day-by-day basis without reference to specific effects they desired
to create.[52]

The full extent of the political climate needs to be incorporated in order
to understand fully the delicate situation NATO was in when it went to war.
Gen. Sir Rupert Smith points out that it is unreasonable for the military to
ask for precise political strategies and end-states: "My personal sense is that
we—the military—are not only unreasonable; I think we are stupid to ask
for that degree of precision. We are demanding a degree of clarity of thought
that is unreasonable to ask the politicians. And we—if we changed positions—would be no cleverer at answering that question than the politicians
are at the moment."[53] Similarly, General Naumann has replied in this way
to the author's expressed astonishment at the lack of strategy and clarity of
thought before OAF commenced: "You can blame us—based on your War
Academy learning—that it was a mistake, and you are right in theory. But if
you are confronted with the option to either tolerate that people were killed
and expelled, or to do something with the vague hope that it might work
even without proper planning—you choose the latter."[54] Still, asked whether
he did not believe that in this particular case there should have been more
clarity than was provided, General Smith replied: "Yes, I would accept that
in the case of the Kosovo bombing. The expectation was that a day or two of
bombing would push Milošević back toward the negotiating table, and that
this would make him more cooperative—and I don't think anybody thought
it through further than that."[55]

The logic of coercion has its limitations, and not all crises can be handled
successfully using this strategy. Thomas Schelling makes an important distinction: it is the expectation of more violence that gets the wanted behavior,
"if the power to hurt can get it at all." Manipulating the risk of violence and
pain comes with a degree of uncertainty:

> Not everybody is always in his right mind. Not all the frontiers
> and thresholds are precisely defined, fully reliable, and known to be
> beyond the least temptation to test them out, to explore for loop-
> holes, or to take a chance that they may be disconnected this time.
> Violence, especially war, is a confused and uncertain activity, highly
> unpredictable, depending on decisions made by fallible human beings
> organized into imperfect governments, depending on fallible commu-
> nications and warning systems and on the untested performance of
> people and equipment.[56]

Therefore, it is quite possible it would have been impossible to coerce Milošević into a negotiated solution to the Kosovo crisis at an earlier stage, but in this particular crisis management, the *effort* was inadequate. In the end, when the first NATO targets were hit in the outskirts of Priština on the evening of 24 March 1999, no one in the military leadership of NATO had received any political guidance or developed any strategy for what the situation in Kosovo would be like after the war. On the eve of conflict, NATO had hardly planned for the war the Alliance itself was about to start.

NOTES

Introduction

1. First war in the history of NATO: Wesley K. Clark, *Waging Modern War: Bosnia, Kosovo, and the Future of Combat* (New York: PublicAffairs, Perseus Books Group, 2001), p. xxiii; Benjamin S. Lambeth, *NATO's Air War for Kosovo: A Strategic and Operational Assessment* (Santa Monica, Calif.: RAND for the U.S. Air Force, 2001), p. xx. The term "war": OAF was never formally declared a war for juridical reasons, but engaging more than a thousand aircraft contributing to the dropping of 23,315 munitions on a sovereign nation suggests otherwise. As General Clark said in his memoirs: "We were never allowed to call it a war. But it was, of course." Clark, *Waging Modern War*, p. xxiii; Lambeth, *NATO's Air War for Kosovo*, p. 88.

2. Lambeth, *NATO's Air War for Kosovo*, summary, p. xx; Roberto Bellini, "Kosovo and Beyond: Is Humanitarian Intervention Transforming International Society?" *Human Rights & Human Welfare*, 2(1) (Winter 2002), www.du.edu/gsis/hrhw/volumes/2002/2-1/belloni2-1.pdf [accessed January 2007].

3. Gen. Jean-Pierre Kelche, interview with the author, Paris, France, 11 April 2005.

4. Daniel Byman and Matthew Waxman define coercion as "the use of threatened force, and at times the limited use of actual force to back up the threat, to induce an adversary to change its behaviour." Daniel Byman and Matthew Waxman, *The Dynamics of Coercion: American Foreign Policy and the Limits of Military Might* (Cambridge: Cambridge University Press, 2002), p. 1. Robert A. Pape defines coercion as "efforts to change the behaviour of a state by manipulating costs and benefits[;] . . . coercion seeks to force the opponent to alter its behaviour." Robert A. Pape, *Bombing to Win: Airpower and Coercion in War* (New York: Cornell University Press, 1996), p. 4. R. J. Art calls coercive diplomacy "the attempt to get a target—a state, a group (or groups) within a state, or a nonstate actor—to change its objectionable behaviour through either the threat to use force or the actual use of limited force. . . . Coercive diplomacy can include, but need not include, positive inducements. . . ." Robert J. Art and Patrick M. Cronin, ed., *The United States and Coercive Diplomacy* (Washington, D.C.: United States Institute of Peace Press, 2003), pp. 6–7.

5. Michael Clarke, "Airpower, Force and Coercion," in *The Dynamics of Airpower*, ed. Andrew Lambert and Arthur C. Williamson (Bracknell, U.K.: Her Majesty's Stationery Office, 1996), pp. 67, 75–85.

6. Clark, *Waging Modern War*, pp. 430–37; Colin McInnes, *Spectator-Sport War: The West and Contemporary Conflict* (Boulder, Colo.: Lynne Rienner, 2002),

pp. 79–82; Eliot A. Cohen, "The Mystique of U.S. Airpower," *Foreign Affairs,* 73(1) (1994), pp. 109–24.

7. *The Mind of Milošević,* Panorama, producer Kevin Sutcliffe, editor Peter Horrocks, reporter Gavin Hewitt, BBC1, 29 March 1999.
8. James Dobbins, telephone interview with the author, 22 September 2004.
9. This includes SACEUR, Commander in Chief Allied Forces Southern Europe, Commander Air Forces Southern Europe, Commander Allied Naval Forces, and Combined Air Operations Center Director.
10. Robert Kagan, *Of Paradise and Power: America and Europe in the New World Order* (New York: Alfred A. Knopf, 2003), p. 3.

Chapter 1. The First Week of OAF

1. W. K. Clark, *Waging Modern War: Bosnia, Kosovo, and the Future of Combat.* (New York: PublicAffairs [Perseus]), 2001, p. 419.
2. *War Room (The Kosovan War),* producers Andrew Bell and Toby Sculthorp, editor Peter Horrocks, BBC1, 19 April 1999; Tim Judah, *Kosovo: War and Revenge,* 2nd ed. (New Haven, Conn.: Yale Nota Bene, 2002), p. 229; Ivo H; Daalder and Michael E. O'Hanlon, *Winning Ugly: NATO's War to Save Kosovo* (Washington, D.C.: Brookings Institution, 2000), p. 18; Dana Priest, "The Battle inside Headquarters: Tension Grew with Divide over Strategy Series: *The Commanders' War: 3/3,*" *Washington Post,* 21 September 1999; Johanna McGeary, "The Road to Hell . . . was paved with good intentions, but muddled planning. Now what?" *Time Magazine,* 153(14) (1999), p. 36.
3. Clark, *Waging Modern War,* p. 170.
4. Michael R. Gordon, "Allies' War by Consensus Limiting Military Strategy," *New York Times,* 4 April 1999.
5. Klaus Naumann, "Interview with General Klaus Naumann," *PBS Frontline,* 2000, www.pbs.org/wgbh/pages/frontline/shows/kosovo [accessed 3 March 2004].
6. John A. Olsen, *From Manoeuvre Warfare to Kosovo?* (Trondheim: Royal Norwegian Air Force Academy, 2001), pp. 266–67.
7. Daalder and O'Hanlon, *Winning Ugly,* p. 90.
8. Ibid., p. 18.
9. Anthony H. Cordesman, *The Lessons and Non-Lessons of the Air and Missile Campaign in Kosovo* (Westport, Conn.: Praeger, 2001), p. 17.
10. "Interview with General Klaus Naumann," *PBS Frontline.*
11. Cordesman, *Lessons and Non-Lessons,* pp. 18–20.
12. Lambeth, *NATO's Air War for Kosovo,* p. 179.
13. Hans Røsjorde, interview with the author, Oslo, Norway, 8 June 2004.
14. Gen. Arne Solli, interview with the author, Oslo, Norway, 9 June 2004.
15. "Interview with Ivo Daalder," *PBS Frontline,* 2000, www.pbs.org/wgbh/pages/frontline/shows/kosovo [accessed 3 March 2004].
16. Dana Priest, "A Decisive Battle That Never Was: *The Commanders' War: 1/3,*" *Washington Post,* 19 September 1999.
17. Clark, *Waging Modern War,* pp. 439–40.
18. Ibid., p. 276.
19. Ibid., pp. 186–87.
20. Ibid., pp. 6–7.

21. *War in Europe,* written and presented by Michael Elliott, film editor John Lee, series producer Eamonn Matthews, MBC with GBH/*Frontline* for Channel 4 (aired January/February 2000).

22. Clark, *Waging Modern War,* p. 188.

23. Kelche interview.

24. North Atlantic Treaty Organization [hereafter NATO], *Press Statement by Dr. Javier Solana, Secretary General of NATO,* 23 March 1999, Press release (1999)040, www.nato.int/docu/pr/1999/p99-040e.htm [accessed 4 May 2005].

25. NATO, *Political and Military Objectives of NATO Action with Regard to the Crisis in Kosovo,* 23 March 1999, press release (1999)043, www.nato.int/docu/pr/1999/p99-043e.htm [accessed 4 May 2005].

26. NATO, *Statement by the North Atlantic Council on Kosovo,* 30 January 1999, press release (99)12, www.nato.int/docu/pr/1999/p99-012e.htm [accessed 4 May 2005].

27. Department of Defense, *Kosovo/Operation Allied Force After-Action Report,* Report to Congress, Washington, D.C., 31 January 2000, pp. 3–4, www.dod.gov/pubs/kaar02072000.pdf [accessed January 2007].

28. "Excerpts from Clinton's Address on NATO Attacks on Yugoslav Military Forces," *Washington Post,* 24 March 1999; William J. Clinton, *My Life,* large print ed. (New York: Random House, 2004), p. 1368.

29. George Robertson, *Examination of Witnesses* (Questions 356–79), London, Parliament Defence Committee, 24 March 1999.

30. Clark, *Waging Modern War,* pp. 423–24.

31. Daalder and O'Hanlon, *Winning Ugly,* p. 19.

32. Brig. Gen. Gunnar Lundberg, interview with the author, Stockholm, Sweden, 25 May 2004.

33. *The Defence Committee Fourteenth Report,* London, Parliament, 2000, point 70 www.parliament.the-stationery-office.co.uk/pa/cm199900/cmselect/cm-dfence/347/34710.htm#a16 [accessed 15 February 2005].

34. Clark, *Waging Modern War,* p. 218.

35. Ibid., p. 248

36. Daalder and O'Hanlon, *Winning Ugly,* p. 99.

37. Clark, *Waging Modern War,* p. 208.

38. Ibid., p. 216.

39. Ibid., pp. 222, 232.

40. Ibid., p. 233.

41. Madeleine Albright, *Madam Secretary: A Memoir* (London: Macmillan, 2003), p. 410.

42. Clark, *Waging Modern War,* pp. 239–40.

43. NATO, *NATO Handbook* (Brussels: NATO Office of Information and Press, 2001), chap. 5.

44. Clark, *Waging Modern War,* p. 271.

45. Gen. Dieter Stöckmann, interview with the author outside Bonn, Germany, 7 December 2004.

46. Parliament, *Fourteenth Report,* point "Strategy," annex A, "Summary."

47. Gordon, "Allies' War by Consensus Limiting Military Strategy."

48. Lundberg interview.

49. Lt. Gen. Michael C. Short, E-mail correspondence with the author, 31 August 2004.

50. Kelche interview.
51. Daalder and O'Hanlon, *Winning Ugly,* p. 104.
52. Clark, *Waging Modern War,* pp. 423–25.
53. Stöckmann interview.
54. Parliament, *Fourteenth Report,* point 301.
55. Ibid., point "Planning and Preparation," annex A, "Summary."
56. Clark, *Waging Modern War,* pp. 183–89.
57. Ingvar Carlson and Shridath Ramphal, "NATO's Vigilante Warfare Gives a Bad Example to the World," *International Herald Tribune,* 1 April 1999.
58. Boris Yeltsin, *Midnight Diaries* (New York: PublicAffairs, 2000), p. 255.
59. Interview with General Klaus Naumann, *PBS Frontline.*
60. David Halberstam, *War in a Time of Peace: Bush, Clinton, and the Generals* (New York: Scribner's, 2001), p. 450.
61. Daalder and O'Hanlon, *Winning Ugly,* p. 117.
62. Department of Defense, *Kosovo/Operation Allied Force After-Action Report,* p. 8.
63. Ibid.; Cordesman, *Lessons and Non-Lessons,* pp. 23–24; Clark, *Waging Modern War,* p. 176; Daalder and O'Hanlon, *Winning Ugly,* pp. 117–18.
64. Department of Defense, *Kosovo/Operation Allied Force After-Action Report,* pp. 17–24.
65. Lambeth, *NATO's Air War for Kosovo,* p. 209.
66. Ibid., p. 185.
67. Ibid., p. 188.
68. Kelche interview.
69. Stöckmann interview.
70. Ibid.
71. Michael C. Short, "Speech to the AFA Air Warfare Symposium 2000," 25 February, www.aef.org/pub/short200.asp [accessed 5 July 2005].
72. Gen. Sir Rupert Smith, telephone interview with the author, 15 March 2005.
73. Short, "Speech to the AFA Air Warfare Symposium 2000."
74. Ibid.
75. Department of Defense, *Kosovo/Operation Allied Force After-Action Report,* p. 23.
76. Paul C. Strickland, "USAF Aerospace-Power Doctrine. Decisive or Coercive?" *Aerospace Power Journal* 14(3) (2000), p. 23.
77. Wing Commander Sean Corbett, e-mail correspondence, spring 2004.
78. Lambeth, *NATO's Air War for Kosovo,* p. 181.
79. Strickland, "USAF Aerospace-Power Doctrine," p. 23.
80. Halberstam, *War in a Time of Peace,* p. 451.
81. Parliament, *Fourteenth Report,* point "Strategy," annex A, "Summary."
82. Col. Tom Johansen, interview with the author, Oslo, Norway, 17 October 2003.
83. Corbett e-mail correspondence.
84. Stöckmann interview.
85. Col. Chris Lorraine, e-mail correspondence, February 2005.
86. Interview with General Klaus Naumann, *PBS Frontline.*
87. Gen. Joseph Ralston, telephone interview with the author, 6 September 2004.
88. Daalder and O'Hanlon, *Winning Ugly,* p. 96.

89. Clark, *Waging Modern War,* p. 176.
90. Daalder and O'Hanlon, *Winning Ugly,* p. 100.
91. Ibid., p. 117.
92. Clark, *Waging Modern War,* p. 178.
93. *Fall of Milošević.*
94. Ibid.
95. *War in Europe.*
96. Clark, *Waging Modern War,* p. 202.
97. Ibid., pp. 224, 429.
98. Kelche interview.
99. Dana Priest, "Bombing by Committee: France Balked at NATO Targets: *The Commanders' War: 2/3,*" *Washington Post,* 20 September 1999.
100. Kelche interview.
101. Lt. Gen. Per Bøthun, interview with the author, Oslo, Norway, 15 April 2004.
102. Clark, *Waging Modern War,* p. 265.
103. Ralston interview.
104. Gen. Wesley K. Clark, e-mail correspondence, 5 May 2005.
105. Clark, *Waging Modern War,* pp. 425–26.
106. Elaine M. Grossman, "Kosovo War Tactics Compensated for Strategy Void, Expert Says," *Inside the Pentagon,* 1 July 1999.
107. Clark, *Waging Modern War,* pp. 202–3.
108. Ibid., p. 211, 216; Daalder and O'Hanlon, *Winning Ugly,* p. 117.
109. Clark, *Waging Modern War,* p. 210.
110. Daalder and O'Hanlon, *Winning Ugly,* p. 118; Cordesman, *Lessons and Non-Lessons,* p. 26.
111. Lambeth, *NATO's Air War for Kosovo,* p. 28.
112. Gen. Klaus Naumann, interview with the author, Berlin, Germany, 30 September 2005.
113. Ibid.
114. Ibid.
115. Norwegian defense minister, Eldbjørg Løwer, interview with the author, Oslo, Norway, 22 March 2004.
116. Norwegian foreign minister, Knut Vollebæk, interview with the author, Oslo, Norway, 26 August 2004.
117. Parliament, *Fourteenth Report,* point 97.
118. Col. Morten Klever, interview with the author, Oslo, Norway, 14 April 2004.
119. Priest, "Bombing by Committee."
120. Corbett e-mail correspondence.
121. Bradley Graham and William Drozdiak, "Allied Action Fails to Stop Serb Brutality," *Washington Post,* 31 March 1999.

Chapter 2. The Airpower Debate and OAF

1. Cohen, "The Mystique of U.S. Airpower," p. 109.
2. Clark, *Waging Modern War,* pp. 122–23; Lambeth, *NATO's Air War for Kosovo,* pp. 33, 66; "Interview with General Michael C. Short," *PBS Frontline;* Short, "Speech to the AFA Air Warfare Symposium 2000," available online; John E. Peters, Stuart Johnsen, et al., *European Contributions to Operation Allied Force: Implications for Transatlantic Cooperation* (Santa Monica, Calif.: RAND, 2001), pp. 58, 67.

3. Phillip S. Meilinger, "Introduction," "Giulio Douhet and the Origins of Air-power Theory"; James S. Corum, "Airpower Thought in Continental Europe between the Wars"; and Peter R. Faber, "Interwar US Army Aviation and the Air Corps Tactical School: Incubators of American Airpower"; all in *The Paths of Heaven: The Evolution of Airpower Theory*, ed. Phillip S. Meilinger (Maxwell Air Force Base, Ala.: Air University Press, 1997), introduction, pp. 1–40, 176, and 183–238. David MacIsaac, "Voices from the Central Blue: The Airpower Theorists," in *Makers of Modern Strategy: From Machiavelli to the Nuclear Age*, ed. Peter Paret (Princeton, N.J.: Princeton University Press, 1986), pp. 624–47; Carl H. Builder, *The Icarus Syndrome: The Role of Airpower Theory in the Evolution and Fate of the U.S. Air Force* (New Brunswick, N.J.: Transaction, 1994), pp. 203–16; Gian P. Gentile, *How Effective Is Strategic Bombing? Lessons Learned from World War II to Kosovo* (New York: New York University Press, 2001), pp. 1–32; Pape, *Bombing to Win*, pp. 55–86, 314–31; John A. Olsen, *Strategic Airpower in Desert Storm* (London: Frank Cass, 2003), pp. 65–72.

4. Meilinger, "Origins of Airpower Theory," p. 2.

5. David R. Mets, *The Long Search for a Surgical Strike: Precision Munitions and the Revolution in Military Affairs* (Maxwell Air Force Base, Ala.: Air University Press, 2001), p. 1.

6. Meilinger, "Origins of Airpower Theory," p. 11; Giulio Douhet, *The Command of the Air* (Manchester, N.H.: Ayer, 1999), p. 50.

7. Meilinger, "Origins of Airpower Theory," pp. 11, 15.

8. Gentile, *How Effective Is Strategic Bombing?* p. 12.

9. Faber, "Interwar US Army Aviation and the Air Corps Tactical School," p. 219.

10. Olsen, *Strategic Airpower in Desert Storm*, p. 65.

11. Haywood S. Hansell, *The Air Plan That Defeated Hitler* (New York: Arno, 1980), pp. 67–93 (quotation on p. 85); Pape, *Bombing to Win*, p. 259.

12. Hansell, *Air Plan That Defeated Hitler*, pp. 84–85; Gentile, *How Effective Is Strategic Bombing?* p. 17.

13. William W. Ralph, "Improvised Destruction: Arnold, LeMay, and the Fire-bombing of Japan," *War in History* 13(4) (2006), p. 509. Ralph refers to Hansell's *The Strategic Air War against Germany and Japan* (Washington, D.C.: Office of Air Force History, 1986), p. 223.

14. Ibid., p. 497.

15. Ibid., pp. 501–3.

16. Ibid., p. 512.

17. Ibid., pp. 513, 517, and 520. Robert S. McNamara, who later was to become Secretary of Defense during the Vietnam War, worked at the Army Air Force's Office of Statistical Control during World War II. McNamara performed analyses of the efficiency and effectiveness of U.S. bombers, especially the B-29 forces commanded by Maj. Gen. Curtis LeMay. Commenting on the bombing of Tokyo, McNamara said: "In that single night we burned to death a hundred thousand Japanese civilians in Tokyo—men, women and children. . . . I was part of a mechanism that in a sense recommended it. . . . LeMay said that if we lost the war we would all have been prosecuted as war criminals, and I think he was right. He, and I would say I, was behaving as war criminals." *The Fog of War: Eleven Lessons from the Life of Robert S. McNamara*, producers Errol Mor-

ris, Michael Williams, and Julie Ahlbergd, distributed by Sony Pictures, released 21 May 2003.

18. Olsen, *Strategic Airpower in Desert Storm,* p. 66.
19. Ralph, "Improvised Destruction," pp. 501–4, 512.
20. Builder, *Icarus Syndrome,* pp. 133–41.
21. Ibid., pp. 145–46.
22. Olsen, *Strategic Airpower in Desert Storm,* p. 71.
23. Colin Powell, *My American Journey* (New York: Random House, 1995), p. 141.
24. Olsen, *Strategic Airpower in Desert Storm,* p. 68.
25. Mark Clodfelter, *The Limits of Air Power: The American Bombing of North Vietnam* (New York: Free Press, 1989), p. 73.
26. Ibid., p. 206.
27. Powell, *My American Journey,* p. 142.
28. Dennis Drew, "Air Theory, Air Force, and Low Intensity Conflict," in *Paths of Heaven,* ed. Meilinger, p. 346.
29. Builder, *Icarus Syndrome,* p. 141.
30. Clark, *Waging Modern War,* p. 5.
31. Ibid., pp. 5–6.
32. Ibid., p. 6. Clark defines deterrence as "causing someone to refrain from doing something by threat of punishment or threat of taking away his means to act," and compellence as "to cause someone to act in a certain way . . . implicit or explicit bargaining through the graduated use of force, inflicting ever increasing punishment to convince an opponent to change his behavior" (p. 5).
33. Priest, "The Battle inside Headquarters."
34. Michael C. Short, "Interview with General Michael C. Short," *PBS Frontline,* 2000, www.pbs.org/wgbh/pages/frontline/shows/kosovo [accessed 20 December 2006].
35. Wesley K. Clark, James Ellis, and Michael C. Short, *Combined Prepared Statement to Senate Armed Services Committee,* 21 October 1999, armed-services. senate.gov/statemnt/1999/991021wc.pdf [accessed January 2007].
36. Robert F. Futrell, *Ideas, Concepts, Doctrine: Basic Thinking in the United States Air Force 1961–1984* (Maxwell Air Force Base, Ala.: Air University Press, 1989), vol. 2, pp. 539–40.
37. John L. Romjue, "The Evolution of the AirLand Battle Concept," *Air University Review* 35 (1984), pp. 4–15.
38. Some, like Gen. Curtis LeMay, claim that the strategic bombing in Linebacker I and II in the Vietnam War proved very effective. Others downplay its effect. Linebacker I and II did, however, not produce a different conceptual approach to strategic bombing, and they did not change the Air Force's doctrinaire perspective on strategic bombing.
39. Benjamin S. Lambeth, *The Transformation of American Airpower* (Ithaca, N.Y.: Cornell University Press, 2000), pp. 1–2.
40. Clodfelter, *Limits of Air Power,* pp. 203–4.
41. Olsen, *Strategic Airpower in Desert Storm,* pp. 86–87.
42. Jeffrey Record, "Into the Wild Blue Yonder: Should We Abolish the Air Force?" *Policy Review* 52 (1990), p. 50.
43. Olsen, *Strategic Airpower in Desert Storm,* pp. 75–76.

44. John A. Warden, *The Air Campaign: Planning for Combat* (toExcel.com, 2000), p. 7.

45. Warden defines *distant interdiction* as "an attack against the source of men and material"; *Air Campaign*, p. 80.

46. John A. Warden, "Employing Airpower in the Twenty-first Century," in *The Future of Airpower in the Aftermath of the Gulf War*, ed. Richard H. Shultz, Jr., and Robert L. Pfaltzgraff (Maxwell Air Force Base, Ala.: Air University Press, 1992), pp. 57–82.

47. Warden, "The Enemy as a System," *Airpower Journal*, 9(1) (1995), pp. 40–55.

48. Ibid., pp. 51–52.

49. Ibid., p. 55. Warden, "Success in Modern War," p. 173.

50. Grossman, "Kosovo War Tactics Compensated for Strategy Void."

51. John A. Warden, e-mail correspondence with the author, 12 September 2005.

52. Olsen, *Strategic Airpower in Desert Storm*, p. 86.

53. Ibid., pp. 91–92.

54. Ibid., pp. 93–95.

55. Halberstam, *War in a Time of Peace*, pp. 48–49.

56. Builder, *Icarus Syndrome*, pp. 179–80.

57. Olsen, *Strategic Airpower in Desert Storm*, pp. 98–100, 107–11.

58. Ibid., pp. 111–14.

59. Powell, *My American Journey*, pp. 472–73.

60. Pape, *Bombing to Win*, p. 211.

61. Peter Kellner, "Blair's Balkan Edge," *New York Times*, 1 April 1999.

62. Halberstam, *War in a Time of Peace*, p. 423.

63. McInnes, *Spectator-Sport War*, pp. 91–93.

64. Byman and Waxman, *Dynamics of Coercion*, pp. 88–89.

65. Cohen, "The Mystique of U.S. Airpower," p. 109.

66. Gordon, "Allies' War by Consensus Limiting Military Strategy."

67. The objectives were to isolate Saddam Hussein, eliminate Iraq's offensive and defensive capability, incapacitate the national leadership, reduce the threat to friendly nations, and minimize the damage so as to enhance rebuilding. Olsen, *Strategic Airpower in Desert Storm*, p. 105.

68. Anthony Lake, telephone interview with the author, 21 September 2005.

69. U.S. Air Force, *Basic Aerospace Doctrine of the United States Air Force* (AF Manual 1-1) (Washington, D.C.: Department of the Air Force, 1992), p. v (foreword).

70. Ibid., p. 17.

71. Ibid., p. 19.

72. AFM 2-11, pp. 9–10, para. 3-3b. AFM 2-11 is an Air Force manual below AFM 1-1 in the doctrine hierarchy.

73. Dennis Drew, "Air Theory, Air Force, and Low Intensity Conflict," in *Paths of Heaven*, ed. Meilinger, p. 346. See Drew's footnotes 91–93, p. 355.

74. Jason B. Barlow, "Strategic Paralysis: An Airpower Strategy for the present," *Airpower Journal* (Winter 1993), p. 5.

75. Ibid., p. 12.

76. David A. Deptula, *Effects-Based Operations: Change in the Nature of Warfare* (N.p.: Air Force Association, Aerospace Education Foundation, 2001), www.aef.org/pub/psbook.pdf [accessed 2006].

77. Ibid.
78. A good commentator on this issue is Phillip S. Meilinger, who writes, "Airmen have always desired to conduct successful effects-based operations. For much of the first century of airpower that aspiration was out of reach because of technological limitations on aircraft and weapons as well as inadequate intelligence and analytical tools. Now those tools and technology are beginning to catch up." "The Origins of Effects-Based Operations," *Joint Force Quarterly,* no. 35 (2003), www.dtic.mil/doctrine/jel/jfq_pubs/2135.pdf [accessed 2006].
79. Effects-based operations were not explicitly included in the 1997 *Air Force Basic Doctrine 1* (AFDD-1), but the sense could be inferred from sentences like, "Strategic attack should produce effects well beyond the proportion of effort expended in their execution.... Strategic attack is a function of objectives or effects achieved, not forces employed.... The means, methods and aim of strategic attack can be tailored to the objective or objectives being sought. Strategic attack can be a practical and potent option and can utilize a variety of weapons, forces, tactics or warfare to attain the desired 'strategic objectives or effects'" (U.S. Air Force, *Air Force Basic Doctrine 1,* AFDD-1 [Washington, D.C.: Department of the Air Force, 1997], pp. 51–52). The 2003 version of the publication declares, "EBO explicitly and logically links the effects of individual tactical actions directly to desired military and political outcomes. By focusing on effects—the full range of outcomes, events or consequences that result from a specific action—commanders can concentrate on meeting objectives instead of managing target lists. Effects-based actions or operations are those designed to produce distinct, desired effects while avoiding unintended or undesired effects" (AFDD-1, 17 November 2003, p. 18).
80. Harlan K. Ullman and James P. Wade, *Rapid Dominance: A Force for All Seasons*, RUSI Whitehall Paper Series (London: Royal United Services Institute for Defence Studies, 1998), pp. vii–xxi.
81. Ibid., p. xi.
82. Robert A. Pape, conversation with the author, Royal Norwegian Air Force Academy, 14 December 2006.
83. John T. Correll, "What Happened to Shock and Awe?" *Air Force Magazine* 86(11) (2003), p. 56, www.afa.org/magazine/Nov2003/1103shock.asp [accessed 2006].
84. Ibid.
85. Ullman and Wade, *Rapid Dominance*, p. vi.
86. Correll, "What Happened to Shock and Awe?" p. 54.
87. AFDD-1, 1997.
88. Ibid., foreword.
89. Ibid., p. 32.
90. Ibid., pp. 37, 40.
91. Tirpak, "Short's View of the Air Campaign," p. 45.
92. Warden e-mail correspondence.
93. Mason Carpenter and George T. McClain, "Air Command and Staff College Air Campaign Course: The Air Corps Tactical School Reborn?" *Aerospace Power Journal* (Fall 1993), www.airpower.maxwell.af.mil/airchronicles/apj/carpent.html [accessed December 2006].
94. John A. Olsen, *John Warden and the Renaissance of American Air Power* (Washington, D.C.: Potomac Books, forthcoming, 2007).

95. Drew, "Air Theory, Air Force, and Low Intensity Conflict," p. 344.
96. Short, "Interview with General Michael C. Short."
97. Warden, "Enemy as a System," p. 45.
98. Tirpak, "Short's View of the Air Campaign," p. 43.
99. Michael C. Short, "An Airman's Lessons from Kosovo," in *From Manoeuvre Warfare to Kosovo?* ed. John A. Olsen (Trondheim: Royal Norwegian Air Force Academy, 2001), p. 260.
100. Tirpak, "Short's View of the Air Campaign," pp. 45, 47.
101. Strickland, "USAF Aerospace-Power Doctrine," p. 14.
102. Ibid.
103. For greater insight in this particular debate, see Robert A. Pape, "The Limits of Precision-Guided Airpower," *Security Studies*, 7(2) (1997/98), pp. 93–114; John A. Warden, "Success in Modern War: A Response to Robert Pape's *Bombing to Win*," *Security Studies*, 7(2) (1997/98), pp. 172–90; Robert A. Pape, "The Air Force Strikes Back," *Security Studies*, 7(2) (1997/98), pp. 191–214; Barry D. Watts, "Ignoring Reality: Problems of Theory and Evidence in Security Studies," *Security Studies*, 7(2) (1997/98), pp. 115–71; Karl Mueller, "Strategies of Coercion: Denial, Punishment and the Future of Airpower," *Security Studies*, 7(3) (1998), pp. 182–228.
104. Robert A Pape, conversation with the author, Royal Norwegian Air Force Academy, 14 December 2006.
105. The term *coercion* means "efforts to change the behaviour of a state by manipulating costs and benefits[;] . . . coercion seeks to force the opponent to alter its behavior," while deterrence seeks "to maintain the status quo by discouraging an opponent from changing its behavior." Pape, *Bombing to Win*, pp. 4, 329.
106. Ibid., pp. 318–19.
107. Ibid., pp. 58–86.
108. Ibid., pp. 55–66, 316.
109. Ibid., pp. 66–67.
110. Thomas C. Schelling, *Arms and Influence* (New Haven, Conn.: Yale University Press, 1966), pp. 2–4.
111. Pape, *Bombing to Win*, p. 316.
112. Ibid., pp. 69–79, 316–17.
113. Ibid., pp. 211, 240–41.
114. Ibid., pp. 55, 79–86, and 316.
115. Stöckmann interview.
116. Clark, Ellis, and Short, "Lessons Learned," p. 2.
117. Naumann interview.
118. Pape, *Bombing to Win*, pp. 66–67.
119. Clark, *Waging Modern War*, p. 449.
120. Ibid.
121. Johansen interview.

Chapter 3. From Vietnam to Kosovo: U.S. Foreign Policy and the Use of Force

1. Stanley Karnow, *Vietnam*, 2nd rev. and updated ed. (New York: Penguin Books, 1997), pp. 14–15; Harvard Sitikoff , "The Postwar Impact of Vietnam," in *The Oxford Companion to American Military History*, ed. John W. Chambers (New York: Oxford University Press, 1999), www.english.uiuc.edu/maps/vietnam/postwar.htm [accessed January 2007].

2. Sitikoff, "Postwar Impact of Vietnam," p. 1.
3. Karnow, *Vietnam,* p. 11.
4. Ibid., pp. 11–14.
5. Colin L. Powell, "U.S. Forces: Challenges Ahead," *Foreign Affairs,* 71(5) (1992), p. 32.
6. Halberstam, *The Best and the Brightest*, p. 41.
7. Karnow, *Vietnam,* pp. 14–16.
8. Ibid., pp. 14–16.
9. Ibid., p. 18.
10. Sitikoff, "Postwar Impact of Vietnam," p. 1.
11. Karnow, *Vietnam,* p. 26.
12. Ibid., p. 9.
13. Ibid., p. 18.
14. Roger J. Spiller, "In the Shadow of the Dragon: Doctrine and the US Army After Vietnam," *RUSI Journal*, 142(6) (1997), p. 43; Karnow, *Vietnam,* pp. 31–32.
15. "Rumsfeld's War." *PBS Frontline, Washington Post,* written, produced, and directed by Michael Kirk, coproduced and reported by Jim Gilmore, 2004. Aired on Norwegian Broadcast (NRK1) 15 February 2005.
16. Spiller, "In the Shadow of the Dragon," p. 42.
17. Sitikoff, "Postwar Impact of Vietnam," p. 1.
18. Clark, *Waging Modern War,* p. 17.
19. Spiller, "In the Shadow of the Dragon," p. 43; Karnow, *Vietnam,* pp. 31–32.
20. "Rumsfeld's War."
21. Karnow, *Vietnam,* p. 31.
22. Ibid., pp. 17, 554.
23. "Rumsfeld's War."
24. Gen. Maxwell Taylor: Vietnam-era adviser to President John F. Kennedy and subsequently Lyndon B. Johnson's ambassador in Saigon.
25. Karnow, *Vietnam,* p. 23.
26. Ibid.
27. Ibid., p. 17.
28. Jeffrey Record, *Making War, Thinking History: Munich, Vietnam, and Presidential Uses of Force from Korea to Kosovo* (Annapolis, Md.: Naval Institute Press, 2002), pp. 18–19.
29. John T. Correll, "About the 'Powell Doctrine' . . . ," *Air Force Magazine,* 82 (1999), p. 8; Jeffrey Record, "Force-Protection Fetishism: Sources, Consequences, and (?) Solutions," *Aerospace Power Journal*, 14(2) (2000), p. 6; Powell, *My American Journey,* pp. 302–3.
30. Record, *Making War, Thinking History,* p. 27.
31. Jim Mokhiber and Rick Young, "The Uses of Military Force," *PBS Online and WGBH/Frontline,* 1999, www.pbs.org/wgbh/pages/frontline/shows/military/force [accessed December 2006].
32. Powell, *My American Journey,* p. 303.
33. Karnow, *Vietnam,* p. 35.
34. Record, *Making War, Thinking History,* pp. 26–27.
35. Ibid., pp. 27–29.
36. Mokhiber and Young, "The Uses of Military Force."
37. Ibid.
38. Powell, *My American Journey,* p. 303.

39. Holbrooke, *To End a War*, p. 217.
40. Halberstam, *War in a Time of Peace*, p. 149.
41. Powell, *My American Journey*, p. 338.
42. Karnow, *Vietnam*, pp. 29–31.
43. Mokhiber and Young, "The Uses of Military Force."
44. Clark, *Waging Modern War*, p. 7.
45. Olsen, *Strategic Airpower in Desert Storm*, p. 71.
46. Ibid., p. 15.
47. Sitikoff, "Postwar Impact of Vietnam," p. 1; Karnow, *Vietnam*, p. 15.
48. "Rumsfeld's War."
49. Ibid.
50. Ibid.
51. Record, *Making War, Thinking History*, p. 30.
52. Halberstam, *War in a Time of Peace*, pp. 12–13.
53. Spiller, "In the Shadow of the Dragon," p. 42.
54. "Rumsfeld's War."
55. Record, "Force-Protection Fetishism," p. 4.
56. Karnow, *Vietnam*, p. 16.
57. Powell, "U.S. Forces," pp. 32–45.
58. Ibid., p. 38.
59. Ibid., p. 40.
60. Record, *Making War, Thinking History*, p. 27.
61. Powell, "U.S. Forces," p. 40.
62. Halberstam, *War in a Time of Peace*, p. 32.
63. Record, *Making War, Thinking History*, pp. 111–12.
64. Warren Zimmermann, *Origins of a Catastrophe: Yugoslavia and Its Destroyers*, 2nd ed. (New York: Times Books, 1999), p. 214.
65. Holbrooke, *To End a War*, p. 360; Albright, *Madam Secretary*, p. 180.
66. Zimmermann, *Origins of a Catastrophe*, pp. 214–15.
67. Halberstam, *War in a Time of Peace*, p. 37.
68. Zimmermann, *Origins of a Catastrophe*, p. 215.
69. Ibid.
70. Halberstam, *War in a Time of Peace*, p. 57.
71. Ivo H. Daalder, *Getting to Dayton: The Making of America's Bosnia Policy* (Washington, D.C.: Brookings Institution, 2000), p. 10.
72. Anthony Lake, "Defining Missions, Setting Deadlines: Meeting New Security Challenges in the Post Cold-War World," remarks at George Washington University, 6 March 1996, www.pbs.org/wgbh/pages/frontline/shows/military/force/lake.html [accessed March 2006].
73. Halberstam, *War in a Time of Peace*, p. 36.
74. Holbrooke, *To End a War*, p. 360; Albright, *Madam Secretary*, p. 180.
75. Albright, *Madam Secretary*, p. 27.
76. Michael Dobbs and John M. Goshko, "Albright's Personal Odyssey Shaped Foreign Policy Beliefs," *Washington Post*, 6 December 1996.
77. Albright, *Madam Secretary*, p. xiii.
78. Ibid., p. 43.
79. Record, *Making War, Thinking History*, p. 114.
80. Albright, *Madam Secretary*, p. 505.

81. Daalder, *Getting to Dayton,* p. 92.
82. Albright, *Madam Secretary,* p. 182.
83. Robert Gelbard, telephone interview with the author, 17 May 2005.
84. Smith interview.
85. Zimmermann, *Origins of a Catastrophe,* pp. 215–16.
86. Les Aspin, "With the Soviets and Cold War Gone, What Is the Future for US Forces?" *ROA National Security Report* (November 1992), p. 23; John T. Correll, "A Strategy of Uncertainty," *Air Force Magazine,* 80(5) (1998), p. 4.
87. Record, "Force-Protection Fetishism," p. 6.
88. Rick Young, "Lessons of Vietnam: A Conversation with Major H. R. McMaster," *PBS Online and WGBH/Frontline,* www.pbs.org/wgbh/pages/frontline/shows/military/force [accessed March 2006].
89. Albright, *Madam Secretary,* p. 178; Carl Bildt, *Uppdrag Fred* (Norstedts, Nor.: Bokförlaget Pan, 1997), p. 113; Daalder, *Getting to Dayton,* p. 13.
90. Albright, *Madam Secretary,* p. 180.
91. Daalder, *Getting to Dayton,* p. 13.
92. Ibid., p. 83.
93. Albright, *Madam Secretary,* pp. 180–81.
94. Ibid., p. 182.
95. Powell, *My American Journey,* pp. 576–77. There is an anecdote regarding this phrase: General Powell, as seen, used this phrase in his memoirs, and Secretary Albright teased him for it. General Powell promptly sent her a copy signed, "Patiently yours, Colin Powell." Later, Madeleine Albright sent him a copy of her memoirs, signed "Forcefully yours, Madeleine Albright"; Albright, *Madam Secretary,* p. 182.
96. Powell, *My American Journey,* pp. 576–77.
97. Ibid.; Albright, *Madam Secretary,* pp. 128–29.
98. Albright, *Madam Secretary,* p. 180.
99. Lake interview.
100. Ibid.
101. Ibid.
102. Halberstam, *War in a Time of Peace,* p. 378.
103. Ibid., p. 323.
104. Ibid., pp. 390–91.
105. Ibid., p. 265.
106. Ibid., pp. 256–58, 377.
107. Daalder, *Getting to Dayton,* p. 20.
108. Ibid., p. 136.
109. Halberstam, *War in a Time of Peace,* p. 286.
110. Clark, *Waging Modern War,* p. 7.
111. Ibid., p. 436.
112. Ibid., p. 39.
113. Halberstam, *War in a Time of Peace,* p. 356; Clark, *Waging Modern War,* p. 42.
114. Clark, *Waging Modern War,* p. 55.
115. Ibid., pp. 39, 42, and 54; Holbrooke, *To End a War,* pp. 142, 175.
116. Holbrooke, *To End a War,* pp. 142, 175.
117. Ibid.; Clark, *Waging Modern War,* p. 54.
118. Gelbard interview.

119. Clark, *Waging Modern War*, p. 54.
120. Ibid., pp. 430, 432.
121. Albright, *Madam Secretary*, p. 192.
122. Mokhiber and Young, "The Uses of Military Force."
123. Holbrooke, *To End a War*, p. 216.
124. Albright, *Madam Secretary*, p. 266; Holbrooke, *To End a War*, pp. 345–48; Clark, *Waging Modern War*, p. 72.
125. Clark, *Waging Modern War*, p. 106.
126. Halberstam, *War in a Time of Peace*, p. 363.
127. Ibid., p. 434.
128. Ibid.
129. Gelbard interview.
130. Halberstam, *War in a Time of Peace*, p. 436.
131. Clark e-mail correspondence.
132. Clark, *Waging Modern War*, p. xxviii.
133. Department of Defense, *Kosovo/Operation Allied Force After-Action Report*, pp. 12, 120.
134. William Cohen, "Interview with William Cohen," *PBS Frontline*, 2000, www.pbs.org/wgbh/pages/frontline/shows/kosovo [accessed December 2006].
135. Zimmermann, *Origins of a Catastrophe*, pp. 225–26.
136. Sitikoff, "Postwar Impact of Vietnam"; Holbrooke, *To End a War*, p. 216.
137. Clinton, *My Life*, pp. 879–86.
138. Holbrooke, *To End a War*, p. 217.
139. Halberstam, *War in a Time of Peace*, p. 263.
140. Record, *Making War, Thinking History*, p. 111.
141. Clark, *Waging Modern War*, p. 437.
142. Clinton, *My Life*, p. 948.
143. Ibid., p. 948.
144. William J. Clinton, "Address to the American Federation of State, County, and Municipal Employees (AFSCME) Biennial Convention," 23 March 1999, www.state.gov/www/policy_remarks/1999/990323_clinton_afscme.html [accessed December 2006].
145. Albright, *Madam Secretary*, p. 265.
146. Ibid., p. 405.
147. Record, *Making War, Thinking History*, p. 116.
148. Ibid., p. 113.
149. Halberstam, *War in a Time of Peace*, pp. 407–8.
150. Record, *Making War, Thinking History*, p. 113.
151. Halberstam, *War in a Time of Peace*, p. 193.
152. Holbrooke, *To End a War*, p. 217; Mokhiber and Young, "The Uses of Military Force."
153. Clinton, *My Life*, p. 948.
154. Gelbard interview.
155. Ibid.
156. Record, *Making War, Thinking History*, p. 116.
157. Daalder and O'Hanlon, *Winning Ugly*, pp. 53–54.
158. Ibid., pp. 54–56.
159. Halberstam, *War in a Time of Peace*, p. 422.

160. Bradley Graham, "Joint Chiefs Doubted Air Strategy," *Washington Post,* 5 April 1999.
161. Albright, *Madam Secretary,* p. 184.

Chapter 4. Lessons from Bosnia

1. *Mind of Milošević.*
2. NATO's website, www.nato.int/docu/update/1990/summarye.htm [accessed March 2004].
3. Zimmermann, *Origins of a Catastrophe,* pp. 157–60.
4. Thorvald Stoltenberg, interview with the author, Oslo, Norway, 8 June 2004.
5. NATO website, www.nato.int/docu/update/1992/summarye.htm. This would later become the "out-of-area concept," which allowed NATO to operate outside alliance territory; Susan L. Woodward, *Balkan Tragedy: Chaos and Dissolution after the Cold War* (Washington, D.C.: Brookings Institution, 1995), p. 397.
6. Albright, *Madam Secretary,* p. 178; Stoltenberg interview.
7. Holbrooke, *To End a War,* p. 28; Stoltenberg interview.
8. Bildt, *Uppdrag Fred,* p. 529.
9. Halberstam, *War in a Time of Peace,* p. 86.
10. Dobbins interview.
11. Thorvald Stoltenberg and Kai Eide, *De tusen dagene: Fredsmeklere på Balkan* (Oslo: Gyldendal Norsk Forlag, 1996), pp. 206, 410; Stoltenberg interview.
12. Holbrooke, *To End a War,* pp. 26–27; Christopher Hill, telephone interview with the author, 8 November 2004.
13. Hill interview.
14. Stoltenberg interview.
15. Woodward, *Balkan Tragedy,* pp. 6–7, 333–34; Clinton, *My Life,* p. 814.
16. Woodward, *Balkan Tragedy,* pp. 7–8, 334–37.
17. Holbrooke, *To End a War,* p. xv.
18. Brendan Simms, *Unfinest Hour: Britain and the Destruction of Bosnia* (London: Penguin Books, 2002), pp. 1–7.
19. Halberstam, *War in a Time of Peace,* pp. 129, 135–36.
20. Ibid.
21. David Owen, *Balkan Odyssey* (London: Victor Gollancz, 1995), p. 13; Clinton, *My Life,* p. 816.
22. Cordesman, *Lessons and Non-Lessons,* p. 6.
23. Albright, *Madam Secretary,* p. 380.
24. Daalder, *Getting to Dayton,* p. 7.
25. Woodward, *Balkan Tragedy,* pp. 7–8, 334–37.
26. Clark, *Waging Modern War,* p. 37.
27. Albright, *Madam Secretary,* pp. 180–81.
28. Halberstam, *War in a Time of Peace,* p. 199.
29. Daalder, *Getting to Dayton,* p. 13.
30. Halberstam, *War in a Time of Peace,* pp. 196–97.
31. Smith interview.
32. Daalder, *Getting to Dayton,* pp. 8–9.
33. Daalder refers to a book by Nelson Drew, *On the Edge,* p. 150 (Daalder, *Getting to Dayton,* p. 14).

34. Powell, *My American Journey*, pp. 575–76.
35. Simms, *Unfinest Hour*, p. 5.
36. Halberstam, *War in a Time of Peace*, p. 227.
37. Daalder, *Getting to Dayton*, pp. 16-17.
38. Rupert Smith, *The Utility of Force: The Art of War in the Modern World* (London: Allen Lane, 2005), pp. 335, 340–41. Smith refers to Shashi Tharoor, "Should UN Peacekeeping Go 'Back to Basics'?" *Survival*, 37(4) (1995/96), p. 60.
39. Smith, *Utility of Force*, pp. 336–37, 353.
40. Daalder, *Getting to Dayton*, pp. 20–1.
41. Ibid., p. 22. Daalder attributes this quotation to Barton Gellman and Trevor Rowe, "NATO Prepares Bosnia Target Lists," *Washington Post*, August 4, 1993, p. A1.
42. Robert C. Owen, ed., *Deliberate Force: A Case Study in Effective Air Campaigning* (Maxwell Air Force Base, Ala.: Air University Press, 2000), pp. 472–73.
43. Smith interview.
44. Daalder, *Getting to Dayton*, pp. 23–24.
45. Simms, *Unfinest Hour*, p. 1.
46. Ibid., pp. 33–36.
47. Stoltenberg and Eide, *De tusen dagene*, p. 172.
48. Woodward, *Balkan Tragedy*, p. 398.
49. Hill interview.
50. Holbrooke, *To End a War*, p. 83.
51. Woodward, *Balkan Tragedy*, p. 6.
52. Clinton, *My Life*, p. 933.
53. Daalder, *Getting to Dayton*, p. 32.
54. Simms, *Unfinest Hour*, p. 131.
55. Daalder, *Getting to Dayton*, p. 33.
56. Ibid., pp. 32–33.
57. Simms, *Unfinest Hour*, pp. 129, 131.
58. Ibid., p. 323.
59. Woodward, *Balkan Tragedy*, p. 2.
60. Bildt, *Uppdrag Fred*, pp. 62–63.
61. Halberstam, *War in a Time of Peace*, p. 126.
62. Misha Glenny, *The Balkans: Nationalism, War, and the Great Powers, 1804–1999* (Penguin Books, 2001), pp. 641–42.
63. Woodward, *Balkan Tragedy*, p. 10.
64. Stoltenberg interview.
65. Woodward, *Balkan Tragedy*, p. 6.
66. Daalder, *Getting to Dayton*, pp. 83–84. The quotation to which Daalder refers is taken from Bob Woodward, *The Choice* (New York: Simon and Schuster, 1996), p. 253.
67. Bildt, *Uppdrag Fred*, p. 27.
68. Halberstam, *War in a Time of Peace*, p. 303.
69. Smith, *Utility of Force*, p. 351.
70. Albright, *Madam Secretary*, p. 186.
71. Daalder, *Getting to Dayton*, p. 80.
72. Ibid., pp. 112–13. The "endgame strategy" included a comprehensive peace

settlement based on the core principles of the Contact Group plan, including a united Bosnia; three-way recognition between Croatia, Bosnia, and the Federal Republic of Yugoslavia; consideration of changes in the Contact Group map to take account of recent territorial changes and to ensure viable and defensible borders; a framework for the long-term constitutional arrangements of a united Bosnia, including the possible scope of the "parallel special relationship" of the two entities with Croatia and Serbia; sanctions relief for Yugoslavia, with the suspension of sanctions once an agreement had been signed and complete lifting of sanctions once the agreement had been implemented; a plan to resolve the situation in eastern Slavonia, a part of Croatia bordering Serbia; and a comprehensive plan for regional economic integration, to be assisted through an international "mini-Marshall" plan. If the diplomatic initiative failed and UNPROFOR had to be withdrawn, the United States would seek to end the arms embargo multilaterally, through a vote by the UNSC; provide arms, training, and support to the Bosnians (whether the arms embargo were lifted or not) in order to assist in establishing a balance of power on the ground; enforce the no-fly zone and conduct air strikes for a nine-month transition period if the Bosnian Serbs attacked; and encourage the presence of a multinational force to assist the Bosnians in defending their territory.

73. Ibid., pp. 102–103. The quotation refers to Ann Blackman, *Seasons of Her Life: A Biography of Madeleine Korbel Albright* (New York: Scribner's, 1998), p. 242.
74. Clark, *Waging Modern War,* pp. 51–52.
75. Albright, *Madam Secretary,* p. 190.
76. Judah, *Kosovo,* p. 121; Bildt, *Uppdrag Fred,* p. 124.
77. Daalder, *Getting to Dayton,* p. 120.
78. Owen, *Deliberate Force: A Case Study,* pp. 496–97.
79. Clark, *Waging Modern War,* pp. 43–44.
80. Ibid., pp. 49–50, 52.
81. Clinton, *My Life,* p. 1068.
82. Halberstam, *War in a Time of Peace,* pp. 338–39.
83. Holbrooke, *To End a War,* pp. 61, 73, 166, and 199. Richard Holbrooke had lunch with the Croatian leader Franjo Tudjman on 17 August, at which time Holbrooke received a handwritten note from Robert C. Frasure [U.S. Deputy Assistant Secretary of State for European and Canadian Affairs, 1994–95] admitting the U.S. contribution: "Dick: We 'hired' these guys to be our junkyard dogs because we were desperate: . . . This is the first time the Serb wave has been reversed. That is essential for us to get stability, so we can get out." Later, Holbrooke gave incentives to the Croats and Bosnian Muslims not to stop the offensive but to continue, in order to provide diplomatic leverage.
84. Judah, *Kosovo,* p. 121.
85. Owen, *Deliberate Force,* p. 28.
86. Holbrooke, *To End a War,* p. 91. Richard Holbrooke himself wondered whether this was a deliberate response to his public warnings the previous day. See also Owen, *Deliberate Force,* pp. 28–29.
87. Daalder, *Getting to Dayton,* pp. 131–34.
88. Cordesman, *Lessons and Non-Lessons,* p. 6.
89. Clark, *Waging Modern War,* pp. 42–43 and 58–59.

90. Ibid., page 63.
91. Holbrooke, *To End a War,* p. 339.
92. Ibid., pp. 83–84, 88, 92, 102–103, 116–17, 185–86, 362, and 367. On p. 191–92, Holbrooke says about this particular phase of negotiations in late September 1995: "I told him that we would then [whether to separate the issues of a cease-fire, peace conference, and location] find ourselves in contentious and time-wasting negotiations within the Contact Group. We had to bypass this step with a package announcement."
93. Albright, *Madam Secretary,* pp. 393–96; Judah, *Kosovo,* p. 219.
94. Owen, *Deliberate Force,* p. 475.
95. Judah, *Kosovo,* p. 150; Daalder and O'Hanlon, *Winning Ugly,* p. 31.
96. Clinton, *My Life,* pp. 1095–96; Albright, *Madam Secretary,* p. 192.
97. Albright, *Madam Secretary,* pp. 382–83.
98. Gelbard interview.
99. Daalder, *Getting to Dayton,* p. 1.
100. Holbrooke, *To End a War,* p. 27.
101. Zimmermann, *Origins of a Catastrophe,* pp. 230–31.
102. Laura Silber and Allan Little, *The Death of Yugoslavia,* rev. ed. (London: Penguin Books, 1996), p. 345.
103. David Rohde, *Endgame: The Betrayal and Fall of Srebrenica, Europe's Worst Massacre since World War II* (Boulder, Colo.: Westview, 1998), pp. 320–21.
104. Albright, *Madam Secretary,* p. 189.
105. Stoltenberg and Eide, *De tusen dagene,* pp. 337–45.
106. Bildt, *Uppdrag Fred,* p. 531.
107. Albright, *Madam Secretary,* p. 192.
108. Daalder and O'Hanlon, *Winning Ugly,* p. 24.
109. Vollebæk interview.
110. J. T. Correll, "The New American Way of War," *Air Force Magazine,* 79(4) (1996), p. 22.
111. Judah, *Kosovo,* p. 122.
112. Clark, *Waging Modern War,* p. 68.
113. Ibid., pp. 67–68.
114. Gen. Wesley K. Clark, e-mail correspondence with the author, 5 May 2005.
115. David Rohde, "Tactics of '95 Bosnia Crisis May Not Fit Kosovo Case," *New York Times,* 2 April 1999.
116. "Interview with Madeleine Albright," *PBS Frontline.*
117. *War in Europe;* Judah, *Kosovo,* p. 229; Daalder and O'Hanlon, *Winning Ugly,* p. 18; Elaine M. Grossman, "Senior General Warned NATO Repeatedly of Prolonged Kosovo Conflict," *Inside the Pentagon,* 22 April 1999. "Interview with Ivo Daalder," *PBS Frontline.*
118. Zimmermann, *Origins of a Catastrophe,* pp. 213–14.
119. Woodward, *Balkan Tragedy,* p. 15.
120. Ibid., p. 260.
121. Rohde, *Endgame,* p. 333.
122. Owen, ed., *Deliberate Force,* p. 497.
123. Ibid., p. 27.
124. Silber and Little, *The Death of Yugoslavia,* p. 356.
125. Rohde, "Tactics of '95 Bosnia Crisis"; Daalder and O'Hanlon, *Winning Ugly,* p. 93.

126. Silber and Little, *Death of Yugoslavia,* p. 383.

127. Judah, *Kosovo,* p. 123.

128. Gelbard interview.

129. Clinton, *My Life,* p. 1068; Rohde, *Endgame,* p. 322.

130. Ibid.; Gelbard interview.

131. Rohde, *Endgame,* p. 359.

132. Owen, ed., *Deliberate Force,* p. 497.

133. Daalder, *Getting to Dayton,* p. 124.

134. Holbrooke, *To End a War,* p. 166.

135. Mark C. McLaughlin, "Assessing the Effectiveness of Deliberate Force: Harnessing the Political-Military Connection," in *Deliberate Force,* ed. Owen, p. 194.

136. Daalder, *Getting to Dayton,* pp. 126–27.

137. Owen, ed., *Deliberate Force,* pp. 193–94.

138. Ibid.

139. Clinton, *My Life,* pp. 1095–96.

140. Rohde, "Tactics of '95 Bosnia Crisis."

141. Gelbard interview.

142. Daalder, *Getting to Dayton,* p. 166.

143. Stoltenberg and Eide, *De tusen dagene,* p. 407.

144. Owen, ed., *Deliberate Force,* pp. 499–501.

145. Clinton, *My Life,* pp. 1095–96.

146. Albright, *Madam Secretary,* p. 189.

147. Rohde, "Tactics of '95 Bosnia Crisis May Not Fit Kosovo Case."

148. Gelbard interview.

149. Owen, ed., *Deliberate Force,* p. 485.

150. Daalder, *Getting to Dayton,* p. 131.

151. Owen, ed., *Deliberate Force,* pp. 498–99.

152. Clinton, *My Life,* pp. 1095–96.

153. Albright, *Madam Secretary,* p. 192.

154. McLaughlin, "Assessing the Effectiveness of *Deliberate Force,"* p. 194.

155. Daalder and O'Hanlon, *Winning Ugly,* p. 93.

156. Owen, ed., *Deliberate Force,* p. 497.

157. Ibid., p. 498.

158. Daalder, *Getting to Dayton,* pp. 43–45; Owen, ed., *Deliberate Force,* p. 506.

159. Smith, *Utility of Force,* pp. 365–68.

160. Holbrooke, *To End a War,* p. 104.

161. Smith, *Utility of Force,* p. 351.

162. Phillip S. Meilinger, "Ten Propositions Emerging from Airpower," *Airpower Journal* (Spring 1996), p. 58.

163. Owen, ed., *Deliberate Force,* p. 514.

164. Judah, *Kosovo,* pp. 123–24.

165. Elaine M. Grossman, "Senior General Warned NATO Repeatedly of Prolonged Kosovo Conflict," *Inside the Pentagon,* 22 April 1999.

166. *War Room.*

167. Ibid.

168. Gelbard interview.

169. Rohde, "Tactics of '95 Bosnia Crisis May Not Fit Kosovo Case."

170. Lake interview.
171. Glenny, *Balkans*, p. 651.
172. *War in Europe.*
173. *Mind of Milošević.*
174. "Interview with Ivo Daalder," *PBS Frontline.*

Chapter 5. The Crisis Emerges: NATO Becomes Responsible for Crisis Management

1. Naumann interview.
2. Albright, *Madam Secretary*, p. 380; Judah, *Kosovo*, pp. 63–64; Zimmermann, *Origins of a Catastrophe*, p. 80.
3. Woodward, *Balkan Tragedy*, p. 340; Zimmermann, *Origins of a Catastrophe*, pp. 234–35; Judah, *Kosovo*, pp. 67, 74–75, and 82; Daalder and O'Hanlon, *Winning Ugly*, p. 8.
4. It should be noted that the opinions of Albanian independence differed, with some Albanians wanting a Greater Albania, some wanting to join Albania, and some wanting outright independence for Kosovo. According to Daalder and O'Hanlon, a 1995 survey showed that 43 percent of the Kosovar Albanians wanted to join Albania, while 57 percent favored Kosovo independence; Daalder and O'Hanlon, *Winning Ugly*, p. 8.
5. Judah, *Kosovo*, pp. 124–25. For further references, see also Albright, *Madam Secretary*, p. 380; Daalder and O'Hanlon, *Winning Ugly*, p. 10; Veton Surroi, "The Albanian National Question: The Post Dayton Pay-off," *Institute for War and Peace Report*, no. 41, May 1996.
6. As to why Kosovo was not included in the Dayton Accords, apparently Kosovo could or would have precluded the agreement ending the war in Bosnia—which was the top priority. The U.S. principal aide to the Dayton Peace Accord process, Christopher Hill, points out that the situation in Bosnia was very nasty and that there were no guarantees that the parties would sign the agreement. To include Kosovo would have overloaded matters and jeopardized the negotiations; Hill interview. The U.S. special envoy to Bosnia and Kosovo, James Dobbins, asserts that it was impossible to include the issue of Kosovo at Dayton. If one were prepared to go back to war for a while, the military situation might have become such that one could press Milošević on the issue, but that seemed not to be the case at the time; Dobbins interview. The UN negotiator in the former Yugoslavia, Thorvald Stoltenberg, gives credit to the Americans for succeeding at Dayton. It was not a perfect peace plan—among other things, it did not include Kosovo—but it managed to end the war and save many lives, and for him that was the most important aspect; Stoltenberg interview. The EU negotiator in the Former Yugoslavia, David Owen, commented in a TV documentary: "Of course it was a mistake not to raise Kosovo at Dayton. I can understand why they didn't. But not to then put Kosovo as the highest priority in the weeks and months after Dayton was a terrible error"; *Mind of Milošević.* Similarly, Daalder and O'Hanlon argue that NATO's tendency to neglect Kosovo in the 1990s was a mistake and that Belgrade should have been pressed more in the period following Dayton; Daalder and O'Hanlon, *Winning Ugly*, p. 14.
7. Glenny, *Balkans*, pp. 652–54.
8. *Fall of Milošević.* The quotation translated from Norwegian to English by the author.

9. Judah, *Kosovo,* p. 118.
10. Albright, *Madam Secretary,* p. 380; Daalder and O'Hanlon, *Winning Ugly,* p. 10; Judah, *Kosovo,* p. 102.
11. Nebojsa Pavkovic, "Interview with Commander Nebojsa Pavkovic," *PBS Frontline,* 2000, www.pbs.org/wgbh/pages/frontline/shows/kosovo [accessed January 2007].
12. Judah, *Kosovo,* pp. 136–37.
13. Ibid., p. 137.
14. Gelbard interview.
15. U.S. Senate Republican Policy Committee, "The Kosovo Liberation Army: Does Clinton Policy Support Group with Terror, Drug Ties?" 31 March 1999, www.fas.org/irp/world/para/docs/fr033199.htm [accessed January 2007]. The text refers to Agence France Presse, 23 February 1998. See also Michael Moran, "Terrorist Groups and Political Legitimacy," *Backgrounder,* 16 March 2006, www.cfr.org/publication /10159/ [accessed January 2007]; Judah, *Kosovo,* p. 138.
16. UN Security Council, Resolution 1160, S/RES/1160, 31 March 1998, daccessdds.un.org/doc/UNDOC/GEN/N98/090/23/PDF/N9809023.pdf?OpenElement [accessed January 2007].
17. Judah, *Kosovo,* pp. 138 and 144.
18. Hill interview.
19. Marcia Christoff Kurop, "Al Qaeda's Balkan Links," *Wall Street Journal Europe,* 1 November 2001, www.freerepublic.com/focus/fr/561291/posts [accessed January 2007].
20. Senate Republican Policy Committee, "The Kosovo Liberation Army." The text refers to *New York Times,* 13 March 1998.
21. Judah, *Kosovo,* pp. 138–40.
22. *Fall of Milošević.*
23. Ibid. The quotation translated from the Norwegian subtext by the author.
24. Ibid.
25. Ibid., pp. 140–41.
26. Judah, *Kosovo,* pp. 146–47.
27. Daalder and O'Hanlon, *Winning Ugly,* p. 38; Judah, *Kosovo,* p. 148.
28. Ibid., pp. 144, 150.
29. NATO, "Council Statement on the Situation in Kosovo, North Atlantic Treaty Organisation," 5 March 1998, press release (98)29, www.nato.int/docu/pr/1998/p98-029e.htm [accessed January 2007]; Daalder and O'Hanlon, *Winning Ugly,* p. 31.
30. Daalder and O'Hanlon, *Winning Ugly,* p. 24.
31. Ibid.
32. Ibid.
33. Albright, *Madam Secretary,* pp. 381–82.
34. Contact Group, "Statement on Kosovo adopted by the members of the Contact Group, meeting in London on 9 March 1998," www.monde-diplomatique.fr/cahier/kosovo/contact-090398-en [accessed January 2007].
35. Ibid.; Daalder and O'Hanlon, *Winning Ugly,* p. 24.
36. OSCE, "Special Session of the Permanent Council of the Organization for Security and Cooperation in Europe (OSCE) of 11 March 1998," S/1998/246, www.un.org/peace/kosovo/s1998246.pdf [accessed January 2007].

37. Albright, *Madam Secretary,* pp. 382–83.
38. Ibid.
39. "Interview with Madeleine Albright," *PBS Frontline.*
40. "Interview with Ivo Daalder," *PBS Frontline.*
41. "Interview with Madeleine Albright," *PBS Frontline.*
42. "Interview with Richard Holbrooke," *PBS Frontline.*
43. Albright, *Madam Secretary,* p. 383.
44. Madeleine Albright, "Transcript: Albright, Dini Briefing in Rome March 7, 1998," telaviv.usembassy.gov/publish/peace/archives/1998/march/me0310a.html [accessed January 2007].
45. Daalder and O'Hanlon, *Winning Ugly,* pp. 22–27. Quotation on p. 27.
46. UN Security Council Resolution 1160.
47. Naumann interview.
48. The text says "Act Toward" but probably refers instead to ACTWARN (activation warning); Samuel Berger, "Interview with Samuel Berger, *PBS Frontline,* 2000, www.pbs.org/wgbh/pages/frontline/shows/ kosovo [accessed January 2007].
49. Albright, *Madam Secretary,* pp. 382–83; Daalder and O'Hanlon, *Winning Ugly,* p. 29.
50. Judah, *Kosovo,* p. 151.
51. Congressional Research Service, *Iraq: Former and Recent Military Confrontations with the United States,* Issue Brief for Congress (Washington, D.C.: 16 October 2002), p. 2, www.gulfinvestigations.net/IMG/pdf/crs-iraq_mil_confr.pdf?PHPSESSID=4d0ac00ce5969b589b2c6be6bedbab51 [accessed January 2007].
52. Elaine Sciolino and Ethan Bronner, "How a President, Distracted by Scandal, Entered Balkan War," *New York Times,* 18 April 1999.
53. Halberstam, *War in a Time of Peace,* p. 376.
54. Albright, *Madam Secretary,* p. 383; Halberstam, *War in a Time of Peace,* p. 376; Gelbard interview.
55. Daalder and O'Hanlon, *Winning Ugly,* p. 30.
56. Gelbard interview.
57. Halberstam, *War in a Time of Peace,* p. 388.
58. Gelbard interview. Gelbard claims that it was he who proposed the air strikes and that Berger became upset with him—that Madeleine Albright had got it backward when later saying in her memoirs that Berger had been angry with her during the meeting.
59. Gelbard interview; Clark, *Waging Modern War,* pp. 117–18.
60. "Interview with General Michael C. Short," *PBS Frontline.* What should be noted in this regard is the immediate choice to establish a no-fly zone. It was to become the first part of OAF about a year later, in which Phase One—together with attacking the FRY IADS and some military forces in Kosovo—sought to establish a no-fly zone south of a latitude of forty-four degrees north. No-fly zones had been used extensively both in Bosnia and Iraq preceding OAF; they were generally perceived as an effective coercive tool for neutralizing an opponent's ambition to use the air to his own military advantage. Interestingly, the U.S. special envoy for Bosnia and Kosovo, James Dobbins, believes that if Milošević had not started a mass expulsion of Kosovars in the beginning of OAF, NATO would probably have been forced to stop the bombing after a period of

time. According to Dobbins, NATO would have opted to create "something like the no-fly zone you had over Iraq for a decade, in which NATO would continue to fly over Serbia and from time to time bomb if some particular activity was found to be objectionable, and the Serbs would just have to live with that rather humiliating situation indefinitely—but from Milošević's perspective, that was not a particularly attractive option either." Dobbins interview.

61. Sciolino and Bronner, "How a President, Distracted by Scandal, Entered Balkan War"; Barton Gellman, "The Path to Crisis: How the United States and Its Allies Went to War," *Washington Post*, 18 April 1999.

62. Daalder and O'Hanlon, *Winning Ugly*, p. 30.

63. Albright, *Madam Secretary*, p. 384.

64. Løwer interview.

65. "Interview with William Cohen," *PBS Frontline*.

66. Daalder and O'Hanlon, *Winning Ugly*, p. 36.

67. Albright, *Madam Secretary*, p. 384.

68. NATO, "Statement on Kosovo," 28 May 1998, press release M-NAC-1(98)61, www.nato.int/docu/pr/1998/p98-061e.htm [accessed January 2007].

69. NATO, *Remarks to the Press by Javier Solana*, press release, 28 May 1998, www.nato.int/docu/speech/1998/s980528a.htm [accessed January 2007].

70. Clark, *Waging Modern War*, pp. 111–12.

71. Ibid., pp. 117–20.

72. Albright, *Madam Secretary*, pp. 382–83.

73. Clark, *Waging Modern War*, p. 119.

74. Ralston interview.

75. Ibid.

76. Clark, *Waging Modern War*, pp. 119–20.

77. NATO, *Statement on Kosovo: Issued at the Meeting of the North Atlantic Council in Defense Ministers Session*, press release M-NAC-D-1(98)77, 11 June 1998, www.nato.int/docu/pr/1998/p98-077e.htm [accessed January 2007].

78. *Statement to the Press by NATO Secretary General, Dr. Javier Solana*, 11 June 1998, www.nato.int/docu/pr/1998/p98-077e.htm [accessed January 2007].

79. Naumann interview; Clark, *Waging Modern War*, p. 120.

80. Naumann interview.

81. Judah, *Kosovo*, p. 166.

82. Smith interview.

83. Daalder and O'Hanlon, *Winning Ugly*, p. 31.

84. Department of Defense, *Kosovo/Operation Allied Force After-Action Report*, p. A-2; Contact Group, "Contact Group Joint Statement: Kosovo, 12 June 1998," www.g7.utoronto.ca/foreign/fm980612_2.htm [accessed January 2007].

85. Judah, *Kosovo*, pp. 165–66.

86. Naumann interview.

87. Klaus Naumann, *Statement to Senate Armed Services Committee*, Washington, D.C., 3 November 1999, armed-services.senate.gov/statemnt/1999/991103kn.pdf [accessed January 2007].

88. Daalder and O'Hanlon, *Winning Ugly*, p. 34.

Chapter 6. Shift in U.S. Policy toward the KLA—and the Summer Offensive

1. *Fall of Milošević.*

2. Clark, *Waging Modern War*, p. 121; Daalder and O'Hanlon, *Winning Ugly*, p. 39.
3. Albright, *Madam Secretary*, pp. 380, 385–86; Daalder and O'Hanlon, *Winning Ugly*, p. 39; Gelbard interview.
4. "Interview with Richard Holbrooke," *PBS Frontline*.
5. *Fall of Milošević*.
6. Judah, *Kosovo*, p. 156.
7. *Fall of Milošević*.
8. The author's interpretation of that conversation is that he clearly meant the United States but that being a career diplomat and the Norwegian ambassador to Washington at the time, he understandably refused to say the name publicly; Vollebæk interview.
9. Hill interview.
10. Dobbins interview.
11. Gelbard interview. It has been impossible for the author to get access to archives that might give insight into the U.S. State Department's policy toward the KLA before and after its shift of policy in May/June 1998. Some sources point to Christopher Hill as the key State Department negotiator from this time until the Rambouillet Conference—in terms of negotiating a deal between the KLA, the Kosovar Albanians, Belgrade, and the United States. Though evidence suggests that direct signals of support concerning Kosovo independence were given by Washington, other evidence suggests that the scope of Ambassador Hill's negotiations was more complex and balanced, and that they reviewed a broader range of possible political solutions to the issue of Kosovo. See, among others, Daalder and O'Hanlon, *Winning Ugly*, pp. 39–40, 47, and 60–61; Judah, *Kosovo*, pp. 170, 200–219; and Albright, *Madam Secretary*, pp. 391, 397–98, and 400–401.
12. Clark, *Waging Modern War*, pp. 122–23.
13. "Interview with General Michael C. Short," *PBS Frontline*.
14. Clark, *Waging Modern War*, pp. 122–24.
15. Ibid.
16. Judah, *Kosovo*, pp. 168–69.
17. *Fall of Milošević*.
18. "Interview with Ivo Daalder," *PBS Frontline*.
19. Judah, *Kosovo*, p. 170.
20. Naumann interview.
21. Daalder and O'Hanlon, *Winning Ugly*, pp. 35–36.
22. "Interview with Ivo Daalder," *PBS Frontline*.
23. Smith interview.
24. Clark, *Waging Modern War*, pp. 124–25; Daalder and O'Hanlon, *Winning Ugly*, pp. 33–34.
25. Judah, *Kosovo*, p. 171; Clark, *Waging Modern War*, p. 129.
26. Cordesman, *Lessons and Non-Lessons*, pp. 10–11; Albright, *Madam Secretary*, p. 380.
27. Albright, *Madam Secretary*, pp. 361, 368.
28. Daalder and O'Hanlon, *Winning Ugly*, p. 2.
29. Cordesman, *Lessons and Non-Lessons*, p. 11; Judah, *Kosovo*, p. 178.
30. Judah, *Kosovo*, p. 176.
31. Daalder and O'Hanlon, *Winning Ugly*, pp. 37–38.

32. Judah, *Kosovo*, p. 176.
33. Daalder and O'Hanlon, *Winning Ugly*, pp. 36, 39–40.
34. Judah, *Kosovo*, p. 179.
35. Bellini, "Kosovo and Beyond," p. 1.
36. Judah, *Kosovo*, p. 179.

Chapter 7. NATO Threatens with Air Strikes: Silence before the Storm

1. *Fall of Milošević.*
2. Clark, *Waging Modern War*, pp. 133–34.
3. Albright, *Madam Secretary*, pp. 387–88.
4. Ibid., p. 388.
5. UN Security Council Resolution 1199, 23 September 1998, S/RES/1199, www.un.org/peace/kosovo/98sc1199.htm [accessed January 2007]; Cordesman, *Lessons and Non-Lessons*, p. 11; Albright, *Madam Secretary*, p. 388.
6. Daalder and O'Hanlon, *Winning Ugly*, p. 43; Clark, *Waging Modern War*, pp. 134–35.
7. ACTWARN is a specific authorization to SACEUR to ask governments to identify the types and numbers of aircraft that they would provide for these operations; Clark, *Waging Modern War*, p. 135. In fact, since ACTWARN—as opposed to an activation request (ACTREQ)—did not bind nations to contributing forces, Secretary Cohen argued for issuing an ACTREQ as well; Clark, *Waging Modern War*, p. 135; Daalder and O'Hanlon, *Winning Ugly*, p. 43.
8. *Fall of Milošević.*
9. Judah, *Kosovo*, p. 182.
10. *Statement by the Secretary General following the ACTWARN Decision*, press release, Vilamoura, 24 September 1998, www.nato.int/docu/pr/1998/p980924e.htm [accessed January 2007].
11. Ibid.; Cordesman, *Lessons and Non-Lessons*, p. 11.
12. *Fall of Milošević.*
13. Judah, *Kosovo*, pp. 150, 226.
14. Ibid., pp. 179–80.
15. Albright, *Madam Secretary*, p. 388.
16. Daalder and O'Hanlon, *Winning Ugly*, p. 43.
17. Judah, *Kosovo*, pp. 181–82; Albright, *Madam Secretary*, p. 388; Cordesman, *Lessons and Non-Lessons*, pp. 11–12; Daalder and O'Hanlon, *Winning Ugly*, pp. 43–44.
18. United Nations, *Report of the Secretary-General Prepared Pursuant to Resolutions 1160 (1998) and 1199 (1998) of the Security Council*, Security Council, S/1998/912, 3 October 1998, daccessdds.un.org/doc/UNDOC/GEN/N98/289/78/PDF/N9828978.pdf? OpenElement [accessed January 2007].
19. Cordesman, *Lessons and Non-Lessons*, p. 12.
20. Judah, *Kosovo*, p. 182; Daalder and O'Hanlon, *Winning Ugly*, pp. 44–45.
21. Albright, *Madam Secretary*, p. 389.
22. Judah, *Kosovo*, p. 183.
23. Ibid., pp. 185–86.
24. Daalder and O'Hanlon, *Winning Ugly*, pp. 47–48.
25. NATO, *Statement to the Press by the Secretary General following Decision on the ACTORD*, NATO HQ, 13 October 1998, www.nato.int/docu/speech/1998/s981013a.htm [accessed January 2007]; *Fall of Milošević.*

26. NATO, *Statement to the Press by the Secretary General following Decision on the ACTORD.*
27. Albright, *Madam Secretary,* pp. 389–90; Cordesman, *Lessons and Non–Lessons,* p. 12; Daalder and O'Hanlon, *Winning Ugly,* pp. 23–24, 48; Judah, *Kosovo,* p. 186.
28. Cordesman, *Lessons and Non-Lessons,* p. 12.
29. *Fall of Milošević.*
30. Cordesman, *Lessons and Non-Lessons,* p. 12.
31. UN Security Council Resolution 1203, 24 October 1998, S/RES/1203, www.un.org/peace/kosovo/98sc1203.htm [accessed January 2007].
32. Clark, *Waging Modern War,* pp. 145–53.
33. Cordesman, *Lessons and Non-Lessons,* p. 13; Judah, *Kosovo,* p. 187.
34. Judah, *Kosovo,* p. 188.
35. Clark, *Waging Modern War,* pp. 137, 140, and 154.
36. Albright, *Madam Secretary,* p. 390.
37. Daalder and O'Hanlon, *Winning Ugly,* p. 49.
38. Gelbard interview; Daalder and O'Hanlon, *Winning Ugly,* pp. 23–24; Judah, *Kosovo,* p. 188.
39. *Fall of Milošević.*
40. Judah, *Kosovo,* p. 189.
41. Daalder and O'Hanlon, *Winning Ugly,* pp. 49, 57–58; Judah, *Kosovo,* p. 230.
42. Daalder and O'Hanlon, *Winning Ugly,* p. 56.
43. Vollebæk interview.
44. Clark, *Waging Modern War,* p. 148.
45. Gelbard interview.
46. *Fall of Milošević.*
47. Alessandra Stanley, "Albanian Fighters Say They Aid NATO in Spotting Serb Targets," *New York Times,* 2 April 1999.
48. William Drozdiak, "War Effort Restrained by Politics, Clark Says; NATO Chief Reviews 'Lessons' of Kosovo," *Washington Post,* 20 July 1999.
49. Priest, "A Decisive Battle That Never Was."
50. Kåre Eltervåg, telephone interview with the author, December 2003.
51. Maj. Gen. Bjørn Nygård, telephone interview with the author, 7 July 2004.
52. Eltervåg interview.
53. Stöckmann interview.
54. Smith interview.
55. Kelche interview.
56. Eltervåg interview.
57. Nygård interview.
58. *Fall of Milošević.*
59. Judah, *Kosovo,* p. 190.
60. Nygård interview.
61. Judah, *Kosovo,* page 190.
62. Ibid., p. 191.
63. Congressional Research Service, *Iraq,* p. 2.
64. Daalder and O'Hanlon, *Winning Ugly,* p. 2.
65. Ibid.

66. John Diamond, "Yugoslavia, Iraq Talked Air-Defense Strategy," *Philadelphia Inquirer,* 30 March 1999; "Is Iraq Helping Serbs?" *Seattle Times,* 29 March 1999.
67. Nygård interview.
68. Tim Weiner and Jane Perlez, "How Clinton Approved the Strikes on Capital," *New York Times,* 4 April 1999.
69. Editorial, "A French spy inside NATO," *US News & World Report,* 16 November 1998, www.findarticles.com/p/articles/mi_m1218/is_1998_Nov_16/ai_n12440819 [accessed March 2005].
70. "French Major Jailed as Serb Spy," *BBC News,* 12 December 2001, news.bbc.co.uk/1/hi/world/europe/1706341.stm [accessed January 2007].
71. Albright, *Madam Secretary,* p. 391; Judah, *Kosovo,* pp. 191–92; Daalder and O'Hanlon, *Winning Ugly,* p. 61.
72. Albright, *Madam Secretary,* p. 392.

Chapter 8. Račak—and the Rambouillet Conference

1. Clark, *Waging Modern War,* p. 170.
2. Judah, *Kosovo,* pp. 193–94; Cordesman, *Lessons and Non-Lessons,* p. 14.
3. *Fall of Milošević.*
4. Cordesman, *Lessons and Non-Lessons,* p. 14.
5. Judah, *Kosovo,* pp. 193–94.
6. Albright, *Madam Secretary,* p. 393; Judah, *Kosovo,* pp. 193–94.
7. "Interview with Richard Holbrooke," *PBS Frontline.*
8. Albright, *Madam Secretary,* p. 393.
9. Halberstam, *War in a Time of Peace,* p. 410.
10. Eltervåg interview.
11. Nygård interview.
12. Bo Adam and Roland Heine, "Račak: Finnish Pathologists Find No Massacre," *Berliner Zeitung,* trans. Sanjoy Mahajan, 17 January 2001, www.campeace.org/yuarchive/racak.htm [accessed March 2005].
13. Petra de Koning, "The Bloodbath in Račak Was a Massacre," *NRC Handelsblad,* 10 March 2001, racak.homestead.com/files/ranta.htm [accessed January 2007].
14. Human Rights Watch, *Yugoslav Government War Crimes in Račak,* press release, 29 January 1999, www.hrw.org/press/1999/jan/yugo0129.htm [accessed January 2007].
15. Tony Blair, "Interview with Tony Blair," *PBS Frontline,* 2000, www.pbs.org/wgbh/pages/frontline/shows/kosovo [accessed January 2007].
16. Halberstam, *War in a Time of Peace,* p. 409.
17. Daalder and O'Hanlon, *Winning Ugly,* p. 64.
18. "Interview with William Cohen," *PBS Frontline.*
19. "Interview with Madeleine Albright," *PBS Frontline.*
20. Albright, *Madam Secretary,* p. 394.
21. Ibid.
22. "Interview with Ivo Daalder," *PBS Frontline.*
23. Hill interview.
24. Ibid.
25. Daalder and O'Hanlon, *Winning Ugly,* p. 71.
26. "Interview with Madeleine Albright," *PBS Frontline.*

27. Albright, *Madam Secretary*, pp. 394–95; Daalder and O'Hanlon, *Winning Ugly*, p. 72. Secretary Albright does not refer to Operation Horseshoe in her memoirs, but her information coincides with a Serb offensive in this period known as "Horseshoe."

28. Daalder and O'Hanlon, *Winning Ugly*, pp. 64–65, 72–73.

29. Yeltsin, *Midnight Diaries*, p. 255.

30. Albright, *Madam Secretary*, p. 397.

31. Cordesman, *Lessons and Non-Lessons*, p. 14; NATO, *Statement to the Press by NATO Secretary General, Dr. Javier Solana*, press release (99)11, 28 January 1999, www.nato.int/docu/pr/1999/p99-011e.htm [accessed January 2007].

32. UN, *Statement by Kofi Annan, Secretary General of the United Nations, Statement to the North Atlantic Council*, 28 January 1999, www.nato.int/docu/speech/1999/s990128a.htm [accessed January 2007]; Daalder and O'Hanlon, *Winning Ugly*, p. 75.

33. This was said privately by U.S. officials for some time, and publicly by President Clinton on 13 February. The United States would contribute some four thousand troops to KFOR; Daalder and O'Hanlon, *Winning Ugly*, p. 74.

34. NATO, *Statement by the North Atlantic Council on Kosovo*. Press release (99)12, 30 January 1999, www.nato.int/docu/pr/1999/p99-012e.htm [accessed January 2007]; Judah, *Kosovo*, p. 195; *Fall of Milošević*; Albright, *Madam Secretary*, p. 397; Cordesman, *Lessons and Non-Lessons*, pp. 14–15; Daalder and O'Hanlon, *Winning Ugly*, pp. 73–75.

35. Daalder and O'Hanlon, *Winning Ugly*, p. 65.

36. Clark, *Waging Modern War*, pp. 164–66

37. Albright, *Madam Secretary*, p. 397.

38. "Interview with General Klaus Naumann," *PBS Frontline*.

39. Madeleine Albright, *Remarks by Secretary of State Madeleine Albright at U.S. Institute of Peace*, United States Department of State, 4 February 1999; Judah, *Kosovo*, p. 197; *Fall of Milošević*.

40. Judah, *Kosovo*, pp. 197–99.

41. Daalder and O'Hanlon, *Winning Ugly*, pp. 78–79.

42. Dobbins interview.

43. Judah, *Kosovo*, pp. 206–8; Daalder and O'Hanlon, *Winning Ugly*, p. 78.

44. Hill interview.

45. Albright, *Madam Secretary*, p. 398; Judah, *Kosovo*, pp. 206–8; Daalder and O'Hanlon, *Winning Ugly*, pp. 79–81.

46. Halberstam, *War in a Time of Peace*, p. 421.

47. Clark, *Waging Modern War*, p. 170.

48. Ibid., p. 167.

49. Sciolino and Bronner, "How a President, Distracted by Scandal, Entered Balkan War."

50. Clark, *Waging Modern War*, p. 171.

51. Albright, *Madam Secretary*, p. 394; Judah, *Kosovo*, p. 207.

52. Dobbins interview; Judah, *Kosovo*, p. 196.

53. Judah, *Kosovo*, pp. 209–10.

54. Clark, *Waging Modern War*, p. 162.

55. Smith interview.

56. The Dayton Peace Accords on Bosnia, annex 1A, "Military Aspects of the Peace Settlement," article VI, "Deployment of the Implementation Force," point 9 (a), www1.umn.edu/humanrts/icty/dayton/daytonannex1A.html [accessed January 2007].
57. Judah, *Kosovo,* p. 210.
58. Daalder and O'Hanlon, *Winning Ugly,* p. 80.
59. Hill interview.
60. Dobbins interview; Daalder and O'Hanlon, *Winning Ugly,* pp. 14–15.
61. Judah, *Kosovo,* p. 212.
62. Ibid., p. 213.
63. Michael Hirsh and John Barry, "How We Stumbled into War," *Newsweek,* no. 133, 12 April 1999, pp. 38–40.
64. Albright, *Madam Secretary,* pp. 402–3; Judah, *Kosovo,* p. 214.
65. *Fall of Milošević.*
66. Judah, *Kosovo,* p. 213.
67. Ibid., pp. 213–14; Daalder and O'Hanlon, *Winning Ugly,* p. 82.
68. Albright, *Madam Secretary,* p. 404.
69. Ibid.; Judah, *Kosovo,* pp. 216–18; Daalder and O'Hanlon, *Winning Ugly,* p. 83.
70. Judah, *Kosovo,* p. 217.
71. Ibid., pp. 209, 218, and 220.
72. Halberstam, *War in a Time of Peace,* p. 421.
73. Judah, *Kosovo,* pp. 222–23.
74. Hill interview.
75. Judah, *Kosovo,* p. 230.
76. Daalder and O'Hanlon, *Winning Ugly,* pp. 84–85.
77. Hirsh and Barry, "How We Stumbled into War," pp. 38–40.
78. Daalder and O'Hanlon, *Winning Ugly,* p. 89.
79. Clark, *Waging Modern War,* p. 173; Cordesman, *Lessons and Non-Lessons,* pp. 15–16; Judah, *Kosovo,* p. 232.
80. Vollebæk interview.
81. Cordesman, *Lessons and Non-Lessons,* p. 16.
82. *Fall of Milošević.*
83. Lambeth, *NATO's Air War for Kosovo,* pp. 20–21.
84. Charles Krulak, "Interview with General Charles Krulak," *PBS Frontline,* 2000, www.pbs.org/ wgbh/pages/frontline/shows/kosovo [accessed January 2007].
85. Ralston interview.
86. Stöckmann interview.
87. Smith interview.

Chapter 9. NATO Crisis Management in Perspective

1. Gen. Wesley K. Clark, Gen. Sir Rupert Smith, and Robert Gelbard, the president's representative for the Dayton implementation in Bosnia, all perceived the U.S. State Department and NSC as the dominant political forces behind the handling of the Kosovo crisis. Clark e-mail correspondence; Smith interview; Gelbard interview.
2. Judah, *Kosovo,* p. 230. See also Daalder and O'Hanlon, *Winning Ugly,* p. 58.
3. Daalder and O'Hanlon, *Winning Ugly,* p. 57.
4. Dobbins interview.

5. Naumann interview.
6. Daalder and O'Hanlon, *Winning Ugly,* p. 91.
7. Halberstam, *War in a Time of Peace,* p. 399.
8. Ibid.
9. Lundberg interview.
10. Bøthun interview.
11. Ralston interview; Lt. Gen. Michael C. Short, e-mail correspondence with the author, 31 August 2004.
12. Ralston interview.
13. Naumann interview.
14. Stöckmann interview.
15. The Interior Minister in Belgrade, Mihalj Kertes, had set up a training camp for irregular forces—called "the Serbian Volunteer Guard"—led by Željko Ražnjatović, better known as "Arkan." A similar force was set up by the Serbian extremist Vojislav Šešelj—a man who had been prosecuted in 1985 for "publishing a demand that Yugoslavia be divided into two states, Croatia and Serbia, with Bosnia shared out between them." In August 1991, the outgoing federal prime minister, Ante Marković, released tapes of a telephone conversation between Milošević and Bosnian Serb leader Radovan Karadžić, in which the former informed the latter that "his next delivery of arms would be supplied to him by General Nikola Uzelac, the Federal Army commander in Banja Luka." Karadžić, who at the time boasted to journalists that he spoke to Milošević "several times a week on the phone," reinforced the link between Belgrade and the Bosnian Serbs. According to Serb nationalist Vojislav Šešelj, the ethnic cleansing of Zvornik (Bosnia) in early April 1992 "was planned in Belgrade." Malcolm, *Bosnia: A Short History* (New York: New York University Press, 1996), pp. 225–26; Silber and Little, *The Death of Yugoslavia,* p. 223.
16. *Mind of Milošević;* Judah, *Kosovo,* pp. 56–57; Malcolm, *Bosnia,* pp. 215–31; Zimmermann, *Origins of a Catastrophe,* pp. 116–17, 160–61; Woodward, *Balkan Tragedy,* p. 355.
17. Judah, *Kosovo,* pp. 56–57; Malcolm, *Bosnia,* p. 215.
18. Zimmermann, *Origins of a Catastrophe,* p. 25.
19. Naumann interview.
20. Judah, *Kosovo,* p. 231.
21. Hill interview; Stoltenberg interview; Naumann interview; Vollebæk interview.
22. Woodward, *Balkan Tragedy,* pp. 6–7, 333–34.
23. Holbrooke, *To End a War,* p. 27; Judah, *Kosovo,* p. 76; Zimmermann, *Origins of a Catastrophe,* pp. 133–34.
24. Warren Zimmermann, John Lampe, and Dragan Cicic, "Interview with Warren Zimmermann, John Lampe and Dragan Cicic," *Online NewsHour,* 2 December 1996, pbs.org/newshour/bb/bosnia/december96/serbia_12-2.html [accessed January 2007]. Warren Zimmermann has previously been introduced. Dragan Cicic was an International Nieman Foundation Fellow at Harvard University and a reporter for the Belgrade magazine *Nin.* John Lampe was director of East European studies at the Woodrow Wilson International Center for Scholars and author of the book *Yugoslavia as History.*
25. British Helsinki Human Rights Group, *Serbia 1997: Parliamentary and Presidential Elections,* www. bhhrg.org/CountryReport.asp?CountryID=20&ReportID= 171&ChapterID=494&next=next&keyword= [accessed January 2007].

26. Gelbard interview.
27. Judah, *Kosovo,* p. 151.
28. Ibid., p. 84.
29. Nygård interview.
30. Woodward, *Balkan Tragedy,* p. 341.
31. Zimmermann, *Origins of a Catastrophe,* p. 80.
32. Cordesman, *Lessons and Non-Lessons,* p. 7.
33. Department of Defense, *Kosovo/Operation Allied Force After-Action Report,* p. 15.
34. Naumann interview.
35. Dobbins interview.
36. Hill interview.

Chapter 10. Diplomacy and Airpower

1. William Drozdiak, "War Effort Restrained by Politics," *Washington Post,* 20 July 1999.
2. Lake interview.
3. Pape, *Bombing to Win,* p. 4; Byman and Waxman, *Dynamics of Coercion,* p. 1; R. J. Art and P. M. Cronin, ed., *The United States and Coercive Diplomacy,* pp. 6–7.
4. Kagan, *Of Paradise and Power,* pp. 3–4.
5. Lake interview.
6. Bildt, *Uppdrag Fred,* p. 534.
7. Naumann interview.
8. Boutros Boutros-Ghali, *Unvanquished: A US-UN Saga* (London: I. B. Tauris, 1999), p. 198.
9. Carl Bildt, "Force and Diplomacy," *Survival,* 42(1) (2000), p. 141.
10. McInnes, *Spectator-Sport War,* pp. 91–93.
11. Tirpak, "Short's View of the Air Campaign," p. 47.
12. Earl H. Tilford, "Operation Allied Force and the Role of Airpower," *Parameters,* 29(4) (Winter 1999/2000), pp. 24–25, www.carlisle.army.mil/usawc/Parameters/99winter/tilford.htm [accessed January 2007]. The article refers to Michael E. Ryan, "Airpower Is Working in Kosovo," *Washington Post,* 4 June 1999, p. 35.
13. Olsen, *From Manoeuvre Warfare to Kosovo?* p. 260.
14. Johansen interview.
15. Halberstam, *War in a Time of Peace,* p. 446.
16. Hansell, *Air Plan That Defeated Hitler,* p. 80.
17. Tirpak, "Short's View of the Air Campaign," p. 43.
18. Gentile, *How Effective Is Strategic Bombing?* p. 191.
19. "Interview with General Klaus Naumann," *PBS Frontline.*
20. John A. Tirpak, "Lessons Learned and Re-Learned," *Air Force Magazine,* 82(8) (1999), p. 24.
21. Halberstam, *War in a Time of Peace,* p. 446.
22. "Interview with General Klaus Naumann," *PBS Frontline.*
23. Smith interview.
24. Kelche interview.
25. Tirpak, "Short's View of the Air Campaign," p. 43.
26. Olsen, *From Manoeuvre Warfare to Kosovo?* p. 264.

27. Priest, "The Battle inside Headquarters."
28. Ibid.; Stöckmann interview.
29. Stöckmann interview; Lundberg interview.
30. Stöckmann interview.
31. Clark e-mail correspondence.
32. Clark, *Waging Modern War,* p. 457.
33. Byman and Waxman, *Dynamics of Coercion,* pp. 18 and 240.
34. Clark, *Waging Modern War,* p. 213.
35. Naumann interview.
36. Judah, *Kosovo,* p. 228.
37. *Fall of Milošević.*
38. Parliament, *Fourteenth Report,* point "Planning and Preparation," in annex A, "Summary."
39. Byman and Waxman, *Dynamics of Coercion,* pp. 10–11; McInnes, *Spectator-Sport War,* p. 95.
40. Department of Defense, *Kosovo/Operation Allied Force After-Action Report,* pp. 15–16.
41. Parliament, *Fourteenth Report,* point "The Future," in "Conclusions."
42. Smith, *Utility of Force,* p. 333.
43. Kelche interview.
44. Smith, *Utility of Force,* pp. 1, 17–18.
45. Martin Creveld, *The Transformation of War* (New York: Free Press, 1991), pp. 224–27.
46. Drew, "Air Theory, Air Force, and Low Intensity Conflict," p. 321.
47. Clark, *Waging Modern War,* p. 418.
48. Naumann interview.
49. Bradley Graham, "Cohen: Airpower Was 'Effective,' 'Successful'; Need for NATO Cohesion Limited Options," *Washington Post,* 11 June 1999.
50. Drozdiak, "War Effort Restrained by Politics."
51. Ibid.
52. Edward Mann, Gary Endersby, and Tom Searle, "Dominant Effects: Effects-Based Joint Operations," *Aerospace Power Journal,* 15(3) (2001), www.airpower. au.af.mil/airchronicles/apj/apj01/fal01/vorfal01.html [accessed January 2007]. The article refers to a quotation by Benjamin S. Lambeth, "Control of the Air: The Future of Air Dominance and Offensive Strike," in a speech delivered at the Rydges Canberra Hotel, Canberra, Australia, 15–16 November 1999, 16 May 2001, p. 14, available from idun.itsc.adfa.edu.au/ADSC/Air/Air_paper_Lambeth.htm.
53. Smith interview.
54. Naumann interview.
55. Smith interview.
56. Schelling, *Arms and Influence,* pp. 3, 93.

SOURCES AND BIBLIOGRAPHY

Books and Essays

Albright, M. *Madam Secretary: A Memoir.* London: Macmillan, 2003.

Andric, I. *The Bridge on the Drina.* Chicago: University of Chicago Press, 1977.

Art, R. J., and P. M. Cronin, eds. *The United States and Coercive Diplomacy.* Washington, D.C.: United States Institute of Peace Press, 2003.

Atkins, D. A. *Air War over Kosovo: Operational and Logistical Issues of the Air Campaign.* N.p.: Writers Club, 2000.

Auerswald, P. E., and D. P. Auerswald, eds. *The Kosovo Conflict: A Diplomatic History through Documents.* Cambridge and the Hague: Kluwer Law International, 2000.

Bildt, C. *Uppdrag Fred.* Norstedts, Swe.: Bokförlaget Pan, 1997. English edition: *Peace Journey: The Struggle for Peace in Bosnia.*

Boutros-Ghali, B. *Unvanquished: A US-UN Saga.* London: I. B. Tauris, 1999.

Brawley, M. R., and P. Martin, eds. *Alliance Politics, Kosovo, and NATO's War: Allied Force or Forced Allies?* New York: Palgrave, 2000.

Bucknam, M. A. *Responsibility of Command: How UN and NATO Commanders Influenced Airpower over Bosnia.* Maxwell Air Force Base, Ala.: Air University Press, 2003.

Builder, C. H. *The Icarus Syndrome: The Role of Airpower Theory in the Evolution and Fate of the U.S. Air Force.* New Brunswick, N.J.: Transaction. Santa Monica, Calif.: RAND study, 1994.

Byman, D., and M. Waxman. *The Dynamics of Coercion.* Cambridge: Cambridge University Press, 2002.

Chomsky, N. *The New Military Humanism: Lessons from Kosovo.* Monroe, Me.: Common Courage, 1999.

Clark, W. K. *Waging Modern War: Bosnia, Kosovo, and the Future of Combat.* New York: PublicAffairs (Perseus), 2001.

Clarke, M. "Airpower, Force and Coercion." In *The Dynamics of Airpower,* edited by A. Lambert and A. C. Williamson. Bracknell, U.K.: Her Majesty's Stationery Office, 1996.

Clausewitz, C. V. *On War.* New York: Penguin Books, 1982.

Clinton, B. *My Life*. Large print ed. New York: Random House, 2004.

Clodfelter, M. *The Limits of Airpower: The American Bombing of North Vietnam*. New York: Free Press, 1989.

Cordesman, A. H. *The Lessons and Non-Lessons of the Air and Missile Campaign in Kosovo*. Westport, Conn.: Praeger, 2001.

Creveld, M. *The Transformation of War*. New York: Free Press, 1991.

Crnobrnja, M. *The Yugoslav Drama*. London and New York: I. B. Tauris, 1996.

Daalder, I. H. *Getting to Dayton: The Making of America's Bosnia Policy*. Washington, D.C.: Brookings Institution, 2000.

Daalder, I. H., and M. E. O'Hanlon. *Winning Ugly: NATO's War to Save Kosovo*. Washington, D.C.: Brookings Institution, 2000.

Deptula, D. A. *Effects-Based Operations: Change in the Nature of Warfare*. Arlington, V.A.: Air Force Association, Aerospace Education Foundation, 2001. www.aef.org/pub/psbook.pdf [accessed 2006].

Doder, D., and L. Branson. *Milošević: Portrait of a Tyrant*. New York: Free Press, 1999.

Douhet, G. *The Command of the Air*. Manchester, N.H.: Ayer, 1999.

Drew, D. M. "Air Theory, Air Force, and Low Intensity Conflict: A Short Journey to Confusion." In *The Paths of Heaven: The Evolution of Airpower Theory*, edited by P. S. Meilinger. Maxwell Air Force Base, Ala.: Air University Press, 1997.

Drew, D. M., and D. M. Snow. *Making Strategy: An Introduction to National Security Processes and Problems*. Maxwell Air Force Base, Ala.: Air University Press, 1988.

Faber, P. R. "Interwar US Army Aviation and the Air Corps Tactical School: Incubators of American Airpower." In *The Paths of Heaven: The Evolution of Airpower Theory*, edited by P. S. Meilinger. Maxwell Air Force Base, Ala.: Air University Press, 1997.

Futrell, R. F. *Ideas, Concepts, Doctrine: Basic Thinking in the United States Air Force 1907–1960*, vol. 1. Maxwell Air Force Base, Ala.: Air University Press, 1989.

———. *Ideas, Concepts, Doctrine: Basic Thinking in the United States Air Force 1961–1984*, vol. 2. Maxwell Air Force Base, Ala.: Air University Press, 1989.

Gentile, G. P. *How Effective Is Strategic Bombing? Lessons Learned from World War II to Kosovo*. London and New York: New York University Press, 2001.

Glenny, M. *The Balkans: Nationalism, War, and the Great Powers, 1804–1999*. New York: Penguin Books, 2001.

Halberstam, D. *The Best and the Brightest*. New York: Ballantine Books, 1993.

———. *War in a Time of Peace: Bush, Clinton, and the Generals*. New York: Scribner's, 2001.

Hallion, R. P. *Storm over Iraq: Airpower and the Gulf War*. Washington, D.C.: Smithsonian Institution, 1992.

Hansell, H. S. *The Air Plan That Defeated Hitler.* New York: Arno (reprint of the first, 1972, edition), 1980.

Holbrooke, R. *To End a War.* New York: Modern Library, 1999.

Hosmer, S. T. *The Conflict over Kosovo: Why Milošević Decided to Settle When He Did.* Santa Monica, Calif.: RAND, 2001.

_____. *Operations against Enemy Leaders.* Santa Monica, Calif.: RAND, 2001.

_____. *Psychological Effects of U.S. Air Operations in Four Wars 1941–1991: Lessons for U.S. Commanders.* Santa Monica, Calif.: RAND, 1996.

Ignatieff, M. *Virtual War: Kosovo and Beyond.* New York: Picador USA, Metropolitan Books, and Henry Holt, 2000.

Judah, T. *Kosovo: War and Revenge.* 2nd ed. New Haven, Conn.: Yale Nota Bene, 2002.

_____. *The Serbs: History, Myth & the Destruction of Yugoslavia.* New Haven, Conn.: Yale University Press, 2000.

Kagan, R. *Of Paradise and Power: America and Europe in the New World Order.* New York: Alfred A. Knopf, 2003.

Karnow, S. *Vietnam: A History.* 2nd rev. and updated ed. New York: Penguin Books, 1997.

Kissinger, H. A. *Diplomacy.* New York: Simon and Schuster, 1995.

Lambert, A., and A. C. Williamson, eds. *The Dynamics of Airpower.* Bracknell, U.K.: Ministry of Defence, Royal Air Force Staff College, Berkshire, 1996.

Lambeth, B. S. *NATO's Air War for Kosovo: A Strategic and Operational Assessment.* Santa Monica, Calif.: RAND, 2001.

_____. *The Transformation of American Airpower.* London and Ithaca, N.Y.: Cornell University Press, 2000.

LeBor, A. *Milošević: A Biography.* London: Bloomsbury, 2003.

Malcolm, N. *Bosnia: A Short History.* New York: New York University Press, 1996.

Mason, T. *Airpower: A Centennial Appraisal.* Rev. ed. London: Brassey's, 2002.

_____. "Rethinking the Conceptual Framework." In *Airpower 21: Challenges for the New Century,* edited by P. W. Gray. London: The Stationery Office, 2000.

_____. "The Technology Interaction." In *Perspectives on Airpower: Air Power in Its Wider Context,* edited by S. Peach. London: The Stationery Office, 1988.

McInnes, C. *Spectator-Sport War: The West and Contemporary Conflict.* Boulder, Colo.: Lynne Rienner, 2002.

McLaughlin, M. C. "Assessing the Effectiveness of Deliberate Force: Harnessing the Political-Military Connection." In *Deliberate Force: A Case Study in Effective Air Campaigning,* edited by R. C. Owen. Maxwell Air Force Base, Ala.: Air University Press, 2000.

McMaster, H. R. *Dereliction of Duty: Lyndon Johnson, Robert McNamara, the Joint Chiefs of Staff, and the Lies That Led to Vietnam.* New York: HarperPerennial, 1998.

Meilinger, P. S., ed. *The Paths of Heaven: The Evolution of Airpower Theory.* Maxwell Air Force Base, Ala.: Air University Press, 1997.

Mets, D. *The Air Campaign: John Warden and the Classical Airpower Theorists.* Maxwell Air Force Base, Ala. Air University Press, 1998.

_____. *The Long Search for a Surgical Strike: Precision Munitions and the Revolution in Military Affairs.* CADRE Paper 12. Maxwell Air Force Base, Ala. Air University Press, 2001.

NATO. *NATO Handbook.* Brussels: Office of Information and Press, 2001.

_____. *The NATO Handbook: NATO 1949–1999.* 50th anniversary ed. Brussels: Office of Information and Press, 1998.

_____. Website, www.nato.int/docu/update/1990/summarye.htm [accessed January 2007].

Olsen, John A., ed. *From Manoeuvre Warfare to Kosovo?* Trondheim: Royal Norwegian Air Force Academy, 2001.

Olsen, John A. *John Warden and the Renaissance of American Air Power.* Washington, D.C.: Potomac Books, 2007.

_____. *Strategic Airpower in Desert Storm.* London: Frank Cass, 2003.

Owen, D. *Balkan Odyssey.* London: Victor Gollancz, 1995.

Owen, R. C., ed. *Deliberate Force: A Case Study in Effective Air Campaigning.* Maxwell Air Force Base, Ala.: Air University Press, 2000.

Pape, R. A. *Bombing to Win: Airpower and Coercion in War.* New York: Cornell University Press, 1996.

Paret, P. *Clausewitz and the State: The Man, His Theories, and His Times.* Princeton, N.J.: Princeton University Press, 1985.

Paret, P., ed. *Makers of Modern Strategy: from Machiavelli to the Nuclear Age.* Princeton, N.J.: Princeton University Press, 1986.

Peach, S., ed. *Perspectives on Airpower: Airpower in Its Wider Context.* London: The Stationery Office, 1998.

Peters, J. E., S. Johnson, et al. *European Contributions to Operation Allied Force: Implications for Transatlantic Cooperation.* Santa Monica, Calif.: RAND, 2001.

Powell, C. L. *My American Journey.* New York: Random House, 1995.

Rajic, L. *Dagbok fra Beograd.* Oslo: Pax Forlag A/S, 2000. English translation (by the author): *Diary from Belgrade.*

_____. *Luftkampen Sett og Vurdert fra Beograd,* vol. 4. Trondheim, Nor.: Royal Norwegian Air Force Academy, 2000. English translation (by the author): *The Air Battle as Seen and Evaluated from Belgrade.*

Record, J. *Making War, Thinking History: Munich, Vietnam, and Presidential Uses of Force from Korea to Kosovo.* Annapolis, Md.: Naval Institute Press, 2002.

Reynolds, R. T. *Heart of the Storm: The Genesis of the Air Campaign against Iraq.* Maxwell Air Force Base, Ala.: Air University Press, 1995.

Ripley, T. *Air War Bosnia: UN and NATO Airpower.* Osceola, Wis.: Motorbooks International, 1996.

Rohde, David. *Endgame: The Betrayal and Fall of Srebrenica, Europe's Worst Massacre since World War II.* Boulder, Colo.: Westview, 1998.

Saxman, J. B. *The Concept of Center of Gravity: Does It Have Utility in Joint Doctrine and Campaign Planning?* Fort Leavenworth, Kans.: U.S. Army Command and General Staff College, 1992.

Schelling, T. C. *Arms and Influence.* New Haven, Conn.: Yale University Press, 1966.

Short, M. C. "An Airman's Lessons from Kosovo." In *From Manoeuvre Warfare to Kosovo?* Edited by John A. Olsen. Trondheim, Nor.: Royal Norwegian Air Force Academy, 2001.

Shultz, R. H., and R. L. Pfaltzgraff, eds. *The Future of Airpower in the Aftermath of the Gulf War.* Maxwell Air Force Base, Ala.: Air University Press, 1992.

Silber, L., and A. Little. *The Death of Yugoslavia.* Rev. ed. London: Penguin Books, 1996.

Simms, B. *Unfinest Hour: Britain and the Destruction of Bosnia.* London: Penguin Books, 2002.

Sitikoff, H. "The Postwar Impact of Vietnam." In *The Oxford Companion to American Military History,* edited by J. W. Chambers. New York: Oxford University Press, 1999.

Smith, Rupert. *The Utility of Force: The Art of War in the Modern World.* London: Allen Lane, 2005.

Stoltenberg, T., and K. Eide. *De tusen dagene: Fredsmeklere på Balkan.* Oslo: Gyldendal Norsk Forlag, 1996. English translation (by the author): *The Thousand Days: Peace Negotiators in the Balkans.*

Strange, J. *Centers of Gravity & Critical Vulnerabilities: Building on the Clausewitzian Foundation So That We Can All Speak the Same Language.* Quantico, Va.: Defense Automated Printing Service Center, 1996.

Thomas, R. *The Politics of Serbia in the 1990s.* New York: Columbia University Press, 1999.

Thompson, W. *To Hanoi and Back: The U.S. Air Force and North Vietnam, 1966–1973.* Washington, D.C.: Smithsonian Institution, 2000.

Ullman, Harlan K., and James P Wade. *Rapid Dominance: A Force for All Seasons.* RUSI Whitehall Paper Series. London: Royal United Services Institute for Defence Studies, 1998.

_____. *Shock and Awe: Achieving Rapid Dominance.* Washington, D.C.: Defense Group, Inc., for National Defense University, 1996.

U.S. Air Force. *Air Force Basic Doctrine 1.* AFDD-1. Washington, D.C.: Department of the Air Force, 1997, and 17 November 2003.

_____. *Basic Aerospace Doctrine of the United States Air Force.* Air Force Manual 1-1. Washington, D.C.: Department of the Air Force, 1992.

_____. *United States Air Force Basic Doctrine.* Washington, D.C.: Department of the Air Force, 1971.

Warden, J. A. *The Air Campaign: Planning for Combat.* toExcel Press, 2000.

Watts, B. D. *The Foundations of US Air Doctrine: The Problem of Friction in War.* Honolulu: University Press of the Pacific, 2002.

Woodward, B. *The Choice: How Clinton Won.* New York: Touchstone, 1997.

Woodward, Susan L. *Balkan Tragedy: Chaos and Dissolution after the Cold War.* Washington, D.C.: Brookings Institution, 1995.

Yeltsin, B. *Midnight Diaries.* New York: PublicAffairs, 2000.

Yost, D. S. *NATO Transformed: The Alliance's New Roles in International Security.* Washington, D.C.: United States Institute of Peace Press, 2001.

Zimmermann, W. *Origins of a Catastrophe: Yugoslavia and Its Destroyers.* 2nd ed. New York: Times Books, 1999.

Journal, Magazine, and Newspaper Articles

Adam, B., and R. Heine. "Račak: Finnish Pathologists Find No Massacre." Translated by Sanjoy Mahajan. *Berliner Zeitung,* 17 January 2001.

Ajami, F. "Under Western Eyes: The Fate of Bosnia." *Survival,* 41(2) (1999), pp. 35–52.

Albright, M. K. "The Testing of American Foreign Policy." *Foreign Affairs,* 77(6) (1998), pp. 50–64.

Anderson, J. H., and J. Phillips. "The Kosovo Liberation Army and the Future of Kosovo." *Heritage Foundation Backgrounder,* no. 1280 (13 May 1999).

Arkin, W. M. "Objective: Kosovo—Inside the Air Force, Officers Are Frustrated about the Air War." *Washington Post,* 25 April 1999.

Aspin, L. "With the Soviets and Cold War Gone, What Is the Future for US Forces?" *ROA National Security Report* (November 1992), p. 23.

Aubin, S. P. "Operation Allied Force: War or 'Coercive Diplomacy'?" *Strategic Review,* 27(3) (1999), pp. 4–12.

Barber, D. "Aerial Coercion: What Does It Mean and Can It Work?" *Airpower Review,* 2(3) (1999), pp. 64–75.

Barlow, J. B. "Strategic Paralysis: An Airpower Strategy for the Present." *Airpower Journal,* 7(4) (1993), pp. 4–15.

Bass, W. "The Triage of Dayton." *Foreign Affairs,* 77(5) (1998), pp. 95–109.

Berger, S. "A Foreign Policy for the Global Age." *Foreign Affairs,* 79(6) (2000), pp. 22–39.

Betts, R. K. "Compromised Command." *Foreign Affairs,* 80(4) (2001), pp. 126–32.

Bildt, C. "Force and Diplomacy." *Survival,* 42(1) (2000), pp. 141–48.

Booth, W. "Bombs Broke Hearts and Minds: In Yugoslavia, Lasting Damage Will Be Psychological." *Washington Post,* 17 July 1999.

British Helsinki Human Rights Group. *Serbia 1997: Parliamentary and Presidential Elections,* www.bhhrg.org/CountryReport.asp?CountryID=20&ReportID=171&ChapterID=494&next=next&keyword= [accessed January 2007].

Broder, J. M. "The Evolution of a President: From a Protesting Dove to a Hesitant Hawk." *New York Times,* 28 March 1999.

Butcher, T., and P. Bishop. "NATO Admits Air Campaign Failed." *Electronic Telegraph,* 22 July 1999, mailman.lbo-talk.org/1999/1999-July/012468.html [accessed January 2007].

Byman, D., and M. Waxman. "Defeating US Coercion." *Survival,* 41(2) (1999), pp. 107–20.

_____. "Kosovo and the Great Airpower Debate." *International Security,* 24(4) (2000), pp. 5–38.

Carlson, I., and S. Ramphal. "NATO's Vigilante Warfare Gives a Bad Example to the World." *International Herald Tribune,* 1 April 1999.

Carpenter, P. M., and G. T. McClain. "Air Command and Staff College Air Campaign Course: The Air Corps Tactical School Reborn?" *Aerospace Power Journal,* Fall 1993. www.airpower.maxwell.af.mil/airchronicles/apj/carpent.html [accessed 2006].

Chipman, D. D. "The Balkan Wars: Diplomacy, Politics and Coalition Warfare." *Strategic Review,* 28(1) (2000), pp. 23–31.

Clark, W. K. "The United States and NATO: The Way Ahead." *Parameters,* 29 (4) (1999–2000), pp. 2–14.

Cohen, E. A. "Defending America in the Twenty-first Century." *Foreign Affairs,* 79(6) (2000), pp. 40–56.

_____. "The Mystique of U.S. Airpower." *Foreign Affairs,* 73(1) (1994), pp. 109–24.

Correll, J. T. "About the 'Powell Doctrine' . . ." *Air Force Magazine,* 82(8) (1999), p. 10.

_____. "Airpower and Its Critics." *Air Force Magazine,* 82(7) (1999), p. 3.

_____. "Assumptions Fall in Kosovo." *Air Force Magazine,* 82(6) (1999), p. 4.

_____. "The New American Way of War." *Air Force Magazine,* 79(4) (1996), pp. 20–23.

_____. "A Strategy of Uncertainty." *Air Force Magazine,* 80(5) (1998), p. 4.

_____. "What Happened to Shock and Awe?" *Air Force Magazine,* 86 (11) 2003, pp. 52–57.

Cviic, C. "The Serbian Exception." *International Affairs,* 75(3) (1999), pp. 635–41.

Daalder, I. H., and M. B. G. Froman. "Dayton's Incomplete Peace." *Foreign Affairs,* 78(6) (1999), pp. 106–13.

Diamond, J. "Yugoslavia, Iraq Talked Air-Defense Strategy." *Philadelphia Inquirer,* 30 March 1999.

Dobbs, M., and J. M. Goshko. "Albright's Personal Odyssey Shaped Foreign Policy Beliefs." *Washington Post,* 6 December 1996.

Drozdiak, W. "NATO leaders Struggle to Find a Winning Strategy." *Washington Post,* 1 April 1999.

_____. "War Effort Restrained by Politics, Clark Says; NATO Chief Reviews 'Lessons' of Kosovo." *Washington Post,* 20 July 1999.

"French Major Jailed as Serb Spy." *BBC News,* 12 December 2001. news.bbc.co.uk/1/hi/world/europe/1706341.stm [accessed 9 March 2005].

"A French Spy inside NATO." *US News & World Report,* 16 November 1998, www.findarticles.com/p/articles/mi_m1218/is_1998_Nov_ 16/ai_n12440819 [accessed January 2007].

Gazzini, T. "NATO Coercive Military Activities in the Yugoslav Crisis (1992–1999)." *European Journal of International Law,* 12(3) (2001), pp. 391–435.

Gellman, B. "Allies Facing the Limits of Airpower: Pitfalls of a Clinton Policy Dubbed 'Immaculate Coercion' Grow Evident." *Washington Post,* 28 March 1999.

_____. "The Path to Crisis: How the United States and Its Allies Went to War." *Washington Post,* 18 April 1999.

Glenny, M. "Will the West Fail Again?" *New York Times,* 31 January 1997.

Graham, B. "Joint Chiefs Doubted Air Strategy." *Washington Post,* 5 April 1999.

_____. "Kosovo Campaign Dwarfed by Gulf War: NATO Officials Acknowledge Underestimating Milošević." *Washington Post,* 2 April 1999.

Graham, B., and J. Lancaster. "All in Favour of This Target, Say Yes, Si, Oui, Ja." *New York Times,* 25 April 1999.

_____. "Most NATO Bombing Raids Target Previously Hit Sites: Latest Belgrade Airstrike Wrecks Ruling Party Offices." *Washington Post,* 21 April 1999.

Gray, P. W. "Air Operations for Strategic Effect: Theory and Practice in Kosovo." *Airpower Review,* 3(1) (2000), pp. 16–31.

Grossman, Elaine M. "Kosovo War Tactics Compensated for Strategy Void, Expert Says." *Inside the Pentagon,* 1 July 1999.

Hedges, C. "Kosovo's Next Masters?" *Foreign Affairs,* 78(3) (1999), pp. 24–42.

Hinman, E. "Airpower's Political-Military Gap." *Strategic Review,* 28(4) (2000), pp. 22–26.

_____. "The Politics of the Air Campaign: Challenges for the US Air Force in the Aftermath of Operation Allied Force." *Aerospace Power Journal,* 14(1) (2000), pp. 82–84.

Hirsh, M., and J. Barry. "How We Stumbled into War." *Newsweek,* 133 (April 12) (1999), pp. 38–40.

"Hope for the Best, and a Spot of Golf: Did Clinton Think It Through?" *Economist,* 351(8113) (1999), pp. 19–24.

Huntington, S. P. "The Lonely Superpower." *Foreign Affairs,* 78(2) (1999), pp. 35–49.

"Is Iraq Helping Serbs?" *Seattle Times,* 29 March 1999.

Jumper, J. P. "Jumper on Airpower." *Air Force Magazine,* 83 (2000), pp. 41–43.

_____. "Kosovo Victory: A Commander's Perspective." *Airpower Review,* 2 (4) (1999), pp. 1–11.

_____. "Rapidly Deploying Aerospace Power. Lessons from Allied Force." *Aerospace Power Journal,* 13(4) (1999), pp. 4–10.

Keegan, J. "How Power from the Air Could Win a Ground War for Nato." *Electronic Telegraph,* 27 May 1999.

Klare, M. T. "The Clinton Doctrine." *Nation,* 1 April 1999.

Koning, P. "The Bloodbath in Račak Was a Massacre." *NRC Handelsblad,* 10 March 2001. racak.homestead.com/files/ranta.htm [accessed 9 March 2005].

"Kosovo Puts Strain on DOD's Two-War Strategy, Cohen Says." *Aerospace Daily,* 15 October 1999.

Krulak, V. H. "A Look Downstream." *Strategic Review,* 27(2) (1999), p. 3.

Lake, A. "Our Place in the Balkans." *New York Times,* 8 October 2000.

Lambeth, B. S. "Bounding the Airpower Debate." *Strategic Review,* 25(4) (1997), pp. 42–55.

Lippman, T. W. "Albright Misjudged Milošević on Kosovo." *Washington Post,* 7 April 1999.

Luttwak, E. N. "Give War a Chance." *Foreign Affairs,* 78(4) (1999), pp. 36–44.

Mandelbaum, M. "A Perfect Failure: NATO's War against Yugoslavia." *Foreign Affairs,* 78(5) (1999), pp. 2–8.

McGwire, M. "Why Did We Bomb Belgrade?" *International Affairs,* 76(1) (2000), pp. 1–22.

Meilinger, P. S. "Air Strategy: Targeting for Effect." *Aerospace Power Journal,* 13(4) (1999), pp. 48–61.

_____. "Gradual Escalation: NATO's Kosovo Air Campaign, though Decried as a Strategy, May Be the Future of War." *Armed Forces Journal International,* 137(3) (1999), p. 18.

_____. "Ten Propositions Emerging from Airpower." *Airpower Journal,* 10(1) (1996), pp. 52–72.

Mokhiber, J., and R. Young. "The Uses of Military Force." *PBS Online* and *GBH/ Frontline*, (1999), www.pbs.org/wgbh/pages/frontline/shows/military/force/ [accessed January 2007].

Mueller, D. K. "The Essence of Coercive Airpower. A Primer for Military Strategists." *Airpower Review,* 4(3) (2001), pp. 45–58.

Mueller, J. "The Banality of 'Ethnic War.'" *International Security,* 25(1) (2000), pp. 43–61.

Mueller, K. "Strategies of Coercion: Denial, Punishment, and the Future of Airpower." *Security Studies,* 7(3) (1998), pp. 182–228.

Murphy, D. J. "The Navy in the Balkans." *Air Force Magazine,* 82(12) (1999), pp. 48–49.

Nye, J. S. "Redefining the National Interest." *Foreign Affairs,* 78(4) (1999), pp. 22–35.

Owen, D. "Kosovo Isn't Bosnia." *Los Angeles Times,* 23 March 1999.

Owen, R. C. "The Balkans Air Campaign Study: Part 1." *Airpower Journal,* 11(2) (1997), pp. 4–24.

_____. "The Balkans Air Campaign Study: Part 2." *Airpower Journal,* 11(3) (1997), pp. 6–26.

Pape, R. A. "The Air Force Strikes Back: A Reply to Barry Watts and John Warden." *Security Studies,* 7(2) (1997–98), pp. 191–214.

_____. "The Limits of Precision-Guided Airpower." *Security Studies,* 7(2) (1997–98), pp. 93–114.

_____. "The Wrong Battle Plan." *Washington Post,* 19 October 2001.

Powell, C. L. "U.S. Forces: Challenges Ahead." *Foreign Affairs,* 71(5) (1992), pp. 32–45.

Priest, D. "The Battle inside Headquarters: Tension Grew with Divide over Strategy Series: *The Commanders' War: 3/3.*" *Washington Post,* 21 September 1999.

_____. "Bombing by Committee: France Balked at NATO Targets Series: *The Commanders' War: 2/3.*" *Washington Post,* 20 September 1999.

_____. "A Decisive Battle That Never Was Series: *The Commanders' War: 1/3.*" *Washington Post,* 19 September 1999.

_____. "Target Selection Was Long Process: Sites Were Analyzed Again and Again." *Washington Post,* 20 September 1999.

Ralph, William W. "Improvised Destruction: Arnold, LeMay, and the Firebombing of Japan." *War in History,* 13(4) 2006, pp. 495–522.

Record, J. "Force-Protection Fetishism: Sources, Consequences, and (?) Solutions." *Aerospace Power Journal,* 14(2) (2000).

_____. "Into the Wild Blue Yonder: Should We Abolish the Air Force?" *Policy Review,* 52 (Spring 1990), p. 50.

_____. "Operation Allied Force: Yet Another Wake-up Call for the Army?" *Parameters,* 29(4) (1999–2000), pp. 15–23.

Rodman, P. W. "The Fallout from Kosovo." *Foreign Affairs,* 78(4) (1999), pp. 45–51.

Rohde, David. "Tactics of '95 Bosnia Crisis May Not Fit Kosovo Case." *New York Times,* 2 April 1999.

Romjue, J. L. "The Evolution of the AirLand Battle Concept." *Air University Review,* 35(4) (1984), pp. 4–15.

Ryan, M. E. "Airpower Is Working in Kosovo." *Washington Post,* 4 June 1999.

Sarkesian, S. C. "Low Intensity Conflict: Concepts, Principles, and Policy Guidelines." *Air University Review,* 36(2) (1985), pp. 4–23.

Scarborough, R. "Officers Criticize NATO's Air-War Strategy." *Washington Times,* 10 May 1999.

_____. "U.S. Pilots Call NATO Targeting a 'Disgrace.'" *Washington Times,* 1 April 1999.

Sciolino, E., and E. Bronner. "How a President, Distracted by Scandal, Entered Balkan War." *New York Times,* 18 April 1999.

Solana, J. "NATO's Success in Kosovo." *Foreign Affairs,* 78(6) (1999), pp. 114–20.

Spiller, R. J. "In the Shadow of the Dragon: Doctrine and the US Army after Vietnam." *RUSI Journal,* 142(6) (1997), pp. 41–54.

Stanley, A. "Albanian Fighters Say They Aid NATO in Spotting Serb Targets." *New York Times,* 2 April 1999.

Strickland, P. C. "USAF Aerospace-Power Doctrine: Decisive or Coercive?" *Aerospace Power Journal,* 14(3) (2000), pp. 13–25.

"Stumbling into War." *Economist,* 350(8112) (1999), pp. 17–19.

Surroi, V. "The Albanian National Question: The Post Dayton Pay-off." *Balkan Crisis Report,* (41) (1996). www.iwpr.net/index.pl?archive/ war/war_41_199605_05.txt [accessed January 2007].

Szafranski, R. "Twelve Principles Emerging from Ten Propositions." *Airpower Journal,* 10(1) (1996), pp. 73–80.

Tamayo, J. O. "Cold War Habits Explain NATO's Cautious Attack on Serbs." *Miami Herald,* 5 May 1999.

Tirpak, J. A. "Lessons Learned and Re-Learned." *Air Force Magazine,* 82(8) (1999), pp. 23–25.

_____. "Short's View of the Air Campaign." *Air Force Magazine,* 82(9) (1999), pp. 43–47.

Tokar, J. A. "Vietnam, the Cold War, and Kosovo: Irony and confusion over Foreign Policy." *Parameters,* 30(1) (2000), pp. 30–37.

Warden, J. A. "The Enemy as a System." *Airpower Journal,* 9(1) (1995), pp. 40–55.

_____. "Success in Modern War: A Response to Robert Pape's Bombing to Win." *Security Studies,* 7(2) (1997–98), pp. 172–90.

Watts, B. D. "Ignoring Reality: Problems of Theory and Evidence in Security Studies." *Security Studies,* 7(2) (1997–98), pp. 115–71.

Weller, M. "The Rambouillet Conference on Kosovo." *International Affairs,* 75(2) (1999), pp. 211–61.

Whitney, C. R. "The NATO General Who Is Intimately Familiar with His Adversary." *New York Times,* 26 March 1999.

Zakaria, F. "The Superpower That Couldn't Say No." *New York Times,* 28 March 1999.

Zimmermann, Warren. "The Demons of Kosovo: Conflict between Serbia and Albania over the Control of Kosovo." *National Interest,* 52 (Summer 1998). www. findarticles. com/p/articles/mi_m2751/is_n52/ ai_20852420/print [accessed 9 May 2005].

Zimmermann, Warren, John Lampe, and Dragan Cicic. "Interview with Warren Zimmermann, John Lampe and Dragan Cicic." *Online NewsHour,* 2 December 1996, pbs.org/newshour/bb/bosnia/december96/serbia_12-2.html [accessed January 2007].

Official Documents, Reports, and Hearings

Clark, Wesley K., James Ellis, and Michael C. Short. *Combined Prepared Statement to Senate Armed Services Committee,* 21 October 1999. armed-services.senate. gov/statemnt/1999/991021wc.pdf [accessed January 2007].

Cohen, William S. *Prepared Statement to Senate Armed Services Committee.* Hearing on Operations in Kosovo. Washington, D.C., 20 July 1999. armed-services.senate.gov/statemnt/1999/990720wc.pdf [accessed January 2007].

Cohen, William S., and Henry H. Shelton. *Joint Statement to Senate Armed Services Committee.* Hearing on Kosovo After-Action Review. Washington, D.C., 14 October 1999. www.aldeilis.net/natofry/cohenshelton.html [accessed April 2005].

Committee on Armed Services House of Representatives. *United States and NATO Military Operations against the Federal Republic of Yugoslavia.* Report. Washington, D.C.: U.S. Government Printing Office, 28 April 1999. commdocs.house. gov/committees/security/has118000.000/has118000_1.HTM#18 [accessed January 2007].

Congressional Research Service. *Iraq: Former and Recent Military Confrontations with the United States.* Issue Brief for Congress. Washington, D.C.: 16 October 2002. www.gulfinvestigations.net/IMG/pdf/crs-iraq_mil_confr.pdf?PHPSESSID= b3fbc28348323 cca 889d34e750a2153c [accessed January 2007].

_____. *Kosovo: Lessons Learned from Operation Allied Force.* Report for Congress, 19 November 1999. www.smallwarsjournal.com/documents/crl1.pdf [accessed January 2007].

Department of Defense. *Kosovo/Operation Allied Force After-Action Report.* Report to Congress, Washington, D.C., 31 January 2000. www.dod.gov/pubs/ kaar02072000.pdf [accessed January 2007].

French Ministry of Defence. *Lessons from Kosovo*, November 1999. Délégation à l'information et à la Communication de la Défense. www.defense.gouv.fr.

Gelbard, Robert S. *Statement before the House International Relations Committee.* Washington, D.C.: U.S. Department of State, 23 July 1998. www.state.gov/www/policy_remarks/1998/980723_gelbard_kosovo.html [accessed January 2007].

General Accounting Office. *Operation Desert Storm: Evaluation of the Air Campaign.* Report to the Ranking Minority Member, Committee on Commerce, House of Representatives, Washington, D.C., 12 June 1997. www.gao.gov/archive/1997/ns97134.pdf [accessed January 2007].

Human Rights Watch. *Civilian Deaths in the NATO Air Campaign,* vol. 12, no. 1 (D), February 2000. www.hrw.org/reports/2000/nato/ [accessed January 2007].

_____. *Federal Republic of Yugoslavia. "Ethnic Cleansing" in the Glogovac Municipality,* vol. 11, no. 8 (D), July 1999. www.hrw.org/reports/1999/glogovac/ [accessed January 2007].

_____. *A Village Destroyed: War Crimes in Kosovo,* vol. 11, no. 13 (D), October 1999. hrw.org/reports/1999/kosovo3/ [accessed January 2007].

_____. *A Week of Terror in Drenica.* 1998. "Gornje Obrinje: Massacre in the Forest." www.hrw.org/reports/1999/kosovo/Obrinje6-02.htm [accessed January 2007].

Independent International Commission on Kosovo. *The Kosovo Report: Conflict, International Response, Lessons Learned.* Oxford: Oxford University Press, 2000.

Jumper, John P. *Statement to House Armed Services Committee.* Washington, D.C., 26 October 1999. www.globalsecurity.org/military/library/congress/1999_hr/99-10-26jumper.htm [accessed January 2007].

Murphy, Daniel J., Jr. *Statement to House Armed Services Committee.* Washington, D.C., 26 October 1999. www.globalsecurity.org/military/library/congress/1999_hr/99-10-26murphy.htm [accessed January 2007].

Naumann, Klaus. *Statement to Senate Armed Services Committee.* Washington, D.C., 3 November 1999. armed-services.senate.gov/statemnt/1999/991103kn.pdf [accessed January 2007].

Organization for Security and Co-operation in Europe. *Kosovo/Kosova as Seen, as Told: An Analysis of the Human Rights Findings of the OSCE Kosovo Verification Mission October 1998 to June 1999.* Warsaw, 1999. www.asylumlaw.org/docs/kosovo/ osce99_kosovo_asseenastold.pdf [accessed January 2007].

Parliament. *The Defence Committee Fourteenth Report.* London, 23 October 2000. www.parliament.the-stationery-office.co.uk/pa/cm199900/cmselect/cmdfence/347/34702.htm [accessed January 2007].

Robertson, George. *Examination of Witnesses.* Questions 356–79. London: Parliament Defence Committee, 24 March 1999. www.parliament.the-stationery-office.co.uk/pa/cm199899/cmselect/ cmdfence/39/9032402.htm [accessed January 2007].

_____. *Kosovo: An Account of the Crisis.* London: Ministry of Defence, 1999. www.kosovo.mod.uk/account/ [accessed January 2007].

Agreement between the Organization for Security and Cooperation in Europe and the Federal Republic of Yugoslavia on the Kosovo Verification Mission, 16 October 1998. www.un.org/peace/kosovo/s98978.pdf [accessed January 2007].

The Dayton Peace Accords on Bosnia, 1995. www1.umn.edu/humanrts/icty/dayton/daytonaccord.html [accessed January 2007].

Kosovo Verification Mission Agreement between the North Atlantic Treaty Organization and the Federal Republic of Yugoslavia, 1998. www.un.org/peace/kosovo/s98991.pdf [accessed January 2007].

Military-Technical Agreement between the International Security Force (KFOR) and the Governments of the Federal Republic of Yugoslavia and the Republic of Serbia, 9 June 1999. www.un.org/peace/kosovo/s99682.pdf [accessed January 2007].

Rambouillet Agreement. Interim Agreement for Peace and Self-Government in Kosovo, 7 June 1999. www.state.gov/www/regions/eur/ksvo_rambouillet_text.html [accessed January 2007].

Text of Kosovo Peace Plan. Transcript, *Washington Post*, 3 June 1999. www.washingtonpost.com/wp-srv/inatl/daily/june99/plantext03.htm [accessed January 2007].

Text of Military Agreement. Transcript, *Washington Post*, 9 June 1999. www.washingtonpost.com/wp-srv/inatl/daily/june99/miltext09.htm [accessed January 2007].

Speeches, Statements, Press Releases, and Resolutions

Albright, Madeleine. *Remarks by Secretary of State Madeleine Albright at U.S. Institute of Peace,* United States Department of State, 4 February 1999.

_____. *Transcript: Albright, Dini Briefing in Rome March 7, 1998,* 10 March 1998. www.usembassy-israel.org.il/publish/peace/archives/1998/march/me0310a.html [accessed January 2007].

Clinton, W. J. *Address to the American Federation of State, County, and Municipal Employees (AFSCME) Biennial Convention.* U.S. Department of State, 23 March 1999. www.state.gov/www/policy_remarks/1999/990323_clinton_afscme.html [accessed January 2007].

_____. *Address to the Nation.* U.S. Department of State, 24 March 1999. beqiraj.com/kosova/de/allied_force/statement/clinton/index.asp [accessed February 2005].

_____. *Excerpts of President Clinton's Address on NATO Attacks on Yugoslav Military Forces: "By Acting Now, We Are . . . Advancing the Cause of Peace."* *Washington Post,* 25 March 1999.

Contact Group. *Contact Group Joint Statement: Kosovo, 12 June 1998.* www.dfait-maeci.gc.ca/g8fmm-g8rmae/joint_statement_ kosovo-en.asp [accessed 7 June 2005].

_____. *Contact Group Statement on Kosovo in London March 9, 1998.* USIS Washington File. canberra.usembassy.gov/hyper/WF980309/epf103.htm [accessed August 2005].

Group of Eight. *Text of the G-8 Foreign Ministers' Statement on Kosovo. Guardian,* 6 May 1999. www.guardian.co.uk/Kosovo/Story/0,2763,207122,00.html [accessed January 2007].

Human Rights Watch. *Yugoslav Government War Crimes in Račak.* Press release, 29 January 1999. www.hrw.org/press/1999/jan/yugo0129.htm [accessed January 2007].

Lake, A. *Defining Missions, Setting Deadlines: Meeting New Security Challenges in the Post–Cold War World.* Remarks at George Washington University, 6 March 1996. www.defenselink.mil/Speeches/Speech.aspx?SpeechID=898 [accessed January 2007].

North Atlantic Treaty Organization. *Council Statement on the Situation in Kosovo.* Press release (98)51, 30 April 1998. www.nato.int/docu/pr/1998/p98-051e.htm [accessed January 2007].

_____. *Council Statement on the Situation in Kosovo.* Press release (98)29, 5 March 1998. www.nato.int/docu/pr/1998/p98-029e.htm [accessed January 2007].

_____. *NATO's Role in Relation to the Conflict in Kosovo,* 15 July 1999. www.nato. int/kosovo/history.htm [accessed January 2007].

_____. *Political and Military Objectives of NATO Action with Regard to the Crisis in Kosovo.* Press release (1999)043, 23 March 1999. www.nato.int/docu/pr/1999/ p99-043e.htm [accessed January 2007].

_____. *Press Conference by Secretary General, Dr Javier Solana and SACEUR, General Wesley Clark,* 25 March 1999. www.nato.int/kosovo/press/p990325a.htm [accessed January 2007].

_____. *Press Statement by Dr. Javier Solana, NATO Secretary General.* Press release (1999)042, 25 March 1999. www.nato.int/docu/pr/1999/p99-042e.htm [accessed January 2007].

_____. *Press Statement by Dr. Javier Solana, NATO Secretary General following the Commencement of Air Operations.* Press release (1999)041, 24 March 1999. www.nato.int/docu/pr/1999/p99-041e.htm [accessed January 2007].

_____. *Press Statement by Dr. Javier Solana, Secretary General of NATO.* Press release (1999)040, 23 March 1999. www.nato.int/docu/pr/1999/p99-040e.htm [accessed January 2007].

_____. *Remarks to the Press by Javier Solana.* Press release, 28 May 1998. www.nato. int/docu/speech/1998/s980528a.htm [accessed January 2007].

_____. *Statement by the North Atlantic Council on Kosovo.* Press release (99)12, 30 January 1999. www.nato.int/docu/pr/1999/p99-012e.htm [accessed January 2007].

_____. *Statement by the North Atlantic Council on the Situation in Kosovo.* Press release (1999)038, 22 March 1999. www.nato.int/docu/pr/1999/p99-038e.htm [accessed January 2007].

_____. *Statement by the Secretary General following the ACTWARN Decision.* Press release. Vilamoura, 24 September 1998. www.nato.int/docu/pr/1998/p980924e. htm [accessed January 2007].

_____. *Statement by the Secretary General of NATO, Dr. Javier Solana on the Initiation of a Broader Range of Air Operations in the Federal Republic of Yugoslavia.* Press release (1999)044, 27 March 1999. www.nato.int/docu/pr/1999/p99-044e. htm [accessed January 2007].

_____. *Statement on Kosovo: Issued at the Meeting of the North Atlantic Council in Defense Ministers Session.* Press release M-NAC-D-1(98)77, 11 June 1998. www. nato.int/docu/pr/1998/p98-077e.htm [accessed January 2007].

_____. *Statement on Kosovo: Issued at the Ministerial Meeting of the North Atlantic Council Held in Luxembourg on 28th May 1998.* Press release M-NAC-1(98)61, 28 May 1998. www.nato.int/docu/pr/1998/p98-061e.htm [accessed January 2007].

_____. *Statement on Kosovo: Issued by the Heads of State and Government participating in the meeting of the North Atlantic Council in Washington, D.C. on 23rd and 24th April 1999.* Press release S-1 (99)62, 23 April 1999. www.nato.int/docu/pr/1999/p99-062e.htm [accessed January 2007].

_____. *Statement to the Press by NATO Secretary General, Dr. Javier Solana.* Press release (99)11, 28 January 1999. www.nato.int/docu/pr/1999/p99-011e.htm [accessed January 2007].

_____. *Statement to the Press by NATO Secretary General, Dr. Javier Solana,* 11 June 1998. www.nato.int/docu/pr/1998/p98-077e.htm [accessed January 2007].

_____. *Statement to the Press by the Secretary General following Decision on the ACTORD,* NATO HQ, 13 October 1998. www.nato.int/docu/speech/1998/s981013a.htm [accessed January 2007].

_____. *The Washington Declaration.* Press release NAC-S(99)63, 23 April 1999. www.nato.int/docu/pr/1999/p99-063e.htm [accessed January 2007].

Organization for Security and Cooperation in Europe. *Special Session of the Permanent Council of the Organization for Security and Cooperation in Europe,* OSCE (S/1998/246), 11 March 1998. www.un.org/peace/kosovo/s1998246.pdf [accessed January 2007].

Short, M. C. *Speech to the AFA Air Warfare Symposium 2000,* 25 February 2000. www.aef.org/pub/short200.asp [accessed January 2007].

United Nations. *Report of the Secretary-General Prepared Pursuant to Resolutions 1160 (1998), 1199 (1998) and 1203 (1998) of the Security Council.* Security Council, S/1999/99, 30 January 1999. www.un.org/Docs/sc/reports/1999/sgrep99. htm [accessed January 2007].

_____. *Report of the Secretary-General Prepared Pursuant to Resolutions 1160 (1998), 1199 (1998) and 1203 (1998) of the Security Council.* Security Council, S/1998/1068, 12 November 1998. www.un.org/Docs/sc/reports/1998/sgrep98. htm [accessed January 2007].

_____. *Report of the Secretary-General Prepared Pursuant to Resolutions 1160 (1998) and 1199 (1998) of the Security Council.* Security Council, S/1998/912, 3 October 1998. daccessdds.un.org/doc/UNDOC/GEN/N98/289/78/PDF/N9828978. pdf? OpenElement [accessed January 2007].

_____. *Report of the Secretary-General Prepared Pursuant to Security Council Resolution 1160 (1998).* Security Council, S/1998/361, 30 April 1998. www.un.org/Docs/sc/reports/1998/sgrep98.htm [accessed January 2007].

_____. *Resolution 1160.* Security Council, 31 March 1998. www.un.org/Docs/scres/1998/scres98.htm [accessed January 2007].

_____. *Resolution 1199.* Security Council, 23 September 1998. www.un.org/Docs/scres/1998/scres98.htm [accessed January 2007].

_____. *Resolution 1203.* Security Council, 24 October 1998. www.un.org/Docs/scres/1998/scres98.htm [accessed January 2007].

_____. *Statement by Kofi Annan, Secretary General of the United Nations, Statement to the North Atlantic Council,* 28 January 1999. www.nato.int/docu/speech/1999/s990128a.htm [accessed January 2007].

Documentaries

BBC1. *The Mind of Milošević.* Panorama. Producer Kevin Sutcliffe, editor Peter Horrocks, reporter Gavin Hewitt, 29 March 1999.

BBC1. *War Room (The Kosovan War).* Producers Andrew Bell and Toby Sculthorp, editor Peter Horrocks, 19 April 1999.

BBC2. *The Fall of Milošević.* Series producer Dai Richards, executive producers Brian Lapping and Norma Percy. Part 1: "Defiance," 5 January 2003; Part 2: "War," 12 January 2003; Part 3: "Finished," 19 January 2003.

Channel 4. *War in Europe.* Written and presented by Michael Elliott, film editor John Lee, series producer Eamonn Matthews. MBC production in association with GBH/*Frontline* for Channel 4. Part 1: "The Road to War," 20 January 2000; Part 2: "Vanishing Targets," 6 February 2000; Part 3: "End Game," 13 February 2000.

Morris, Errol. *The Fog of War: Eleven Lessons from the Life of Robert S. McNamara.* Director Errol Morris, producers Errol Morris, Michael Williams, and Julie Ahlberg. Distributed by Sony Pictures, released 21 May 2003.

PBS. "Rumsfeld's War." *PBS Frontline, Washington Post.* Written, produced, and directed by Michael Kirk, coproduced and reported by Jim Gilmore, 2004. Aired on Norwegian Broadcast (NRK1) 15 February 2005.

PBS Frontline Interviews

Albright, Madeleine (2000). "Interview with Madeleine." www.pbs.org/wgbh/pages/frontline/shows/kosovo [accessed January 2007].

Berger, Samuel "Sandy" (2000). "Interview with Samuel 'Sandy' Berger." www.pbs.org/wgbh/pages/frontline/shows/kosovo [accessed January 2007].

Blair, Tony (2000). "Interview with Tony Blair." www.pbs.org/wgbh/pages/frontline/shows/kosovo [accessed January 2007].

Chernomyrdin, Viktor (2000). "Interview with Viktor Chernomyrdin." www.pbs. org/wgbh/pages/frontline/shows/kosovo [accessed January 2007].

Clark, Wesley K. (2000). "Interview with General Wesley Clark." www.pbs.org/ wgbh/pages/frontline/shows/kosovo [accessed January 2007].

Cohen, William (2000). "Interview with William Cohen." www.pbs.org/wgbh/pages/ frontline/shows/kosovo [accessed January 2007].

Daalder, Ivo (2000). "Interview with Ivo Daalder." www.pbs.org/wgbh/pages/front-line/shows/kosovo [accessed January 2007].

Holbrooke, Richard (2000). "Interview with Richard Holbrooke." www.pbs.org/ wgbh/pages/frontline/shows/kosovo [accessed January 2007].

Krulak, Charles (2000). "Interview with General Charles Krulak." www.pbs.org/ wgbh/pages/frontline/shows/kosovo [accessed January 2007].

Naumann, Klaus (2000). "Interview with General Klaus Naumann." www.pbs.org/ wgbh/pages/frontline/shows/kosovo [accessed January 2007].

Pavkovic, Nebojsa (2000). "Interview with Commander Nebojsa Pavkovic." www. pbs.org/wgbh/pages/frontline/shows/kosovo [accessed January 2007].

Short, Michael C. (2000). "Interview with General Michael C. Short." www.pbs.org/ wgbh/pages/frontline/shows/kosovo [accessed January 2007].

Talbott, Strobe (2000). "Interview with Strobe Talbott." www.pbs.org/wgbh/pages/ frontline/shows/kosovo [accessed January 2007].

Thaçi, Hashim (2000). "Interview with Hashim Thaçi." www.pbs.org/wgbh/pages/ frontline/shows/kosovo [accessed January 2007].

Walker, William (2000). "Interview with Ambassador William Walker." www.pbs. org/wgbh/pages/frontline/shows/kosovo [accessed January 2007].

Young, R. (1999). "Lessons of Vietnam: A conversation with Major H. R. McMaster." *PBS Online and WGBH/Frontline.* www.pbs.org/wgbh/pages/frontline/shows/ military/force [accessed January 2007].

Author Interviews and Correspondence

Bøthun, Per. Lieutenant General, Royal Norwegian Air Force (Ret.). Former Nor-wegian chief of defense representative in NATO's Military Committee through Operation Allied Force. Interview (taped), Oslo, Norway, 15 April 2004.

Clark, Wesley K. General, U.S. Army (Ret.). Director for Strategic Plans and Policies (J-5) in the Pentagon's Joint Staff (1994–96), part of Richard Holbrooke's nego-tiation team leading to the Dayton Peace Accords (1995), Supreme Allied Com-mander Europe (SACEUR) (1997–2000) and Commander, European Command (1997–2000) during OAF. E-mail correspondence, 5 May 2005.

Corbett, Sean. Wing Commander, Royal Air Force. Leader of the NATO targeting cell in CAOC Vicenza during OAF. In this capacity he had insight into the con-duct of and guidance given to this targeting cell and was responsible for decon-fliction between the U.S. and NATO targeting effort during OAF. Telephone conversation and e-mail correspondence spring/summer 2004.

Dobbins, James. Former U.S. Special Envoy for Bosnia, Somalia, Haiti, and Kosovo, Assistant Secretary of State for Europe, U.S. ambassador to the European Community, and President Bill Clinton and Secretary of State Madeleine Albright's special adviser for Kosovo and Bosnia and Herzegovina. Telephone interview (taped), Norwegian Air Force Academy, Norway, 22 September 2004.

Efjestad, Svein. Director General, Security Policy at the Norwegian Department of Defence through Operation Allied Force. Interview (transcript), Oslo, Norway, 14 April 2004.

Eltervåg, Kåre. Former political adviser to William Walker (head of KVM), 1998–99, and leader of a small team that wrote KVM's daily reports to the OSCE headquarters in Vienna and the monthly reports to the UN secretary-general. All information gathered by the KVM field presence was fed into his reporting cell. He reestablished the OSCE's presence in Kosovo in mid-June 1999, a few days after Operation Allied Force ended. Telephone interview (transcript), Trondheim, Norway, December 2003.

Gelbard, Robert. U.S. State Department's Deputy Director for Western European Affairs (1982–84), U.S. ambassador to Bolivia (1988–91), president's representative for the Dayton implementation in Bosnia (1996-99) and involved in the diplomatic handling of the deteriorating situation in Kosovo (1996–99). Telephone interview (taped), Norwegian Air Force Academy, Norway, 17 May 2005.

Hill, Christopher. Principal aide to the Dayton Peace Accord process (1995), office director of the U.S. State Department's Bureau of European Affairs (1995–96), U.S. ambassador to Macedonia (1996–99), involved in the negotiations leading to the October Agreement with Slobodan Milošević (1998), and part of the troika who coordinated the day-to-day negotiations at the Rambouillet Peace Conference (1999). Telephone interview (taped), Norwegian Air Force Academy, Norway, 8 November 2004.

Johansen, Tom. Colonel, Royal Norwegian Air Force (Ret.). Battle staff director (responsible for minute-to-minute decisions related to air operations on behalf of the Joint Force Air Component Commander (JFACC), Gen. Michael C. Short) in CAOC Vicenza during OAF. Interview (taped), Oslo, Norway, 17 October 2003.

Kelche, Jean-Pierre. General French Marines (Ret.). Former French chief of defense through OAF, leaving the position in 2002. Interview (taped), Paris, France, 11 April 2003.

Klever, Morten. Brigadier General, Royal Norwegian Air Force. Offensive tasker (planner) for offensive air operations in Bosnia-Herzegovina, coordinator between UN headquarters in Zagreb (Croatia) and CAOC Vicenza, 1994–95, and deputy to the Norwegian National Representative in CAOC Vicenza during OAF. Interview (taped), Oslo, Norway, 14 April 2004.

Lake, Anthony. U.S. vice consul in Saigon, South Vietnam, 1963, and in Hue, 1964–65; special assistant in the Nixon administration, 1969–70; PhD Princeton University, 1974; director of policy planning for President Carter, 1977–81; senior foreign policy adviser to the Clinton/Gore campaign, 1991–92; and national security adviser for President Clinton, 1993–97. Telephone interview (taped), Norwegian Air Force Academy, Norway, 21 September, 2005.

Lian, Jakken Bjørn. Political director in the Norwegian Ministry of Foreign Affairs (1992–94), Norwegian ambassador to the United Nations (1994–98) and to NATO from 1998 and through OAF. Interview, Oslo, Norway, 22 March 2004.

Lorraine, Chris. Colonel, Royal Netherlands Air Force. Worked with targeting and planning at the CAOC Vicenza during OAF. E-mail correspondence, February 2005.

Løwer, Eldbjørg. Norwegian minister of defense (1999–2000) during OAF. Interview (taped), Oslo, Norway, 22 March 2004.

Lundberg, Gunnar. Brigadier General, Royal Norwegian Army (Ret.). Chief of the Nordic-Polish Brigade (NORDPOL BDE) in Bosnia (1996–97) and deputy chief of operations in SHAPE from 1997 and through OAF. Interview (taped), Stockholm, Sweden, 25 May 2004.

Naumann, Klaus. General, German Army (Ret.). Chairman of NATO Military Committee (1996–99) during OAF. Interview (taped), Hotel Marriott, Berlin, Germany, 30 September 2004.

Nygård, Bjørn. Major General, Royal Norwegian Air Force (Ret.). Former Norwegian military attaché in Washington and deputy head of mission/chief of staff, Kosovo Verification Mission (KVM) in Priština, Kosovo, 1998–99. Telephone interview (taped), Norwegian Air Force Academy, Norway, 7 July 2004.

Olsen, Ove Sten. Rear Admiral, Royal Norwegian Navy (Ret.). Norwegian National military representative at SHAPE, 1996–99, responsible for day-to-day information from SHAPE to the chief of defense in Norway. E-mail correspondences, spring 2004.

Pape, Robert A. Professor of political science at the University of Chicago. Generally considered one of the most important contributors to modern airpower thinking. His book *Bombing to Win: Airpower and Coercion in War* (1996) represented an important contribution to modern airpower thinking. Lecture and conversation, Royal Norwegian Air Force Academy, 14 December 2006.

Rajic, Ljubisa. Professor at the University of Belgrade, editor in chief of the magazine of the first oppositional organization in Yugoslavia, the Association of Yugoslav Initiatives for Democracy, and one of the leaders of the democratic and anti-nationalistic university protests at the University of Belgrade in 1992, 1996–97, and 1998. Professor Rajic reported regularly from Belgrade to the Nordic media during OAF and has been a critic of both the Serbian leadership and the international community's handling of the Kosovo crisis, as well as of the NATO air campaign. Interview (transcript), Trondheim, Norway, October 2003.

Ralston, Joseph. General, U.S. Air Force (Ret.). Vice chairman of the Joint Chiefs of Staff (1996–2000) during OAF; SACEUR, 2000–2003, and Commander, European Command, 2000–2003. Telephone interview (taped), Norwegian Air Force Academy, Norway, 6 September 2004.

Røsjorde, Hans. Former leader of the Defense Committee in the Norwegian Parliament (Stortinget) during the crisis. Interview (taped), Oslo, Norway, 8 June 2004.

Short, Michael C. Lieutenant General, U.S. Air Force (Ret.). Commander, Air Forces Southern Europe (NATO), 1998–2000; Commander, Sixteenth Air Force, 1998–2000; CFACC during OAF. E-mail correspondence, August 2004.

Smith, Rupert. General, British Army (Ret.). Commander United Nations Protective Forces (UNPROFOR) in Bosnia-Herzegovina (1995; Commanding General in Northern Ireland, 1996–98; and Deputy SACEUR, 1998–2001, during OAF. Telephone interview (taped), Norwegian Air Force Academy, Norway, 15 March 2005.

Solli, Arne. General, Royal Norwegian Army (Ret.). Norwegian chief of defense, 1994–99, and member of NATO's Military Committee through OAF. Interview (taped), Oslo, Norway, 9 June 2004.

Stöckmann, Dieter. General, German Army (Ret.). Commander in Chief, Allied Forces Central Europe (NATO), 1996–98; chief of staff of SHAPE, 1998–2001, during OAF; and Deputy SACEUR, 2001–2002. Interview (taped), outside Bonn, Germany, 7 December 2004.

Stoltenberg, Thorvald. Norwegian minister of defense, 1979–81; foreign minister, 1987–89 and 1990–93; UN High Commissioner for Refugees (UNHCR), 1990, and UN peace negotiator in the former Yugoslavia, 1993–96. Interview (taped), Oslo, Norway, 8 June 2004.

Svingen, Bjørn. Brigadier General, Royal Norwegian Air Force (Ret.). Assistant to the chairman of NATO's Military Committee, 1989–93; assistant chief of staff, International Military Policy Division, Plans and Policy Staff, HQ Defence Command Norway, 1994–99, through OAF. Interview (transcript), Royal Norwegian Air Force Academy, Trondheim, Norway, 1 July 2004.

Vollebæk, Knut. Norwegian foreign minister, 1997–2000, during OAF; member of the OSCE leadership troika (preceded by Poland), 1998, and succeeded by Austria, 2000; chairman in office of OSCE, 1999, through OAF. Interview (taped), Oslo, Norway, 26 August 2004.

Warden, John A., III. Colonel, U.S. Air Force (Ret.). Generally considered one of the most important contributors to modern airpower thinking, one of the principal architects of the Desert Storm air campaign, 1991. His book *The Air Campaign: Planning for Combat* (1988) is considered one of the most important contributions to modern airpower thinking at the operational level of war. E-mail correspondence, 12 September 2005

INDEX

ABOUT THE AUTHOR

Dr. Dag Henriksen was born and raised in Trondheim, Norway, where he currently lives with his fiancée, Anne Katrine, her daughter, Maren, and their son, August. He enlisted in the Royal Norwegian Air Force (RNoAF) at the age of nineteen and specialized in Air Battle Management (Fighter Controller, Fighter/SAM Allocator, Weapons Allocator). He served in NATO operations in the Baltics (Baltic Accession) in 2005 and in Afghanistan (International Security Assistance Force [ISAF]) in 2007.

Dr. Henriksen studied political science and history at the Norwegian University of Science and Technology (NTNU) in Trondheim, graduated top of his class after four years at the RNoAF Academy, and graduated from the University of Glasgow, UK, with a Ph.D. in military studies in 2006. The title of his doctorate thesis was "Operation Allied Force: A Product of Military Theory or Political Pragmatism? An Examination of the Role of Air Power in handling the Kosovo Crisis, 1998–99." Dr. Henriksen holds the rank of captain and is currently working as a lecturer in airpower at the RNoAF Academy.

THE NAVAL INSTITUTE PRESS is the book-publishing arm of the U.S. Naval Institute, a private, nonprofit, membership society for sea service professionals and others who share an interest in naval and maritime affairs. Established in 1873 at the U.S. Naval Academy in Annapolis, Maryland, where its offices remain today, the Naval Institute has members worldwide.

Members of the Naval Institute support the education programs of the society and receive the influential monthly magazine *Proceedings* or the colorful bimonthly magazine *Naval History,* and discounts on fine nautical prints and on ship and aircraft photos. They also have access to the transcripts of the Institute's Oral History Program and get discounted admission to any of the Institute-sponsored seminars offered around the country.

The Naval Institute's book-publishing program, begun in 1898 with basic guides to naval practices, has broadened its scope to include books of more general interest. Now the Naval Institute Press publishes about seventy titles each year, ranging from how-to books on boating and navigation to battle histories, biographies, ship and aircraft guides, and novels. Institute members receive significant discounts on the Press's more than eight hundred books in print.

Full-time students are eligible for special half-price membership rates. Life memberships are also available.

For a free catalog describing Naval Institute Press books currently available, and for further information about joining the U.S. Naval Institute, please write to:

Member Services
U.S. NAVAL INSTITUTE
291 Wood Road
Annapolis, MD 21402-5034
Telephone: (800) 233-8764
Fax: (410) 571-1703
Web address: www.usni.org